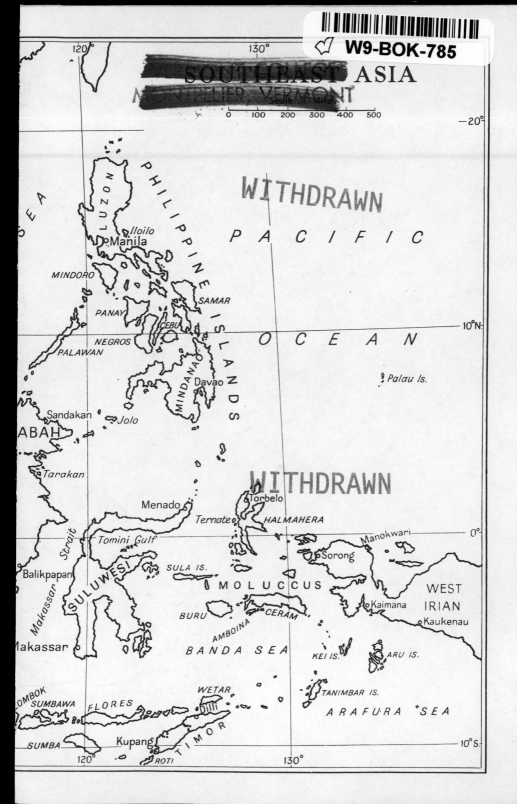

SOUTHEAST ASIA

Scale of Miles

0   100   200   300   400   500

—20°

120°   130°

WITHDRAWN

P A C I F I C

LUZON

Iloilo
Manila

PHILIPPINE ISLANDS

MINDORO

SAMAR

PANAY
CEBU

NEGROS

PALAWAN

MINDANAO

O C E A N   10°N

Davao

Palau Is.

SEA

Sandakan   Jolo

ABAH

Tarakan

WITHDRAWN

Menado   Torbelo

Ternate   HALMAHERA

Manokwari   0°

Tomini Gulf

Strait

Sorong

Balikpapan   SULA IS.   WEST
                                            IRIAN
SULUWESI   M O L U C C U S   Kaimana
Makassar
                BURU   CERAM   Kaukenau

Makassar   AMBOINA

        B A N D A   S E A   KEI IS.   ARU IS.

LOMBOK   WETAR   TANIMBAR IS.
SUMBAWA   FLORES   A R A F U R A   S E A

SUMBA   Kupang   TIMOR   10°S
120°   ROTI   130°

SOUTHEAST ASIA

SOUTHEAST ASIA

E. H. G. DOBBY
B.A. Ph.D.

Sometime Professor of Geography at the University of Malaya,
Singapore, and at the University College of Ghana

UNIVERSITY OF LONDON PRESS LTD

SBN 340 09098 7

First published 1950
Tenth edition
Copyright © 1967 E. H. G. Dobby

University of London Press Ltd
St Paul's House, Warwick Lane, London EC4

Printed and bound in Great Britain by
Hazell Watson & Viney Ltd, Aylesbury, Bucks

PREFACE

THE aim of this book is to present a picture of environmental conditions and human adaptations in Southeast Asia which shall provide the student with a basic text and at the same time stimulate the sociologist, the administrator, the politician and the businessman to see the relation of their work to the general field. It is assumed that readers will already know modern writings on the physical, environmental and social aspects of geography, and the text dwells at length only on those circumstances peculiar to Southeast Asia and its people.

This book is not a dictionary, a gazetteer or an encyclopaedia. It is one of the first studies of locational perspectives in Southeast Asia, the critical importance of which became apparent during the last war when the scarcity of information demonstrated how little study had been given to the region as a whole.

The book is divided into three parts. The first pictures the natural setting, the second gives a regional treatment of the human details of each political unit, and the third ties together the social geography of Southeast Asia, to pose some of its present problems.

All money references are in Malaysian dollars (2s. 4d. or U.S. 33 cents) partly because this currency had wide pre-war usage in the region, partly because it is the one with a simple and fixed relation between its post- and pre-war values. The object has been not to overload the text with statistics, which are best obtained fresh from the latest year-books. At every stage in reading this book, reference should be made to the topographic maps of Southeast Asia, which now exist in fair quantity.

The author thanks Professor E. G. R. Taylor for her advice on this work and her encouragement at many stages of his career, and Professor L. D. Stamp for his kindness in reading and advising on the manuscript. Those pioneer scholars of the area, whose papers are listed in the bibliography, and upon whose work the author has of necessity drawn liberally for facts, are also thanked. In addition he is heavily indebted to his wife for her continued patience and co-operation at every stage in the production of this book.

If the result of this work is to stimulate a flood of critical studies of Southeast Asia, however much later workers may question its statements, the author will be satisfied, especially if it encourages and helps students living in Southeast Asia to write about their own countries.

E. H. G. DOBBY

SINGAPORE, 1950

PREFACE TO THE TENTH EDITION

Further amendments have been made to reflect conditions in 1966.

E. H. G. DOBBY

March, 1967

CONTENTS

PART II

THE COUNTRIES OF SOUTHEAST ASIA

Contents 9

LIST OF MAPS AND DIAGRAMS

Front endpaper—Southeast Asia

PART I
THE NATURAL LANDSCAPE OF SOUTHEAST ASIA

Chapter One

THE NATURAL LANDSCAPE OF SOUTHEAST ASIA

SOUTHEAST ASIA is a term which became popular during the Far Eastern War 1941–45, to describe those territories of Eastern Asia which lie south of the Tropic of Cancer (Burma, Thailand, Indochina and Malaysia) and the nearby islands spreading eastwards from the Asiatic continent towards Irian (New Guinea). The archipelago section merges eastwards into island groups of the West-Central Pacific, for which reason West Irian itself may best be considered outside the definition "Southeast Asia," an exclusion justified (*a*) by its closer physical association with the Australian Continent, (*b*) by its sparse population of distinctive anthropological type now found principally in Australia, and (*c*) by the close affinities of its flora and fauna with those of Australia. The northern limit of Southeast Asia extends beyond the Tropic of Cancer to include Upper Burma on the western side, and withdraws south of the tropic to the political boundaries of Thailand and Indochina farther east. By this definition, "Southeast Asia" and its off-lying islands sprawl asymmetrically across the Equator and cover a zone not far short of 1,500 miles in radius from a point off the mouth of the Mekong, an area comparable to all Europe and its seas north of the African coast. Thus isolation by great distances, as well as by physical obstructions, is a constant factor in the geographical relation between the various parts of Southeast Asia.

In Southeast Asia, that which forms its core and constitutes the geological link between its chief parts is the Sunda Platform, the southernmost continental block of Asia, whose integrity as a land mass has continued, with only minor tectonic disturbances on its fringes, through such long geological periods that it may be compared with those other "permanent" massifs, the Deccan, the Arabian Block and the Laurentian Shield. It is this physical feature which underlies Borneo, Eastern Sumatra, Northern Java and Malaysia.

A somewhat similar platform is the common physiographic basis of Australia and West Irian, forming what is known as the Sahul Shelf, to the east of the East Indian Archipelago.

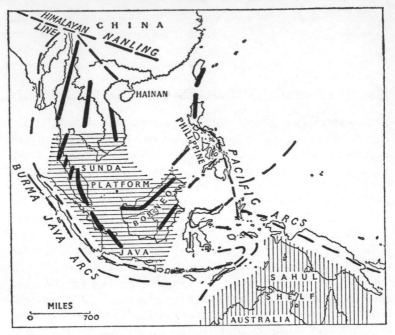

FIG. 1.—Landforms of Southeast Asia

The three basic physical units (Fig. 1) of this region are, then:
1. The Sunda Platform
2. The Sahul Shelf
3. A "ground swell" of young mountain arcs fringing and lying between the two other units.

1. THE SUNDA PLATFORM

The line of the Himalayan mountain formations extends eastwards to the China Sea to appear in South China as the Nanling and as that line of W–E. mountains forming the watershed between the Red River of North Viet Nam and the Sikiang of Canton. This chain of fold mountains of Alpine type delimits Southeast Asia geologically from the rest of Asia and is accepted as evidence of mountain building processes related to forces operating from the north.

South of this marginal zone of latitudinal alignments, the structural trends, although varying from place to place, are mainly meridional and modulate the surface of the Sunda Platform itself on similar lines. These roughly N–S. ranges are described by Suess as the roots of ancient mountains. They are to be thought of as the denuded vestiges of mountain systems, the inner crystalline cores of which stand revealed by prolonged erosion of the sedimentaries within whose folds they were primarily intruded. These stumps of mountains are typically free from precipices and crags, have gentle slopes but are still fairly high because the parent mountains were huge, probably of Himalayan proportions. Today these "Altaid" relief features, apparent in that mountainous

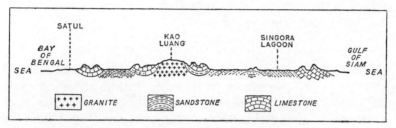

FIG. 2.—A section of the Kra Isthmus

country between Burma and Thailand, in Indochina, in Malaysia and in Borneo, by no means approximate to the towering heights of Himalayan and Alpine mountains, having been denuded to little higher than some 10,000 ft.

Towards the centre of the Platform, in Malaysia and Borneo, the characteristically senile, denuded relief (Fig. 2) is most emphatic, extending into the islands of the Lingga and Rhio Archipelagoes, which may be considered as monadnocks. The Altaid trend lines, while mainly meridional, are least so in Borneo, where NE–SW. alignments are apparent. In Indochina, Thailand and the Kra Isthmus, the N–S. line is well developed and very pronounced in that closely packed series of ranges among which the Irrawaddy, Salween, Menam, Mekong and Red Rivers have parallel courses. While the Sunda Platform has had a prolonged history of stability, at the present moment it is extensively inundated, so that only its higher parts stand above sea level. The advanced peneplanation of the Platform as a whole is evidenced by the uniformity in depth of the shallow seas, the South China Sea, Malacca Strait and Java Sea, now spread across the continental shelf.

The Sunda Platform is characteristically free from active

volcanism or frequent earthquakes, though relics of old seismic activity are present.

2. THE SAHUL SHELF

Similar to the Sunda Platform in its morphology, the Sahul Shelf is best considered as a northern extension of the Australian continental mass, partially inundated by the shallow Arafura Sea, and terminating south of the main E–W. range of middle New Guinea. This stable land mass is, like the Sunda Platform, free of recent volcanic forms. Evidence of active mountain building on its fringe, in the north of Irian (New Guinea), suggests stresses from the Sahul Shelf towards the north.

3. YOUNG MOUNTAINS AND INSULAR ARCS

The festoons of mountains which enfold the Sunda Platform and the Sahul Shelf provide much scope for theories about mountain building processes, a matter outside the immediate field of geography. These mountains in many cases rise steeply from the floor of the Indian and Pacific Oceans to heights over 15,000 feet above sea level; in other localities, the greater part of the mountain system is below sea level and only its topmost points emerge as strings of islands. Fault and fold systems on several lines curve and recurve over one another to make an exceptionally involved pattern, in which certain well marked alignments may be distinguished.

(a) The Burma–Java loop starts from the India–Burma border and runs through the Arakan Yoma, disappears for some distance as a topographic feature and then continues as the complicated fold-fault systems of Western Sumatra, South Java and eastwards as a string of islands curving back from the Sahul Shelf through the Kei Islands to Ceram. This series on the Indian Ocean fringe of Southeast Asia is paralleled seaward first by a deep oceanic trough and then by an oceanic ridge showing as the Nias-Mentawei Islands off West Sumatra and as the islandless submarine ridge south of Java.

(b) The arcs on the Pacific margins run through the Philippines and Northern West Irian, creating lines of islands enclosing small, deep, square-shaped, oceanic basins. Troughs or trenches much deeper than the Pacific average are situated on the Pacific side of these arcs (the Philippine Trench is over

7 miles deep), and these resemble in form and location the
oceanic trenches off Sumatra and Java.

(c) The complex of short arcs and knots showing in the Suluwesi
Moluccas groups have alignments which repeat the patterns of
the Pacific and Indian Ocean fringes, and of the inner edges of
the Sunda Platform and the Sahul Shelf. Here, too, the arcs

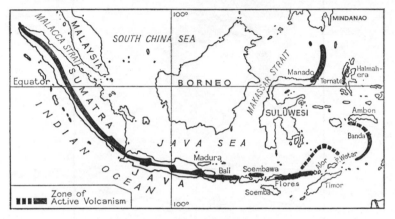

FIG. 3.—East Indies Volcanic Zones

enclose deep geosynclinal oceanic basins, such as the Molucca
Sea which is over 16,500 ft. deep. The intersection of these
alignments produces the curious shapes of Suluwesi and Halmahera. This zone may be likened to the "mediterranean
seas" between Europe and Africa and between North and
South America; in this case it is a mediterranean sea between
Asiatic and Australian continental blocks.

Throughout these zones of contemporary crustal deformation,
the longitudinal and transverse fractures are dotted with volcanoes,
many of which are still active (Fig. 3). Their ejecta further complicate the land forms already made complex by the ravages of
violent erosion (Fig. 4). Lava and igneous materials of widely
varying ages have flowed over large areas and even on to parts of
the Sunda Platform, as in Sumatra. Within the oceanic deeps
marginal to these zones of crustal stress are the epicentres of most
of those major earthquakes whose frequency is yet another symptom of the instability surrounding the shelves.

Thus the geomorphology of this third zone is transitional,

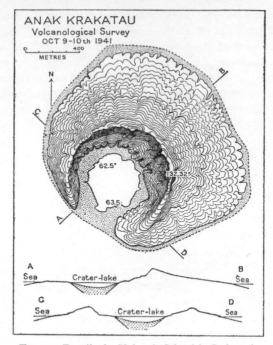

ANAK KRAKATAU
Volcanological Survey
OCT 9-10th 1941
0 _____ 400
METRES

N

B

C

62.5°

132.32

63.5

A

D

A
Sea   Crater-lake

B
Sea

C
Sea   Crater-lake

D
Sea

FIG. 4.—Detail of a Volcanic Island in Indonesia

reflecting at once the influence and forms of continental Asia and continental Australia, and of the Indian and Pacific Oceans.

ROCK TYPES

Profound chemical action caused by tropical and equatorial weathering has two effects on most of Southeast Asia; the destruction of readily accessible fossils by weathering and the concealing of native rocks by great thicknesses of weathered material. Thus the historical geology of Southeast Asia, the dating of the rocks, is not yet fully studied, and the geological interpretations of local rocks are by no means unanimous.

So far as their general character is concerned, however, no appreciable difference can be noted between the rocks of Southeast Asia and those of more intensively studied areas in Europe and North America. The effects of each rock type in conditioning landscape forms appear to be much the same throughout the world, differing in degree, not in character.

The pattern of rock types may be summed up thus:

1. Within the Sunda Platform quartzites and shales are prominent over large areas, generally producing subdued relief, not closely allied to the fold lines of the strata. These metamorphics often appear at the surface close to a group of limestone rocks of which a calcareous shale, much of it in areas of low elevation, is most extensive. Massive limestone is most common as a landscape feature where least subject to solution weathering,

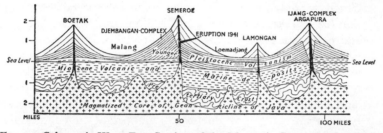

Fig. 5.—Schematic West–East Section of the Mountain Structures in Malang

towards the drier margins of the Platform (as in East Java and Tonkin) where it stands out as gaunt hills whose features recall those of the Karst, though partly disguised by a wilder profusion of vegetation. Small, slightly metamorphosed limestone formations retain this karstic character even under equatorial rains, as in West Malaysia where they still rear prominently above the horizon. A large part of Borneo, the biggest single exposure of the Platform, is built of old sandstone, establishing a flat-topped landscape through which ravine-like valleys have been cut. The higher mountains of the Sunda Platform, the Altaids of Suess, are invariably elongated intrusions of igneous rock, mainly granitic, and this material forms the chief heights of a relief otherwise gently modulated.

2. Upon the young mountain systems marginal to the Platform, the landform owes more to recent tectonic activity than to the nature of the constituent rocks, most of which are also represented on the Sunda Platform. Complex fracturing and folding produce on the young mountains a wild steep landscape which here and there encloses fragments of older continental blocks. The vents and caldera of volcanoes (Fig. 5) add their special forms built from looser, easily eroded rock materials of lava

type which have been severely scarred by denudation. Magmatic rocks have flowed extensively from these volcanoes, spreading over a large area and serving to mask relief forms developed upon underlying earlier structures. As a result of these igneous formations throughout the region, contact metamorphosis has taken place on a large scale, which has a major bearing on the frequency of metallic minerals and helps to account for the scarcity of coal formations.

3. The detail of much of the Southeast Asia landscape is conditioned by contemporary river alluviation and coastal sedimentation (as in Eastern Sumatra and Kalimantan) whose thickness and profusion relate to the rapidity of tropical erosion on the one hand and to the stability of the continental platform on the other. Relief upon the great alluviated landscapes is slight. In this zone where there is so much coastline in proportion to the land area, marine accumulations of spits, bars and off-shore beaches are both prominent and important in conditioning coastal topography and the location of settlements. Marine loads tend to be heavy in this zone of violent terrestrial erosion and under certain conditions sediment accumulates quickly owing to the speed with which mangrove establishes itself upon any bank or spit which is built up, thereafter further hastening deposition by hindering the free scouring of normal wave action. Marine sedimentation is greater upon the inner coasts of the Sunda Platform and less upon those coasts facing the Indian and Pacific Oceans where the shore profiles are steep and the waves have maximum drive of wind behind them.

CHARACTER OF SEAS

Three types of seas may be distinguished by the criterion of depth:

1. Shallow seas of the Sunda Platform
2. Shallow seas of the Sahul Shelf
3. The Austro-Asiatic "mediterranean" basins between the Sunda Platform and the Sahul Shelf, and subdivided by island festoons. In this group may be provisionally placed the Sulu Basin, though the South China Basin between the Philippines and the Asiatic mainland may only be included by considerably stretching the "mediterranean" conception.

1. *Sunda Platform Seas*

These seas, the Malacca Strait, the southern portion of the South China Sea, the Sunda Sea and the Java Sea, are remarkable less for their shallowness than for the uniformity of their shallowness, which is mostly about 120 ft. and only in a few places reaches depths exceeding 150 ft. This derives from the long history of peneplanation of the whole platform prior to its present partial inundation, which has fairly conclusively been shown to be due to eustatic rather than tectonic changes. The small islands (the Rhio, Lingga, Banka and Billiton islands) within these seas are generally of monadnock type and they have granitic cores. Low profiles characterise the adjoining shore lines where broad estuaries carry low topography far inland and where flat coasts of sedimentation, backed by marshes, are more common than those of marine erosion. Such shallow seas are affected strongly by currents arising from winds and less by the circulatory systems of the surrounding oceans, so that monsoonal wind reversals are the major influences on water movement. The drift of surface water thus relates closely to the wind systems described in Chapter 2. Out of contact with oceanic circulations by reason of the disposition of islands athwart the lines of Indian and Pacific Ocean water movements, and located between equatorial land-masses with a very heavy rainfall draining into them, these shallow seas are abnormally fresh and remain abnormally warm: from salinities of 31 per mille and sea temperatures of 70° F., few parts of the surface waters show any significant deviation from place to place or from season to season.

Enclosed between the Andamans, Burma, Kra and Sumatra is a sea steadily being encroached upon by the Irrawaddy Delta, yet its depth and connection with oceanic circulations external to the Platform relate it chiefly to the Bay of Bengal, except that the huge outpouring from Burmese rivers lowers its surface salinity to figures even below those of the Platform seas.

Further evidence that the existence of these seas derives from eustatic rather than tectonic changes is found in the loose gravels, sands and muds which form most of the beds of Sunda Platform waters and in the absence of raised wave-cut terraces along the coasts. Attached plants may be found almost everywhere on the sea floor, which is entirely eulittoral in character.

2. *The Sahul Shelf*

The Arafura Sea and its extension to the Gulf of Carpentaria have been only sketchily studied and are properly outside Southeast Asia. They broadly repeat the features of the Sunda Platform seas except that the salinities are not so abnormally low because the freshwater inflow is less abundant, since the Australian margin has a lower rainfall.

3. *The "mediterranean seas" of the Indies*

The Snellius Expedition catalogued twenty-six distinct basins and trenches in the "mediterranean seas" of the Indies, excluding the deep between the Philippines and China which scarcely belongs to the region. Of these, eight are deeper than 15,000 feet while the sills between them are not less than 4,000 feet deep. Within each basin there tend to be two circulatory systems:

(a) the surface circulation, relatively fast-moving, connected freely with circulations in adjoining basins and thence with currents in the open ocean. It is confined to an upper layer reaching from the surface to approximately the depth of the sill surrounding the basin, that is, to an average depth of about 5,500 feet. The location of the main island barriers is such that the upper waters are strongly influenced by water from the North Equatorial Current of the Pacific, which presses into the "mediterranean seas", through those many gaps between Mindanao and New Guinea. Scarcely any similar currents derive from the Indian Ocean, in the direction of which the basins are almost isolated by the continuous Sumatra-Java obstruction. In temperature, these basins have a surface warmth similar to that of all equatorial waters, the great difference between their surfaces and those of the Platform seas being a higher salinity—generally 34.5 per mille—and a diminished influence of monsoon winds.

(b) the circulation at depth, a movement so slow that the expression "creep" might be substituted. This movement takes place within each basin or trough, isolated from circulation in neighbouring deeps by the sill, and from the surface movements by a discontinuity plane which develops owing to the greater density of the deep water. For the most part, however, the water moving in these isolated deeps originates from the

Pacific by creeping into the Northern Banda Basin, than passing through the Southern Banda Basin and the Weber Deep, the Sawoi Basin and the Weker Basin out into the Indian Ocean deeps. All these lower waters have characteristically high salinity and low temperatures, which prevent any continued outward movement from the basins, though there is a steady removal of water drawn in from deep-level Pacific Equatorial water, whose feature is low temperature by comparison with adjoining water at the same depths within the sills. Inside the basins, minimum temperatures are found just below the level of the lowest sill. Farther down this temperature increases adiabatically but the potential temperature (i.e. reduced to sea level) remains low, so that no convectional circulation is induced. Under these conditions of dense water stably stratified, the profound deeps tend to accumulate hydrogen sulphide.

The margins of these "mediterranean seas" commonly show raised beaches and wave-cut terraces uncorrelating in altitude from point to point owing to the wide variation of amplitude in the tectonic changes over short distances. Shore profiles are normally steep with the result that estuarial sedimentation is negligible.

TIDES

Within these partially enclosed seas, tidal impulses come from both the Pacific and the Indian Oceans. Whatever the character of tides in the open oceans or in the mediterranean basins, the impulse is for the most part converted into progressive waves by the shallowness of seas upon the Platform (Fig. 6).

Tidal waves from the Pacific advance westwards through the Luzon Strait and the many channels between Irian and Taiwan. Those from the Indian Ocean progress eastwards along the Malacca Strait and also northward through the passages between Sumatra and Irian. In the deep basins and troughs of the "mediterranean" section, tides appear to behave as standing oscillations, whose periodicity depends on the form and size of the deeps.

Conditions on the Sunda Platform are best known along only the major shipping lanes. In the deep northern part of the South China Sea, tides resemble standing oscillations and are almost simultaneous. The southern part is shallow, causing tides

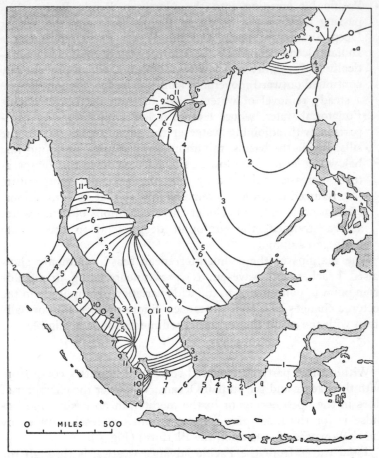

FIG. 6.—Co-tidal Lines (hourly intervals) in Southeast Asia seas for
14th March 1956

to travel slowly southwards and even through the Sunda
Sea.

From the west, Indian Ocean tides move down the funnel-shaped
Malacca Strait, steadily increasing in range. From the east,
comes the tide from the Hongkong Basin, which is of Pacific
origin. The tide in the Java Sea derives from the southernmost
"mediterranean seas", which take their main impulse from Indian
Ocean by way of the Timor Sea and the Lesser Sundas.

Just south of Singapore Island, the Malacca Strait and the South

China Sea tides converge, locally retarding the scouring capacity and assisting heavy marine sedimentation derived from the adjoining land masses. Among the Lingga and Rhio Islands, the tidal movements are extremely complicated due to convergent tidal waves from neighbouring seas. Tidal values in all these seas are modified seasonally by winds which practically reverse through the year, working to augment or reduce the water level. The South China Seas, whose length parallels the direction of the seasonal wind streams, changes level as much as 1.5 ft. due to the Northeast Monsoon.

The range of the tides here varies from less than 2 ft. over the deep basins to 10 or 12 ft. in the shallow seas. Around most coasts, the usual range is below 5 ft.

CORALS

The polyps and other organisms whose skeletons accumulate to form coral reefs, live in colonies which within four years may grow to two inches in diameter from a single individual. They are exacting in their environmental requirements, needing sea temperatures of at least 68° F. throughout the year, shallow clear water to permit their food processes, which are largely photosynthetic, and fairly high salinity. A live coral colony has a slimy surface which is in fact the living matter; the live cells die if exposed to the air, or if covered with mud. Corals establish themselves for the most part on rocky foundations. Off Southeast Asia distinct differences can be seen in their regional distribution.

On the Sunda Platform as a whole corals are only developed well beyond easy access from the shore. The relatively fresh seas with swampy margins heavily charged with fine silts and humic acids are unfavourable to the polyps and the recent history of slow inundation of the Platform operates against them as well, though corals are found at depth along its margins and in broad belts round the rocky islands off Singapore. Platform corals are exclusively submarine and generally stand below sea level well offshore, so that they are never prominent on a coastal landscape. The great development of coral is on the eastern edge of the Platform, running parallel to the east coast of Borneo and well out into the Macassar Strait (Fig. 7), where broad reefs occur whose proportions resemble those of the Great Barrier Reef on the

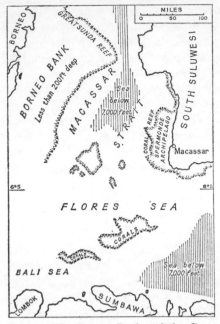

FIG. 7.—The Borneo Bank and the Great Sunda Barrier Reef on the East of the Sunda Platform

eastern edge of the Sahul Shelf. These locations are favourable because they are washed by the warm onshore equatorial currents; similar extensive developments on the western side of the continental shelf are prevented by slight upwellings of water produced behind offshore currents.

Within the "mediterranean seas", the occurrences of coral are less extensive at any one point but they show much greater variety of form. Atolls, barriers and reefcaps at varying levels above, below and inclined to present sea levels and in varying degrees of symmetry to existing islands, may be found in this zone where there has been steady and repeated displacement of the geanticlines which form the chains of islands.

Several theories have been devised to account for the formation of coral. All of them start from the environmental requirements of the live polyp (i.e. sunlit waters below low-tide), and relate the shape and extent of the accumulations of skeletons to some change of water level. In the Southeast Asia seas may be found examples to support those coral formation theories stressing sea level or eustatic change, a dominant process on the Sunda Platform; and also examples of corals associated with slow movements of the earth's crust, the chief physical factor operating among islands of the "mediterranean seas" and the basis of theories attributing coral formations to submarine tectonic changes.

Chapter Two

CLIMATIC FACTORS IN SOUTHEAST ASIA

FEW regions comparable in size to Southeast Asia have so uniform a temperature régime over the whole area and throughout the year. Apart from those local variations due to altitude, and in Northern Burma and Thailand to continental influences from Tibet, Southeast Asia from Lower Burma to South Viet Nam and Irian has average monthly temperatures which remain within ten degrees or so of 80° F. at all seasons. Symmetry about the Equator and a set of land units thoroughly broken up by water bodies of greater area than themselves account for this uniformity of warmth in time and from place to place, and in turn mean that the broad human and vegetation variations do not correlate closely with variations of warmth from place to place, nor is the rhythm of vegetation and cultivation in the region as a whole set by an annual procession of temperature changes.

The basic rhythm of plants and agriculture through most of Southeast Asia is dominated by rainfall—by its incidence rather than by its volume, though considerable differences in volume make distinct climatic sub-divisions away from the axis of the Equator. Köppen's classification emphasises these climatic differences. In this broken terrain, the pattern of the rainfall and the pattern of its variations within short distances, are set by the wind systems. To understand these is to see the operative factor behind the local differences in rainfall periodicity which very much depend on the aspect of the land masses in relation to the seasonal air currents and to local water areas.

THE WIND RÉGIME

Two similar air masses move across Southeast Asia:

(a) The Northern Tropical Air Mass which normally moves from the Tropic of Cancer towards the Equator as the Northeast Trades;

(b) The Southern Tropical Air Mass, originating over the Tropic of Capricorn and normally moving towards the Equator as the

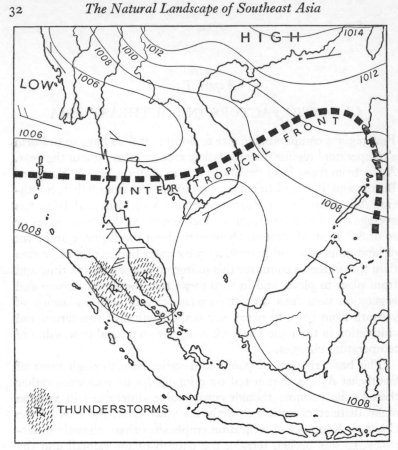

FIG. 8.—Daily Weather Chart of Southeast Asia with isobars in millibars
at 12.00 on 28th September 1946

Southeast Trades.

The physical character of the air is much the same in these two masses, which each have long courses across extensive warm seas, so that each is uniformly warm and uniformly damp. Furthermore, the air masses are both losing impetus as they move into lower latitudes. Where the Northern and Southern Tropical Air Masses converge is thus a front, by analogy with conceptions regarding air convergences worked out in other parts of the world, e.g. the Polar Front. The surface of convergence of the two tropical air-streams may be called "The Intertropical Front" and it shows on the weather map as a line.

The similarity of physical conditions in these airstreams means that the Intertropical Front is less sharply defined at any one time by comparison with the Polar Front which separates air masses in different physical states. The warmth, the humidity and the loss of horizontal impulse in each of the Tropical Air Masses mean that vertical impetuses are increasing so that the Intertropical Front is marked by upward movements on both sides, tending to a vigorous convectional action. This explains the frequent calms along the Intertropical Front when strongly developed in what may be called its "ideal position," i.e. roughly along the Equator. In the older terminology, the zone of convergence of the Trade Winds was called the Doldrums. Just as the Polar Front has been found extremely useful in forecasting depressions in more northern latitudes, so also the Intertropical Front is a valuable line for forecasting weather, since along it move mild depressions and squalls which may assume great violence. Daily weather charts (synoptic charts) in this zone have so far only been prepared for official use and are not sold publicly (Fig. 8).

This relatively simple pattern is complicated by two other influences. Firstly, the two air masses are displaced across the Equator by the annual migration of the sun. The Intertropical Front is thus pulled south during the Southern Hemisphere summer and north of the Equator during northern summer. When the airstreams cross the Equator, Ferrell's Law operates upon them differentially so that Southeast Trades moving into the Northern Hemisphere become southwesterly winds and Northeast Trades become northwesterly winds when moving into the Southern Hemisphere.

Secondly, the low pressure areas developed over the continents to which Southeast Asia is marginal, induce certain seasonal deviations in the air streams. Summer low pressures over Australia are just strong enough for the Intertropical Front to be pressed abnormally far south over Northern Australia in December. But the summer low pressures over India and the margins of continental Asia, particularly over Central Burma and Thailand, have more dramatic effect: the Northern India low pressure system draws parts of the South Tropical Air Mass over the Equator in late northern spring, to maintain a parabolic path over the North Indian Ocean until November. The low pressure system which becomes established over the eastern parts of Asia two or three

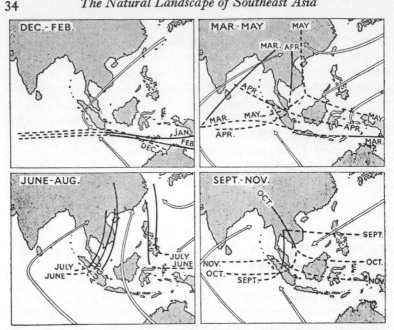

FIG. 9.—The Intertropical Front in Southeast Asia. The front is shown by a heavy line, drawn as continuous where it is sharply defined and persistently located; as an interrupted line where the front is weakly defined and subject to considerable variation in position. The open lines show diagrammatically the manner in which the air masses move

months later than that over India, has a somewhat similar effect, drawing Southern Tropical Air far northwards through the South China Sea during June–July–August.

These influences produce the air streaming analysed in the accompanying four maps (Fig. 9), each representing conditions over three-month periods, which may be summarised thus:

1. December to February. The Southern and Northern Tropical Air Masses at this period move almost on ideal lines. The northern air streams cross the Equator as northwest winds reaching to about 7° S. where the Intertropical Front runs almost latitudinally except for a sag farther south towards the Australian low pressure zone.

2. March to May. Three air streams interact at this time. The Southern Tropical Air presses northward but does not substantially cross the Equator near Southeast Asia. The Northern Tropical Air Masses withdraw towards the northeast and in

places move towards East Asia as east winds. Over mid-Indian Ocean, a first part of the Southern Tropical Air Mass (under the influence of Indian low pressures) crosses the Equator to blow across the Bay of Bengal as southwest winds, reaching farther eastwards as the season advances. The Intertropical Front at this time has branched form; its trace becomes roughly a cuspate curve pointing northward and prolonged in that direction by one or two arms which mark the convergences of air streams from the Bay of Bengal and from the West Pacific. The crux of this front is over the Central Indian Ocean in March, moving to positions eastward and slightly northward to one off Labuan in May.

3. June to August. Southern Tropical Air increases its migration north and a second major transfer of it into the Northern Hemisphere takes place, driving through the Java Sea and the South China Sea, drawn far northwards by East-Central Asia low pressures. At this time Northern Tropical Air does not reach Southeast Asia. The Intertropical Front opens into two almost symmetrical fronts of hyperbolic shape as a result of the second streaming of South Tropical Air. The double arms of the Fronts are close together at first but the distance between them increases until during August only the western portion lies over Southeast Asia as a roughly N–S. curving front off the coast of Indochina. The Intertropical Front persists over the Malaysia-Indochina area throughout this quarter, delimiting two air streams both of which are Southern Tropical in origin yet which have acquired different physical characteristics and directions by taking different courses.

4. September to November. At this season the Northern Tropical Air rapidly increases its pressure from the north, extending its coverage westward and southward. Southern Tropical Air continues to cross the Equator over the Indian Ocean but diminishes in drive, to cease as an air transfer by November. The streaming of Southern Tropical Air through the South China Sea becomes completely occluded and is finally confined below the Equator as the Southeast Trades. Moving southward, the Intertropical Front reverts to the cuspate form of March–May, flattening to a latitudinal alignment. At this transitional period the cuspate curve is much sharper at its beak and less symmetrical than in the spring.

In considering this analysis of tropical air masses, it must be remembered that the Intertropical Front varies in its preciseness and the positions given here are tendencies often disguised in practice by broad zones of calms. Thus the Doldrums should be considered as the zone within which is located the Intertropical Front, characterised by highly unstable air conditions and traversed by weak depressions moving sometimes westwards, sometimes eastwards, or at certain seasons polewards under the influence of the adjoining continents.

RAINFALL

In Fig. 10 the generalised effect of aspect, relief and these air streams may be seen to produce a rainfall above 80 in. per annum upon large areas of Southeast Asia. The zones of low rainfall are the dry belt of Upper Burma and Central Thailand which are shielded by relief barriers athwart the air streams. Moreover the total precipitation lessens eastward through Indonesia, particularly in the territories and islands east of Central Java.

North of a line from Achin through South Kra to Mindanao, and east and south of Central Java, very distinct dry seasons appear, the criterion being that of Köppen: at least one month of these areas has less than 2.4 in. of rain. The disposition of these dry zone areas is related to latitudes beyond the equatorial belt and towards the tropical limits. Towards the Equator, precipitation varies seasonally, generally with double wet seasons, though no season is sufficiently rainless to be called dry.

The tropical air masses operating over Southeast Asia are characterised by high temperatures and humidity, coupled with a physical instability which is greatest towards the Equator and decreases towards the continent of Asia. As a result of this instability, relatively weak depressions, small relief features and local overheating by insolation in, say, a town or in bare fields, can act as triggers to stimulate violent vertical air movements. Altitude thus has greater effects proportionally than is normal in other latitudes. Under these conditions cumulo-nimbus clouds of as much as 10,000 ft. depth may develop within half an hour and vertical air currents of 100 m.p.h. inside such clouds are quite

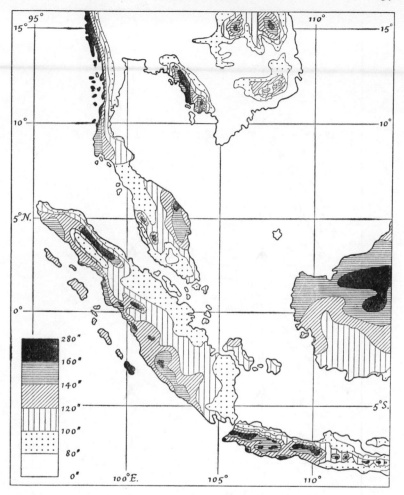

FIG. 10.—Mean Annual Rainfall of Southeast Asia

common. With the parent air so humid, the precipitation consequent on such updraughts is very heavy (often as much as 2 inches
within an hour) even though localised over a small area, and the
latent heat deriving from precipitation serves to perpetuate the
uprush of air. While all types of initial cause of precipitation occur
over Southeast Asia, they tend always to be accompanied by

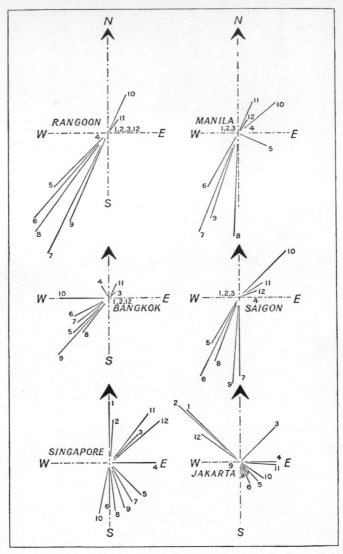

FIG. 11.—Correlation of Rainfall and Wind Direction in Southeast Asia. The bearing of each arm represents the mean monthly direction of the wind (blowing towards the centre) and the length of each is proportional to the mean monthly rainfall. Months of no rainfall are thus no more than points at the compass centre. The numbers on each arm indicate the month (1 Jan., 2 Feb., etc.)

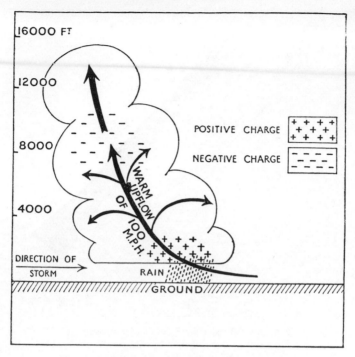

FIG. 12.—Structure of a Tropical Thunderstorm

thunderstorms, which towards the Equator are of daily occurrence and great violence (over 320 storms occur round Bogor each year). Thunderstorm frequency decreases in those sub-regions where winter dry seasons are pronounced, yet even there the rainy months have high thunderstorm frequency. These Southeast Asia thunderstorms resemble those of middle latitudes (Fig. 12) and are accompanied by a "chimney" of rapidly rising air at the core, often with downflows of cooler air just in front of the storm. While the up-current of these thunderstorms is strong enough at times to tear an aeroplane apart, the freezing level is so high (above 25,000 feet) that hail, a common feature of similar storms in other latitudes, is here rare. The degree of correlation between rainfall and wind is evident from the combination of wind-roses and rainfall data in Fig. 11 which also demonstrates how emphatic is the dry season at places away from the Equator.

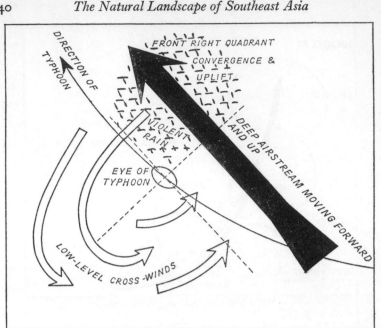

FIG. 13.—Theoretical Structure of a Typhoon

TYPHOONS

"Typhoon" is the name given to tropical cyclones which occur off East Asia. Only the northernmost parts of Southeast Asia come under the influence of typhoons which are most frequent over the Philippines and Indochina. A few have been known to cross the Kra Isthmus and pass over Bengal. The Bay of Bengal typhoons, frequenting a restricted area well north in the Bay, do not normally affect Burma, so that only the South China Sea typhoons strongly influence the weather conditions of Southeast Asia territories.

While theories about the origin of typhoons do not reach general agreement in detail, partly due to the difficulty of obtaining full meteorological data about these phenomena whose violence so often destroys instruments and whose variable paths defy advance preparation for tests, they seem to result from a widespread convection of hot, moist, unstable air and may represent extreme variants of the forces arising from convergent air currents. Much has been done to accumulate data about sea level features of

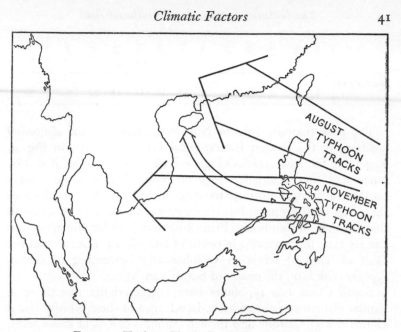

FIG. 14.—Typhoon Tracks in the South China Sea

typhoons, but little information is available about their vertical structure apart from navigators' notes on cloud formation. Clines, writing on the basis of U.S. data, seems to have established that typhoons are in fact largely self-perpetuating from the release of much latent heat due to violent precipitation in the front right quadrant, where he suggests a point above the ground at the precipitation level is in effect a constant generator of heat, and a constant low pressure focus towards which the sea-level barometric centre is always moving (Fig. 13). A close relation between the path of typhoons and a front between air masses has also been suggested.

Typhoons of the South China Sea normally originate somewhere east of the Philippines and travel towards those islands and Indochina, along paths which gradually assume that parabolic line peculiar to all tropical cyclones, so that between the Philippines and North Viet Nam they begin to recurve on a line towards the northeast (Fig. 14). The seasonal incidence varies. In the period 1918–29, ninety-eight South China Sea typhoons were distributed thus through the year:

	Jan.	Feb.	Mar.	Apr.	May	June	July	Aug.	Sept.	Oct.	Nov.	Dec.	Total
Number of Typhoons	2	0	0	0	4	6	22	17	11	15	15	6	98

The peak periods, July to November, relate to the abnormal positions of the broken Intertropical Front as shown in Fig. 9. Regarding the mean tracks of these East Asia typhoons, it will be noted that they normally move on paths shifting progressively northward from February to August and shifting southwards thereafter until January, but they never reach much farther south than the Cape of Cambodia. From July to September the maximum danger zone for typhoons is north of latitude 15° (Luzon and the Gulf of Tonkin) while in October and November maximum typhoon risk is on the coasts of South Viet Nam.

South China Sea typhoons have characteristics like those of similar disturbances elsewhere. In advance of them whispy cirrus clouds at high altitude and broken cumulus clouds at lower levels drift across the horizon, the latter becoming dark rugged clouds, more numerous and coalescent in the centre as the typhoon approaches. About 100 miles from the centre, dark nimbus clouds develop and produce torrential rains moving forward with the whole typhoon at rates from 10–20 knots, while the constituent winds often increase to speeds reaching and exceeding 80 knots. Each typhoon has an "eye" of comparatively small area, perhaps 5 miles in diameter where the sky is relatively clear, calmer or only lightly squally and no rain falls, resembling an intensified form of the quiet conditions between the warm and cold fronts of a middle latitude cyclone. Behind the "eye" of the typhoon winds again blow with devastating violence, in a reverse direction to winds in advance of the "eye", with nimbo-strutus clouds producing torrential rains which reduce visibility to nil. These gradually lose intensity and the typhoon passes over, leaving a trail of high cirrus.

In these deep tropical depressions, the great force of the winds involved causes widespread damage in built-up and cultivated areas. Their violence and frequency is particularly great in Luzon and they appear to lose violence over Indonesia. They form one of the major hazards of shipping in the South China Sea, particularly for native sailing vessels. Most of the first study of these typhoons was contained in European seamen's handbooks which were chiefly concerned with rule of thumb methods by which ships unlucky enough to be caught in a typhoon could avoid the most dangerous parts of them. The coastal zones of Tonkin and Annam experience severe floods in low-lying areas when the typhoon winds set in certain directions which augment the tides. Typhoon winds can, at their worst, lift trains from their rails and cast steamers several hundred yards inland from the shore.

The French observers, Bruzon and Carton, describe thus a typhoon over Nha Trang and Hon Ba in 1926: "The typhoon appeared first on 2nd November, WNW. of Yap and on the 3rd was 700 km. east of Manila. During the night of 5th–6th November it crossed south of Manila. Over the China Sea, its course changed from west to west-southwest and the typhoon struck the coast of Annam on the 7th. At Nha Trang about 16.00 hours on that day, the wind blew violently from WSW. During the night its violence increased and its course changed through NW. and N. to NNE. Minimum pressure was experienced that night (980 m.b.) but at Hon Ba in the mountains (1,480 m.) pressure went down two hours later to 818 m.b. During that one night pressures dropped about 30 m.b. in the path of the typhoon but after a few hours reverted to normal again. Considerable damage was done to Hon Ba forests, many trees were uprooted and in some places entire groves were destroyed. The typhoon brought torrential rain to the whole Annam coast from Faifoo to Cap Padaran."

Certain line squalls moving eastwards to West Malaysia at very low latitudes in the Malacca Strait have a violence at times approaching that of typhoons and the squalls are in fact related to disturbances on the Intertropical Front: they are not circular in character, have no "eye," are not extensive or persistent features and they have no connection with true typhoons.

SUNSHINE

Over most Southeast Asia territories for much of the year, the cloud cover is very heavy and the sunshine period is low. This is most emphatic towards the Equator away from which a season of clear skies and continuous sunny weather occurs. The effective sunshine is rendered even less by the high humidity which cuts off many actinic wavelengths. In Singapore for over half the day the sun is obscured by clouds; in Jakarta less than 70 per cent of the possible sunshine hours are sunny. A distinct diurnal rhythm of sunshine incidence is characteristic of the Equator; during the mornings, which frequently begin clear and sunny, cumulus clouds steadily increase to a maximum in the afternoon, when convectional influences are at their peak, often producing thunder-showers followed by a clearing of the sky towards sunset. The amount of sunshine received is normally greater at sea level and decreases with altitude. On the other hand, those districts with distinct dry seasons have high sunshine values in the dry periods, often offset on the average by prolonged obliteration of the sun during the rainy season. These factors have considerable agricultural significance.

HUMIDITY

High average humidity values are normal everywhere in Southeast Asia, but they are subject to frequent variations. Coasts are damper than interiors and highlands are damper than plains. Localities with marked dry seasons have periods of low humidity accompanied by high temperatures. In any one place a few hours sunshine rapidly lowers the relative humidity and it is a fact that even in the wettest places, the ground and wet clothes dry out under direct sunshine. Comparatively minor humidity variations have considerable effects on plants, and from the point of view of human beings it is the humidity rather than the temperature which produces feelings of body heat or body cold. When the relative humidity drops a few points, the skin sensation is one of coolness, due to easy evaporation of perspiration. By the same cause, a site exposed to regular breezes feels drier and cooler than the actual humidity or thermometer figures justify. The generalised rainfall and seasons map (Fig. 10) is a convenient guide to the distribution of humidity.

ALTITUDE EFFECTS

Throughout the region altitude is an important factor varying the local weather conditions. While the land masses are relatively small, they are orographically very broken so that (apart from

East Sumatra) no very extensive plains have developed and mountains are visible from most points. Even the highest peak known (Kinabalu, Br. Borneo, 13,681 ft.) lies well below the snow line but those highlands adjoining Yunnan do receive a brush of snow in winter. The average highland is, however, more

FIG. 15.—Köppen's Climatic Regions in Southeast Asia

of the order 8,000 feet and continuous areas at a high altitude are quite small. These altitudes induce local temperature reduction, more evident at night than during the day, and local high humidities. They cause local rain shadows which, owing to the differing winds through the year, are seasonal rather than permanent, except where double ranges give the intervening lowland a fairly constant rain shadow, as in Central Burma. A major function of the higher altitudes is to cause orographic rains and to lower the temperatures, which latter has less geographical significance than the overall raininess.

CLIMATIC REGIONS

Raininess is the basic criterion between major parts of this climatic area where temperatures are for most regions never less than warm. Two broad rain types may be distinguished:

(a) heavy rains at all times of the year (over 80 inches per annum). In detail there are peaks of raininess, generally double peaks, but between these peaks is a season less rainy, though still without any month which may be called dry. This region is mainly equatorial.

(b) rains through most of the year, with at least one month with less than 2.4 inches during these cooler months, the length of dry seasons increasing with latitude and the limits being roughly latitudinal as in Fig. 10. The dry seasons are normally related to wind streams at various times of the year. This zone subdivides into:

  1. A subdivision where total rainfall is exceptionally low (below 60 inches per annum) and the drought season long, as in Central Burma and East Thailand.

  2. A subdivision where the dry season is long and altitude reduces the temperature to less than about 60° for the cool season, but not reaching freezing on the average.

Köppen's classifications for this zone are a convenient but by no means fully checked scheme (Fig. 15).

Chapter Three

THE DRAINAGE PATTERNS OF SOUTHEAST ASIA

THE Irrawaddy, Salween, Menam Chao Praya and Mekong are remarkable for their length compared with most Southeast Asia rivers, which rarely exceed a few hundred miles long. Those four major rivers are associated with tectonic basins; relief elsewhere only permits short streams. All districts marginal to the Sunda Platform have experienced relatively recent tectonic changes and the rivers developed upon them are youthful as well as short. Upon the Platform itself much more advanced landscape maturity is evident but because this older surface has only limited areas exposed, rivers even there are short.

CHARACTERISTICS OF TROPICAL RIVERS

In the régime of tropical rivers several factors have distinctive emphasis compared with conditions in temperate latitude rivers. Firstly the volume of water precipitated into and to be carried from any drainage basin is several times that of equivalent temperate latitude rivers as a result of the much higher rainfall. Moreover the precipitation is more intense. Even the dry interior of Burma experiences falls of rain averaging .6 inches per rainy day. The water content of those Tropical Air Masses over Southeast Asia is so high and the rising air currents so strong and sustained that several Javanese stations have recorded falls of over 16 inches per day. These violent torrential downpours are often very localised at any one time, yet on an average they affect large areas. Thus the volume of rainwater in any drainage basin is enormous and fluctuates widely within short periods of a few hours.

A further consequence of these great rainstorms is their powerful erosive effects. Upon cultivated land the force and volume of these downpours cause surface downwash to be large, the soil rapidly washes away and whole hillsides may slip, so that the run-off has a high mud content. Because the rivers are mostly immature, this heavy load may be sustained by turbulence for considerable

47

distances. In areas of alternating wet and dry seasons, drought cracks the ground, loosens the top surface and thereby increases the available load when the rains begin. The Dry Zones of Burma and Thailand are therefore areas of most violent surface removal. The very heavy load of Southeast Asia rivers gives them a great capacity for rapidly building up deltas, sedimenting the estuaries and at times causing heavy deposition of silt well inland. Furthermore the rainfall is not only violent and intense, it is also variable in seasonal incidence; thus many streams of Upper Burma, Central Thailand and Eastern Java are for months almost dry and then come into spate within a few hours, not unlike the wadis of North Africa. Landform combined with the seasonal rains causes the Salween, for instance, to vary its level 50 feet within a few hours. Such variability of volume induces deposition well inland. Huge silt banks lie across many watercourses, vast alluvial fans develop at the debouchment to plains, and even at the junction of tributaries.

The Irrawaddy presents an example of how the drainage conditions differ at different points in the course of a tropical river. Near and above Bhamo changes of Irrawaddy level directly parallel changes of rainfall. As the stream passes through the Dry Zone of Burma it receives no significant additional water from the tributaries after it passes the confluence of the Chindwin and it is effectively losing water by evaporation. Stamp estimates 45 per cent of Irrawaddy water has been lost by evaporation when the stream finally reaches the head of the Delta. Evaporation rates in the Burmese Dry Zone are little, if at all, less than the precipitation. Farther downstream, in the Delta, heavy precipitation occurs again, so that the Irrawaddy floods arrive at the Delta roughly a month after peak rains in the reaches above Bhamo, to find it already suffering from floods due to local rains and small local streams. These floods of local origin effectively oblige the Irrawaddy water to remain within the main distributaries. Even more interesting is Stamp's evidence that the average annual silt load at the Delta head is 261 million tons, whereas at Mandalay it is only 32 million tons, showing that 229 million tons of silt is added in the Dry Zone. Since the Chindwin provides 109 million tons of silt, the balance of 120 million tons derives from the wadi-like, highly variable streams (chaungs) joining the Irrawaddy in its driest section.

LOAD AND THE EROSION OF BASINS

Acting as a brake on the destructiveness of the rivers and on the changes of river levels, the dense forest cover of most of the landscape breaks the force of the downpours and provides roots and undergrowth to act as a spongelike retainer of water and as a partial filter of sediment. Under natural conditions, where the forest is undisturbed by man, this influence is so strong that even minor brooks are relatively clear, but where the natural cover is removed by burning to permit cultivation or mining, the brooks are thick and opaque with sediment, a condition rapidly extending as more and more surface is exposed for farming or for alluvial mining. Wherever there are active volcanoes, great quantities of loose ash are thrown out regularly; Southeast Asia volcanoes typically eject ash rather than lava. Unconsolidated ash without vegetation cover is rapidly washed into the streams and by these agents spread out over the estuaries. A new volcanic outburst is at once followed by heavier loads in the local rivers and increased estuarial deposition (Fig. 19) and greater danger of silting up irrigation and drainage canals which may have been built downstream for cultivating rice. That so much of Java's volcanic ash cones are terraced may only partly be ascribed to agricultural pressure; the terracing is equally necessary to control slip of the ash and to prevent sedimentation by waterborne ash from completely overwhelming the lowlands. Largely as a result of heavy ash loads, the Solo River, for example, carries some sixty times as much sediment as the Rhine, though it is 60 per cent shorter.

The heavy load being carried away by the rivers lowers the surface of the drainage basin over most of its area, even though part of the lower basin is being built up a little by sediment. The rate of destruction of the drainage basin in the tropics is far higher than anywhere else. The Chindwin is removing the surface of its basin by .78 mm. per annum, the Irrawaddy above Prome by .52 mm. per annum, the Loesi in Java by .87 mm. In some small Javanese streams the destruction of the drainage basin has reached as much as 3 mm. per annum. As standards of comparison, the annual lowering of the Danube basin is at the rate of .006 mm., and of the Marne, .005 mm.

As a region, Southeast Asia is thus one of the least stable in the world, as far as orographic form and drainage patterns are concerned. Erosion here works faster and the associated deposition occurs at a greater rate than temperate latitude geographers allow for. This adds only a further variant to the general tectonic instability of all the zone fringing the Sunda Platform, but in the case of the Platform itself, its great age and relative stability plus the intensity of river erosion, provide an excellent case of a landscape exposed continuously to subaerial erosion for a period long enough to indicate an approach to mature peneplanation. The West Malaysian landscape, central to this continental Platform and exposed fully to continuous, powerful and prolonged river action, has special interest in this connection. In W. Malaysia, large alluviated plains dominate the landscape and the hills rise sharply from these plains, yet the features of normal river types still persist. Rapids exist in a number of Malaysian rivers, profiles are slightly broken at a number of levels, trellis drainage patterns have persisted on tilted strata (Fig. 32) and river capture goes on even at this advanced stage, as in the capture of the Bera headwaters by the Muar (Fig. 16). Lakes, however, are unusual on the main Sunda Platform; this negative point is at once a symptom of erosional senility and of the ability of tropical vegetation to build out into the lakes, hastening their sedimentation until the standing water disappears. Thus the Bera Lake of W. Malaysia is really a large swamp periodically inundated; the Tonle Sap of Indochina is rapdily filling to become a similar swamp-lake varying with the seasons. Infilled swamp-lakes appear also in Borneo and the Shan Plateau.

THE GLACIAL PERIOD AND SOUTHEAST ASIA DRAINAGE

While tectonic and erosional changes have produced most variations in river forms of those parts of Southeast Asia fringing the Sunda Platform, *upon* the Platform itself, rivers have been more recently affected by a process of marine inundation. There is general agreement that the history of the Platform is one of stability or possibly of slight sinking; the uniform depth and terrigenous bottom material of the Sunda Platform seas, and also the full-developed river valleys upon their floors, combine to support the view that a rise of sea level has taken place, associated with continental icemelt which took place in northern lattitudes when the last Glacial Period closed. De Geer estimates that the last Scandinavian glaciation reached its peak some 25,000 years

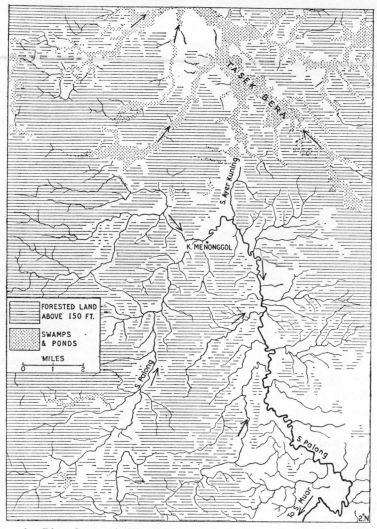

Fig. 16.—River Capture in West Malaysia. The Palong, tributary of the Muar, is drawing off headwaters of the Bera system

ago, at which time maximum water would be withdrawn from oceanic circulation and locked up as ice, thereby lowering the average sea level. Daly calculates that this withdrawal of water would mean a lowering of sea level (relative to present level) at the Equator by between 250 ft. and 300 ft. The average depth of water in the Sunda Platform seas today is 180 ft., so that on Daly's figures the whole Platform would be exposed and drainage lines developed upon it. Molengraaf's work (Fig. 18) suggests the drainage lines of the exposed Sunda continental surface formed two river systems flowing roughly north-eastwards from the Singapore area and roughly due east through what is now the Java Sea. To support this conception he instances the striking likeness between fish of the Moesi in Sumatra and those of the Kapuas in Kalimantan and suggests the similarity derives from association through the main stream developed during the Glacial period. Because there have been in fact several glacial advances in northern latitudes (the Gunz, Mindel, Riss and Wurm Glaciation) his theory implies at least four periods of water withdrawal from the Sunda Platform (and of course from all equatorial areas): that is, four periods when the Sunda sea-floors were exposed to subaerial erosion.

Thus the broad history of recent river development has been one of periodical lowering of sea level, in effect a lowering of erosion base levels for all Sunda Platform rivers, which means four intervening periods of rejuvenation of Southeast Asia rivers and corresponding periods of rising sea level when rivers diminished their cutting power and became senescent, owing to rising erosional base level (Fig. 17). While the world glacial periods varied in duration, they appear not to have differed very widely in extent of greatest development, so that present sea level at the Equator probably represents roughly the level towards which the erosional base rose at each interglacial phase. Those early periods of rising sea could not, on present facts, have reached higher than 100 ft. above present sea level and it is almost certain the variation was much less. It is therefore difficult to accept any theorising which postulates during the last million years over the Sunda Platform, sea level positions 100 ft. higher than the present one.

The landscapes carved by river systems over the older parts of Southeast Asia are conditioned in their recent forms by circumstances of a rising sea level, quite different from Europe and North America where a relatively rising land surface has had the latest influence on landscape form. A recent history of rising sea level implies:

(*a*) rising base levels to river erosion;

(*b*) diminution of downcutting power by existing streams;

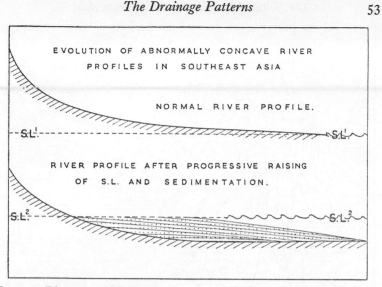

FIG. 17.—Diagram explaining the Development of Inselberge and Concave
Profiles typical of the Sunda Platform

(c) diminution of load-carrying power and an increase of upstream
sedimentation, due to loss of grade in the theoretical profiles;

(d) shallow offshore coastal profiles and consequent increase of
coastal sedimentation;

(e) detrunking of streams as the inundation formed new marine
gulfs (see Molengraaf);

(f) the rapid sedimentation of the estuaries produces in river
profiles an abnormal flattening at lower levels while the upper
profile retains the acute forms developed at lower sea level
positions. This produces "sagging profiles," concave or
flattened outlines (Fig. 17), as contrasted with kinked, faceted
and convex profiles of contemporary streams in Europe;

(g) mountains in the form of "inselberge," that is, standing like
islands surrounded by low-level alluvial plains.

During the glacial periods, when downcutting to a lower base
level was the major influence, considerable upstream terraces
could develop at all altitudes, but this aspect of Sunda Platform
geography is difficult to study owing to the intensive weathering
since that time and the heavy vegetation now masking any benches
built or carved during the period. Such upstream terraces have
been noted by Richardson and Scrivenor in West Malaysia.

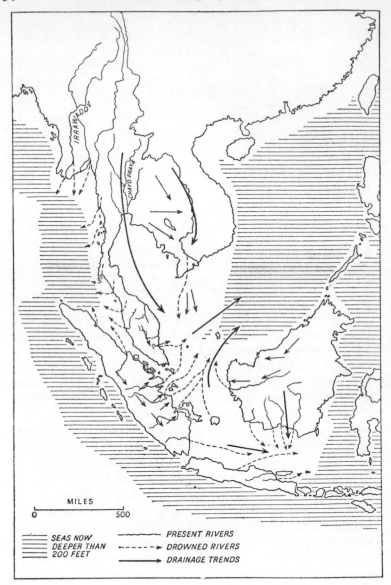

FIG. 18.—Drainage and Shallow Seas of Southeast Asia. Seas now shallower
than 200 ft. were probably land areas in the Glacial Periods

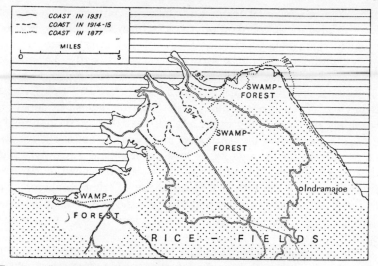

FIG. 19.—Coast Changes at the Mouth of R. Tjimanoek. This shows the rapid changes of the Java coast as a result of sedimentation

The history of inundation at first glance makes it surprising that ria forms have not appeared on the Sunda Platofrm; the explanation lies in the heavy sedimentation by the rivers and in the relatively soft laterised surface which would be presented to the rising sea and quickly moulded by it.

The glacial periods had little other effect in Southeast Asia; Weissman estimates the snow line in Northern Burma to have descended to about 9,000 ft. during the Glacial Periods. If this lowering of the snow line by about 3,500 ft. compared with today roughly indicates the condition for all Southeast Asia at the time of maximum glaciation, then in the equatorial zone where the present snowline is about 16,000 ft., no mountain tops of Borneo, Java, Sumatra and Malaysia could have been seriously affected by snows, let alone by mountain glaciation. Interpretation of land forms in these units on the assumption of glaciation must therefore produce overwhelming evidence to counter such arguments.

SEDIMENTATION

Very heavy river loads, the decreasing carrying power of rivers, and the shallow seas of the Platform zone, combine to make rapid sedimentation of estuarial and coastal regions the characteristic of contemporary relief forms and drainage patterns. The rate of coastal advance seaward upon the Platform is in places phenomenally rapid; the Tjimanoek (Fig. 19) and Solo deltas in Java are extending at the rate of 100 metres annually, the Mekong at 60–80 metres annually. An outburst of volcanic ash increases the deposition by neighbouring rivers at the coast, though the behaviour of sea currents moulds the riberine deposit in detail on reaching the sea. Mangroves and associated vegetation quickly establish themselves on sandbanks and cays so that at the mouth of the Perak, for example, an exposure of a bank for only a few days at a low water season is enough to permit vegetation to start there, hastening the rate of deposition by offering an abstraction to river outflow and thereby perpetuating the bank which in other settings might disappear by erosion during the next high water spell.

Where streams debouch into deep seas the rate of coastal extension is inevitably less, due to the greater thicknesses which must be laid for every outward extension, yet the Irrawaddy Delta is building outward at the rate of about 60 metres per annum; that the Irrawaddy can maintain this rate of building into a deep basin reflects its tremendous load and a physical condition which concentrates the deposition of this load at the outer edge of the Delta rather than over its surface. (See Chapter 9.)

Because the rivers are steadily sedimenting the bed of their lower reaches, these are in fact generally being raised in level. Such a process cannot continue very far; when its bed is raised slightly above the surrounding land, the river easily changes course, and every large delta of Southeast Asia shows signs of frequent migration of distributaries. Old channels and distributaries in various phases of abandonment may be seen at nearly every river mouth. Most deltas suffer regular inundation at various times of the year facilitating farming for rice, which depends on either natural or artificially induced floods, in most cases derived from rivers. The process of spreading sediment over the whole delta zone goes on both by migration of distributaries and by seasonal inundations, so that the deltaic surface over a wide area is being slowly raised by sedimentation, making it progressively more difficult to irrigate the inner and higher sections of the deltas and in the long run causing the centre of gravity of irrigation steadily to move

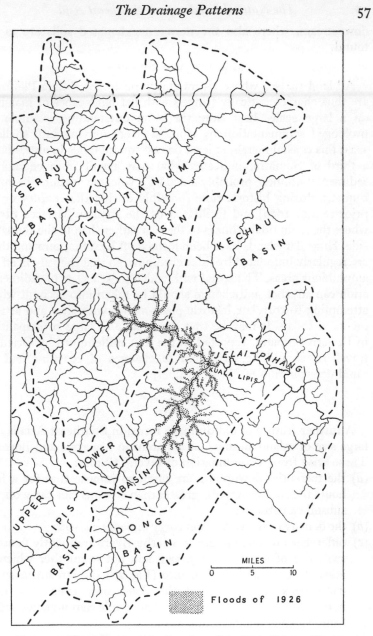

Fig. 20.—Flood Zones at the Junction of the Lipis-Pahang Rivers

downstream, where also the newer unexhausted soils are to be found.

MARSHES AND SWAMPS

All land masses whose rivers empty on to the Sunda Platform are thus characteristically fringed with flat landscapes of marshes on a large scale. East Sumatra is an outstanding example of prolonged sedimentation by tropical rivers moving into shallow seas; this coastal marsh, at least 60,000 square miles in area, about a third of Sumatra, indicates what may result from equatorial sedimentation, here probably aided by a volcanic outburst in inner Sumatra during historic time (possibly during the century or so prior to A.D. 1000) and facilitated by the shallow Malacca Strait where the main tidal scour is to the east rather than to the Sumatra side. Huge flat islands have been formed off East Sumatra and they are regularly inundated by tides even now, so that they are in effect amphibious areas. The speed with which these coasts of sedimentation can advance and change should be taken into account when attempting to correlate historic place-names with sites and settlements of today. It may be that the decline of large principalities in Eastern Sumatra, reported in the first millennium by Oriental travellers, should be attributed to changes of coastline and to rapid deterioration of old site values.

FLOODS

A further feature of old drainage forms in Southeast Asia is the large size of inland swamps, as apparent in Malaysia and Borneo. These arise from a combination of several factors:

(*a*) the torrential downpours are often so intense that for a few hours the surface water is greater than streams can carry off, or subsoil can absorb;

(*b*) the density of the vegetation cover impedes run-off;

(*c*) differences of downpours in nearby rivers frequently cause a swift rise of level in one stream and not in another which it joins, so that at the confluence (Fig. 20) the stream in spate dams back the other and the flood may even flow into it, or build bars of silt across it. The Tonle Sap marshes suffer from Mekong floods in this way;

(*d*) where a drainage system has cluse (as in Malaysian streams) or similar constrictions (as in the Irrawaddy gorges) these features may induce flooding of the valley above the narrows. The Tasek Bera of W. Malaysia in this way reflects constrictions in the Pahang Valley;

(e) the presence of levees means that the zone between them and the foothills has difficulty in draining to the river after a flood or during a downpour, so the levees are generally lined landwards by broad freshwater marshes, as by the rivers across the Korat Plateau in Thailand (Fig. 90);

(f) where local rain seasons coincide with the arrival of spates, originating elsewhere in the local rivers, the landscape cannot shed the direct rainfall rapidly and it induces marshes.

Most of the freshwater marshes are seasonally flooded, drying out quickly in spells of drought, draining when local streams are low, but then flooding to depths up to 10 ft. during wet seasons.

Some types of swamp are man-induced. When alluvial mining is being carried on, dredges and gravel pumps effectively stir up large quantities of river sediment which is carried downstream as the mining effluent (Fig. 21).

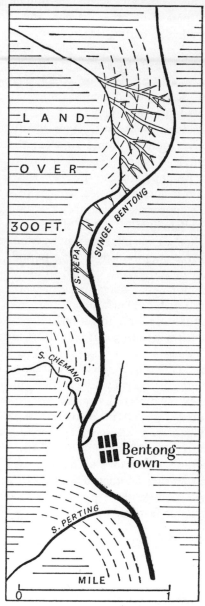

FIG. 21.—Alluvial Fans being thrust across Bentong Valley

This artificially stirred sediment is agriculturally negative and it penetrates the ditches and drains of rice growing areas, gradually silting them up, often spectacularly raising the local river bed (at Serendah in W. Malaysia, the river bed was raised 21 ft. by sedimentation over the decade 1923–33), as well as sterilising fields on which the silt spreads so that cultivation becomes more difficult as the river can no longer be kept out. The yields decrease and the fields are abandoned, swamp vegetation gradually obliterating signs of cultivation. Round the lower Malacca River may be found signs of the old field bundings within the tangle of swamp vegetation now growing there, a sign of the effects of mining higher in the river whose effluent is obliterating cultivation in lower areas. This type of swamp comes slowly and has all the appearance of nature overcoming men's efforts to farm, but it is fundamentally a result of man-induced erosions or abrasions elsewhere. Thus interference, by mining and forest clearing, with landforms stabilised over long periods, not only goes on by removal of silt and gravels carried from mining areas and topsoils removed by torrential rains on clean-weeded agricultural areas as a mark of transfer of surface materials from one area, but it also causes the obliteration of cultivation and an extension of useless marsh in the areas where this material is deposited.

Because these tropical marshes occur in zones of human significance, that is, in the flatter areas with agricultural possibilities, and along the coasts where settlement from overseas might take place, they have played a major part in conditioning the distribution of human beings in Southeast Asia. Both the coastal and inland marshes are tree-covered, making it even more difficult to penetrate, control, or cultivate them. Varying degrees of swampiness often account for the ease of development of farming in one place rather than another in Southeast Asia and a broad belt of marsh has generally proved a greater human impediment than any other topographic feature.

Chapter Four

SOUTHEAST ASIA'S NATURAL VEGETATION

TROPICAL FOREST FACTORS

THE heavy, evenly distributed rainfall and constant high temperatures of most of Southeast Asia encourage continuous plant growth and a profuse, very varied flora. Because the whole year is here a growing season, plant life becomes almost overpowering in its rate of growth. This region contains more species than any other; the flora is not yet completely known, but some 35,000 species of flowering plants alone are thought to exist there (van Steenis). On Borneo at least 11,000 species have been listed, according to Merrill. This contrasts with the parallel figure of 13,000 species for the whole of Tropical West Africa (Good). Woody plants predominate and 15 per cent of the species are trees whose mature trunks are over 16 in. in diameter. The profusion of species is due to (a) the predominantly warm, moist climate, (b) the constancy of this climate over long geological periods, (c) the variety of relief and islands producing minor adaptations, (d) the rapidity with which selective and adaptive evolutionary processes can establish new characteristics in a tropical climate which has no resting season, and (e) the migrations of plant types from both Asia and Australia.

Southeast Asia was originally clothed by nature almost entirely by a tree cover. Only in modern times has there been any extensive clearing because apart from firing, primitive people were technically incapable of removing the forest. Some clearings became permanent for cultivation, in recent centuries, but the majority have been temporary and partial clearings, later left to natural replacement by a selective vegetation such as grass, savannah or scrub. Temporary clearings resulted largely from systems of shifting cultivation which finally abandon an area, partially cleared by fire, to a series of quick-growing plants, becoming after a few years a secondary forest which may, over prolonged periods, evolve to be scarcely distinguishable from primary forest.

The system of migrant agriculture or shifting cultivation, in W. Malaysia called *ladang* and in Burma *taungya*, is widespread throughout Southeast Asia and it may be this form of nomadism has in fact operated so long that it affects nearly every acre of the region, thereby exercising a distinct selective action on the whole forest (Sauer). Much forest which we call "primary" may be senile secondary. This is evident in more densely populated areas such as Java and Viet Nam, and over the centuries may have no less influenced the forest types of even thinly populated zones, as Borneo still is. In this sense "primary forest" is a relative term, to be retained for convenience rather than as presupposing an absolutely virgin tropical forest.

Two main types of primary lowland forest may be distinguished, the critical factor being drought:

1. In those zones astride the Equator where no season may be called dry, the natural forest is a tall, leafy, congested and evergreen type known as Tropical Rain Forest, sometimes called Equatorial Rain Forest. It may even occur well away from the Equator, towards the northern limit of Southeast Asia, where certain local conditions create a more continuously wet climate than is normal for the latitude.

2. In localities where there are several consecutive months practically without rain, a shorter and more open forest type develops: it has deciduous foliage on the whole, and considerably fewer species. Deciduous Tropical Forest is more generally known as "Monsoon Forest" and occurs over huge areas in eastern Java, Burma, Thailand and Indochina.

Between these Tropical Rain Forests and Monsoon Forests, there are intermediate types and transitional areas where no single meteorological criterion can be used to define the boundary sharply. Within both types, local peculiarities of soil porosity, number of rain-days, relief, exposure and aspect all induce minor variations. In any given unit of this mountainous region, three zones of vegetation may be distinguished within both main forest types, these zones being more distinctive in their differences than the variations of vegetation from one part to another of this huge region. These zones are: (1) coastal vegetation, (2) lowland vegetation, (3) mountain vegetation.

(1) COASTAL VEGETATION

On shores predominantly sandy, short herbs, grasses and shrubs with creeping stems and fleshy leaves are found; these plant groups resemble those of salt-tolerant vegetation on European beaches of which spinifex is a sample. Behind this shore grows a distinctive strip of what may be called *beach woodland*, sometimes referred to as beach forest. On reefs, on muddy shores and estuaries, where there is diurnal flooding at high tide, the *mangrove* forest develops. When the shore is rocky, lowland forest may reach high tide mark. In this vegetation seeds and fruit are water-borne so that currents are an important means of dispersion.

Well-developed beach woodland forms as a ribbon rarely more than 200 ft. inland from the shore and contains tree types not usually seen elsewhere and often reaching 90 ft. in height. The typical tree, the casuarina (Equisetifolia, rhu, ru, tjemara) is rather like a conifer to look at and is related to Australian she-oaks. Sometimes the casuarina is in pure stands; at places the strip includes screw pines (Pandanus), the leathery-leaved Calophyllum, Inophyllum and Barringtonia. Coconut palms, which can take root after nuts have been dispersed by sea-currents, are now prominent in beach woodland areas as a planted crop, but they occur self-sown everywhere through the islands.

Mangrove forests are widely distributed on sedimenting shores throughout Southeast Asia. The fringe of mangroves is interrupted where rocks or cliffs come to the sea and when drainage control has diminished the silt from terrestrial sources. Where mangroves develop, silt is being deposited at a fast rate (sometimes to a thickness of $1\frac{1}{2}$ in. annually); the mangrove thus both raises the surface level and progressively presses farther seaward. Whether mangroves grow only where silt is being deposited or whether they cause silt deposition by their root system, obstructing tidal currents and flood run-off, is still disputed. Possibly both processes operate together. The net effect is one of raising the land level and reclaiming land from the sea. In addition, the wood of mangroves is valued for firewood and charcoal; the bark is sold extensively for tanning. The mangrove trees are of some thirty species, all with structural adaptations enabling them to root in unstable muds and to tolerate daily inundation of their root system by saline tidal water. In addition to the tree, there are shrubs, herbaceous plants and ferns (particularly Aerostichum aureum). The trees are evergreen, sometimes 100 ft. tall, mostly with shining, leather-like leaves, small flowers, and unusual root systems. Some (as Rhizophora) have many roots supporting the trunk which begins well

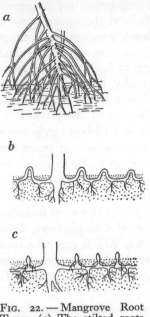

FIG. 22. — Mangrove Root Types. (*a*) The stilted roots of Rhizophora. (*b*) The knee-roots of Bruguiera. (*c*) The up-growing roots of Avicennia

above mud level, as though supported by flying buttresses (Fig. 22). In others (Avicennia and Sonneratia), the main roots are horizontal with many small branches exposing themselves through the mud to stand up above its surface in great numbers covering a wide area round the tree. Another mangrove, Bruguiera, has lateral roots which bend in loops showing above the mud; these loops are called knees and make a great obstacle to movement between the trees. These special root adaptations protrude through the mud to reach free air and they have breathing pores (lenticels); their function may be to oxygenate the roots but they also enable fresh rootlets to be put out at higher and higher levels as the mud and silt increases and stifles the older roots. Many mangrove plants have seeds which germinate before leaving the parent tree. Being heavy and fleshy, they can stick firmly in the mud at low tide or may float away in the tidal currents for considerable distances; other germinated seedlings are shaped like darts to pierce deeply into the mud when they fall.

The main differences between mangrove species are the result of selection according to the amount of tidal inundation they can tolerate; the tide is the chief selective factor in the vegetation pattern from place to place in any one mangrove forest and results in a belt zonation of types roughly paralleling the shoreline. The seaward plants, the pioneers, are most tolerant of salt water; the inland fringe is of the least salt-tolerant types and, as the silt is progressively built up, tidal effects diminish and the vegetation gradually turns into a freshwater swamp with different associations.

The nipa palm (Nipa fruticans), with short stem and feathery leaves often 18 ft. long, lines many estuaries where tidal influence is weakening. It is a palm of brackish but not saline preferences and is extensively used for thatching huts.

(2) Lowland Vegetation

Tropical Rain Forest.—This primary forest is evergreen, tall and profusely-leaved, but by no means gloomy; the forest floor is usually dappled with sunlight at midday and the undergrowth is fairly thin, except at the edges of roads, paths or rivers, where extra

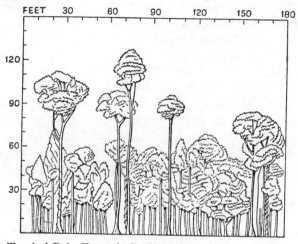

Fig. 23.—Tropical Rain Forest in Profile. The diagram represents a strip of forest 180 ft. in width. Note: (i) the height of the trees; (ii) the crowns are represented in a conventional manner

light induces dense ground vegetation. Within the forest, air is still and constant at temperatures as much as 10° F. below those at the top of the forest. Plants with showy flowers are unusual; variegated and multicoloured foliage is common, while not modifying the general impression of a dark green landscape.

It is the Tropical Rain Forest which most often gets called "jungle." This word, however, has been applied so loosely from district to district, to vegetation types ranging from forest to dry scrub, that it has lost precise meaning and should be avoided.

A distinct structure shows in Tropical Rain Forest, based on height and light. Trees some 190 ft. high are scattered throughout the forest, jutting their isolated heads through a layer of foliage some 60 ft. high, where the crowns of trees touch one another to form a canopy or storey (Fig. 23). Below this are shrubs, saplings and herbaceous plants, all shade-loving types and thinly scattered. On the whole the trees are evergreen, though there are distinct leaf changes in individual trees. This change of leaves is not regional and some trees retain old leaves until new ones are well formed. The general impression of evergreen persists as a result of a non-synchronous leaf rhythm. The degree of correlation between flowering, leafing and climate varies considerably; certain of the forest plants flower after a few days of drought or a slight local drop of temperature, as in thunderstorms, others persist in annual rhythms whatever the local weather may be, some correlate with the local peaks of rainfall, and some assume a fifteen months' periodicity. Each storey of trees has special features; the topmost storey has thin straight boles despite the great height of the trees, and is inclined to flattened crowns of undivided, tough, oval leaves. Many of the tall trees have plank buttresses, thin outgrowths extending up to 15 ft. from the ground, stabilising the relatively thin boles in soils not well suited for root anchoring, and presenting a major difficulty when the trees are to be felled. Second storey trees are in general smaller in every respect; their leaves are proportionately larger, extending to long fine points.

Two groups of plants fit into this tree ecology: (*a*) the lianes, (*b*) the epiphytes.

Lianes are woody creepers, often several hundred feet long, which climb from the ground using hooks and tendrils on the tree-trunks in order to reach the sunlit crowns. They use trees as supports only and spread in great festoons from tree to tree; their flowers are in the upper storeys and their stems may be from finger thickness to as much as 10 in. in diameter. Rattans are typical lianes, their strong thorny stems being much used as native ropes and wires.

Epiphytes include orchids, ferns and wild figs. Their seeds become established in high branches and are adapted either to live self-contained above ground, or as in the case of the strangling fig (Fiscus), to send down very long roots which ultimately fasten in the ground. Only certain of these epiphytes are truly parasitic, feeding on the sap of a host; most of them are merely supported by the host-tree. The fig sends down tough quick-growing roots round the trunk of another tree, finally strangling the host until it rots away, leaving the fig tree sustained by a hollow network of roots. This particular plant, the seeds of which are both bird-carried and wind-borne, may prove highly destructive to stone structures, as in the case of the Angkor temples.

Tropical Rain Forest is remarkable for the number of tree-types which go to make it and for its heterogeneous composition. Continuous stands of any single tree species very rarely occur, and often thirty may be found in a forest patch 100 yds. square. While the trees differ widely, the family group Dipterocarpaceae, gigantic in dimensions and bearing winged seeds like shuttlecocks, is the most prominent. Within the forest individual trees are restricted by the congestion so that the shape of high trees in tropical gardens or along roads is no guide to their shape when in their natural setting.

From the thousands of tree types in this forest some commercially valuable timbers, gums, resins and camphor can be obtained. Most of the trees, however, are commercially useless; the heterogeneous composition and density of the forest operates against exploitation of even those species which could prove useful.

Within the Tropical Rain Forest, several subsidiary types may be recognised.

(*a*) Parts of Borneo, Sumatra and W. Malaysia have a white, porous, sandy subsoil thought to be a tropical podsol (see Chapter 5). Upon this, pitcher plants, conifers and a treeless, heathlike ecology of grasses and shrubs may develop.

(*b*) Upon porous limestone landscapes, the trees are short and epiphytic plants are most common, since these can tolerate the absence of groundwater.

(*c*) Behind the mangroves and transitional between them and the true lowland Tropical Rain Forest, are Freshwater Swamp Forests, extensively developed in Sumatra, W. Malaysia and Borneo. The plants peculiar to this swamp setting vary with the duration of freshwater flooding. Trees here are shorter, fewer in species, well-buttressed and often stilt-rooted. Over considerable areas stands of a single type of palm may occur and palms of short varieties cover the ground to impede movement. Sometimes on the east coast of Sumatra the Freshwater Swamp Forest produces a tropical bog on peat soil formed by rotting vegetal remains several yards deep.

Secondary Forest.—The sequence of vegetation which replaces Tropical Rain Forest after removal is called Secondary Forest, made up of ferns, tropical grasses and scrub. It may be subdivided into distinct vegetation types which are various stages in the transition from naked ground to tropical forest. The process of replacement depends for its character in detail on the length of time the forest clearing has continued in cultivation, the extent of soil erosion, the clearing suffered, the original soil type and the proximity of natural forest from which seeds may be derived. To go through these replacement phases, natural vegetation is thought to need at least two centuries of most favourable conditions before it will become anything like Primary Tropical Rain Forest again. During the transitional stages spontaneous fires often occur, to prolong the replacement period; grazing animals have similar selective effects.

The normal replacement succession is first herbaceous grassland, then shrubs and finally trees. Tropical grasses, coarse, tough and in tussocks, quickly appear on any newly exposed ground and reach a height of 5 ft. These grass landscapes, on which Imperata Cylindrica is typical, often resemble savannah. The grass burns rapidly and regrows quickly because it spreads by subsurface root runners shielded from the effects of burning. Quick-growing tropical grass stifles most other vegetation, so that it is both a sign of inferior soils and may even be the cause of them. While grass is the most prominent type, sometimes wild sugar canes establish themselves.

The scrub consists of wild ginger and a tropical rhododendron (Melastoma malabathricum). Giant ferns spread rapidly and compactly in some districts as pure stands in which bracken (Pteridium) appears prominently.

Young Secondary Forest develops trees some 30 ft. high in a few years but the earlier successions leave behind a dense undergrowth and many giant creepers. Stands of the same species persist for some time and the trees are at first of fast growing, soft wooded varieties. Pines are fairly common in some local secondary vegetation, the older types of which are scarcely distinguishable from Primary Forest except for the thick undergrowth.

Monsoon Forest.—Because Monsoon Forest has a distinct dry season, it is subject to widespread and frequent fires which exercise a selection in favour of deep-rooted or thick-seeded types which can regrow after a forest fire. Shifting cultivation is thought to have had a greater effect in Monsoon Forest areas than on the Tropical Rain Forest, so that Monsoon Forest may be largely a secondary rather than a primary forest type. The type stretches across Southeast Asia in two broad zones, roughly symmetrical to the Equator. The largest zone covers Burma, Thailand and Indochina, while the counterpart in Eastern Java, the Sunda Islands and Irian covers a much smaller area, with local variants due to insularity. These zones are identical with the dry areas of Fig. 10.

In the rainy season, Monsoon Forest resembles Tropical Rain Forest. Its tree heights are less, the foliage not so profuse, and the spacing more open. Only the undergrowth remains fairly green for the whole year; the rest of the vegetation sheds leaves in the dry season, when the forest has a bare, stark appearance. Herbaceous plants, lianes and bamboo are common but epiphytes are unusual and the herbs almost disappear in the very hot dry season. Among the trees, Acacias and Albizzias are especially common and Leguminosae are prominent.

Some observers distinguish between wetter and drier types of Monsoon Forest, both transitional from Tropical Rain Forest to Tropical Desert, the latter being outside Southeast Asia.

Monsoon Forest is mostly of mixed species but sometimes a single species dominates, possibly as a result of selection through repeated burning. Of these, teak forests (Tectona grandis) are characteristic and important commercially, occurring in North Burma, North Thailand, Eastern Java and the Moluccas. So valuable has teak proved itself that some existing forest areas are actually re-plantations of it. Teak has thick hard-cased seeds which are fire resistant. Its saplings come through fire successfully and the pure stands are thought to have been the result of natural selection on these lines, since it is fairly certain that forests of teak alone do not occur under normal conditions. Teak reaches to heights of over 120 ft., the lower half of the tree being straight and unbranched under forest conditions. Undergrowth is negligible and the ground is covered with brittle teak leaves which often cup, forming mosquito-breeding places in the wet season.

Resembling the teak forests in origin, eucalyptus forests have developed in the eastern islands as migrants from Australia, occurring naturally only in Irian, Timor, the Lesser Sundas, Suluwesi and the Philippines.

Another single stand deriving from the Monsoon Forest by selection, is bamboo forest. Considerable areas almost exclusively occupied by bamboos are found in the northern parts of Southeast Asia, with small patches in East Java. Bamboos in great variety grow everywhere in Southeast Asia and they have been planted

extensively because of their usefulness structurally and domestically, but continuous stands become established only where the
dry season is very marked and where shifting cultivation is known
to have been practised extensively. Bamboos are giant perennial
grasses of about a hundred species, with woody stems and woody
roots. They grow in clumps and may be evergreen or deciduous.
Some bamboos flower at long intervals (25–70 years) and their
seeds are fire-resisting. Constant friction between the dry woody
stems may cause forest fires and help to produce that selective
process which leads to stands of bamboo.

Monsoon Dry Forest, an open wooded landscape containing
very few species, may be found on large areas of Burma, Thailand
and Indochina in association with poor soils. Known as *indaing*
in Burma and *padeng* in Thailand, this forest develops where rainfalls are not much above 40 in. per annum, and it may merge on
the equatorial side into Tropical Rain Forest and on the other into
dry or thorny savannah vegetation. Within Monsoon Dry Forest
trees are widely spaced, tending to be stunted forms of Dipterocarpaceae and distinctly deciduous.

Secondary Monsoon Forests.—Considerable areas of savannah
found in Burma, Thailand, Indochina and Eastern Indonesia are
secondary growths after a removal of the natural Monsoon Forest.
Savannah is open country of tall, coarse grasses, occasionally having
a few scattered bamboos or low trees and very much associated
with long dry seasons whose effects are aggravated by poor or
porous soils. Savannah merges into Monsoon Dry Forest and
is often covered with low palms (Borassus flabellifer), and
contains prickly pears, spiny cactus-like plants, and similar
thorny scrub.

(3) Mountain Vegetation

Vegetation steadily and often imperceptibly changes with
altitude and the resulting types are much the same, level for level,
throughout Southeast Asia. All but the very highest mountains
are forested, though the trees on exposed summits are dwarfed;
only parts of Irian and Yunnan have heights great enough entirely
to prevent tree growth and produce an alpine vegetation. Young
volcanoes may be treeless for pedological, rather than for climatic
reasons.

Above about 2,000 ft., at most points of Southeast Asia, large trees of Dipterocarp type gradually disappear and temperate trees of the oak and chestnut type become commoner, though the landscape continues full of giant bracken and tree ferns. Higher still the vegetation dwarfs considerably, shadiness diminishes, and woody plants become twisted and gnarled. This often turns into a moss or "elfin" forest above 5,000 ft., in localities where the air is constantly cool and saturated, to produce thick blankets of wet mosses and liverworts upon all other vegetation. Mosses hang in fantastic festoons everywhere and sometimes (as in E. Malaysia) form walls or platforms under which other vegetation, such as dwarf oaks and rhododendrons, may be buried (Harrison). Moss forest will not occur in localities with a noticeable dry season: in monsoon areas it is replaced in succession by pine forest, in which, however, some broadleaved trees persist. Above both these mountain forest types (above 6,500 ft.), mountain grasses and shrubs form landscapes of rolling downlike appearance.

FAUNA

Between the western and eastern fringes of Southeast Asia there are greater differences zoologically than between Asia and South America, even though these are separated by the Atlantic (Merrill). The differences derive from the long separation of Australia from Asia. Migration has gone on from Asia and Australia into the islands and peninsulas of Southeast Asia which is thus a transitional zoogeographical region (Fig. 24).

The Tropical Rain Forest has complicated ecologies of living creatures associated with the various storeys and the variety of these creatures parallels the variety of vegetation. Large animals such as elephants, tigers, rhinoceros, etc., are relatively few and confined to the coastal sections. Specially numerous are arboreal and flying creatures, butterflies, birds, moths and insects. These are able to migrate from place to place with considerable ease so that the convergence of Asiatic and Australian species has gone on fairly freely. The contrasting zoological types are summed up in the difference between mammals; in Australia, except for a few bats and rodents, mammals are marsupial (pouched) or monotreme (single vented); in Asia these groups are entirely lacking and are prelaced by placental mammals, monkeys, shrews, squirrels and ungulates.

By far the richest zoological group is that spreading from Asia.

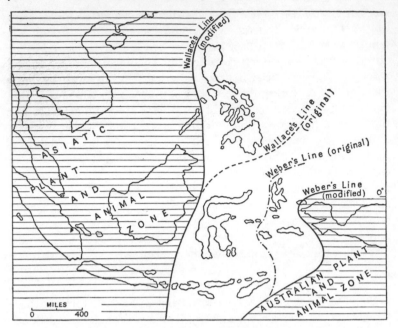

FIG. 24.—Biological Regions of Southeast Asia

For a long time Wallace's Line was held to demarcate these zoological types; Wallace himself drew the boundary just west of Lombok and Celebes but Huxley later extended it to include the Philippines in the "Australian" zone. Geographically the boundary clearly correlates with the limits of the Sunda Platform and the interglacial connection between Malaysia, Borneo, Sumatra and Java appears to have permitted zoological migration fairly uniformly among them, whereas there has been no continued land connection between the "mediterranean islands" east of the Platform. Later more detailed study of the fauna has produced criticisms of the Wallace Line. The steady pressure of zoological types eastward has been demonstrated and Weber laid down another limit which he showed more closely to accord with the balance between Asiatic and Australian fauna. East of it Australian types dominate. Wallace's Line thus is now best thought of as the eastward limit of the typically Asiatic zoological types; it is matched by a line just west of the Sahul Shelf which is the westward limit of exclusively Australian and New Guinea faunal types.

Between this and the Wallace Line is the zone of tectonic instability, the "mediterranean" zone, where faunal destruction followed by re-population from nearby continents has gone on fairly frequently, but irregularly and without uniformity from place to place; Weber's Line is roughly marginal to this "mediterranean" faunal zone.

Chapter Five

SOUTHEAST ASIA SOILS

FACTORS IN TROPICAL SOIL DEVELOPMENT

WHILE most soils of Southeast Asia have in common the fact that they have been evolved under conditions of plentiful moisture, they vary very considerably and the term "laterites," frequently used to describe them, is so broad that it misleads. In the tropics, as elsewhere, soils represent a synthesis of the inter-related factors of climate, parent rock, plants and animals, relief and drainage; a change in any one of these factors will cause a change of soil character. Time, too, plays a considerable part. If the factors operate for a period indefinitely long, the soil type conditioned by them will evolve until the soil represents a perfect balance or end product of them. When the forest cover is removed or a volcanic eruption throws out new rock material, certain of the factors are changed, the soil reverts to a more juvenile stage and its evolution begins again on different materials and may take a different form. Thus soil differences from place to place are often due to differences in stage of evolution, in the time factor.

Southeast Asia weathering is fairly uniform from place to place. It occurs without exposure to frosts or to wide alternations of heat and cold, but under conditions of warmth and heavy rainfall. Hence the weathering process is chemical rather than mechanical.

Those regions of Southeast Asia away from the Equator and having a markedly seasonal rainfall (as in the dry belts of Burma and Thailand) may be described as subject for part of the year to equatorial soil processes where surface evaporation is nearly nil and for part to desertic soil processes in which surface evaporation is at a maximum.

The warm rainwater of tropical conditions, well carbonated and charged with the biochemicals of vegetal disintegration, breaks down the silicates, which form most rocks, into salts which are leached away, leaving the complex sesquioxides to accumulate in the soil. These may in turn undergo selective changes, all leading to the accumulation of clays. In the tropical heat of Southeast Asia

74

lowlands these changes, known as the hydrolysis of the silicates, most involved phases of soil chemistry, take place very fast compared with those of European latitudes or of high mountains, and reach the "end-product" or mature stage quickly. On the Sunda Platform and the Sahul Shelf, prolonged geological stability has in any case brought the mature stage in local soils, but even the more juvenile types of soil on the younger volcanic structures are rapidly evolving towards maturity. Adding further to the complexity of Southeast Asia soils is the variety of rock types and the varied lengths of dry season towards the margins of the region. Thus the diversity is great, although differences in the soil endproducts is lessened to some extent by rapid maturity under a single broad weathering type—the warm, damp tropical.

TROPICAL GROUNDWATER

With certain local exceptions, Southeast Asia experiences an annual excess of rainfall over evaporation. This means that there is a steady movement of rainwater downwards, percolating through the soil as a dilute solution of chemicals from the air and from plants, capable in turn of dissolving some solids in the soil. While some of the soil compounds are produced by the decay of vegetation, the plants depend on the groundwater to dissolve those which become plant nutrients and are absorbed through the root systems. Not all solubles enter plants; most of them are just carried away. The continued downward movement of the soil water effects a steady removal (leaching) of the solubles in Southeast Asia soils. While a thick vegetation cover continues to be in place upon the surface, replacement of some solubles by humus renewal goes on all the time, but once that vegetation is removed, the surface soil rapidly loses its existing soluble elements, receives no renewals, and becomes infertile, a factor making continuous agriculture a drain upon the soil which not only loses its qualities by greater leaching but in addition loses by that which is absorbed into the cultivated plant. Where, however, there are breaks in the cycle of leaching, as in areas having a dry season, the soil water is for a time subject to a condition where evaporation exceeds rainfall, the leaching ceases and there begins the accumulation of soluble plant nutrients or even the drawing up of solubles from depth by capillary processes. These zones, where soil impoverishment is seasonally checked, are those with dry seasons, i.e. from Central Java eastwards, in the monsoon zones of the Kra Isthmus and northward into Burma, Thailand, Indochina, a factor in the greater fertility, agriculture and population of those zones compared with the equatorial areas.

Solution by groundwater, however, is not peculiar to tropical latitudes—it goes on elsewhere. The distinctive point is that high tropical temperatures and heavy rainfalls give groundwater great power both to dissolve and to carry away special selections of the solubles. Easily soluble components of the soil disappear wherever rainfall and groundwater are ample, but the order in which sandy elements, clay elements and iron oxides (the main colouring element) are leached depends on the organic content and temperature of the groundwater. Water containing large quantities of organic material is a rapid solvent of clay and iron compounds; when groundwater is of this type, the silica occurring in the soil in the form of quartz remains scarcely touched for a long period, according to Glinka, causing the mature topsoil to consist largely of sandy elements bleached white by the removal of iron oxide colouring and the mature subsoil to show signs of re-precipitation of the iron oxide at lower levels. This is the process of *podsolisation*. On the other hand, where its organic content is low, groundwater breaks down any silica in the form of complex aluminium silicates faster than the other compounds and removes certain elements of it, so that there remains an upper soil consisting at maturity largely of stable clays and iron compounds, strongly coloured red, yellow or brown. This process is *laterisation*, the dominant soil process in Southeast Asia. The end-product of laterisation may be called laterite, a porous, crumbly-textured, bright red soil often hardening on exposure to the air and composed almost exclusively of clays and iron compounds, and much the same whatever the parent rock. Only in limited areas is this laterite fully developed; elsewhere the process has not reached its final or mature stages so that most Southeast Asia soils may more aptly be called laterised, that is, at an intermediate stage of laterisation. This stage may be assessed by measuring the proportion of silica to the alumina; the higher the silica content, the less laterisation has taken place (Polynov).

The whole process of laterisation involves very special aspects of complex chemical and physical changes which await the researcher for clarification.

The organic content of soils depends in turn on temperature

which conditions the rate at which soil bacteria and fungi can break down dead leaves and other plant remains, first to the dark-coloured humus and then to chemical compounds. Thus there is a steady addition of decaying vegetable matter to the soil as trees and plants drop their leaves or die, and a continuous depletion of it as bacteria complete its breakdown. The balance between them is established by temperature and in the tropics where soil temperatures remain so steadily above 75° F. the breakdown by micro-organisms is considerably faster than the vegetation, profuse as it may appear, can replace. Thus the organic content of laterised soils is relatively small, and confined to a few inches of topsoil, beneath which practically no humic solids or liquids will be found. In vegetation-covered localities, shielded by the canopy of trees, where average soil temperatures may be well below 75° F., accretion of organic matter exceeds depletion, enabling humus to accumulate and form black-coloured soils.

Where the soil is waterlogged, a widespread condition in western Southeast Asia, bacterial action is hindered by the exclusion of oxygen so that, whatever the soil temperature, dead vegetation accumulates, often in the form of thick layers of peat. Altitude, by lowering the soil temperature for periods below the critical 75° F. (Glinka), is also responsible for variations in the humus content of soils. In Preanger (Java) for example, the top soil gradually changes from one with a slow humus content and red colour on the foothills, through brownish, with an increasing humus content at altitudes of 5,000 ft., to become dark brown or black at higher levels on mountains. The relative subsoils are red in the foothills, where laterisation predominates, and gradually change to dirty white at higher levels where podsolisation and bleaching are aided by the lower temperatures.

Examples of local podsolisation in the tropics have been observed upon parent rocks of exceptionally porous character, as in the coarse sands and sandstones of Banka, Borneo and Malaysia over which distinct bleached earths occur. Why laterisation should be replaced by podsolisation under these conditions is not clear, but the sandy, white or bleached soils are unmistakable. Thin Secondary Forest is normally the vegetation cover of such districts, whether as cause or effect of the podsolisation has not been determined. Glinka quotes examples where excessive moisture and humus have bleached certain soils among laterites and notes that

podsols developed under these conditions in the tropics differ
chemically from analogous types in temperate climates. He reports
the possibility that white laterised soils may derive from rocks containing magnetite forms of iron, which will not break down into
ordinary brownish oxides under weathering.

LATERISED SOILS

While the characteristic colour of laterised soils is red, some of
them have bright yellow colours which, however, do not indicate
major chemical differences, except that the various types of iron
oxide are more intensely hydrated. The colour distinction is now
held to be of minor importance. Sometimes a red mottling breaks
the uniformity of the yellow colouring; this is thought (Pendleton)
to be connected with aeration along dead roots of plants, which
have now disintegrated. Occasionally the fine channel of a root can
be seen at the core of such mottlings, cross-sections of which often
have ringed or oyster-shell patterns.

Laterisation produces end-products not materially differing however different the parent rocks may be, so that tropical red soils
develop to much the same appearance over granite and over limestone, although the rate of maturing varies. On the other hand, the
chemical character of parent rock may show for a considerable time
in the laterised soils. Thus, the igneous rocks of Sumatra and Java
are in some regions basic and in others acid. The more acid type of
igneous rock contains very little calcium and phosphorus, weathering slowly into poor soils, whereas the basic rocks initially contain
more of these elements and release them readily, to weather in the
tropics into soils whose composition makes them more fertile. The
leaching continues rapidly, and at a more advanced stage of weathering the soils from basic rocks are no richer in these solubles than
those from acid extrusions. This accounts for great differences in
the agricultural potential of the flanks of different volcanoes in
Java, where any thinly populated zone may safely be interpreted as
a zone of soils lying over acid igneous parent rocks, or of over-
mature soils upon basic parent rocks. Pedologists disagree as to
whether mature laterites can be derived from every type of rock
but the majority incline to accept this point of view. Pure quartz
sandstone, however, resists laterisation and quartz veins persist
unweathered long after the original rocks containing them have
broken down.

The term "laterite" (from L. later, brick), now limited to mature laterised soils, has had a history confused by varying definitions. It was used in India by Buchanan in 1807 to describe a tropical soil containing large quantities of iron, soft enough to be cut with a spade or mattock, yet rapidly hardening on exposure to sun and air into an excellent constructional material much used for tropical buildings. Afterwards the term became loosely used for any reddish

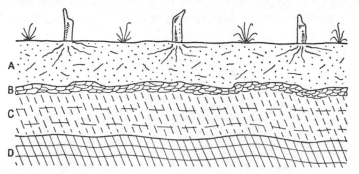

Fig. 25.—Section of Laterised Sandstone, Korat. Surface burnt for shifting cultivation. (*a*) Reddish-yellow sandy layer with tubular ironpan along old root-lines. (*b*) Lateritic ironpan and granular concretions, 6–12 inches thick. (*c*) Weathered sandstone, some bedding still showing, tubular passages (old roots), brownish-red. (*d*) Red sandstone of Korat, lightly consolidated, hardly deformed

tropical soils. Discrimination in the use of the word is modern and the standards are by no means uniform.

At best, only certain layers or horizons of laterite will harden on exposure. When this type of laterite is used structurally, being an end-product of weathering, it resists further weathering and buildings made of it stand up to the tropical climate better and longer than any other local material, evidenced by the old fort at Malacca and the temples of Angkor whose laterite slabs are firm and square after centuries of exposure.

Mature laterites may be up to 100 ft. thick, all weathered *in situ* and justifying the word "soil" to describe it. Several distinct horizons occur within this thickness. On top is a few inches of forest soil, dark with humus and partially decayed matter (Fig. 25). Under this is red earth, crumbly and sticky to the hand, permeable to water yet easily "baking" if ever exposed to the direct sun. Much of the water is held colloidally so that percolation wells can rarely be used in laterised ground. Four or five feet below the surface a distinct cellular structure develops, consisting of a coarse network of iron compounds round softer cores of clay. This is the horizon which may be of that hardening type suitable for a structural material. Sometimes the iron compounds at this level change *in situ* into hard concretions like a pan roughly paralleling the surface and looking like a lustrous slag. These crusts or concretions ring like hollow iron and might be mistaken for volcanic material. Containing up to 30 per cent of iron, they have at times been smelted, but extensive use for this purpose awaits development of a suitable

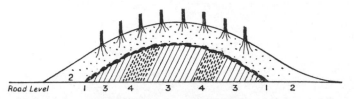

FIG. 26.—Section in West Singapore: Hill with Partially Removed Rubber. 1. Lateritic ironpan running across bedding planes. 2. Red subsoil, 3 feet thick. 3. Partially removed shale. 4. Conglomerate

process. Oxide of manganese occurs in these concretions as well. The pan may be continuous beneath a large area and prevent percolation, and in deforested areas the softer topsoil may be washed away, or slide down the surface of the iron pan which then shows as a compact platform inhibiting secondary vegetation.

The concretion of iron compounds is thought to be connected both with seasonal variations of the subsoil water level and with electrolytic changes in descending water heavily charged with solvents. Fracture planes, by creating internal drainage lines, encourage panning to follow lines unrelated to the surface contours. Skew-panning may also develop strongly along lines of quartz which persists undecomposed through thick laterites. While the iron concretion layer has special interest because of its resemblance to pan layers in other latitudes, it is by no means ubiquitous and some writers relate the pan to igneous parent rock. The stratifications of laterised soils are more related to the relief of the surface than to stratifications of the parent material (Fig. 26).

Beneath the concretion layer is another horizon of almost continuous saturation where the coloration tends to be less red and more yellow or whitish right down to the horizon of decomposing rock. These deeper horizons represent less advanced stages of weathering, repeating at depth some of the variations noted at the surface in less maturely laterised soils elsewhere.

Cuttings through laterised soil, as for roads and railways, frequently develop a dark crust after exposure, giving the sides of the cuttings an appearance of hardness belying the soft soil beneath it. Occasionally these exposures are honeycombed where softer parts have been washed away by rains, leaving the cellular structure of iron compounds fully evident. Because laterised soils are so wet and thick, the destructive processes of slumping and slipping assert themselves strongly. Soil creep on slopes operates relatively fast, particularly if an iron pan exists not far below the surface. Whole sections of a hillside may thus slump down into a valley leaving a scar which wild vegetation needs a long time to conceal. Road cuttings frequently slump at the sides as though huge spoons had been used upon them. Almost any ditch will show soil creep in the form of root-matted topsoil hanging well out over the side of the ditch.

POLYNOV AND LATERISATION

Polynov in his "Cycle of Weathering" has discussed a new interpretation of lateritic soils. Previous pedologists have considered laterisation to be a process peculiar to the high temperature and heavy rainfalls of the tropics. Polynov produces an argument to show that laterised soils may result as the end-product of weathering in any latitude, given a sufficiently long time for the process to operate. In his view the frequency with which laterites occur in the tropics now is due less to the special character of weathering there, and more to its rapidity, which brings soil maturity very much faster than in cooler latitudes. The age and stability of the Sunda Platform and the Sahul Shelf fit into both schemes since soils upon them may be considered to be brought to maturity by uninterrupted weathering during prolonged geologic time, and by the intense and continuous nature of tropical weathering. Whatever the value of Polynov's theory from the soil chemist's point of view, it helps to account for red soils of lateritic aspect outside tropical areas without needing to postulate major climatic changes.

SOILS IN THE DRIER ZONES OF SOUTHEAST ASIA

Northward from the Equator, Southeast Asia is subject to a longer and longer dry season during which soil leaching diminishes. On exposed soils, the high surface evaporation of dry periods even induces an upflow of groundwater which evaporates and thereby precipitates solubles in the topsoil. These have sometimes been called the Savannah Soils, found widely in Thailand and Indochina. The type occurs not only where the climate permits but also where destruction of marginal Tropical Rain Forest has gone on at a rate faster than natural replacement. Because tropical forest soil works with a very small quantity of plant nutrients circulating rapidly in a cycle from soil to leaves and back again to soil, the balance is delicate. Where the forest is almost virgin, natural fires do little damage, but persistent burning by men may break the cycle of nutrients and release altogether the small initial capital of solubles. The iron concretions under such conditions become firmly cemented into subsurface platforms inimical to anything except coarse tropical grass and the topsoil is exposed to rapid removal by torrential storms. The more accessible laterites which received early examination were often under vegetation of the savannah type and they were thought at one time to be signs of a change of local climate, from Equatorial to Savannah, whereas in fact they reflect over-destruction of the original tropical forest, followed by such a change of soil type that the forest cannot re-establish itself. Because laterite is very porous, rain falling upon it may be heavy yet quickly passes beyond the reach of plants, carrying all plant nutrients away, thereby preventing regrowth of the original vegetation cover.

Natural savannahs in Southeast Asia are noteworthy for their extensive iron concretion layers which provide support for the view that vertical fluctuation of subsoil water is a factor in the formation of lateritic iron-pan.

Soils and Agriculture

The different types of tropical forest induce minor differences in the soils beneath them, which assume major significance when the forest is cleared for cultivation. The limited supply of plant nutrients explains that paradox between the apparent fertility of an elaborate and profuse forest vegetation and the poverty of the soil when the forest is removed, the cycle of nutrients broken and most solubles washed away. Eventually clearances in the forest mean an increase in the outflow of nutrients in solutuon or suspension which are finally distributed into the swamps, the estuaries and the sea. To some extent the practice of burning, which reduces the forest to ash, lying for a while upon the surface, returns to the soil part of the chemicals of plant structure, yet unless steps are taken to retain this "capital" by terracing or cover crops, the ash quickly dissolves and disappears into the streams. Good crops may be obtained by utilising this soil capital immediately, but it can last only for a season or two, after which the natural infertility of laterised soils becomes apparent. It is not so serious with isolated native clearings, done under the shifting cultivation system, because each clearing is so small, and surrounded by forest, that lost soil nutrients are not carried far before they are recaptured into the forest ecology by the tangle of adjoining vegetation. When shifting cultivation is done too frequently over the one patch, that is, more frequently than, say, once in twenty years or so, then progressive impoverishment of the soil takes place. Maintenance of fertility in clearings is easier in less maturely laterised areas and where there is at least a short, dry season to interrupt the depletion processes.

The basic volcanic rocks of Java as well as the recent ash and mud flows contain chemicals which weather to plant nutrients and, being in addition very young in the laterising cycle, they produce fertile soils. On the older lavas and on the acid outpourings, a maturer stage of laterisation has been reached to produce soils no better for agriculture than other parts of the Sunda Platform. A new volcanic outburst, while creating temporary havoc, may ultimately produce local agricultural prosperity because it brings a new supply of plant nutrients. The elaborate terracing of new volcanic ash landscapes is only partly due to population pressure: it equally reflects the need to restrain the run-off and to hold back the solubles as long as possible.

Apart from the loss of soil fertility due to rapid solution, all bare or clean-weeded soils in the tropics suffer from mechanical erosion by the violent torrential rainstorms. Rainfall of tropical intensity rapidly gullies all bare landscapes and is particularly evident on the less cohesive ashes of volcanic cones, so that another reason for terracing is to offset gullying. Tangled vegetation prevents mechanical soil erosion having any great significances in forested areas, but in Java, where recent ash and intensive cultivation combine to facilitate this type of erosion, rivers contain from 300 to 2,000 gms. of silt per cubic metre; the Irrawaddy has about 750 gms. suspended in each cubic metre. (The Seine and Rhine only contain about 50 gms. of silt per cubic metre.) From tropical forest in a natural state the soil loss is mainly by solution, and streams running from the jungles are either clear or black with humus content. From clearings, whether natural or artificial, subsoil solution is supplemented by violent mechanical erosion, and streams from these zones are thick and muddy, often tinted red.

Since both the subsoil processes and the surface erosion have water as their principal vector, the solubles and the silt are carried to the deltas and to the freshwater swamps which are the depositories of plant nutrients from all the forested soils. The coastal and freshwater swamps are not subject to rapid decomposition and they progressively accumulate plant foods, hence they function as the chief agricultural areas, continuing to produce without serious soil exhaustion through years of productiveness, as in the Irrawaddy and Menam Chao Praya valleys. These sticky wet soils are black or dark brown, often containing lenses of peat, and completely unlike the laterised soils around them. They are all transported soils, both fluvial and marine sedimentation playing some part in building and shaping them.

PART II
THE COUNTRIES OF SOUTHEAST ASIA

Chapter Six

THE NATURAL LANDSCAPE OF WEST MALAYSIA

SITED roughly at the middle of the Sunda Platform, W. Malaysia has special interest as a sample of a very ancient landscape scarcely disturbed by tectonic changes which have gone on close to the margins of the Platform. In addition, W. Malaysia is almost entirely equatorial in climatic character, accentuating the maturity of the landscape forms. It also exemplifies the surface effects of that process of marine inundation which followed the glacial epochs of northern latitudes.

RELIEF

Broadly, the country is mountainous. Wide plains, scarcely above sea level, surround the ranges and caused early explorers approaching Malaysia from the sea to think the Peninsula was a string of islands. Yet the mountains have no great altitude: Gunong Tahan is only 7,186 ft. and just breaks the continuity of the forest cover, so that Tahan is sparsely covered with thin shrubs through which quartz crystals gleam, an unusual phenomenon in this otherwise tree-covered country, giving rise to the Malay legend that the mountain is made of diamonds guarded by demons.

The mountain ranges stand up most strongly in the northern half of the country but their altitudes diminish southwards where their line disappears beneath the sea to the south, to continue in the hills of the Lingga, Rhio and Banka islands. In Central Malaysia meet two sets of ranges; the northern ranges, which lie staggered *en echelon* and skew-wise across the peninsula on NNE–SSW. lines, and the southern ranges of lower altitudes which are less skew to the peninsula and have a NNW–SSE. pattern, apparent also in the Trengganu Highlands. Of the ranges, one called the Central Range, though it lies well to the west, running from Patani in Thailand to Malacca, is the most continuous. While differing slightly in detailed structure, all these ranges dominating the Malaysian topography have igneous cores which were intruded into very ancient (late Mesozoic) fold mountain systems, possibly

87

fan-folded with the Central Range as the middle fold, so extensively eroded over long periods that the intrusive granitic rocks within them are now exposed and stand out as the greatest heights.

The ranges are, from west to east:

1. *The Nakawn Range,* reaching the seas as a limestone ridge on the Perlis-Thailand border.
2. *The Western Range,* from Singgora through west-central Kedah to the western border of Province Wellesley, with minor outliers in Penang, at Kedah Peak and extending to hills round the Dindings.
3. *The Bintang Range,* from Thailand nearly to Bruas.
4. *The Kledang Range,* east of the Perak River and west of Kinta, breached by the Sungei Plus.
5. *The Central or Main Range,* sometimes called the Kerbau or Korbu Range after the highest peak (Gunong Kerbau, 7,160 ft.), stretching in an arc from Thailand to Malacca.
6. *The Benom-Mt. Ophir Range,* whose continuity is much broken by east-flowing streams from the Central Range.
7. *The Tahan Range,* running from the Trengganu Highland through Johore and continued through Singapore to the archipelago southward. It is interrupted by the Pahang and Rompin rivers.
8. *The Eastern Range,* the least known, evident from Kelantan to the Pengerang Peninsula in SE. Johore and considerably interrupted by transverse drainage lines.

On either side of the ranges are hills taking their form and pattern from scarps developed upon the folded sedimentaries flanking the lines of granite.

MALAYSIAN ROCKS

Much of the Malaysian rock structure (Fig. 27) is concealed by a thick cover of weathered material and this in turn by the Tropical Rain Forest; only in streambeds, in hills and in mining areas does it show clearly. The main rock formations are:

1. Limestone and calcareous shale: marked on the geology map as a single formation, it may be subdivided into:
    (a) massive, resistant, jointed limestone, greyish when newly cut, with minor intercalations of shale. Those parts in contact with the intrusive granite of the ranges have been metamorphosed into marble; partially metamorphosed examples

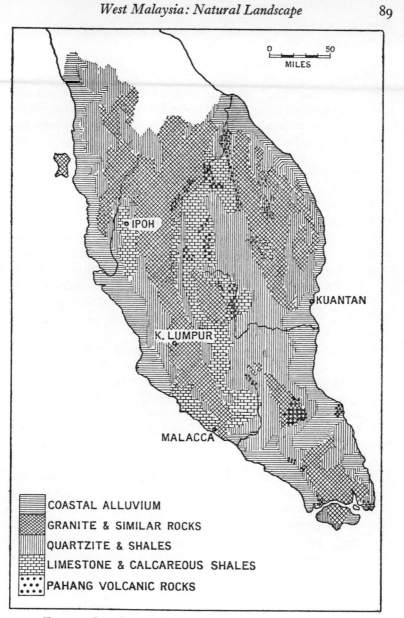

COASTAL ALLUVIUM

GRANITE & SIMILAR ROCKS

QUARTZITE & SHALES

LIMESTONE & CALCAREOUS SHALES

PAHANG VOLCANIC ROCKS

FIG. 27.—Location and Distribution of West Malaysian Rocks

have resisted weathering and stand up as cliff-like hill masses repeating the solution features of karst landscapes, as in Langkawi, Kinta, Perlis and Kelantan.

(b) calcareous shales, containing only thin beds of limestone. They have in places been metamorphosed by contact and pressure into schists, phyllites and slates. Most of this formation has suffered from equatorial weathering and now has low altitudes often blanketed by alluvium; frequently the subsurface limestone continues to dissolve, causing slips of the overlying rocks.

2. Quartzites, conglomerates and shales normally lie upon (1). They form highlands to the north where they often constitute the ranges (as in Tahan) but elsewhere have been partially removed, to remain on the flanks as foothills, standing up because of the resistance of quartzites to equatorial weathering. Jointed and severely folded, the beds often dip steeply, frequently forming steep relief with precipices. The formation contains some purple-green shales, often almost black and with a high carbon content, which quickly weather except where metamorphosed to a glossy schist. Some chert beds, fine textured and flinty, occur among the shales in South Kedah and Selangor.

A few outcrops of hard quartzite (sandstones whose silica grains have been cemented together by additional silica or by recrystallisation into a resistant mass of interlocking quartz crystals), formed before (1) and (2) and with a few beds of shale, have been proved in small areas of the Langkawis, in North Perlis and near Baling in Kedah. These are the oldest rocks of Malaysia but they cause no significant relief differences.

3. The Pahang Volcanic Series is a mixed group of igneous rocks, mainly of volcanic ash, cemented pumice beds and coarse fragments from explosive volcanoes, together with lavas varying from cream or purple rhyolites to dark greenish basaltic rocks. Some of these have metamorphosed into very resistant rocks. This group, whose age is greater than that of Malaysian granites, and whose origin has not been fully studied (Scrivenor), is found within the bedding of (1) and (2) and is therefore younger than those formations. It occurs scattered through those parts of Malaysia east of the Central Range, except for a few small outcrops west of the Central Range. No volcanoes, active or extinct, have been found in Malaysia; the Pahang Volcanic Series is

unrelated to the existing volcanoes of Sumatra and it is difficult to connect them with the long-extinct ones of Borneo which are so far away.

4. Granites, mostly coarsely crystalline intrusive types marked on the geology map variously as syenite, hornblend-granite, granite and granite-porphyry, are generally grey, with large crystals of felspar set among finer crystals of quartz, mica and various dark minerals. Strongly jointed, the granite contains veins of quartz and metallic ores from which derive many of the exploited minerals of Malaysia. These granites form the structural framework of Malaysia, outcropping as low hills particularly in the south, but also as the major heights of Bintang and Benom (over 6,000 ft.); younger than any of the formations so far described, they assume smooth outlines and gentle curves, emphasised by the thick layer of weathered material which invariably lies upon them.

5. Deposits of soft shale, sandstone and coal occur at Batu Arang in Selangor, on the Thai border of Perlis, near Kepong and Niyor in Johore and at Enggor in Perak. The coal is a high-grade brown lignite, tending to crumble and with a high moisture content. Its principal deposit is at Batu Arang where there were easily accessible seams 45 ft. and 25 ft. in thickness (output in 1959 about 6,100 tons monthly; the mine closed in 1960).

6. Great deposits of alluvium, brought by rivers flowing from the other formations, have been spread along the valleys in belts of varying thickness through the foothills, and along the coasts.

The coastal deposits, of dark blue clays containing lenticulate sands and peats, stretch inland for up to 40 miles, as flat swampy ground, at the coast thickening to as much as 400 ft. (as indicated by borings in Selangor). Formed by both river and marine action, these coastal alluvials represent the effects of progressive postglacial inundation together with the effects of rapid sedimentation among mangrove and swamp vegetation, which seems often to have maintained the coastline despite eustatic change, so that today the general trend is an advance of the coastline seaward.

Inland alluvial belts at the foot of the ranges and along the valleys vary according to rock of origin and the degree of sorting done by rivers and torrents. Clays, sands, gravels, thin peats (old marsh or lake remains) and thin ironstone bands are common, but adjoining the granite outcrops occur "granite-wash," of white kaolin-like clays containing coarse quartz grains, the first sorting of disintegrating granite. Among the alluvials from metalliferous parent rocks, metallic ores have been segregated by flowing water and from these most Malaysian tin derives. The alluvials vary in thickness, probably reflecting differences in erosion rate: in Kinta thicknesses from 60 ft. to 200 ft. have been verified. Partial dissection of older alluvial deposits has left scattered patches of high-level alluvials, remnants of river terraces (Richardson).

CLIMATE

Two factors dominate the Malaysian climate:

(*a*) Low latitude, which gives uniformity of high temperatures throughout the year and from place to place. Even at places of high altitude such as the Cameron Highlands in the Central Range, the uniformity is still characteristic though at somewhat lower temperatures. The absence of continuous high altitudes and of large settlements there makes this lowering of temperature of little human significance.

(*b*) The movement of tropical air masses to and fro across the Equator, which causes seasons to depend on wind reversal rather than on temperature changes. In the northern winter, winds from northeasterly points cover the whole peninsula; in the summer, the incidence of wind varies, being southerly towards Singapore and westerly over North Malaysia, which makes for minor differences in local climates.

The movement of air masses affects the incidence and distribution of rainfall, variations in which are the chief characteristics of the seasons. Rainfall, however, is not at its peak during any one of these seasons. Maximum rains occur in the Doldrums at the periods between the wind seasons. The belt of equatorial calms is well established over Malaysia during April–May and during October–November, bringing rainfall peaks separated from one another by drier (though not dry) seasons when the wind systems are well established (Fig. 31). Thus the rains are largely of instability type, depending on local influences acting upon unstable warm, damp air masses. Hence the importance of aspect, local relief, local convection over bare paddy fields and over bare tin mines, and land and sea breezes in establishing the detailed pattern of rainfall.

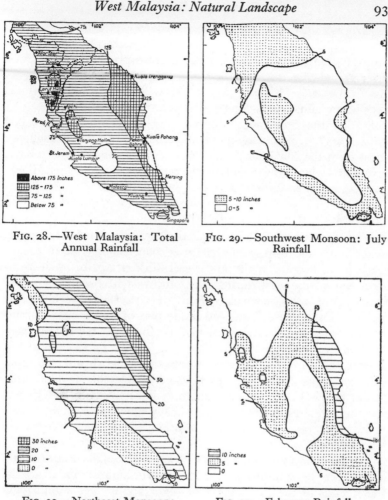

FIG. 28.—West Malaysia: Total Annual Rainfall

FIG. 29.—Southwest Monsoon: July Rainfall

FIG. 30.—Northeast Monsoon: November Rainfall

FIG. 31.—February Rainfall

Frequent storms, generally accompanied by lightning, bring very localised rains, typically though by no means always occurring in afternoons, so that the diurnal rhythm (cool clear nights and mornings, hot thundery afternoons) in the weather is often more emphatic than the seasonal rhythm of change.

The seasons are: (1) Northeast Monsoon, from late October to the end of March, when strong winds blow from the South China Sea, bringing heavy rain and low cloud to the east coast and to the eastern side of mountains, while elsewhere winds are lighter and the rainfall less (Fig. 30). (2) Southwest Monsoon, from the beginning of June to September, bringing generally light winds and a drier period (Fig. 29). (3) The Doldrums or transitional seasons of April–May and October–November, with light variable winds, very heavy rain, much cloud and violent electric storms.

During the Southwest Monsoon small intense storms called "Sumatras" occasionally move towards the Malacca-Singapore coast from the Malacca Strait. They are line-squalls in character, bringing violent winds and heavy rains for a few hours. These storms rapidly lose force after crossing the coast.

RAINFALL

W. Malaysia's rain falls mainly in torrential showers (often an inch in an hour) and during the late afternoon, though the incidence tends to be after midnight on the east during the Northeast Monsoon and on the west during the Southwest Monsoon. The total rainfall (Fig. 28) varies widely from year to year, a reflection of its origin in instability storms, and at any part of the year heavy rains and dry spells are equally possible. To the west, rainfall averages are high from October to January and least in July or February. To the north August to October brings intense rains and December to February is distinctly dry. To the east October to December brings heaviest rain, with minimum in February (Fig. 31). Severe flooding often results from the very heavy showers which may bring 15 inches in one day; 17 inches in 8 hours have been recorded in Penang.

The east coast is a belt where high annual rainfalls occur (mostly over 125 in. per annum) but the localities of highest rainfall are the Larut Hills of the Bintang Range (over 200 in. per annum) and that part of the Central Range between Kampar and Tanjong Malim (over 150 in. per annum). The driest district is the sheltered one just southeast of the Central Range, centring on Kuala Pilah (below 75 in. per annum).

Humidity for most of the year remains high and, while the relative figure for daytime may fall to 65 per cent, the wet bulb is usually above 75° F. for most days, nights and seasons, which produces enervating conditions. In these circumstances, human comfort depends on the cooling effect of evaporating perspiration and this, in turn, on movement of air, so that on shores and windy places the enervating effect is not strong, though it may become overpowering in closed or sheltered places.

AVERAGE MONTHLY RAINFALLS (in inches)

	Aver. heavy rain days	*Jan.*	*Feb.*	*Mar.*	*Apr.*	*May*	*June*	*July*	*Aug.*	*Sept.*	*Oct.*	*Nov.*	*Dec.*	*Total*
Alor Star	58	1.7	1.2	5.3	10.5	8.6	7.5	6.6	10.6	10.2	13.7	8.3	6.2	90.4
Trengganu	59	9.2	3.4	7.3	4.6	4.7	5.1	6.2	7.0	5.8	14.7	27.2	24.7	119.9
Cameron Highlands	68	6.0	5.1	6.8	12.4	10.7	5.1	3.7	7.8	8.9	13.1	12.3	9.8	101.7
Kuala Lipis	61	10.1	3.5	6.9	8.0	8.4	5.8	5.1	6.6	7.7	11.5	11.8	9.8	95.2
Kuala Lumpur	62	6.6	6.1	8.8	10.5	8.5	4.9	4.3	6.3	7.3	11.1	9.9	9.7	94.0
Kluang	55	8.6	4.1	8.7	9.9	10.0	6.5	3.9	6.3	6.5	9.3	10.1	8.4	92.3
Singapore	58	9.9	6.9	7.6	7.4	6.8	6.8	6.7	7.7	7.0	8.2	10.0	10.2	95.2

(By "heavy rain days" is meant "days receiving 0.5 inch and over")

More significant from the agricultural point of view is the cloud cover, upon the absence of which largely depends the ripening of fruits and paddy. Clouds, mostly cumulus, vary very much during the course of any one day, though October and November are decidedly the cloudiest months and February the clearest. Over the interior and the west, January to March is a period of moderately clear skies. At all times Singapore and the mountains have denser and more prolonged cloud cover. In part the rainfall map reflects the cloud cover which is significantly small over the rice areas of Kelantan and Kuala Pilah.

DRAINAGE SYSTEM

High rainfall and low evaporation cause Malaysian rivers to have great volume relative to their length or catchment areas; they contain more organic solubles and colloidals than solids, they change rapidly in volume within hours or days and so encourage levees. While the drainage system is of great antiquity and far advanced in development, there are discordances in Malaysian river profiles which relate to a remoter history, the more recent physical history (Fig. 17) being one of progressive inundation which has over-flattened the lower profiles in relation to the upper profiles. Changes of landscape due to solution of limestone massifs have also caused drainage readjustments. The rising sea level has not caused ria estuaries owing to rapid sedimentation, but rivers have not developed normal delta form because strong seasonal onshore winds spread the sediment as spits and lines of offshore drift, flattening the plan of deltas on their seaward side.

FIG. 32.—Drainage Lines of West Malaysia

The plan of Malaysian rivers (Fig. 32) is a product of several in-fluences, each of which varies in proportion from place to place:

(*a*) The tectonic pattern of the ranges tends to produce longitu-dinal streams running on broad meridional lines through the strike-vales. This is apparent in the Kelantan, Perak and Johore rivers and in the middle course of the Pahang.

(*b*) The orographic influence produces streams on latitudinal lines consequent to the slopes of the ranges and sometimes breaking through the adjoining ranges in cluse. Under this influence the Upper Pahang tributaries, for example, flow east.

(*c*) The continental submergence has induced premature precipitation upstream and created meanders and vague drainage far inland.

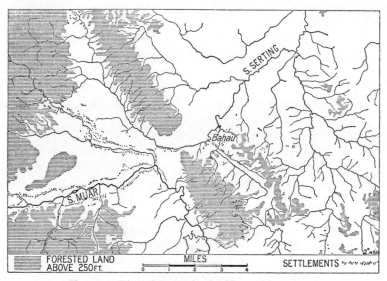

FIG. 33.—River Capture in the Upper Muar Area

Where (*a*) and (*b*) predominate, as in most of Central and North Malaysia, the river pattern becomes trellis-like with broad marshes in the meridional sections and sharper relief at the transverse courses in the cluse. Senile versions of the pattern familiar in uniclinal structures show fairly symmetrically on each side of the ranges. Towards the south, the factor (*c*) is dominant with some erosional competition between the Malacca Strait and South China Sea drainage systems; the upper Muar shows signs of capture of the latter by the former (Fig. 33). Capturing of upper courses and shifts of lower courses are widespread, as in the Kinta and Pahang rivers.

In the limestone zones a fourth influence comes into play: the drainage orginally developed on the limestone rapidly changes as solution removes the formation, which factor, for example, has re-aligned the Kinta streams from being tributaries of the River Pari to being Perak tributaries, as at present (Fig. 37).

SOILS

Rocks differ in their reaction to equatorial weathering, which tends to be one of laterisation, though there are considerable areas of podsolisation which produces bleached grey or white subsoils that have complicated the interpretation of high level soils found in many places.

(a) On granite, weathering first breaks down the felspar crystals to kaolin, leading to a mixture of fine clay and coarse sand which may be 50 ft. thick. Squared blocks of fissured granite disintegrate into rounded boulders within the clay-sand mass. High precipitation aids slipping and slumping of this weathered surface so that bare slopes of granite appear in parts of W. Malaysia.

(b) Quartzites and conglomerates weather chiefly into loose sands and pebbly gravels, generally not weathered so deeply as in granite. Chert rapidly bleaches into dull angular fragments. Ease of drainage through such loose materials appears to encourage podsolisation rather than laterisation (Glinka).

(c) On shales, slates, schists and phyllites the laminated structure breaks down easily into a soft tenacious clay, often containing mica flakes. The carbon compounds in these rocks bleach white. The clay may take on a wide range of colours, yellow, brown, green or blue. Core boulders of fresh rock are found within this weathered material and laterised ironstone concretions commonly occur close to the surface, often forming a surface athwart the structural lines.

(d) Limestone weathers by solution and little residuum is left except from the calcareous shales. Pinnacles and knife-edge ridges, the normal superficial effects of limestone undergoing solution, have been preserved beneath the alluvials of the Kinta Valley which also conceal old drainage channels, incised into the limestone. Solution still goes on under the alluvial blanket which is constantly subsiding. Cave systems occur in all stages of development from fissures to enclosed basins (*wangs*) formed from collapsed areas, and stalactites are found everywhere in association with the caves.

(e) Most rocks of the Pahang Volcanic Series resist weathering and stand up as bare outcrops with only an inch or two of bleached surface like a rind above the original rock. Rhyolites, however, weather down into silts and volcanic explosive agglomerates into loose boulders. Certain local zones of weathered basic igneous rocks produce fertile soils though these are not particularly significant in W. Malaysia owing to their inland location and the absence of adequate incentive to exploit fully the soil resources. They are attracting some cacao-growing trials.

(*f*) Quartz veins, which run through and beyond the granites, resist weathering and may persist as lines of broken crystals within masses of weathered material. Where the quartz is continuous and thick, as near the Klang Gates, it stands out as a topographic feature.

Within the valleys and marshes and along the coasts, soils are transported, consisting of fine sticky clays with a high vegetal content; these are depositories of river-borne topsoil from the uplands. Outside these areas soils have mostly developed *in situ* to produce only a few inches of humus-bearing topsoil overlying a thick laterised subsoil. The agricultural value of the *in situ* soils is invariably very low; that of the transported soils varies enormously, a fertile loam often deriving from the calcareous shales. The major fertility factor is less the soil itself and more the location of the watertable. Cleared, drained and cultivated, the transported soils of the estuarial zones represent the accumulation of fertile elements from the whole interior and maintain production for long periods without noticeable deterioration, largely because at this stage and at such low levels weathering does not leach them. Elsewhere solefluction, slipping and slumping combine to hasten the removal of both top and subsoils, aided by the high proportion of water within the ground and by the characteristic panned structure of laterised soils which are very fully developed in W. Malaysia where both climate and tectonic history have together induced advanced laterisation.

The flow of subsoil water varies considerably, though under most areas such water is held colloidally rather than interstitially, so that wells are only rarely of the percolation type. Large areas of the Malaysian surface are so waterlogged that the watertable lies only an inch or so from the surface. Local artesian conditions have been met within the lenticular alluvials along the coast. Most water supply, however, is from surface sources and wells accumulate surface run-off rather than fill by percolation from below. Hot springs near Malacca and Kuala Lumpur and in Perak have low pressure issues of water at about 100° F.; these are probably from great depth, deriving their heat from pressures rather than from vulcanism and for this reason are known technically as "juvenile" waters.

FOREST LANDSCAPE

While certain types of Malaysian natural vegetation occupy too small an area to be easily mapped, they merit special consideration because they stand in just those marginal zones where population concentrates and because the Malaysian natural landscape is more sharply differentiated by the forest types than it is by any other single factor. To some extent the forest types relate to the relief and location so that a dual tag aptly describes them.

The Casuarina Beach Woodlands.—An almost continuous casuarina fringe some 60 ft. broad stretches just above high water level and above the level of fresh-water swamp, along the coast from Trengganu to Johore and in patches along the west coast. These trees, often 80 ft. tall, have needle leaves which fall to make a bed, obliterating other vegetation, though other gnarled trees, like *penaga laut* (Calophyllum) and *ketapeng* (Terminalia Catappa) may accompany it. The tree establishes itself quickly upon exposures of marine sands and dunes, often acting as pioneer for mangrove. Behind it, inland, usually stretches a few hundred yards of scrub, tropical grass (*lalang*, Imperator cylindrica) and Straits rhododendron (Melastoma). This beach forest provides some timber for building fishing boats.

Mangrove Sea-Swamp Forest.—Forming a seaward belt from Kedah to Singapore, the mangrove forest ranges from 50 yds. to 12 miles in width and extends farther inland along rivers. Within it, river estuaries provide waterways and sometimes the forest subdivides into islands with deep channels between them, as round Port Swettenham. These mangrove swamps develop from river muds, often infilling lagoon-like spaces between offshore bars of marine sands thrown up persistently by Malacca Straits currents. They shelve gently on the seaward side so that even small sea-going boats must keep hundreds of yards from shore at low tide. Mangrove banks become convex, the slightly higher part being less frequently and less deeply inundated, which exercises a selection of species. Deposition quickly raises the surface level, a process aided by burrowing prawns (Thalassina).

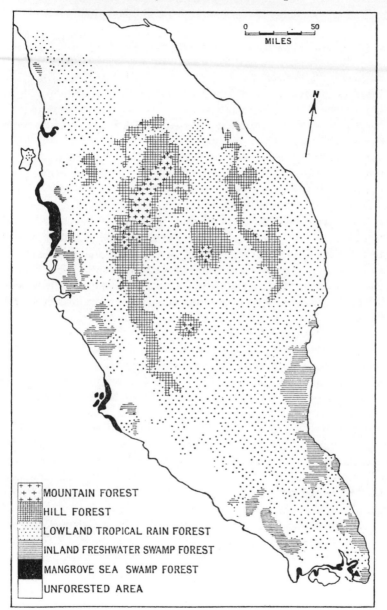

FIG. 34.—Forest Types of West Malaysia

The trees are uniform dense growths averaging 40 ft. high, with dark shining foliage. The *Api-api* (Avicennia), with typical greyish leaves, is an early coloniser, capable of establishing itself upon banks exposed by the sea only for a few days; it binds and builds up the surface, making possible the setting of other species. Fireflies frequent this tree, which is traditionally a guide to sailors. Behind the *Api-api* in situation, and succeeding it in progression, come *Bakau* (Rhizophora), and *Lenggadai* (Bruguiera). Away from the estuaries in Selangor, Perak and Province Wellesley there are acres of swampy scrub enclosed by small bunds built to exclude tides from farmlands and often the sign of land which has gone out of cultivation.

Mangrove forests of the east coast are confined to estuaries and colonise somewhat differently upon sandspits driven southward from the river mouth. These banks are colonised by casuarinas and then the creek or laggon behind is converted into mangrove swamp and gradually filled by tides through some breach in the sandspit. Remnants of successive spits and mangrove swamps may be traced inland for several miles in some places and the swamps at a later stage frequently become lines of paddy fields. Similar successions may be met in Kedah.

Mangrove covers over 460 square miles and is well worked over for firewood, charcoal and poles for which the trees are particularly suited. Some parts of the mangrove zone are well peopled. Villages in them may have several thousand people in settlements built on piles and lapped by the tides, or in lines on old beach sands. Fishing, fish drying, pig keeping and crocodile hunting (for the skins) are the human activities in mangrove settlements, which usually avoid sandy stretches of the west coast owing to the high incidence of malaria and sandfly fever. That pigs are so frequently kept is sign that these villages are often non-Muslim and the people more primitive than Malays.

Lines of nipa, nibong (Oncosperma) and pandanus develop along estuaries where water is fresher; the nipa is highly valued for thatching and the pandanus leaves are woven into sleeping mats and bags.

Inland Freshwater Swamp Forest.—The recent history of rising sea level, together with the torrential rains of today, cause the extensive alluvial lowlands to be frequently under water, to form Inland Freshwater Swamp Forest. In these places the soil is a viscous mud covered with peat which may, as in Kuala Selangor, be as thick as 30 ft., the greater thicknesses normally being well inland. While the trees of this Freshwater Swamp Forest are below the Malayan average for height, the sodden ground has a thick undergrowth mainly of palms, pandanus and thorny plants, making the forest almost impenetrable. *Lopak* is the local name for those marginal areas which are occasionally rather than regularly flooded. *Permatang* are low ridges of slightly drier land running through the swamp, probably old levees or beach lines. In Kedah and Perlis the swamps contain considerable pure stands of *gelam* (Melaleuca) which can grow in water up to 3 ft. deep. The types of tree are relatively few though they include commercial trees which remain untouched because of inaccessibility over the swamp ground.

Lowland Tropical Rain Forest.—This forest type in Malaysia differs little from the one usual to similar areas of Southeast Asia (see Chapter 4). It persists from the coastal plains to heights of 2,000 ft. and occupies 60 per cent of the peninsula. While there are thorny types of undergrowth, such as *bertram* (Eugeissona), rattans (climbing palms) and *kelubi* (Zalacca), access is not generally difficult, which makes the extraction of *chengal, balau, kapur, keruing* and *meranti*, the chief Malaysian timber trees, commercially practicable, though difficulties of haulage, extraction and labour shortage prevent extensive exploitation. These timbers are used domestically, yet W. Malaysia is a net importer of timbers. The collection of gums and similar products from wild trees has always gone on, but has rarely exceeded a third of a million dollars annually; of this *jelutong* for chewing gum was always the greatest single item.

Malaysian timbers are:

1. *Chengal* (Balanocarpus), a very strong, hard, heavy structural timber.
2. *Balau* (Shorea) similar to, but less durable than *chengal*.
3. *Merbau* (Afzelia) strong, hard and heavy for internal construction because it resists white ants although liable to quick decay.
4. *Kapur* (Dryobalanops), strong, moderately hard, durable, for buildings; especially abundant in Trengganu and East Johore.
5. *Keruing* (thirty species of Dipterocarpus), strong, moderately durable, shrinks greatly, very abundant but needs treating unless used for covered constructions; mainly extracted from Johore.

6. *Meranti* (several types of Shorea), generally reddish, moderately hard, not very durable; for light or temporary constructions or cheap furniture.

Secondary Forest.—This has no natural location since it originates from clearings man-made, from forest fires, and from abandoned farms. Known in Malaysia and the Indies as *belukar*, it is a forest type whose stages of growth vary enormously from initial long tropical grasses (*lalang*) to a forest not clearly distinguishable from lowlands forest. Patches of it may be exclusively *resam* (impenetrable climbing bracken), but it is generally mixed with heavy undergrowth.

It is commonest near *kampongs* and in northeast Kedah where jungle tribes have almost over-worked the forest with their temporary clearings. *Belukar* has no commercial use, apart from the extraction of a little bamboo; it is, however, a heritage of other uses.

Hill Forest.—This is a type of Tropical Rain Forest which is adapted to the slightly different weather of the hills. It develops on uplands and ridges from 2,000 to 4,000 ft. high. Most *keruing* (Dipterocarpus) disappear at this altitude. The *serava*, a grey-leaved tree, is prominent, together with the thorby *bertam* palm. Nothing of value comes from these forests though they are threaded by tracks of many wandering tribes.

Mountain Forest.—Above 4,000 ft. the mountain forest of Malaysia is that normal to similar heights in Southeast Asia (see Chapter 4), being a transition varying from mountain oak forest (Pasania) at lower altitudes to xerophytic scrub at greater altitudes. The only tree of commercial use is "mountain oak" for local firewood and hill station structures.

MALAYA, MALAYSIA, MALAY, MALAYAN

Malaya *is used to describe the peninsular region originally of sultanates south of the Thai border and once organised into the* Federation of Malaya. Malaysia *is a portmanteau word first used by Emerson in* 1937 *for the region of Malay-speaking peoples (including Malaya, Indonesia and parts of the Philippines) and later restricted to the political organisation of Malaya, Sarawak and Saba into the* Federation of Malaysia. *The peninsular part of this federation is now officially* West Malaysia *and the Borneo part is* East Malaysia. *A Malay is a person of one ethno-linguistic group in the Peninsula; a* Malayan *is a person irrespective of race who was a national of the Federation of Malaya; a* Malaysian *is any national of the Federation of Malaysia.*

Chapter Seven

THE CULTURAL LANDSCAPE OF WEST MALAYSIA

THE Malaysian natural landscape has only on a lesser part (about 34 per cent of the total area) been greatly modified by human activities and both the intensities and the age of the modifications are dominated by two distinct objectives; to obtain food, and to obtain money.

Activities associated with obtaining food are still the chief concern of indigenous peoples, whose ways, traditions and patterns of settlement and distribution have been much the same for centuries and are closely integrated in detail with the subtle variations of local environment. On the other hand, those parts of the landscape devoted to obtaining money, by the sale and export of produce, are recent innovations by foreigners whose ways and patterns of settlement relate more to conditions overseas than to the Malaysian landscape. These latter areas show the influence of recent diffusions of modern technique and modern economic organisation, immaturely modified to the setting though varying in impact upon and interrelation with the older cultural landscape forms. Thus the cultural landscape may be divided into two, the food producing and the money producing; to a certain extent there are marginal overlaps between these landscape types.

THE LANDSCAPE OF FOOD PRODUCTION

The large-scale food-producing activities in Malaysia are rice farming and fishing. All are overwhelmingly Malay activities, so that traditional Malay houses (stilted, thatched wooden huts), costume (loose skirtlike *sarong* and black fezlike *songkok*) and cultural centres (mosques) characterise the associated landscapes in degrees varying with the prosperity of the region and with its isolation.

Fishing.—While fishing is most developed and specialised on the basis of sea fishing, all rivers, streams and even canals are fished for local use, and fish form the second staple in the Malay diet. Along the East Coast, villages are often nearly entirely devoted to fishing and to drying the fish into forms suitable for transport in this hot climate; round Pangkor Island and the Dindings there are similar specialisations. In those places the fishing village occupies a part of the coast fairly sheltered from the violence of the sea during the worst monsoon storms, and its houses are often partly hidden under coconut palms, grown as adjunct to fishing and as source of cooking oil. Malaysian fishing is inshore work using drift, seine and lift nets and lines in waters less than 20 miles from the coast. In the shallow fringes of the calmer West Coast thousands of long screens of bamboo stakes are built in the water to lead the fish into traps; these are mainly used by Chinese fishermen. Fishing tends to be an exclusive occupation, other food needs of fishing families being obtained by sales of fish; on the East Coast, where November to March is a closed season due to the violent weather, fishermen may also be paddy farmers or coconut smallholders. The frequence of coastal swamps tends to isolate fishing villages from the interior and their communications are normally by water, except in Malacca and on the Perak coast where there are major interior markets for fresh fish chilled with ice and transported by road.

The chief fish edible in Malaysia are, in order of weight caught, *Kembong* or mackerel (Scomber) especially from the Dindings; *Bilis* or whitebait (Stolephorus), chiefly from Trengganu; *Udang* or prawns (Peneus), from the West Coast; *Tamban* or sprats (Clupea) from northern coasts; *Selar* (*Selayang*) or horse mackerel (Caranx) mainly from the East Coast; *Parang* or Dorab (Chirocentrus) from the southern coasts; *Delah* or seabream (Caesio), coming to Singapore from deep sea fishing among islands farther south than Malaysia.

In 1965 the catch totalled 229,000 tons, of which 105,000 tons was from the West Coast where fishing is more commercialised, with 10,600 tons at Singapore; on the East Coast much goes unrecorded. About 57,000 persons and over 5,000 powered boats were then employed in fishing.

Rice Farming.—Whether or not the theory that Malays were originally seafarers, fishermen and sailors can be maintained, they have mostly become the paddy-farmers of the Peninsula. Of some six million acres of agricultural land, about 970,000 acres now normally carry rice, the chief states concerned being Kedah, Kelantan and Perak in that order; these three states contain over two-thirds of W. Malaysian paddyfields. At least 94 per cent of Malaysian paddy is wet, so that hill or dry paddy contributes negligibly to the landscape and the production. Dry paddy is sown to a small extent in the small clearings of shifting cultivation and also as a catch crop on land being newly cleared and prepared for other agricultural uses. On the land utilisation map only wet paddy is sufficiently large to mark, occupying a small part of W. Malaysia as a whole and best examined on the regional maps of land use (Figs. 35–43).

Wet paddy depends on water control which in Malaysia varies from primitive arrangements for holding or restraining local rainwater run-off to ingenious Malay devices for directing river water, and to modern engineering schemes. Kedah, Province

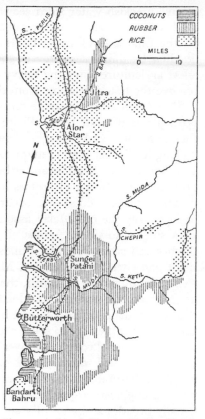

FIG. 35.—Land Use in Perlis, Kedah and Province Wellesley

Wellesley, Krian in Perak, and Kelantan have extensive and continuous areas under rice, all of them in the lower deltaic zones of large streams. Elsewhere units of paddy-land tend to be small, stretched along the flood plains of the larger rivers, the Perak and Pahang (Fig. 42), and in thin ribbons among hill valleys (Fig. 38). Scarcely any wet paddy grows above the 50 ft. level anywhere in Malaysia. In the coastal belts of Kelantan, Trengganu and in parts of Province Wellesley, the rice is in innumerable small areas mostly of the order 10 acres, lying between the sandy ridges of old spits which once enclosed mangrove creeks and lagoons. These are areas of coastal advance under continual river deposition, moulded by marine currents. During dry periods, the fields in such areas receive brackish water from seawater percolating inland through old beach sands as the water-table lowers; bunds of 2 ft. are built on the tidal side of these fields to reduce this risk. Occasional flooding by dilute seawater in some of these areas seems not to affect agriculture since the heavy torrents of fresh rainwater later remove the brackish water from the surface.

These paddylands provide on the Malaysian landscape the only open plains without trees. There is rarely any settlement within them, houses and villages being characteristically marginal, seeking levels just high enough to be free from normal flood risk. The houses are, in addition, stilted to stand some 3 ft. from the ground. This stilting of houses has become a tradition, based no doubt on present flood risk, security from wild animals, coolness, and possibly the old Malay association with coastal and estuarial sites subject to tides. Across all paddyland run shallow control ditches and canals lined by bunds which become tracks of movement and sites for settlement. Malay-built canals have been dug to 4ft. depth and 18 ft. width, the bunds being perhaps 3 ft. high, 10 ft. broad and unsurfaced. Heads of water in the canals are often formed by dams of faggots and boulders. They are filter-dams in the sense that they are to some extent permeable, allowing a gentle trickle of water through and over the dam. These are easily built, quickly removed during unexpected floods and they do not significantly diminish the silt load. Modern canals constructed by western engineers are similar in size but the bund on one side is usually broader and carefully surfaced as a track. In these canals the dams are generally permanent cement structures, often with sluices at the bottom. By stopping water completely they tend to retain the silt content and the violent outflow from the sluices has in some cases bitten deeply into the valley below the dam, causing progressive lowering of the water-table in the adjoining fields, which thereafter become more critically dependent on irrigation rather than on natural water.

Fields are subdivided with small bunds 9 in. high, to mark property limits and to facilitate water control. They give a shallow-stepped or terraced appearance though it is rare to have more than a few inches difference of level between adjoining fields. At most stages of paddy growth these fields are flooded; in the off season they bake hard and the bare ground under the sunlight works up to very much higher temperatures than is customary elsewhere, a factor which may act as a "trigger" in local convectional storms.

In Kedah, Perlis, Kelantan, Trengganu and most of Malacca, paddy stands growing in the fields during the wet phases of the year from September to January. Where seasonal water is ample, as in Kedah, even in June planting may take place. Reaping, by hand methods, generally cutting head by head, goes on variously from January to March, after which the ground lies fallow. Where there is little noticeable rainfall rhythm, planting depends on irrigation from rivers whose flood peaks harmonise with heavy rains in a remoter part of the country; planting is then timed by official announcements based on information about heavy rains round the headwaters. Few areas cultivate more than one crop of

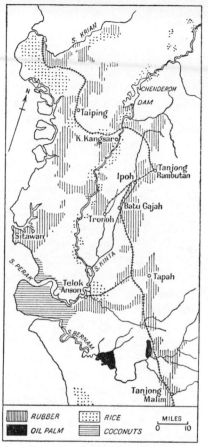

FIG. 36.—Land Use in Perak

rice a year, the local explanation being that the ground and the shortage of water will not permit a second crop. Over the paddy areas, roads invariably stand upon embankments above normal flood levels.

Considerable variation in the rhythm of cultivation may be noted from district to district, depending upon the incidence of floods either from torrential rains or from the river. While these rhythms of activity relate to solar rhythm affecting the rainfall, the local calendar is lunar, and the festivals associated with it are not closely connected with the rhythm of agricultural life of the seasons, a discordance matched also by the Muslim religious festivals which relate more to Middle East events than to those of Southeast Asia. Geographically, the persistence of seasonal rhythms in food agriculture is an interesting contrast with the ill-defined character of local seasons. Despite the absence of strongly marked seasons, leaving an equable condition which better matches a yam agricultural system, the average yields of Malaysian paddy (some 1,400 lbs. of cleaned rice per acre for 1963) are higher than those of most Southeast Asia territories.

CYCLE OF WEST MALAYSIAN PADDY FARMING

	Kedah	Kelantan and Trengganu	Inner Pahang (Temerloh)	Malacca	Negri Sembilan
Preparing fields	Early Aug.	Early Aug.	July	Early July	March
Setting seedbeds	Mid Aug.	Mid. Aug.	Late July	Mid July	April
Transplanting	Early Oct.	Early Oct.	September	August	Mid May
Harvesting	January	March	Early Feb.	January	November
Expectation of heaviest rain	Oct.	Dec.	Dec.	July	Mar.
Length of time in ground	7–8 months	8–9 months	8–9 months	7–8 months	6–8 months

The West Malaysian rice production now normally exceeds 600,000 tons, which is roughly one-half of the population's requirements. Much of Malaysian rice is locally consumed by the Malay farmers and scarcely enters the trading system. Often the milling and processing of paddy is done on the farms by hand methods. Because these methods suit only small quantities at one time, paddy is often stored in the husk (it keeps better that way) in large thatched bins of woven palm leaves standing upon rat-proof legs in front of the farmhouse. A few official power mills have been set up to encourage large-scale rice production in the more extensive areas such as Kedah, Perlis and Perak but there are very few huge mills such as those of the Burma-Thailand-Indochina rice-producing landscapes.

Because buffaloes are used to pull the ploughs, they are common in all paddy areas, where Thai-type oxen may also be used. Over two-thirds of Malaysia's oxen and buffaloes are distributed in the paddy areas. Inadequate local fodder restricts these animals in number and size and they play little part in the economy of farming apart from haulage; they graze on paddyland after harvesting and upon young shoots of tropical grasses.

Settlement in the paddy areas is in villages (*kampongs*) of Malay houses standing a little apart from each other and surrounded by a few coconut or fruit trees which both conceal and shade the houses. There is little nucleation in the European sense; not even the mosque acts as focus to the house groups and the typical long string of houses may have different place names in different parts of the same line. Settlements of this open type have clearly no defensive outlook and the lines of houses run (*a*) along the edges of paddylands, so that the kampong has the form of the contour, (*b*) along bunds or canals, in straight lines, (*c*) along roads, mostly linear but occasionally cruciform, where roads cross. To some extent the dispersed settlement form offsets and makes innocuous the absence of any sanitation and the dependence for potable water on local streams or canals.

Few supplementary food crops are grown by the Malay farmer: he plants small patches of coconut for his cooking oil and illuminant, a few areca palms and some fruits, but vegetables are neither widely grown nor prominent in his diet.

THE LANDSCAPE OF PRODUCTION FOR CASH

Whereas food production is an indigenous activity, production for money is an innovation by foreigners upon parts of the Malaysian surface which previously had had no production value. Thus the two forms of production have been able to go on side by side with relatively little mutual interaction in techniques, in peoples or in tradition.

Two distinct types of landscape have evolved with the object of production for cash sales—one an agriculture for commerce, the other mining. The former is mainly concerned with rubber and the latter with tin, though there are variants.

(a) Cash Agriculture

Rubber.—Over the last fifty years, the rubber tree has become the most important crop in Malaya both by area (about 3½ million acres out of a total agricultural area of 6½ million acres), in value, and in numbers of people directly employed (.5 million out of roughly 1.4 million agricultural workers at 1957 census). All figures except those for area alter only slightly over the years without changing the outstanding position of rubber farming.

Until the introduction of *Hevea Braziliensis* as a British experiment over several years from 1879, Malaysia had never been concerned even with collecting wild rubber and no local latex-producing plant had attracted major interest.

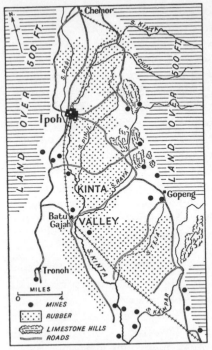

FIG. 37.—Land Use in the Kinta Valley

The *Hevea* was particularly suited to the poor lateritic soils and the climate of Malaysia, both of which resemble those in the Amazon Valley, and its introduction met several needs—the need for an agriculture to open up Malaysia's virgin forests, the growing needs of the electrical industries in Britain, and the new needs for rubber tyres as the car industry developed in the United States and Europe. It was, however, a tree requiring at least seven years to reach maturity which, together with the heavy initial labour costs of jungle clearing and of recurrent maintenance costs during growth, implied substantial financial backing.

Hence the rubber plantation became a highly capitalised, company-promoted operation of long-term planning, something as foreign to Malaysia as the new tree and the people who worked to cultivate it. As a result, the cultivation of rubber represents an outstanding example of large-scale human intervention in plant geography so that Malaysia and Southeast Asia are now more linked with the *Hevea* than is the Amazon Forest which was its home, and large portions of Malaysian land have been converted from its natural heterogeneous forest to a homogeneous forest of rubber trees with an artificially limited undergrowth retained as erosion control.

At various times other crops were tried in Malaysia to establish commercial agriculture—gambier, coffee, tea, sugar—to be virtually abandoned for different reasons of soil poverty, labour scarcity and competitive production elsewhere. Only tea continues as a minor commercial crop.

Originally all rubber was "clean-weeded," kept free from undergrowth in the manner of orchards in temperate latitudes.

This caused rapid erosion of topsoil by torrential rains and led to experiments to control and improve the soil. It culminated in the technique of letting undergrowth develop as a soil protector, a device hastened by neglect during the Japanese Occupation, so that most plantations now have considerable scrub undergrowth through which run paths for the labourers to reach each tree.

When the rubber-growing became well established as a highly capitalised agriculture run by plantations normally covering about 2,000 acres each, Asiatic smallholders took up the crop in units mostly of less than 100 acres. These smallholdings are of two types: larger ones organised as miniatures of the estates, and smaller ones run by paddy-farmers or fishermen as an adjunct to their food producing activities and drawing them, to a degree varying with the price of rubber, into the system of production for cash. More than 45 per cent of rubber acreage is now in this smallholding category, which produced 43 per cent of Malaysian rubber in 1964.

While rubber fits the Malaysian ecology by being almost constantly productive through the year and continuously growing and producing over many years, it needs an equally continuous labour supply for the tapping and collection routines. In this sense the rubber plantation by its regularity of rhythm throughout the year resembles the dairy farm. On an average one worker is needed for each six acres though this proportion is less where workers contract to tap by area rather than by time and varies considerably from estate to estate. These workers are at wages, and purchase their food from distant producers, a factor which operates to keep rubber costs relatively inflexible except in the case of smallholders who can grow food to feed themselves and thereby lessen their immediate dependence on rubber prices. But the total labour force needed for rubber growing is clearly heavy. There was no labour force in Malaysia, so that the whole of the rubber system came to depend upon imported labour, partly Indian, partly Chinese. In 1962, 2 million acres of rubber estate employed 286,000 workers of whom 46 per cent were Indian and 31 per cent Chinese. These live in small squalid hamlets scattered within the plantation which has one central nucleus round the factory where the latex is coagulated, formed into sheets and smoke-dried for sale off the plantation. Only in a few large scientific estates such as those pioneered by Dunlops, has it become the practice to move liquid latex from the plantation to the ports for shipment in that form to processors overseas. Except at the factory, the workers' settlements have every sign of their unattached, floating lives; their quarters are almost makeshift, they have tolerated monotony and crudity to accumulate money to set them up elsewhere. When foreign labourers immigrated, they often went to the estates as their first experience of work in Malaysia and generally graduated to other less austere types of employment later or caused sons to do so.

The factory is the managerial centre, but is no more integrated to the population and the setting than the tappers' hamlets, because the managerial group is mostly transitory as well. Everything on the landscape tends to be impermanent, crude, unshapely and artificial, without any mature cultural or communal living at all. Thus the cultural landscape of a rubber estate bears little resemblance in its structure to that of Europe where the technicians came from, or to that of South India or China whence the labour comes, though an occasional Tamil shrine or Chinese temple stands among the trees. The atmosphere of makeshift and impermanence is in contrast to the actual outlook of a rubber plantation which is above all long-term. Other crops, like rice, leave the ground cleared and ready, at the end of each year's harvest, for replacement by new sowings; the rubber tree and its work goes on regularly and the costs of making a change would be almost as great as the original cost of clearing the primary forest—for which reason the Japanese Occupation and the war leading up to it, failed to cause the destruction or change of more than a few per cent of the rubber acreage. Just as the dairy farm centring on the cow has produced a distinct cultural landscape and tradition elsewhere, so rubber is ripe for creating around it traditions and associations more intimately and permanently linked to the setting than is the case now in W. Malaysia. That type of smallholding exclusively concerned with rubber differs from the large estate only in proportion, not in style, but the small-holding of two or three unevenly planted acres adjoining paddy or vegetables and cultivated on a family basis is more closely integrated to the environment, giving rise to family or co-operative tapping groups sometimes selling the latex to a larger factory. In total this last type of holding covers large areas though individual units are very small.

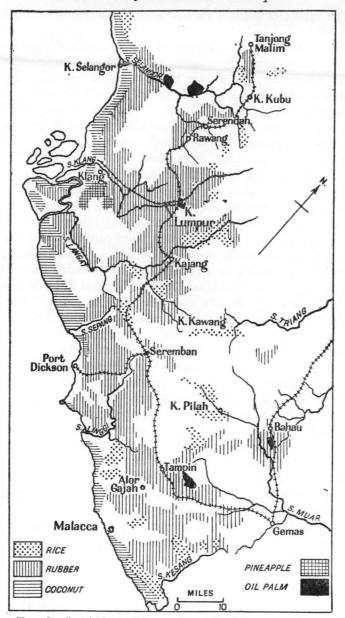

Fig. 38.—Land Use in Selangor, Negri Sembilan and Malacca

The aspect of planted rubber is one of a uniform crop from trees which, when fully matured, represent only a variant of the otherwise ubiquitous landscape of forest. Rubber trees to the south are not markedly seasonal in their leafing, though to the north where the dry season becomes more emphatic, rubber foliage turns red and then drops for some four weeks, about February; elsewhere the fall takes place sporadically and the estates as a whole appear evergreen. Controlled undergrowth has become widespread now that rubber can be called fully mature. The regular alignment of trees allows visibility within a plantation for as much as a quarter mile. Properly cultivated, rubber roots are not far below the surface, yet if soil erosion takes place roots appear to lie upon the surface itself. Silt pits along contours are customary erosion precautions, made necessary by the rolling or lightly hilly country which best suits rubber, whose vitality lowers if the roots are in soggy ground. Some rubber trees acquire a gnarled appearance as a result of careless cutting of the bark during tapping. Where rubber has been planted in badly drained lowlands, drainage ditches have been dug to lower the watertable. Roads through plantations, essential because of the coagulant acid, finished rubber and food supplies going to and from the plantation, are invariably of red pounded lateritic ironstone which makes a fair surface from easily accessible local materials. Isolation obliges most plantations to provide their own power either from diesel engines or from wood-burning steam engines.

Because external contact is necessary both for the sale of rubber and for bringing in the food of the labour force, rubber plantations need main road or railway communications. Hence the distribution of rubber relates to the pattern of highways and railways, as well as to the better drained lowlands or foothills. Association with immigrants who come in for other activities accounts in part for the concentration of rubber in the western peninsular belt where at the same time the lowland forest zone is better accessible to port facilities, the last and essential stage in the export of rubber, which has practically no use locally.

Coconut and Oil Palm Plantations.—Besides being grown in small units for direct local consumption, coconut has developed as a plantation crop on large estates close to the coast where the necessary deep drainage is maintained by ditching with sluices to keep out the tide. Beneath the palms only short Victoria grass grows without other undergrowth, so that the plantations seem light and open, although the ground is not worked. The labour used is much less than that in rubber growing and it is regular throughout the year because the tree fruits continuously. About 10,000 people were employed on coconut production at the 1957 census, which was less than the number of market gardeners. Many

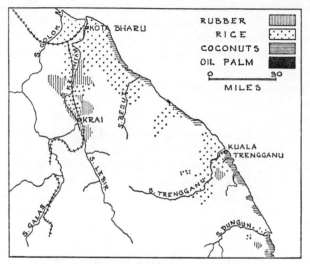

FIG. 39.—Land Use in Kelantan and Trengganu

of those employed are Malays who usually build villages and houses within the plantation on traditional Malay lines so that the whole integrates well with the Malaysian landscape. To convert the coconut meat into copra, either sun drying, smoke drying, or kiln drying is used, depending on the size of the plantation, but for this also the labour required is small in volume and unskilled in character. Smoke kilns predominate and they are fuelled by burnt husks; early drying is essential and must take place on the estate, which always ships its crops in the form of copra. Coconut oil is expressed from copra generally at portside, particularly at Singapore and Penang, or even overseas.

Coconut production for trade is an unstable activity. The price and demand fluctuates considerably and freight charges can easily squeeze away the profit from this low-grade, bulky commodity. Moreover it is highly competitive because part-time growers, already assured of their food supply by other work, can sell their copra individually in small units which make a large total, at rates below those of wage-paying plantations. Altogether about two-thirds of a million acres of coconut stand in W. Malaysia, mostly in units too small to appear on the land utilisation map except on the Perak coast (Fig. 36). W. Malaysian figures for copra and coconut are difficult to assess owing to the high local consumption and the entrepôt trade in those commodities at Singapore. For 1963 W. Malaysian production was 136,000 tons of copra and 80,000 tons of coconut oil, smallholdings accounting for 47 per cent of the whole.

The Oil Palm (*Elaeis guineeniss*), transferred from West Africa, and not indigenous, is grown only in large plantations on riverine and coastal flats. These palms branch fairly close to the ground and the dead fronds persist for a long time, so that the plant has a more solid, compact appearance than the coconut, and although to each acre there are only about the same number of palms as in a coconut plantation, the estates appear denser and more continuous. Though there is neglible undergrowth, it is not possible to see far. As in the case of coconuts, practically no cultivation of the ground is done. The plam fruits continuously giving a regular daily labour rhythm. These plantations are large units, exclusively foreign, mainly British, generally employing South Indian labour in the same proportion per acre as the coconut plantation and there is no competitive smallholder production. A good transport system on the estate is essential and may be either road, light railway or canoe on the drainage canals; the nuts, which are fairly small and very numerous, must be treated immediately at a large, expensively equipped factory on the estate; the process is mostly expressive but several minor processes have to be used to prevent chemical changes. The oil moves from the estates as liquid, some going to Singapore by sea; special storage tanks are necessary for handling the commodity which has the same broad industrial uses as coconut oil.

Oil palm estates are distributed through Johore (half of all in Malaysia), Perak and Selangor in that order of acreage (Figs. 36, 38, 43). After steadily extending to 121,000 acres, production had reached 101,000 tons of palm oil in 1965 (cf. 51,000 tons in 1938).

Other Cash Crops.—Pineapples, which fruit in December and June, eighteen months after planting, were at one time extensively planted by canning-factory owners in Singapore and Johore, where they were sometimes used as a catch crop in young

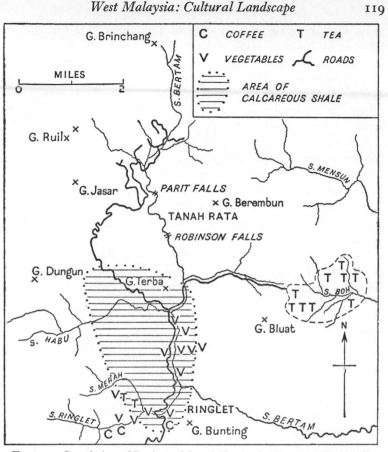

FIG. 40.—Correlation of Rocks and Land Use in the Cameron Highlands

rubber. It was essentially an industrialised activity, closely integrated with Chinese canners and exclusively using Chinese labour in a fluctuating and seasonal activity, which made very little impact on the landscape as a whole. The canned output goes very largely to the British and Canadian markets.

After its disappearance during wartime, pineapple-growing abandoned the now costly hillside locations favoured by the *Singapore* variety and was re-established in a new terrain, the peaty soils of SW. Johore, where about 17,500 acres were planted in 1954, mostly as smallholdings involving some 5,000 Chinese families, but production has now substantially dropped.

Market gardening occupies fairly extensive areas round every town though it ranks very low in total area. Almost entirely Chinese in character, it is the most intensive form of cultivation in Malaysia, worked mainly on a family basis and essentially a cash occupation needing at least two persons per acre. In the Cameron Highlands, many smallholders produce temperate climate vegetables for consumption in the towns of the lowlands which are served daily by road transport (Fig. 40).

A number of minor crops for sale show in the list of normal Malaysian production, though many continue only as catch crops. Of them, tapioca ranks exceptionally large in acreage, partly because it is a rice substitute and partly because it has a sale value for commercial starch. Sugar, maize, gambier, tea, coffee, spices, tobacco, derris and groundnuts are also grown on a small scale for cash sales. Almost all these minor crops are Chinese or Indian activities and their total significance on the Malaysian landscape is negligible; they inject little into the stream of trade. In Trenggannu, an estate is growing Amelonado cacao commercially.

(b) Mining

Tin.—Except for lode tin mines in Sungei Lembing (near Kuantan) and gold mines at Raub (Fig. 42), Malaysian mining is characteristically operated as various types of open-cast and is mostly alluvial, especially in tin mining. Thus mining occupies an area out of proportion to the tonnage produced and only 62,000 tons of tin were extracted from about 700 mines in 1956 before international restriction began, the effect being to close about half the mines. Production then increased to 63,000 tons in 1965.

The tin ore (cassiterite, containing about 75 per cent tin) occurs mostly in weathered grains scattered through gravels and sands; it may be eluvial (weathered *in situ*) but the majority is alluvial, that is, originally water-borne and partly sorted by flowing water. The principle of mining remains the same—removing a "dead" surface, breaking up the tin-bearing alluvials and washing away the sands, clays and gravels by a water method which leaves behind the heavy cassiterite grains. Techniques vary, however, and make different impressions on the landscape.

1. *Dredging:* This method has been the most productive and labour-saving since 1929. The dredge floats in a pond (technically called a paddock) covering about 4 acres and its steam or electrically-driven buckets on an endless chain draw up

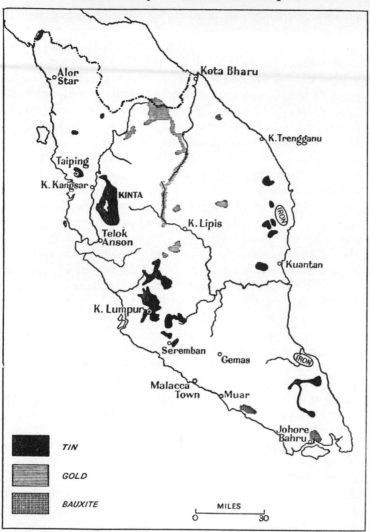

FIG. 41.—Locations of West Malaysian Minerals

from underwater the alluvium. As this is removed the dredge moves on, progressively excavating the bottom and sides of the pond. Within the dredge, the alluvium is screened to remove the tin and any other minor minerals, and the rest passes out as tailings which are spread by sluices behind the dredge. Thus the dredge transfers its pond slowly from place to place. The tailings lie only a little above the surface of the water to form loose swamps for hundreds of yards behind the dredge. Being soilless, these tailings can only be slowly colonised by vegetation.

To build a dredge is expensive (often over £250,000 each), so that this technique is confined to large-scale, heavily capitalised mines, chiefly European. By dredges a high extraction rate can be assured and alluvials once dredged are not worth going over again. As relatively few labourers, of the skilled artisan type, are employed, such mines have few buildings round them and these are often temporary, so that labour can move closer to the dredge as it moves on. Dredge mines are located in or close to river beds, but they do not make great demands on water supply—the same water is being used over and over again and fill-in by the tailings goes on automatically. Cheap tin may always be expected from dredges, which need very little labour. Some dredges were destroyed during the war and were not quickly replaceable owing to the demands for heavy equipment in other parts of the world; 71 were operating in 1957, employing 16,000 people, but by 1963 only 62 were in use.

2. *Gravel pump mines:* These tin mines open great pits in the alluvials to form scars on the landscape for long periods at a time. They can conserve the topsoil separately from the rest and spread it again over the alluvials once the mine is filled in, so that they need not permanently affect the landscape, though in point of fact careless infilling has mutilated large areas of landscape by preventing regrowth.

The pumping, by steam, diesel or electric power, is part of the process of raising a mixture of water and tin-bearing gravels by wide pipeline to the top of a high-level sloping sluice, built on tall timber trestles which stand everywhere on a Malaysian mining landscape. The sluice upon these trestles is stepped and the tin ore collects in the steps while the gravels are washed away by the continuously pumped water. Gathered from the sluice, the cassiterite is rewashed before drying and sacking for shipment. The tin-bearing alluvials are mixed with water by jets (monitors) playing on the sides of the pit, and the water carries the alluvials in a muddy stream to a "gravel pump" at the bottom of the pit. Tailings on these mines are derived from chutes here and there along the sluice and from its lower end; they are spread out loosely round the mine to form a landscape of dead land covering greater areas than those left by dredges. Considerably more labour per unit output is needed and round gravel pump mines lie haphazard groups of thatched, wooden, earth-floored miners' huts. Nearby there must be a pond or impounded stream to provide water for the monitors and when mines are abandoned the pits often fill with water and remain as deep lakes.

The proportion of extraction by this method varies and often the tailings merit being worked over several times by successively better methods. Some Malaysian areas have already been worked over four times. Work often goes on continuously day and night. Such mines go in and out of production fairly quickly, need less machinery than dredges do and are not confined to heavily capitalised undertakings. Ownership is very mixed; European, Chinese and Indian firms own gravel pump mines, and in 1956 about 620 Chinese gravel pump mines were operating with 19,000 labourers; half these mines closed in 1957, but most reopened by 1963.

3. *Other forms of Tin Mining:* Hydraulic mines (13 in 1960) resemble the gravel pump mine in most respects as far as technique, layout and form are concerned. They differ chiefly in using a pipeline from the hills to supply the head of water for the monitors and to motivate the gravel pumps.

Several true open-cast mines are operated, the Hong Fatt at Sungei Besi, being the outstanding example; in these, the alluvials are mechanically excavated from spiral terraces round the sides on which run rails for trucks and mechanical grabs. After being hauled to the surface the alluvials are treated with water as in gravel pumping.

The primitive method of panning by hand, to separate the cassiterite grains from the other gravels, better known in connection with gold prospecting and mining, has also been extensively used by small free-lance miners employing Chinese women coolies. In Malaysia, panning is known as *dulang* mining, much used by miners during slumps when larger concerns closed down.

At the Sungei Lembing lode mines, not far from Kelantan, the usual system of vertical shafts (to 1,200 ft. depths) is used, and the ore comes to the surface for crushing and roasting, an unusual technique in Malaysia. This particular installation of the Pahang

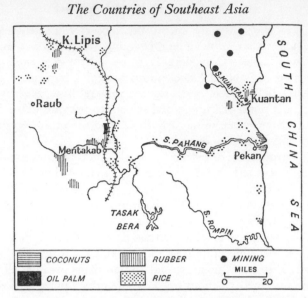

FIG. 42.—Land Use in Pahang. Areas left blank are forested

Consolidated Mining Company is large, heavily capitalised, elaborately equipped and a sign of the future of Malaysian tin-mining.

Most of the labour on tin mines has always been Chinese, supported in immediately pre-war years by Indians in the proportion roughly nine to one. Only a few Malays worked in this industry. The number of people employed varied with the prosperity of the industry which has changed considerably; in the six years 1933–38, annual production varied from about 25,000 tons to over three times that figure, and labour was recruited or discharged accordingly. There were about 35,000 workers on the mines in 1964 when Malaysian production was 60,000 tons (cf. 83,000 workers for 85,000 tons in 1940). In 1959, restriction reduced the workers to 21,000 for 32,500 tons. For labourers, the industry was a gamble; some were employed on daily wages, though housing and food were provided; others worked on contract and were paid according to the volume of ground cut away. A few groups of miners worked as a form of co-operative, sharing profits after the tribute (royalty) of the actual lessor had been paid.

From the human geography standpoint, the cultural landscape of mining was transient in most respects, except that the industry in boom years attracted mining rushes and it left relatively permanent scars of tailings and ponds on the worked-over landscape. This last was not in general serious from the agriculturists' point of view, since only occasionally had suitable alluvials been found under land already intensively cultivated. As a remoter effect, by altering the rate and incidence of natural sedimentation, tin mining has changed water-courses, increased deposition and clogged estuaries, particularly on the west coast, in Lower Perak and Selangor.

The pattern of Malaysian tin mining is thus set by alluvial deposits which have brought cassiterite from its veins at contact zones and fissures in the rocks adjoining the igneous intrusions. These deposits lie predominantly among the foothills to the ranges, where break of slope has lowered the capacity of streams to continue carrying heavy cassiterite. Thus, the mining zones flank the Central Range throughout its length, more especially on its west side, in the Kinta Valley and round Kuala Lumpur, where about three-quarters of Malayan tin is produced, but there are workings at Bentong and a few other points east of the Range to the south (Fig. 41). Other workings flank the Nakawn Range in Perlis, the Western Range and the Bintang Range (chiefly round Taiping). On the extreme East, workings are few, largely due to inaccessibility, and are scattered on the coastal side of the Eastern Range all the way from Besut River to Johore; of these, the Sungei Lembing lode mines are the most important.

Although tin once played a major part in Malaysian external trade, it has only a subdued rôle on the landscape and in human activities within the country, which are more extensively affected by the rubber and paddy. On average, West Malaysia has produced the world's cheapest tin; exhausting the dredgable land will make its tin more costly than in any other country. In 1946, the "life" of Malayan mines was given as 24 years, but output remains high beyond that term due partly to better extraction methods.

Cassiterite leaves all mines in granular form to be transported in sacks by rail to Penang and Singapore where two furnaces up to 1942 handled about half the world's tin, importing ore from surrounding countries in addition to handling Malaysian ore. Thus tin smelting was a more stable industry than mining itself. To smelt tin the ore is mixed with limestone and anthracite, the former gathering the non-tin minerals and the latter reducing the tin which is further refined to over 99 per cent pure in cast-iron

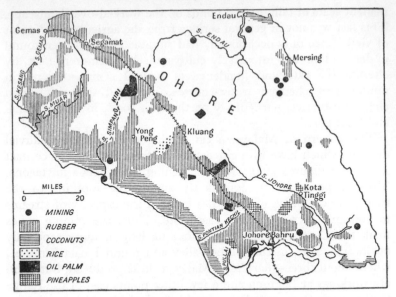

FIG. 43.—Land Use in Johore

kettles before flowing into moulds. A new smelter opened in 1955 at Butterworth intended to replace that at Singapore. The smelters handle Thai and Burmese ores, producing altogether 79,000 tons refined tin in 1965, but likely to suffer from the new smelter in Kra.

Iron.—By 1940 Malaya was annually producing nearly 2 million tons of iron ore derived from haematite deposits in Johore, Kelantan, Pahang and Trengganu, which have an iron content of 50–65 per cent, thereby ranking as high quality ores (Fig. 41). The Johore deposits (at Batu Pahat and Endau) (Fig. 43) and the Trengganu deposits (at Dungun and Kemaman) (Fig. 39) produced over 80 per cent of the whole. The mines were worked on the open-cast system, using Chinese labour, and causing considerable local landscape changes in what had been virgin territories. The great bulk of the production made a substantial labour demand, out of proportion to the low value of iron ore production compared with tin. Since the majority of mines were on East Coast sites, they had to devise their own transport system which was chiefly by river barges down to the coast. They faced difficulties of harbourage (no major steamers can come inshore for loading on the East Coast and they must anchor offshore to load from barges), difficulties of transhipment during the heavy Northeast Monsoon seas, and remoteness from suitable coal deposits. Before 1941, iron mining was exclusively Japanese-financed and the whole production shipped to Japan for smelting. The Trengganu mines were reopened by an Australian company in 1949 for export to Japan. A new iron mine developed along the Rompin River involved building a new railway and ore port in Pahang. The combined iron ore production for 1965 was 7.2 million tons (cf. 2.4 million tons 1956), mostly shipped to Japan.

Gold.—Small quantities of alluvial gold occur at many places in Kelantan and northwest Pahang, and in tin alluvials of the Bidor-Tapah area, Malacca and parts of Selangor. No major undertaking is concerned with gold except at Raub, where lode mines with shafts as much as 1,000 ft. deep produced about 7,300 ozs. troy in 1964 (cf. 20,000 ozs. during 1960), the whole process of crushing and amalgamation being done at Bukit Koman: large quantities of scheelite are mined incidentally.

Other minerals.—Low grade manganese ores have been mined in conjunction with the iron ores in the northeast and sent to Japan. In Kedah and Trengganu, small tungsten ore (wolfram) deposits were regularly worked for sale to the United Kingdom and the United States. Superficial and shallow deposits of bauxite were quarried immediately pre-war by Japanese firms at Batu Pahat and just east of Johore Bahru; no facilities for extracting the aluminium existed locally and the total export of ore did not exceed 60,000 tons per annum. Aluminium works in Australia are now absorbing most Malaysian bauxite (464,000 tons in 1964). As a by-product of tin mining, ilmenite (titanium ore), together with monazite (a source of thorium) are recovered magnetically from the refuse. The ilmenite (29,000 tons 1964, cf. 80,000 tons 1960) comes from Perak and Selangor tin-fields, promising to be a profitable export so long as world use of titanium is expanding. Columbite, a rare metallic mineral needed for alloy steels in jet engines and a by-product of West Malaysian tin-mines, was being shipped at the rate of about 12 tons monthly in 1957 but this proved a short-lived development.

In 1965, the peninsular outflow of primary products was worth $2,700 million.

Chapter Eight

THE SOCIAL GEOGRAPHY OF WEST MALAYSIA

BECAUSE the development of West Malaysia into the forms of today has taken place within the last 150 years, it exemplifies geographical factors involved in changing the ecology and associations of life in tropical areas.

THE EVOLUTION OF MALAYSIAN LIFE

Before the end of the 18th century, the pattern of Malaysia was simple and Malays lived as self-supporting rice farmers and fishermen with only a little interchange between these groups in a few districts of specialised activity. Probably a population of no more than a quarter million was involved, and people lived in settlements strung along the coasts and rivers where transport by small boat, drinking water and irrigation water, were available. The dense forest seems to have repelled the Malay no less than it repelled the foreigners who occasionally passed by on the high seas, and it was left as a negative no-man's land between the settlement lines of rivers and coasts. Thus Malay political units, sultanates, chieftaincies and so on, were shaped round estuaries where rice growing was easy and where the coastal and riberine strings of villages met. The interfluve was a forested frontier zone to political units undefined by boundaries and among its forests wandered a few poorly-organised debilitated aborigines.

Malay society was communally self-sufficient, a nice balance between the amount of food needed and growable and the number of hands available to produce it. All the Malaysian agricultural products grown for sale today and at various times tried commercially, are foreign innovations. Apart from spices, nothing cultivated by the local people then had exportable value; even rice, which had become their staple food, was introduced by first millennium Indian colonists to this setting which is more naturally fitted for yam cultivation. The trade in spices which developed round medieval Malacca was of small volume, and depended on a few trees in native gardens rather than on large-scale plantations.

Equally repelled by the Malaysian surface, the first modern settlements concentrated on the coast, where position relative to the whole region attracted Arabs, Indians, Chinese, and Europeans in succession. The Portuguese and Dutch trading post was Malacca; the first British posts were on the Islands of Penang and Singapore, isolated from the peninsula, and following until 1874 a general directive of avoiding political ties or mainland responsibility.

When interest turned to the Malaysian mainland, its physical difficulties and their variations from place to place had to be taken into account. There are four main types of surface: unpopulated forest-covered ranges of which the Central Range is the most prominent; foothills flanking these ranges, forest-covered but well-drained and partly broken up by lines of pioneer Malay settlements: a badly-drained zone of freshwater swamp forest, forbidding to settlement and to cultivation and penetrable only along the rivers; and a healthier coastal strip of mixed farming and fishing, with here and there an intensively cultivated plain or a rocky outlier which sedimentation had converted from an island to part of the mainland. This fourfold pattern is arranged roughly symmetrically to the Ranges, but the Central Range is nearest the west coast at certain points, serving to narrow that repellant unit, the marsh zone.

In the foothills lay Malaysia's great attraction to external interests, alluvial tin, and accessibility to the foothills was the most important consideration to the western tin belt, which is richest and nearest to the coast. To these foothills, only the rivers provided access and along them the first outsiders were able to move through the marshes, concerned with rivers not only as a means to travel inland, but also as a means for sending out the heavy, bulky tin and for bringing in the food for miners who were working in areas generally far from local agriculture. Local agriculture was in any case closely involved in a tight subsistence ecology without appreciable surplus for sale.

At two places, on the Larut coast and at the mouth of the Klang River, ranges came so close to the coast that the tin belt in their foothills could be easily and quickly reached by poling shallow-draught canoes and boats along streams too shallow for large ships and never very significant even for Malay settlement. The first two mining settlements inside West Malaysia were round what are now Taiping and Kuala Lumpur where the first mining was exclusively Chinese.

The opening up by mining did not produce an economic struggle between Chinese miners and Malay farmers because in those zones Malay settlement was negligible. The state of Selangor (around Kuala Lumpur) had an extremely small Malay population when mining began to assume importance and the sultanate capital of the time, Bandar Termasa, was a poor unhealthy village resembling those primitive settlements to be seen today on lonely parts of the Borneo coast. The Chinese miners worked on lease from the sultans against a royalty on production. Disorders on the early mining regions arose from disputes among rival prospectors to whom Malay chiefs granted unsurveyed and often overlapping concessions. Malays declined to do mining labour, which was done by Chinese, who were often imported under dubious conditions. Friction was aggravated by banditry and clan fighting which the Chinese brought with them; the clans of South Chinese were often as unintelligible and foreign to one another in speech as they were to the Malays. What the number of immigrant Chinese was before 1870 is not known. In 1891 alone nearly 90,000 Chinese arrived to work in the peninsula, where there were probably well above 100,000 miners already.

The Chinese miners depended on imported food and to cater for them other Chinese set up shop. Malay villages had no shops. The advent of miners and, later, planters, working a trade economy, introduced money into rural Malaysia, accompanied by the creation of rural shops and trading centres into which the Chinese quickly fitted, helped by earlier experience elsewhere in East Asia where certain types of them had already a long tradition as traders and middlemen. As a result, in Malaysia today shops and retail businesses are largely Chinese, although a few Indian traders came when Tamil labourers were brought into the rubber estates.

The tin rush had little effect on Malay food agriculture though it might have been expected that the presence of so many extra rice-eaters would stimulate local cultivators. The Malays remained tied to their original system: having increased probably sevenfold since 1874, their farming skill was sufficiently strained to keep pace with their own natural increase.

At Kuala Lumpur and Taiping, the inflow of people and supplies, and the outflow of tin ore led to building short railways to the nearest coastal points (Klang and Port Weld), to replace poling along the streams, which were unsafe and quickly inadequate as they silted with tailings. Later a railway was built longitudinally to link these early mines and made it possible for other mines to develop along the western foothill belt.

Despite increasing British interest after 1874, Malaysian tin mining continued to be a Chinese activity. European finance, management and techniques came in when mining needed heavy equipment, high capitalisation and competitive costs.

Kuala Lumpur in 1874 was a few squalid thatched huts at the Klang-Gombak confluence. Today the municipality contains over 350,000 people, having doubled since 1947 due to guerrilla fighting. From being a sleepy market, it has become a capital linked by roads, railway and air services to Federation state capitals and has an international airport. Beside office blocks of the Selangor state and Federation governments and of businesses, terrace dwellings and shops are a feature of its central area cramped either side of the now embanked Klang River, and congested with motor traffic. Outside this area are modern residences of wealthy businessmen, administrators, politicians and foreign diplomats. New housing estates have mushroomed over old mining land or converted rubber estates. After 1949 at least six "new villages" grew alongside the municipality: one of these, Petaling Jaya, located 12 miles south-west, is the most spectacular planned satellite town in Southeast Asia, now exceeding 50,000 people. The centrality of Kuala Lumpur is increased by the "Gap Road," the only route over the Central Ranges and about ten miles to the north. Kuala Lumpur has a population largely Chinese (62 per cent), Malays forming only 15 per cent though this is their largest urban concentration.

Gradually the Taiping–Kuala Lumpur railway line was extended during the nineties to link Malacca and Prai (for the ferry to Penang) and ran completely to Singapore by 1909. The line initially and in extension kept well inland to the foothills and away from the marshy forests behind the west coast. It was characteristically a national railway, capitalised and run without resort to publicly raised external capital. Inspired by and located for the tin areas, the railway both encouraged speedier development of that activity and fixed the pattern for future opening up of the mainland. It assured export of commodities from the interior and import of food for immigrants. When the time came for new agricultural plantations and associated industries, they gravitated towards the railway, which moulded them into a longitudinal pattern round the railway as axis. Bridle paths through the forest were the early feeders to the first railway. The present road system developed later than the railways, to feed them; roads came later than the railways because in the forest where indigenous draught animals were negligible and horses unsuitable, roads could have little value until motor transport evolved. When they became practicable roads followed patterns roughly complementary to the railways.

Roads were first designed in Malaysia to serve the railway rather than to compete with it or duplicate it. Only when oil-driven vehicles came into general use were longitudinal roads constructed through the west coast zone. Even by 1942, no through road paralleled the east coast but an eastern railway through the mountains and valleys from Gemas to Kota Bahru followed principles worked out on the other side of the Central Range. It was linked to the east coast by a long road to Kuantan and by the old river route down the Pahang, whose middle course was not far from the railway (Fig. 36). This line had only a limited service before 1942 when the Japanese removed its rails for use in Thailand, and it was fully restored in 1948 when services into Kra resumed.

Two zones of comparatively dense road network now spread out, bounded in each case by the Malaysian ranges:

(*a*) From Butterworth south to the Kinta Valley;

(*b*) From Kuala Selangor to Muar.

These are both zones of old-established and elaborate development in mining and planting. Elsewhere, except on Singapore Island, the road network is very open and has frequent dead-ends. The absence of coastwise roads reflects the difficulty of crossing the wide, swampy estuaries which mostly still have to be ferried. Where N–S. roads do exist, they are generally confined to foothill zones and do not in any case link with road systems through the Kra Isthmus where the railway has a monopoly beyond Singgora. Only two highways cross the Central Range, linking the mining and planting settlements on either side and encouraging the development of hill stations, one of which, Cameron Highlands, has become a producer of vegetables (Fig. 40), using a daily road service to the lowlands.

In 1890, after the major tin rush, there began the move towards cultivating rubber and the locations sought by British planters for this purpose were close to those originally sought by the Chinese tin miners. There were two reasons. The foothills where the tin occurred had the advantage of good natural drainage and therefore suited rubber trees, which had to be out of the swampy lowlands. Moreover, the railway built for the tin mines provided the communications which were needed for rubber plantations, whose supplies, particularly rice for their Indian labourers, had to be brought in from outside, and whose rubber needed to be sent abroad. The rubber plantations gravitated to the western foothills as ribbon developments along the railway lines and although plantations gradually fanned out from the railway, even today the land utilisation map shows how closely the distribution of rubber correlates with the railway and the road system.

The Malay tradition of self-sufficiency presented a wall of opposition to the introduction of exportable crops, whether of the outstandingly successful rubber or of the less successful sugar, coffee, gambier, coconuts and oil palms, which Europeans introduced, with the result that, failing to get the innovations taken up by local farmers, Europeans took to farming themselves in contrast to the turn of events in Burma and resembling those of the Indies. Even this was no easy solution because the plantations had to be in virgin country to get suitable soils, and at the same time needed labour which local communities were ill-adapted to supply because every hand was needed for food production. Planters here remedied the situation by bringing in agricultural labourers from abroad. Thus the South American Hevea was first grown here by European methods with predominantly Indian labour, and the Malay was not involved until the First World War, when he tried a little rubber planting, more in the spirit of gambling than of farming. So far as most Malays were concerned the innovation caused little disturbance in their way of life, since it occurred on land which had been forest and not on lands engaged in their rice ecology. They steadily drifted into wage-earning occupations, so that Malays formed 12 per cent of the estate labourers by 1954, or 18 per cent if with them be included Indonesians.

All these influences have worked to establish the greatest concentrations of people and the exploitative industries (rubber and tin) in the middle belt of West Malaysia, running from Malacca, through Kuala Lumpur to Ipoh and Taiping (Fig. 44). To this belt of immigrant peoples and foreign innovations, Kuala Lumpur is as focal as midpoints of a belt can be, thereby justifying its selection as capital of the first independent Federation of Malaya (1957). It has assumed this rank because it is the old-established focus of a wealthy, commercially active tin and rubber zone and it was exclusively peninsular in interest, by constrast with coastal towns. Its choice as a federal capital was aided by not being an old sultanate seat and thereby not the traditional focus of one state. Kuala Lumpur is not particularly central to the peninsula yet no other point rivals it for centrality in view of the configuration which disperses rather than focuses natural routes. Since 1925, the Klang railway has been extended to Port Swettenham, 24 miles from the capital beside a deep channel in the Klang Delta, to make an outport for the bulky freight of the middle "Tin and Rubber Belt."

The other dense population centre, Singapore Island, is less a focus for West Malaysia and more an entrepôt for Southeast Asia; for years it was foreign to the peninsula both in population (1,270,000 Chinese out of 1,670,000 in 1961) and in economic interests, which are trade rather than production.

In the far northwest and northeast of the peninsula, the Malay continues his life much as before, fishing, farming for his rice and nearly self-sufficient; very little change has come to him through the great and speedy immigrations of Chinese and Indians in the peninsula. Though the Second World War stirred Malay nationalism, it has not given him means or numbers to balance, rival or subdue the newcomers in a combination of West Malaysia and Singapore, though in the Peninsula the Malays in conjunction with "Malaysian" or Indonesian immigrants roughly equal in numbers the combined Chinese and Indian population. Broadly speaking, this has created a cellular society of different cultural, linguistic, ethnic and economic communities living their separate ways in different parts of the Peninsula and stratified socially within themselves. The Peninsula was united into an independent Federation of Malaya in 1957, separate from self-ruling Singapore until 1963 when these voluntarily linked with Sarawak and Sabah to form the Federation of Malaysia. In 1965, Singapore Island was again outside the Federation, the peninsula part of which was renamed West Malaysia.

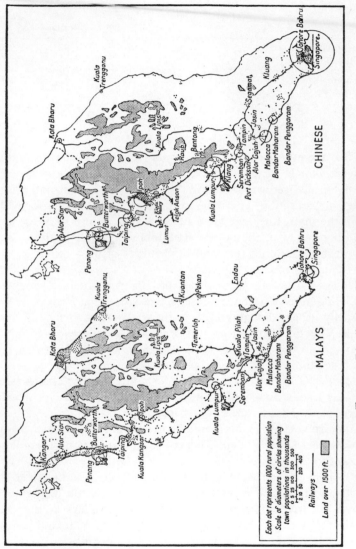

Fig. 44.—Distribution of Population in West Malaysia

COMPOSITION OF POPULATION
(in thousands, 1961 census)

	Malays	Chinese	Indians and Pakistanis	Europeans and Eurasians	Total
West Malaysia	3,500	2,600	787	82	7,050
Percentage	50	39	11	1	100
Singapore Island	237	1,270	142	21	1,670
Percentage	14	76	8	1	100

DISTRIBUTION OF ETHNIC GROUPS

Thus the ethnic groups of Malaysia have taken on a distinctive pattern, which, although modified to some extent by the war which emphasised population in the west and the south and accentuated urbanisation, continues to have much the same form. In detail the intensities may have altered a little, more so in the case of Indians than in the others. The following brief analysis from the censuses assumes that only settlements of over 10,000 people may be called towns.

Malays.—Only three towns, Kota Bahru, Kuala Trengganu and Dungun have Malay majorities, indicating that Malays are not normally urban, though groups of them live on the fringe of most towns. The greatest densities of Malays in rural areas are:

1. In the northeast, on the rice-growing plains of Kelantan and Trengganu.
2. Along the northwest coast from Taiping to the Thai border, where rice farming and fishing draw Malays into relatively dense groups over fairly large continuous areas.
3. A narrower fringe of more dispersed and less homogeneous Malay settlements from Malacca southwards along the Johore coast to Singapore.

Nowhere else are there high densities of Malays, although all the coasts and rivers have scattered Malay hamlets, too dispersed to appear on any but inch to the mile maps. Malays at the 1960 census totalled over 3.5 millions, 50 per cent of mainland people. Malacca has some Eurasians of Portuguese descent.

Immigrant Peoples.—Malaysian non-indigenous people, principally the Chinese and Indians have settled densely in a belt about 40 miles wide down the west coast, where concentrate 90 per cent of the Chinese and 95 per cent of the Indians living on the mainland. In this belt are 26 of the peninsula's 35 towns (of over 10,000 each) and these 26 contain nearly a million Chinese.

The immigrants are unevenly spread. Chinese have settled least on the east coast (though this faces their homeland) and Kedah. East of the Central Range only Raub, Bentong, Kuantan and Kota Bharu each contain over 10,000 Chinese. In the west, over 20,000 Chinese townees live in each of Klang, Kuala Lumpur, Ipoh, Telok Anson, Kampar, Taiping, Butterworth, Georgetown, Seremban, Alor Star, Batu Pahat, Muar, Kluang and Johore Bahru. Ipoh, northern capital of the "Tin and Rubber Belt," is focus of the tin-rich Kinta Valley where a quarter million Chinese live. Kuala Lumpur district contains more Chinese than any other (about 300,000) and southward from it along road and railway to Singapore are extensive Chinese rural developments. As an anti-bandit measure from 1950, half a million rural Chinese were compulsorily resettled into about 450 new villages, changing the countryside by eliminating scattered immigrant farming families and providing them with social organisation and modern utilities. Many new villages have intensive vegetable garden economies and are the scene of rapid cultural and political change.

Security resettlement since 1950 has also nucleated rural Indians, but 78 per cent of these are outside the 35 towns, rubber plantations and unskilled trades continuing to attract them. Kuala Lumpur contains 54,000 Indians (as against 124,000 in Singapore). No town has an Indian majority. The Kuala Lumpur-Klang-Malacca zone of old and extensive rubber estates has high Indian density and there is another concentration from Kinta to Butterworth.

The non-Malays were by 1960 at least 85 per cent locally born.

REGIONAL GEOGRAPHY

In subdividing West Malaysia into regions, the following factors have to be considered:

1. Because dense forest covers highlands and lowlands alike, it makes them equally difficult to human activity, so that orographic delimitation is not a primary consideration.
2. Marsh and swamp forest have obstructed human activities more than any other landscape type.
3. Climatic distinctions are subdued and condition only the incidence, not the character of local rhythms.

4. The cultural landscape is more differentiated than the physical.
5. Indigenous groups used interfluves as boundary zones and rivers have had major significance as lines of entry and development at all stages.
6. Lines of transport not only establish coherence but also set the pattern of actual and potential development.
7. External considerations have been at least as strong as internal factors in Malaysian development.

Population distribution and economic development justify a primary division into Western and Eastern Regions, using the Central Range as main boundary, extended south along the watershed between rivers leading to the Malacca Strait and South China Sea and terminating at the Johore Strait between Johore Bahru and the Johore River. To the Western Region the railway and road system forms the main artery; to the Eastern Region the line of movement mainly eastwards along rivers and then coastwise. Singapore Island is best treated separate from these two primary peninsular regions, which subdivide thus (see end-paper):

Western Region

(*a*) The Northern Coastal Plain, west of the Western Range from the Thai border to just south of Province Wellesley, a zone where Malays predominate and subsistence farming on a rice basis is the development type in a climate with a slight dry season. The Langkawi Islands, best thought of as outlier of Malaysia, resemble the Nakawn Range, and they are more interesting geologically than geographically, since they support only a few thousand people in small bays on a karstic limestone landscape.

(*b*) The Mountain and Valley zone of broken, isolated, little-developed country between the Western Range and the Central Range, terminating north of the Taiping-Kuala Kangsar railway.

(*c*) The Tin and Rubber Belt, in the foothill zone from Larut and the Kinta Valley southwards to include the coast south of Port Dickson and stretching to Singapore. A zone of intense tin and rubber activities, linked throughout by railway and a dense road network, it has developed on the basis of production for export and is populated by Chinese in large pioneer nuclei and by Indians dispersed in the rural areas. Only in Malacca and in Negri Sembilan are there small enclaves of the Malay sub-sistance-farming landscape.

(*d*) The West Central Marshy Coast, including the Perak, Bernam, Selangor and Langat River estuaries; an undeveloped, repel-lant zone typically fringed by mixed fishing and coconut-growing colonies on the coast itself where there are distinct rocky island zones (the Dindings) now silted up to link with the mainland. On this coast are outports. Telok Anson for Ipoh and the Kinta Valley, Port Swettenham for Kuala Lumpur, the latter port used by 1,500 vessels in 1964.

(*e*) Penang; entrepôt for (*a*) and the Kinta Valley portions of (*c*).

Originally established as a centre for buying spices and selling textiles and opium to the peninsula, Penang Island, a granite-cored outlier of northwest Malaya's ranges (area 110 square miles, maximum height, 2,722 ft.), was acquired uninhabited (1796) as a potential mercantile and naval base, a pawn in the competition between the rival British and Dutch East India trading companies. It provided one of the few available deep water anchorages for sailing ships coming before the wind across the Indian Ocean, but did not protect them from the violence of storms from east and west. As long-distance shipping displaced trade routes across the Kra Isthmus into Thailand, Penang lost its earlier significance as fulcrum of Malay, Burmese and Thai interests and became an entrepôt, yet its location finally proved inconveniently far from direct routes between East and West. Development of the Peninsula gradually shifted south so that while the port increased its population and trade, Singapore outpaced it, handling ten times its tonnage in 1964. Deserted in 1790, the island of Penang carried 20,000 people, mostly Chinese, by 1801 and by 1960 had 363,000 people, 70 per cent Chinese, 11 per cent Indian, as well as admini-stering another 223,000 people across in Province Wellesley. From these Chinese came those who made the first tin rush to Taiping so that Penang was from the beginning the "outport" of the northern mining interests, emphasised today by the presence of two smelters. Rubber plantations centred much farther south, and as rubber boomed, Penang's trade became half Singapore's by 1825, and one-third by 1864, shrinking in proportion, yet grossing about $1,800 million in 1964 when one-sixth was entrepôt with Sumatra and Burma, and 2,000 vessels used the port.

The railway into Thailand brought a considerable tin and rubber trade from Kra to Penang, yet even in this trade Penang suffered from the increasing hold of Singapore as the greatest entrepôt for the South China Sea. Although the town occupies only a small fraction of northeastern Penang, very little farming is done now, though sugar, tapioca and spices were cultivated at the end of last century. The town functioned as a stepping stone for much of the Indian coolie labour from Madras. A new satellite township is developing north of Butterworth opposite George Town.

Eastern Region

(*a*) The Kelantan-Besut delta zone north and east of Kuala Krai is a densely populated rural zone concerned almost exclusively with Malay self-contained farming for paddy with subsidiary fishing.

(*b*) The East Coast Fringe, isolated from the mainland by a difficult terrain of broad marshes, occupied by discontinuous Malay fishing communities with subsidiary subsistence farming and linked by coastwise shipping in small boats.

(*c*) The mountains and valleys of West Pahang, running from the Middle Kelantan Valley along the east of the Central Range as far as inner Negri Sembilan. A complicated terrain of mountains with two sets of emphatic valleys on N–S. and E–W. lines, sporadically developed for mining by Chinese in the Raub-Bentong district, with a few Malay subsistence paddy farming valleys towards the south (Kuala Pilah). The developed areas are linked by roads across the Central Range to the Western Region. The N–S. link of the railway from Gemas to Kuala Lipis has been restored and lies well east of the mining areas, though it has attracted rubber plantations along its track.

(*d*) The Trengganu Highlands, an isolated, almost uninhabited, forest-covered area has only been developed by foreigners on the easternmost fringe where the Dungun-Kemaman iron mines until the war exported to the coast, as does the big tin mine of Sungei Lembing behind Kuantan, all employing Chinese or Indian labourers.

(*e*) The Pahang-Rompin Valleys, including the Pahang from Jerantut southwards and the Sungei Bera. This is an isolated, undeveloped, thinly populated area. Along the middle and lower

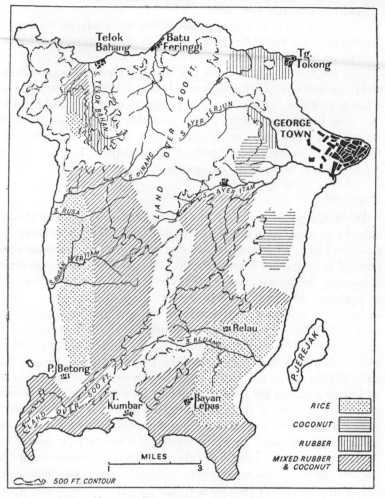

Fig. 45.—Penang: Land Use and Relief

Pahang, Malay villages have evolved a little subsistence paddy farming between the riverside levees and the marshes adjoining them. The Pahang itself is a transport link, though its traffic has no great commercial significance.

(*f*) East Johore, a zone of hills isolated by marshes and very thinly populated, had in the inter-war period developed tin mines (behind Mersing), iron mines (near Endau), and rubber plantations towards the south. The original outlet from these production points was the east coast, but roads to Singapore increasingly carry tin and rubber in that direction. Chinese labour preponderates.

The roughly E–W. lines of the Muar-Simpang Kanan-Endau river marshes virtually divide south Johore from both Western and Eastern Regions. This isolation was significant historically and in our own times and might justify delimiting Johore as a region transitional between the Western and Eastern Regions and forming the immediate hinterland of Singapore, towards which Johore's roads and railways converge.

Singapore

While the physiography and development of the Malay Peninsula have been centrifugal in their effects, Singapore may be described as representing the climax of routes and relations centripetal to Singapore Strait, though it is only since 1819 that these influences finally focused in Singapore itself, being centred in Palembang, Malacca, Jakarta and Penang at previous periods in history. For over sixty years from the year Raffles took it over as merely one of those almost unpopulated, undeveloped and unproductive little islands scattered thinly south of Malaya, Singapore in fact was concerned with nothing else except trade upon the basis of these centripetal influences, which made it the port of call and of interchange for Indian, Chinese, European and East Indian commodities; during that time Singapore was solely an entrepôt. Later, Malaysian tin came into its commercial sphere, yet this was for a long time only an extra aspect of the entrepôt trade. As Malaysian tin and rubber rose into world-wide prominence in the present century, trade in these products from the peninsula began to pass almost entirely through Singapore, establishing the port as the tin and rubber market for the world. Gradually it drew to itself more of these commodities as the East Indies and other parts of Southeast Asia imitated Malaysia's successful innovations and added them to their stream of trade with Singapore. On this basis, Singapore was started as a free port and has remained so, the fiscal dues on Malaysian trade being paid at the Johore Strait and not in Singapore itself, which was not in fact linked to the peninsula by causeway until 1918 and is even now administratively distinct from it. There was no sustained success in cultivating pepper, spices or rubber on Singapore Island which has increasingly concentrated on its commercial life.

Within four months after establishing his port at Singapore, as another development in the rivalry of British and Dutch East India companies, Raffles reported the arrival of 5,000 Chinese, whom he deliberately encouraged because he thought their business-like

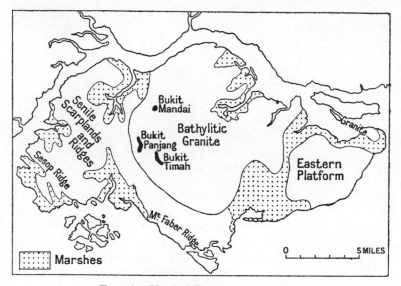

FIG. 46.—Physical Features of Singapore

astuteness and hard-working character fitted well with British mercantile interests, and because he had an eye on the China trade and the part Chinese merchants were already playing in the trade of the archipelago. It was, in fact, something of a paradox since the main interest of the British East India Company was India, from which base Singapore was controlled until 1867.

The accompanying maps (Figs. 46, 47, 48) summarise the geographic facts about the island (area 220 square miles) and show how it subdivides into three parts on the basis of physical and land utilisation differences; these are largely delimited by deep mangrove indentations. The south and eastern portions of the island have been tending for years to become largely urbanised as a result of repeated expansion. Small specialised towns serve the Naval Dockyard to the north, the air base at Changi and the

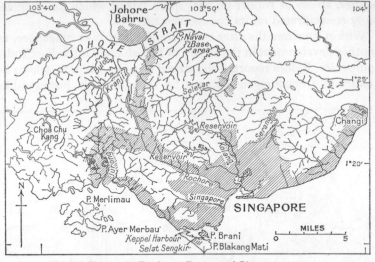

FIG. 47.—Drainage Pattern of Singapore

Pasir Panjang militarised area to the west—well away from the city to whose suburban growth the central reservoir zone sets limits which make satellite development inevitable. The population now exceeds 1¾ million with 63 per cent in the built-up "city" zone.

The city itself is built on the rectangular street pattern common to most pioneer towns of the peninsula, with house forms and layout very westernised in character though the population is overwhelmingly Chinese. To these, the focus of activity is the waterfront where dozens of ocean-going vessels and hundreds of small inter-island ships are always assembled, some transhipping offshore, others by the quayside—for Singapore has the deepest harbour and dock facilities within a thousand miles radius, as well as elaborate warehouses and a complicated network of largely Chinese shipping services, both steam and sail, connecting it to all Southeast Asia and the archipelagos. Its street life is Chinese but dressed European; its commerce is largely Chinese, but the commercial language is English, supplemented by bazaar Malay, though Chinese still use their dialects, and the Chinese national language is taught.

Two-thirds of Singaporeans live in 38 sq. miles round the waterfront, but major suburbs are to the east; the western sector is thinly peopled yet an industrialised satellite town, Jurong, is

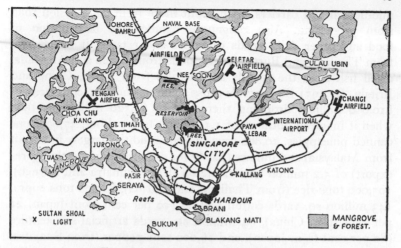

FIG. 48.—Land Utilisation on Singapore

The area left white represents patches of rubber, coconut, scrub and vegetable gardening together with the rapidly extending suburban "garden zone" of residential development round the closely built-up urban core (marked black and adjoining the harbour).

rapidly growing west of the river of that name. Though immigration has ceased, Singaporeans have a nett increase of 4.8 per cent p.a.—over twice the rate for all Southeast Asia.

Local transport is complex. Road traffic is very dense. The railway serves almost exclusively for mainland trade, the freight each way being roughly equal in 1958. A huge two-way flow moves by long-distance road services. Over 7,800 foreign ocean-going vessels and 9,000 coastal and native craft used the harbour in 1962. A third of the island's trade by value derives from the Peninsula though it remains fiscally separate. A quarter of Singapore's inflow usually comes from Indonesia, also a major absorber from the island. Manufactured goods are imported in bulk largely by European traders, but retail distribution is by Chinese and Indians. Tin smelting is little evident because the one old smelter is on a small offshore island, near other islands which are the oil storage depots. In few cases has Singapore added any stage of manufacturing to materials passing through; its function is that of handling, forwarding, shipping, reshipping, breaking bulk, grading, distributing and collecting. Its commerce is of go-betweens, middlemen and carriers, with profit more from commission than from processing. Also Singapore handles the distribution of food and other daily needs of mines and estates; it brings rice from Thailand and Burma, other foods from China and Australia, dried fish from the islands and textiles from Japan, China and Britain. By 1951 Singapore's gross trade reached a record peak of $10,000 million, dropping thereafter to $7,520 million in 1960 when it involved outflows of 1.1 million tons rubber, 37,000 tons canned pineapples, 20,800 tons tin (commodities largely in transit from Malaysia) and inflows (partly for consumption, partly for re-export) of 5.2 million tons crude oil (from Sumatra and Borneo), 105,000 tons rice (from Thailand and Burma), 88,000 tons copra, 143 million sq. yards cotton textiles (50 per cent from Japan, 25 per cent from China), 84 million sq. yards artificial silk textiles (80 per cent from Japan), and 16,000 tons pepper (from Sumatra, Sarawak, Banka and Billiton). This pattern was increasingly disturbed by the nationalist trend for trade to be handled at its own ports, yet in 1965 it continued to be the world's fifth busiest port, Asia's busiest port, handling 90 million tons shipping, employing 12,500, and moving 23 million tons freight worth $7,100 million.

Singapore's stability amid a region of insecurity brought prosperity and expansion for years. Asian wages rose and capital was attracted. Expanding local markets led to minor industrialisation. Engineering workshops (connected with shipping and road transport) flourished. Factories spread along the arterial road north to Johore and west to a new industrial satellite at Jurong. Here are made metal boxes and cappings, electric batteries, glassware, foods and sauces, industrial gases, furniture, bricks, pipes and plywood, diversifying Singapore's activities whose high labour costs and weakness in water, food and power supplies operate against it. A major change is the huge amount of oil converging on Singapore Harbour as a result of expanding production in Seria and Sumatra which has led to a great tanker trade and to building a local refinery on Pular Bukum, processing 2 million tons crude annually.

[*One Malaysian dollar was 33 U.S. cents or 2s. 4d. in 1966.*]

Chapter Nine

THE NATURAL LANDSCAPE OF BURMA

WEST MALAYSIA represents the Sunda Platform environment; Burma exemplifies conditions marginal to that Platform and to the Himalayan systems, a region transitional in type between geographical environments of Southeast Asia archipelagoes, of mountainous Western China, and of India.

PHYSIOGRAPHY

The physiography of Burma, less simple than it appears at first sight, and particularly complex in the human reaction to its various parts, is laid out with a relief-pattern shaped like an asymmetrical inverted V.

(*a*) The relief stems from a nameless mountainous core north of Putao, rising to heights of more than 20,000 ft. as a complex structural knot where the typical W–E. Himalayan trend lines branch into a great loop of fold systems which run southwards on a great arc, forming the mountain system of West Burma (mainly the Arakan Yoma), and thence as the southern and western margins of the Sunda Platform in Sumatra and Java.

(*b*) On the extreme east are the Shan Highlands; from the Putao Knot mountainous relief continues southward into the Shan Highlands, though the orographic continuity has no basis in structural uniformity.

(*c*) Between the Western Mountains and the Shan Highlands lies the Irrawaddy Basin, broadening and sloping southward to become the Gulf of Rangoon.

(*d*) Modern Burma as a political unit tapers towards the Kra Isthmus, where the ranges *en echelon* of the Malay Peninsula are repeated northward to merge into the Shan Highlands; this isthmus section of Burma is Tenasserim.

Thus there is a triple physiographic division, the Western Mountains, the Shan Highlands and their continuation into Tenasserim, and the Irrawaddy Basin (Fig. 49). Of these the best studied, the most elaborately developed and highly organised is the Irrawaddy Basin.

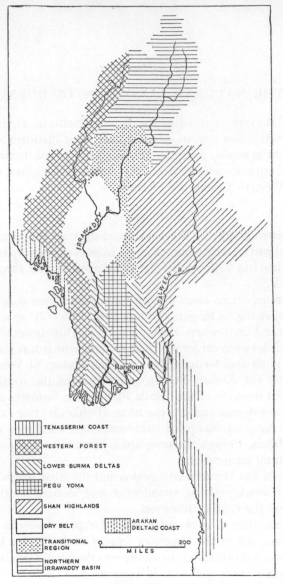

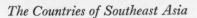

FIG. 49.—The Regions of Burma

1. The Western Mountains

The knot north of Putao is complex but its form lines in Burma run predominantly N–S. The thinness of peopling and poor development cause it to be more interesting geologically than geographically, though it has functioned as a bridge for peoples moving from Asia southwards.

More significant for Burma is the main Western Mountain group (highest peak, Mt. Sarametti, 12,557 ft.) through which runs the India-Burma border. This arcuate set of ranges which includes the Arakan Yoma and is mostly above 6,000 ft., is broad to the north, tapering in width southward to become Negrais Point and later a submarine section, showing above the sea as the Andaman Islands. It is largely a series of parallel ranges through which rivers have in places cut transverse valleys to produce a trough and cluse drainage-pattern resembling a trellis in plan. To the north the ranges are called the Patkoi, Lushai, Naga, Manipur and Chin Hills, becoming more compacted at the centre as the Arakan Yoma. Between the Patkoi Hills and the Arakan Yoma is the intermontane basin of Manipur, lower than the surrounding country yet called "The Highland of Manipur," an important channel of entry of ethnic groups moving into Burma. Some of the mountain masses are possibly fragments of older structures caught up in the western mountain building processes. In its northern section, this unit on the east breaks sharply to the Hukawng alluvial valley, but the Arakan Yoma proper abuts an area of hilly dissected upland shaped from pitching synclines to produce in places a series of boat-shaped scarps as in the Lower Chindwin. The Arakan coast, a group of narrow alluvial flats laid down by short, violent streams, and dominated by forest-clad hills often reaching to the sea as cliffs, is of the type called "Pacific Coast," where the fold-structure lines parallel the coast. Though the northern end has considerable heights, glaciated relief is found only north of latitude 27° and has not been proved to exist in the Arakan Yoma itself.

2. The Shan Highlands

A deeply dissected plateau, the Shan country, averaging 3,000 ft. high, rises abruptly, often in single steps of 2,000 ft., from the Sittang-Irrawaddy Basin. It is, however, intensely folded on N–S. lines and consists of rocks and structures much older than most in

Burma and more closely related to those of the Sunda Platform; great stretches of massive limestone, sandstones and metamorphic rocks and granite repeat on a larger scale at sustained higher altitudes the rock types and relief forms already described in Malaysia. Granites are not prominent at the surface of the structures here in Burma, except to the south and on the western fringe where the Highlands narrow and break down into the Tenasserim Ranges lying skew-wise to the Isthmus. The Shan Highlands merge northwards into the mountainous uplands dissected on N–S. lines by deep river gorges, a landscape which increases in altitude to the Putao Knot and extends eastwards through Thailand and beyond the Mekong into Laos. Over large areas compact limestone provides excellent examples of landscape, developed on this relatively soluble rock, whose usual valleys are broad, shallow and with gently sloping sides, now undergoing solution; through them streams meander sluggishly, often edged by marshes. Where several streams combine to give a powerful flow of water, down-cutting exceeds the rate of solution of the sides and leads to narrow gorges choked with masses of limestone fallen from the precipitous sides. Sometimes the dissolved limestone is redeposited from the groundwater to form travertine or calcareous tufa which looks rather like pumice; should this form rapidly, a natural dam may be built up. Later the stream will break this dam and take another course, resulting after a time in a network of small watercourses, not all of them full, surrounded by marshy ground—as at Hsum Hsai on the Mandalay–Lashio railway. Enclosed drainage basins (polje) are also very common, together with the other evidence of subterranean river systems. Extensive limestone caves are found at Moulmein, Kalaw, Gokteik, Singgu (above Mandalay) and Myitkyina.

3. *The Irrawaddy Basin*

Located between the two higher landscape types to the east and west, the Irrawaddy Basin, while also primarily a folded structure, though of less amplitude, has in addition the remnants of local volcanic land forms. It is by no means merely a large river valley or an old gulf of the sea: its rocks and structures are distinctive and in places of great thickness, considerable age and of successions peculiar to this area, so that there are special rock groupings called the Irrawaddy Series and the Pegu Series. Though partly concealed by terraces of Chindwin, Irrawaddy and Sittang river alluvials, the folded substructure of this Basin appears dissected at the surface in the Pegu Yoma which runs lengthwise through the middle, from the Myingyan District to the low ridges overlooking Rangoon, continuing far northward as a double line of dissected hills across the Irrawaddy and Chindwin rivers as the Sagaing-Mingin-Zibyun hills. Originating in connection with the folding of the Pegu Yoma and their extensions in the northern hill ranges is the line of extinct volcanoes now showing as the eroded cones and lavas of Mount Popa on the northwest flank of the Pegu Yoma, of Wuntho's jade mining district, and of Taungthonlon in the Mingin Hills. Once thought to be a tectonic rift flanked by faults, the Basin is accepted as mostly a fold structure, developed on alternating beds of clays, shales and sandstones, the varying characters of which produce great variations in the surface according to their exposures.

The Irrawaddy Series of rocks consists essentially of sands with subordinate conglomerates and clays which have been folded and eroded into a landscape of strike ridges and valleys. In the Dry Zone round the Chindwin-Irrawaddy junction, the series is capped by looser gravels and lateritised soils over a wide area (Fig. 56).

The Pegu Series includes thick, massive but easily eroded sandstones forming long continuous escarpments on N–S. lines, the lowest sandstone forming the impressive scarp overlying the Ponnyadaung Range, clays and shales with thin interbedded sand stones forming low ridges above clay lowlands (as at Pyawbwe). The Pegu and Irrawaddy Series of folded, younger rocks have produced under erosion some of the best Southeast Asia examples of scarped landforms.

Farther south over the Basin are spread alluvial deposits of many types and thicknesses, varying in character from coarse gravels near the hills to fine clays and silts towards the centre and south. While these deposits, interpreted by de Terra as a succession of river terraces, vary too much for generalisation, their different qualities and texture condition the pattern and intensity of cultivation.

CLIMATE

Several factors modify in Burma those climatic influences common to most of the rest of Southeast Asia.

1. Higher latitudes and altitudes and more continental location produce in parts of Burma lower temperatures than those normal for Southeast Asia, so that freezing in January may be met

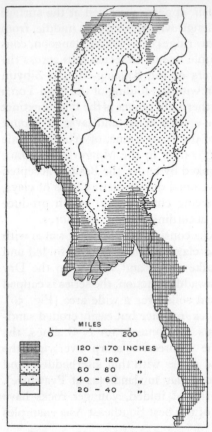

MILES
0   200

120 - 170 INCHES
80 - 120   "
60 - 80   "
40 - 60   "
20 - 40   "

FIG. 50.—The Rainfall of Burma

on altitudes over 3,500 ft.; the Shan Highlands experience light frosts at that time and higher still, above 10,000 ft., farther north, snow falls for about two months a year. A cool season is noticeable throughout Burma.

2. A distinct dry season occurs in most districts except where on the coastal fringe or on uplands local influences may cause sufficient precipitation to minimise the drought. The dry season tends to be more emphatic in areas where annual precipitation is lower than the average for Burma. Rain comes on with the abrupt violence characteristic of an Indian monsoon, starting fairly generally towards the end of May and ending in the third week of October. During the dry season sunshine periods and temperatures are high, until the coming of the rains brings a sharp drop in daily maxima which are highest in April and May.

3. The N–S. arrangement of the relief runs athwart the airstreams sweeping over Burma, so that the central Irrawaddy Basin is in a rain shadow for most of the year and has a Dry Zone of elongated, lobate shape roughly centred on Pagan. The dryness of this zone is emphasised by föhn winds produced as the airstreams move into it from the Arakan Yoma and the Shan Highlands. When rain does fall in the Dry Zone it comes chiefly from southerly sectors of the summer airstream.

Relief dominates the pattern of rainfall (Fig. 50). During the period of southwesterly winds, the warm damp air masses impinge on the Western Mountains and the isthmus coast to produce heaviest rainfalls in Arakan and Tenasserim where over 200 in. per annum may be recorded. On the eastern flanks of the Arakan Yoma at that time considerably less rain falls, but precipitation increases again in the eastern highlands. Northern Tropical Air, in this latitude flowing over Burma in winter, is not particularly rainy except where altitude induces precipitation in the eastern highlands and on the western side of the Irrawaddy Basin.

MONTHLY RAINFALLS (in inches) AND PREDOMINANT WINDS OF MONTH

	Aver. No. of rainy days	Jan.	Feb.	Mar.	Apr.	May	June	July	Aug.	Sept.	Oct.	Nov.	Dec.	Total
Rangoon	122	.2	.2	.3	1.4	12.0	18.0	21.4	19.4	15.3	6.9	2.8	.4	98.3
		NNE	NNE	SW	WSW	SW	S	SSW	SSW	SW	NE	NNE	NNE	
Thayetmyo	73	.1	.1	.2	.8	4.5	6.7	6.8	6.5	6.1	4.1	1.7	.2	37.8
Moulmein	139	.2	.1	.5	2.8	20.3	37.2	46.2	43.6	27.7	8.7	2.2	.3	189.6
Mandalay	51	.1	.1	.2	1.1	5.8	5.5	3.3	4.6	5.7	4.7	1.6	.4	33.1
		N	SSE	SSE	SSE	SSE	SSE	SSE	SSE	SSE	SE	NE	N	
Minbu	57	0	0	.3	.8	5.6	5.7	4.5	5.3	6.2	4.5	1.8	.5	35.3
		NW	NW	SE	SE	SE	SE	SE	SE	SE	SE	NW	NW	

The Dry Zone, focal area of Burmese life and development, has much of its scanty rain (in places less than 25 in. per annum) concentrated in a few torrential storms (Fig. 52). Moreover the fall is less reliable here than elsewhere in the country, a critical factor since the most elaborate and complicated agricultural development has taken place in the Dry Zone. The unreliability of rains has been countered to some extent from the human angle by a diversified agriculture so that whatever the particular rainfall of one year, at least one crop may be expected to be satisfactory. Fine clear weather, with many calms, continues from November to March though in river valleys morning mists may lie; during the rains (June to September) which reach the Dry Zone rather later than elsewhere, winds are weak and daily cloud densities are high. Violent thunderstorm-rains arrive in May and October. While the Dry Zone is strictly confined to Inner Burma, the tendency to drought is apparent even in the Irrawaddy Delta (Fig. 59) which has a longer dry season than either Arakan or Tenasserim. On the Delta, rainfall diminishes rapidly inland from 200 to 100 in. per annum at the coast, to about 40 in. inland; at Thayetmyo rainfall is 38 in. per annum, and at Prome 47 in.; July is the rainiest month and December–March the driest season.

During the period November–May cyclonic disturbances streaming across northern India eastwards cause minor deteriorations of the otherwise fine weather over northern Burma. Minor depressions from the South China Seas sometimes cross north Burma from July to September, producing local rains. Tropical cyclones also move over the Bay of Bengal between April and December, moving westwards away from Burma but occasionally striking the Arakan coast. In the last sixty years, the totals of tropical cyclones of various intensities striking the Arakan and Martaban coasts were:

Season	Arakan	Martaban
December–March	—	—
April–May	21	15
June–September	2	1
October–November	24	—

In Burma, close correlations between climate and tropical diseases have been demonstrated. Inland, malaria increases in the wet season but on the coast it is more frequent in the dry season. Cholera is a feature of the early rains, while smallpox reaches its peak at the end of the dry season. Dysentery peaks are associated with disrupted sanitation during floods early in the wet season.

DRAINAGE PATTERNS

While two-thirds of Burma's surface drains into the Irrawaddy, which therefore ranks as by far the most important Burmese river system, there are several subsidiary river systems.

Arakan Rivers

The Kaladan, Lemyo, Mayu and Naaf rivers flow on N–S. lines separated by abrupt, high and forbidding watersheds related directly to the fold structure. Their courses become trellis patterns and they have all built broad deltaic forms at the coast where the streams debouch after taking sharp bends out of the structural alignment. Apart from the lower zones of sedimentation, tending to delta form, though much flattened against the coast by onshore winds, the streams are immature and unusable for navigation, except the Kaladan which can be used almost to Paletwa. These streams rank as important because only on their estuaries can settlement reach any great density. Their headwaters lead to the passes through the Arakan Yoma which have had negligible modern significance.

Tenasserim Rivers

On the Burmese part of the isthmus, relatively short streams follow lines resembling those of Malaysia, between ranges slightly skew to the coast and continuing out to sea as a string of offshore islands which has facilitated coastal sedimentation (Fig. 55). Often the rivers, while otherwise mature in form, pass through narrow rocky gorges at gaps in the ranges. Tenasserim streams frequently make right-angled bends to reach the sea. As in the case of the Arakan streams, these are short tropical streams bringing heavy silt loads in their fairly constant flows and the rate of coastal sedimentation is rapid. Some were used by earlier merchants for harbourage and a trans-isthmus route, but most are no longer usable even for sailing craft. A fluvial sorting of the sediments, varying from gravels to fine silts, may be observed from the ranges to the coast and in Tavoy the gravels are tin-bearing under much the same physical circumstances as in West Malaysia.

The Salween River

Paralleling the Irrawaddy for much of its course, the Salween crosses the Shan Highland in a series of deep gorges whose lengths are unequalled even by the Yangtze gorges. Coming from Tibet, the Salween draws close to the Mekong and Yangtze, all three lying within 42 miles of one another at some points.

Until it reaches the Shan country, the Salween has no tributaries apart from torrents, but there it receives many streams as much as 300 miles long. Its deep, rocky trough-like valley reaches within 50 miles of the sea, so that the Salween's erosive power remains strong almost to the coast. The greater incision of the Salween compared with the nearby upper Mekong is due to its greater rainfall; the narrowness of its long, ribbon-like drainage basin is thought to be due to encroachment and capture of its tributaries by neighbouring rivers, of which the Irrawaddy and Mekong have been particularly active as captors. Many Salween tributaries, of which the largest are the Yungzalin, Gyaing and Attaran, enter the parent stream with a cataract or cascade, caused partly by more intense erosion by the main stream, partly by the enormous variations of water level in it. The average seasonal change of the Salween level is 65 ft. which dams tributaries and induces them to drop gravels and boulders not far from

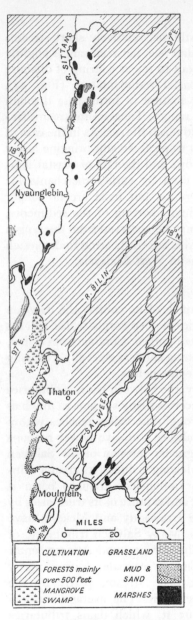

FIG. 51.—The Sittang and Salween
Deltas

the confluence. Despite its size, the Salween has so broken a course, is so deeply incised and suffers such enormous changes in level that it is probably the least useful major river in Burma. Its only value has been for floating teak logs, yet it might with major engineering works be made a source of hydro-electric power. A quick and constant building of shoals and bars with a resulting frequent change of distributaries goes on at its mouth (Fig. 51) which is becoming silted up beyond possibility of use as an entry for steamers, though its outlets near Moulmein were extensively used for harbourage earlier this century. The great volume of the Salween in spate is the cause of inundations in rivers like the Attaran, an otherwise stable stream in a mature valley. During the rainy season, when the Salween runs faster than its choked outlet can discharge, widespread floods develop behind the coast.

At Inle, between the Salween and Irrawaddy watersheds, is a small area of inland drainage into a lake 14 by 4 miles at 3,000 ft., varying greatly in depth according to the season. It drains southward but the outflowing streams quickly disappear into a limestone substructure, probably to discharge ultimately into the Salween.

The Irrawaddy River System

In the Irrawaddy Basin we see the effects upon drainage pattern of subdued tectonic foldings which took place on a landscape where a complete river system had already been established. Following the upfolding of the Pegu Yoma, two streams drained into the basin:

(a) A western stream, formed of what is now the Chindwin, together with that part of the Irrawaddy below Pakokku; this river has been named the Proto-Irrawaddy.

(b) An eastern stream, formed of the present Irrawaddy above Mandalay continued south into the present Sittang, to constitute the Proto-Sittang.

The capture of the headwaters of the Proto-Sittang by the Proto-Irrawaddy near the great bend at Mandalay seems to have resulted from structural warpings within the basin and from an outburst of volcanism, which has now become extinct (Stamp). The Sittang (Fig. 56) neatly demonstrates the normal symptoms of capture, i.e. conformity between its profile with the Upper Irrawaddy, irregular and reversed drainage near the elbow of capture, disproportion between the Sittang stream and the alluviated valley it now occupies, and a much reduced vertical erosive power of the river. Rapid silting up of the Sittang still goes on as a result of cultivation and forest clearing, so that while forty years or so ago the river at Toungoo averaged 18 ft. deep, it now averages scarcely 3 ft. and the water has been forced to fan out to at least double its previous width (Fig. 51).

The Irrawaddy itself varies so much in different parts of its course that its features will be best described in subdivisions:

(a) The Irrawaddy above "the confluence" (north of Myitkyina) does not carry that name. Two mountain streams partly draining the southern snows, the Mali Hka and the Nmai Hka, combine at this confluence. Of these the Mali seems the maturest and is probably an antecedent stream.

(b) From the confluence to Bhamo, the name "Upper Irrawaddy" is used. Over this 150 miles the current is usually strong yet permits navigation, except at a dangerous point below Sinbo where the river enters a gorge only 50 yds. across and becomes violent and dangerous (known to rise as much as 80 ft. in one night). Through it passes water which even at low levels back at the confluence is already a quarter mile broad and 30 ft. deep. The gorge (Third Defile) has over its 40 miles of length immediate cliffs of 60 ft. height between mountains over 2,500 ft. high. East of the defile and paralleling it, is a broad, low valley, once the Irrawaddy watercourse. Why the river was diverted from it to the present defile has not been convincingly explained.

(c) At Bhamo the Irrawaddy spreads across an alluvial basin about 12 miles broad, and this plain continues as a bend to the west.

The Irrawaddy takes a different bend to the west, avoiding the plain and passing into its Second Defile through a massive limestone. Here the gorge is sometimes 250 ft. deep and 100 yds. wide. Again this entry into a gorge and evidence of an easier alternative course cannot readily be explained; Stamp suggests it evolved not as a drainage line antecedent to the present relief but as a capture by rivers originally underground in solution channels within the limestone. After this defile, the Irrawaddy re-enters the alluvial plain westwards to reach Katha, whereafter it resumes its southerly course. From its source to Katha, the Irrawaddy is broadly antecedent to existing structural forms.

(d) From Katha to Mandalay the Irrawaddy follows a strike valley. East of it are the crystalline hills of the Shan Highlands which thereafter continue southwards in almost a straight scarp as much as 2,500 ft. high for about 500 miles to the sea, probably representing a faulted limit of the Sunda Platform and conditioning the pattern of the Proto-Sittang. Near Thabeikkyin the river enters a sandstone gorge (First Defile) whose sides are forested and less precipitous than the other defiles. At Kabwet a lava sheet, probably poured out in historic times, has diverted the river to the west, which after it rapidly widens southward to the Mandalay Basin, where a few crystalline hills (outliers of the Shan Highlands) occasionally show through the alluvials as inselbergen. The one bridge across the Irrawaddy at Ava was built to benefit from a local inselberge.

The great swing westwards of the Irrawaddy near Mandalay in preference to what appears an easier route southward to the Sittang is one of those puzzles so often associated with capture processes. The swing may have been connected with that period of vulcanism producing Mt. Popa which, rising now to some

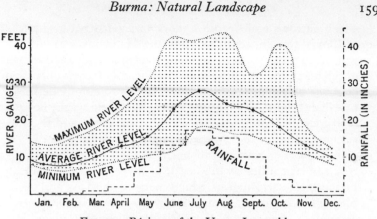

FIG. 52.—Régimes of the Upper Irrawaddy

5,000 ft., overlooking the Irrawaddy from the south, was still active a few centuries ago. At its turn the Irrawaddy has a huge discharge of water (about 900,000 cusecs—cubic feet per second—for ordinary wet seasons).

Mandalay is chief focus of the Burmese people and their tradition. By location it functions as a convergence centre dominating human movements along the Chindwin-Irrawaddy-Sittang corridors and the valleys through the Shan country.

(e) From Mandalay to Thayetmyo, the Irrawaddy passes through the Dry Zone, a landscape where low terraces and degraded scarps flank the flat Irrawaddy alluvials and generally stand up sharply without much vegetation (Fig. 56). The long dry season and the violence of a few rainstorms each year make this zone one of powerful erosion, producing "bad lands" terrain whose deeply scored hillsides witness the heavy load of silt which each storm adds to the Irrawaddy. Many side streams here are dry for most of the year, to become seething torrents of dirty brown muddy water within a few minutes during the brief wet season. Throughout this Dry Zone, the evaporation rate is high, so that the river volume is not usually very great, emphasised by the fact that the river is here losing grade because it is less than 200 ft. above sea level and has over 450 miles more to go to reach the sea (Fig. 52).

(f) From Thayetmyo to the Akauktaung Ridge below Prome, the Arakan Yoma and Pegu Yoma approach one another fairly closely and spurs from both lie across the Irrawaddy Valley.

which narrows and becomes more variegated because pockets of alluvial terrain, reminiscent of the Mandalay area, alternate with steep rocky sections recalling the Upper Irrawaddy; in one of the narrower sections stands Prome, a key river port. Some 90 miles below it, the Irrawaddy begins to subdivide into its first distributary, the Bassein River. Even below this, however, sandstone cliffs still occur to constrict the river, and the valley section continues to Myanaung, the apex of the delta.

(g) The delta, 180 miles from north to south and fanning to a width of 150 miles at the coast, is covered by a complicated braiding of distributaries which merge, subdivide and recombine until nine mouths empty into the sea. Most water passes out through the Eya mouth. While the Bassein and Rangoon rivers connect with the Irrawaddy distributaries, they are really separate streams, the Bassein draining the southern Arakan Yoma, the Rangoon River the Pegu Yoma, whose respective deltaic fans have merged into the main delta. The delta is less noteworthy for its flatness and more for its low altitude; about 2,000 square miles (of its total 12,000 square miles) are below high spring tide level and another 2,000 square miles are only one foot above that level. The heavy rainfall in violent showers and the fineness of the silts which form this landscape combine to produce rapid erosion of the deltaic surface despite its being so little above sea level. Hence the surface is not being built up vertically, especially where cleared for cultivation, but it is extending horizontally seawards at about 3 miles per century (about 50 metres per annum) as lines of spits built by onshore drift from deltaic sediments are fixed by vegetation growing upon them, so that the lagoon or creek behind each spit becomes gradually filled by mangrove to rise above sea level by the process explained in Chapter 4. Thus the landscape has a very low relief, slightly modelled by levee banks arranged radially across the delta and parallel to the distributaries, and by lines of casuarina-covered low ridges paralleling the lobate coast, the vestiges of old spits now continuous with the mainland.

Tributaries of considerable complexity resulting from an interaction between antecedent drainage lines and the tectonic drainage lines of the present Basin, join the Irrawaddy above Mandalay. These, of which the Shweli and Myitnge are the longest, have highly irregular courses with frequent captures, diversions and gorge features.

The Chindwin (drainage basin 44,000 square miles) is, however, the main tributary of the Irrawaddy. Its headstream in the Hukawng Valley rises close to the Upper Irrawaddy, and then moves westwards in a great arc with frequent rapids and waterfalls until it takes on the southerly course which it maintains until it joins the Irrawaddy in a group of distributaries and a landscape like an inland delta. Such a form at the junction indicates the loss of grading experienced by the Chindwin on reaching the Irrawaddy Valley. The Upper Chindwin runs through a wide syncline flanked by bold scarps, mostly fan fold structures, though there is a great fault line east of the Shwebo Hills; north of Kalewa the river has scarp falls to the east and dip slopes on the west. Near Mingin the Chindwin breaks out of the tectonic basin it has flowed through and penetrates scarps to reach a depression between the anticlinal domes of Medin and Palusawa after which its southward course as a calm wide stream is interrupted only near Shwezaye where barriers of volcanic ash from extinct volcanic craters, on either side of the river, for some miles constrict the Chindwin into a narrow cliffed channel.

FORESTS AND VEGETATION

Tropical Rain Forest covers the whole length of western Arakan Yoma, the southern part of the Pegu Yoma, the western edge of the Shan Highlands overlooking the southern half of the Sittang Valley, a narrow belt astride the Salween as far north as 25° N., and the whole of Tenasserim (Fig. 53).

The 80 in. isohyet chiefly delimits forms of deciduous (monsoon) forest containing ironwood (Pyinkado, Xylia dolabriformis) and teak. These have sparse bush and ground vegetation giving an open aspect, and they are mixed with some evergreen trees and bamboo, almost ubiquitous in Burma. Two types of teak forest have been distinguished, the drier one with thickets of bamboo and a wetter type, source of most commercial teak, in north Tenasserim, Pegu Yoma, and near Bhamo and Katha in Upper Burma. Where heights increase, this type of forest merges above 3,000 ft. into one dominated by oaks. Conifers appear on the higher Arakan Yoma and over the Patkoi Ranges.

Savannah mixed with forest, the effect of porous subsoils and

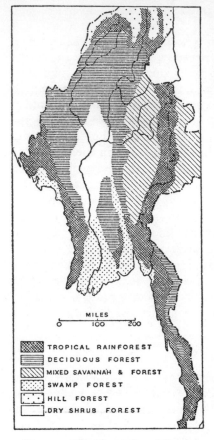

MILES
0   100   200

▨ TROPICAL RAINFOREST
▤ DECIDUOUS FOREST
▧ MIXED SAVANNAH & FOREST
▨ SWAMP FOREST
▨ HILL FOREST
☐ DRY SHRUB FOREST

FIG. 53.—The Vegetation of Burma

overcutting by shifting cultivators, is very extensive over
all the Shan Highlands.

The Dry Zone of the Irra-
waddy basin has dry scrub
forest within the 35 in. isohyet.
A form of ebony (Diospyros)
in stands pure enough to be
attractive commercially, extends through the Yaw Valley
west of Pakokku. South of
Mandalay, particularly on the
Pegu Yoma, low-branching
short types of trees, the teak
species and acacias grow, with
some cycads towards the
wetter limits. At the middle
of the zone short thorny
acacias and euphorbias are
most common, with toddy
palms (palmyra) along water
lines.

In the far north, altitude
and a more continental climate
induce a "rhododendron
forest," where rhododendrons,
magnolias and maples are common, together with firs and
tall Formosan pines. Even
here, above 8,000 ft., scattered short bamboos persist. Higher
still this forest merges into an alpine vegetation of mossy heaths,
dwarf junipers and rhododendrons, and a wealth of small ever-
greens and perennials.

On the coasts and over the deltas, the mangroves and swamp
vegetations repeat features common to similar parts of Southeast
Asia.

Commercial Work of Forests

Teak and ironwood constitute the bulk of commercial timber
extracted in Burma, where, however, there is in addition

considerable local use of many other timbers. Bamboo and various palm leaves are prominent in Burmese domestic life.

Teak, known to Burmese as *Kyun*, occurs over large areas and has proved to be one of Burma's valuable commercial assets, capable of sustained annual yields of over 500,000 tons of timber. The main areas exploited are the Tharawaddy-Prome forests, Pyinmana, Toungoo, Katha, Shwebo, Chindwin Valley, Myitkyina, Minbu, the Shan Highlands, and the lower Salween. Careful planning of the extraction is made necessary by the scarcity of labour and the timing of spates for transport. Teak in most of these forested areas is hauled to water-edge by elephants and floated downstream. Waterways like the Irrawaddy, Sittang and Salween take down great rafts of teak during the rainy season from July to October, and deliveries of the timber at the chief commercial centre for it, Rangoon, normally go on through the period November–February. The assembling of teak rafts is done at Mandalay, Pakokku, Prome and Toungoo, and the milling into commercial boards mostly at Rangoon and Moulmein, though there were scattered local mills elsewhere along the rivers. Burma's production of teak declined after 1946, but rose to 580,000 tons in 1965. Large quantities of the teak exported go to India and much of the rest to the United Kingdom. The annual output of teak from all other Southeast Asia areas amounted to about equal that of Burma in 1964.

Over recent years the cut of other timber (605,000 tons in 1965) has exceeded that of teak but the other timber was mostly consumed within Burma. The output of timber seems less than proportionate to so forested a territory, but the difficulties of extraction are high and some of the best "other timbers" are heavier than water (e.g. *pyinkyado* or ironwood, invaluable for sleepers on tropical railways and heavy structures) and can only be floated if buoyed with other wood, which means it can only be floated down the deeper streams which give the suspended logs clearance. About 100,000 tons per annum of ironwood are cut and Mandalay is the chief milling centre for it.

Forest provides a significant part of the Burmese revenue and teak ranks second only to rice, providing 13 per cent of current exports—contrasting with the lack of interest in most forests close to the Equator and in spite of civil insecurity.

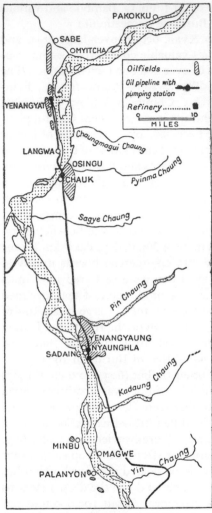

FIG. 54—.The Oilfields of Middle Irrawaddy

MINERALS

The absence of suitable coal has operated against attempts to industrialise Burma; low grade lignitic coals occur in the Northern Shan States, near Lashio and Namma and in the Arakan Yoma foothills near Minbu and Henzada. Burma's chief mineral is petroleum, found in the anticlinal and dome structures northwest of the Pegu Yoma where a line of oilfields from Indaw (Upper Chindwin) through Sabe (west of Pakokku) and Singu to Yenangyaung is being operated and the output piped to Syriam across the river from Rangoon. The installations were destroyed in 1942 as a denial action and restored by 1952. The yield is small (less than 1 per cent of Asian production), roughly only enough for domestic petrol, paraffin and candles. The Yenangyaung-Syrian industry is national-ised, crude output in 1965 being 537,000 tons and de-clining; Syriam refining capacity is 1,200 tons daily.

Precious stones, particularly rubies from the Mogok mines northeast of Mandalay, have a reputation in Burmese tradition, but Burmese jade has greater value today. Following the older Chinese workings, modern mining at Bawdwin in the Shan States, produced in 1964 ore for 14,000 tons lead and 58 tons silver (a fraction of 1940 output). Tin gravels in the western foothills of the granite formations in Tenasserim and Karenni (Fig. 55) repeat conditions found farther down the peninsula in Malaysia, while east of Tavoy tin and tungsten occur together, between Mergui and Victoria Point the mines are exclusively for tin. Most tin concentrates (about 600 tons in 1965) move from Tenasserim to Rangoon and thence to smelters at Penang or Singapore. Tin mining is quickly fading out as alluvial gold near Myitkyina has done.

In total, Burma's primary mineral production is relatively small, not particularly important for the national welfare, and inadequate for industrialisation, more especially since the means of production were destroyed during the war. While there are great reserves of lead-silver at Bawdwin, it is clear that the cream of Burma's other minerals has already been skimmed and that the possibility of exploiting these productions will be small until methods of solving the labour difficulties are devised. These are by no means new difficulties: Burmese agriculture faces acute labour shortages during sowing and harvesting seasons.

FIG. 55.—The Mines of Lower Burma

Soils

Burmese soils mostly repeat features common to Southeast Asia *pari passu*, except for those of the Dry Zone where climatic conditions are abnormal for this region. In the Dry Zone, while laterisation processes are apparent peripherally, high evaporation rates cause accumulation of solubles to be dominant in the topsoils. Two distinctive soil types have evolved in this Dry Zone:

(a) *Black Cotton Soil.*—Known as *tane*, it forms to depths of about 2 ft. upon some older Irrawaddy alluvials and is remarkable for its black colour (though when dry it may be straw yellow) which intensifies when moist. Its texture is claylike, though clay is not predominant in its composition (about 45 per cent) and its stickiness and tenacity derive from a high calcium and magnesium content which accumulates as the result of prolonged evaporation. Associated with cotton cultivation, and difficult to work, Black Cotton Soil occurs on either side of the Chindwin at Monywa and round Shwebo, and small patches are widely distributed through the central parts of the Dry Zone. Its retention of moisture makes it a reliable producer even during abnormally dry seasons and suitable for winter cropping.

(b) *Saline and alkaline soils* develop under high evaporation where the clay content is low; capillarity causes the accumulation of carbonates and sulphates of sodium, calcium and magnesium which colour these soils yellow or brown. Generally inimical to vegetation, saline soils develop southeast of Shwebo and in northern Sagaing where even salt lakes occur (Halin, Yemyet In). Saline efflorescences also appear round the Selingyi Volcanic Uplands.

Chapter Ten

THE CULTURAL LANDSCAPE OF BURMA

THERE are three distinct types of agriculture in Burma. They are: (1) Hill agriculture, (2) Dry Zone agriculture, (3) Delta agriculture. Of these, the Dry Zone agriculture has had special significance for Burmese people, establishing their traditional way of living and conditioning their integration as a nation. The delta agriculture has most interest for the outside world since it produces that surplus of rice which goes into the export trade. The hill agriculture is restricted both in the number of people concerned with its direction and its external interest.

DRY ZONE AGRICULTURE

At first glance it appears anomalous that the nursery of Burmese people since about the ninth century should be the Dry Zone where the landscape has the features of aridity for most of the year and where, as soon as population density approached optimum for the environment, at the beginning of last century, the Burmese suffered from the agricultural risks attendant on unreliable rainfalls (Fig. 61). The explanation for development in the Dry Zone rather than in what have become the more productive ricelands of the southern deltas, is a complex of environmental and traditional influences, and not one of conscious choice of the Dry Zone in preference to the deltas. Burmese people came to this region from the north, from the landward rather than from the seaward side, and they brought agricultural conceptions from dry rather than from wet environments. In these circumstances, the Dry Zone was within their technological range; they could cope with the conditions of cultivation there and probably find them considerably easier than farther north. This Zone of undulating plains and irregular rivers, low hills and very varied light soils has proved capable of a very mixed agriculture and is still essentially a mixed farming area. Quite clearly too, the Dry Zone, sited midway along the Irrawaddy Basin and at an area of convergence of people moving along the Chindwin, Upper Irrawaddy, Lower Irrawaddy and

Sittang valleys, was one of centripetal influence which at once conserved and strengthened Burmese traditions, enabling them to retain a firm hold against later intruders who followed them from the inhospitable north.

Agriculture in this dry area is at once diversified and broken into relatively small units of property. Paddy grows only in scattered areas, to take advantage of water in narrow valleys, and where some local catchment basin may be used to supplement the rainfall. Small-scale irrigation systems of distributary type (as opposed to storage type) have been developed since the eleventh century, particularly in Kyaukse, and as a whole the Zone became practically self-sufficient in paddy. Irrigation from tanks (natural run-off water impounded inside shallow bunds) is quite common, the small streams of the Zone being too incised, violent and erratic in flood to be controllable or stored by smallholder techniques. The degree of self-sufficiency grew less as the pressure of population increased, but the principle of self-sufficiency continues to be strong in the farming tradition. About two and a half million acres are normally under paddy and a portion of this is planted in April–May for harvesting after July, a rhythm different from that of most of Burma.

Upon the Black Cotton Soils of this region, cotton has been placed on up to half a million acres, in small fluctuating units. It remains a crop of peasant farmers and the possibility of extension or elaboration of cotton growing is impeded by the difficulty of obtaining harvesting labour. Cotton is sown in May for harvesting usually in late September, which is generally the end of the local paddy harvest. Often it is intersown with lines of pigeon peas (*pesinngon*) which ripen after the cotton and form a dietetic staple in this country of vegetarian people. Cotton is cultivated on 580,000 acres near Myinyan, Thayetmyo, Meiktila and Pakokku, producing 23,000 tons of low-grade lint in 1965. At one time exclusively despatched overland to Yunnan by way of Bhamo, more recently it has gone to Japan. 45,000 tons cotton seed is pressed for oil.

Since the Zone has low rainfall and light alluvial soils, dry, deep-rooted crops like groundnuts and sessamum are an important part of the Burmese farming system, very variable but each averaging about $1\frac{1}{4}$ million acres yearly, though broken into very small lots. These oil seeds supply the staple cooking oil of nearly all Burma in normal times. Sessamum, the most important of

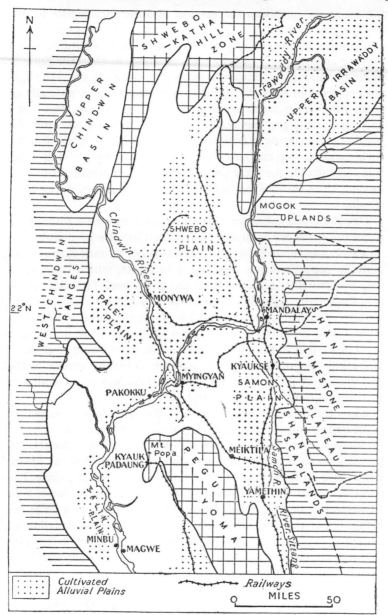

FIG. 56.—The Dry Zone of Burma

the oil seeds, goes into the ground in June for reaping in early September. In addition, there are ranges of beans, grams, pulses and chillies, all with an important place in local foodstuffs. Widely varying areas, about 360,000 acres in 1965, in the Dry Zone are planted with millet, which at once reflects the aridity and the lightness of some of its soils. Reliable as a crop even in specially dry years when unirrigated paddy fails, millet goes into local diet to varying extents and has the advantage of being sown later than paddy for harvesting in November, which means farmers who find their paddy failing can cover their loss quickly by planting millet; this accounts for the great fluctuation of millet acreages from year to year, since for most farmers millet is an insurance rather than a staple.

Dry Zone diversified farming would be impossible without bullocks and buffaloes as draught animals. They are bred and reared on a scale large enough to permit sale to other parts of Burma where climatic conditions are less suited to cattle, which must therefore be constantly replaced from the Dry Zone. This activity (see also the relation between Korat cattle and Lower Thailand) is not highly organised yet it is essential in the agricultural ecology of all Central and Southern Burma. It has little significant influence on local diet either in the Dry Zone or in the delta owing to Buddhist and Hindu prejudices. Loss of cattle consumed by armies for food and transport proved a most difficult problem in rehabilitating Burmese agriculture after the war.

Thus the diversified agriculture of the Dry Zone is in the first place largely subsistence farming, providing most of what is needed for domestic use locally, and the farmers, small landholders, depending on their families and neighbours for help, have an assured livelihood, buffered against most vagaries of external prices. They invariably own their land-holding, which everages between 5 and 15 acres per family; a holding of 80 acres ranks as a large one. Roughly one-third of each holding in any one year is left fallow and a method of tilth ploughing (*t'ayee t'unde*) is used, which resembles the water-conserving device of dry farming in such settings as Spain. Rotation of crops is regularly practised.

Farming for money is, however, also carried on as a subsidiary activity. Oilseeds, cotton, cattle and pulses are the money producers, mostly going into commerce within Burma, though not exclusively within the Dry Zone. Despite the erratic rainfall, therefore, Burmese farmers of the Dry Zone have an agriculture more constant in its effects than at first appears because, being diversified, it is rare that all crops fail in any one year. In any case, double cropping is sufficiently common to act as a further crop assurance. Because so strong an influence of subsistence farming may be traced in the Dry Zone, it follows that, though buffered from the effects of crop failures or abnormally low prices in the external world markets, the Dry Zone Burmese are also buffered from the occasional boom. There is never much money about in Dry Burma and, to that extent, its standard of living is normally lower and the way of living less elaborate than that elsewhere in Burma. Life there in the arid tropics is simple yet exacting, with a pace entirely set by natural conditions and therefore seemingly slow. The peasants live in nucleated, fenced villages and not upon their farmland.

Most settlements have domestic industries based on handweaving of cotton and silk from fibres that are generally imported; over 200,000 handlooms, generally one loom per family, are still thought to be in use, scattered through Central Burma, and official policy is to increase them.

Some exclusively commercial activities are carried on: the milling of rice and oilseeds, the transportation of teak through the zone on the main rivers, the working of the Chauk-Yenangyaung oil wells. From here chiefly were produced from small farms in 1965 about 345,000 tons groundnuts and 100,000 tons of sessamum.

Thus Dry Burma forms an admirable example of a mature and highly developed indigenous agriculture producing enough margin of food and allowing enough personal time to encourage a ripe and imaginative culture expressed in wood and stone carvings and paintings, centring on Buddhist ceremonials, a complex tradition of music, dancing and drama, and a highly decorative dress of the skirt and jacket type which relates to similar modes through Southeast Asia. All of this fits into a balanced ecology which continues to be almost on a subsistence basis, showing considerable caution towards farming for money and interchange with the rest of Burma.

Delta Agriculture

This broad type includes the form of agriculture carried on along the Arakan and Tenasserim coasts and upon the deltas of the

Irrawaddy, Sittang and Salween. The whole character is set by
the Irrawaddy Delta where the bulk of agricultural land outside
the Dry Zone is located.

The Irrawaddy Delta Agriculture is based on the cultivation of
a single crop—rice—on a large and extensive scale with the object
of selling the bulk of it. It is monocultivation of the staple Asiatic
cereal. Farmers depend on sales of rice to purchase their other basic
food needs and only a few fruit trees and vegetables are grown on
delta farms to supplement the rice. This monoculture of rice has
evolved under circumstances of special geographical interest because, as a result, the Irrawaddy Delta (followed historically by
agricultural developments on the Menam Chao Praya and Mekong
deltas) has had the same significance for the world's rice-eating
peoples as the Argentine, North American and Australian wheatlands have for bread-eaters. Over half the total rice in international trade for the decade 1930–40 originated on the deltas
of Burma where some ten million acres of one-time swamp
were planted with rice, which occupied the whole agricultural
landscape.

This specialised agriculture on a money basis is so new that
Lower Burma must be thought of in the same terms as the pioneer
agricultural areas of other continents. At the beginning of last century, although rice was the staple food of Burma, it was farmed
entirely on a subsistence basis, almost exclusively in the Dry Zone,
and the export of rice from there was in fact forbidden by Burmese
kings, so that the scanty surplus of Lower Burma at that time went
inland to supplement the already inadequate production of the Dry
Zone. A little rice trickled from Arakan into Assam, then a province
of Burma, but to all intents and purposes, Burma was merely self-
supporting in rice and the great deltas were negative areas,
undeveloped and covered with forms of swamp forest. Such terrain
throughout Southeast Asia continues to be repellent, but the only
large-scale examples of still untouched deltaic swamp may be
found in Borneo and East Sumatra where may be seen something of the conditions prevailing on the Irrawaddy and other
Burmese deltas only 150 years ago.

Penetration of the deltaic zone began just before the middle of
the 19th century, but reliable statistics are available only since
1870. The following figures sum up the development of Burmese
ricelands:

Year	Acres of Burma under rice (millions)	Lower Burma only
1866	1.75	1.44 (1865)
1886	4.00	3.70 (1885)
1896	5.75	5.00 (1895)
1910	9.95	7.81
1920	10.30	8.59
1930	12.37	9.91
1940	12.80	9.95
1950	9.30	6.70
1960	10.45	7.51

These figures of expanding acreage under rice are the more astonishing because the expansion implied the clearing, flattening, draining and organising of freshwater swamp terrain, processes carried out exclusively by manual methods without any mechanical devices or elaborate equipment. The vast acreage of riceland in the Deltaic Zone now is a monument to the sustained effort of millions of peasants working only with bullocks or buffaloes and simple, locally-made ploughs and implements. Too little attention has been given to large-scale pioneering squatters in the virgin swamps of Lower Burma, an amazing development at roughly the same time as the pioneering on the world's wheatlands and well in advance of similar developments in the deltas of the Menam Chao Praya and Mekong which were imitative of the success achieved in Burma. The rates of annual increase of rice acreage rose to a peak between 1883–1902, and the much higher 1958–65 rates indicate renewed pioneering with mechanisation.

RATE OF EXPANSION OF RICE ACREAGE IN LOWER BURMA

Period	Average annual increase in acres
1852–72	63,577
1873–82	117,490
1883–92	164,041
1893–1902	162,595
1903–12	136,888
1913–22	78,867
1923–32	84,105
1933–37	14,385
1948–57	115,000
1958–65	420,000

Paralleling this agricultural expansion on the deltas, people migrated southwards because the development in the first instance was essentially by the hands of Burmese peasants who took up

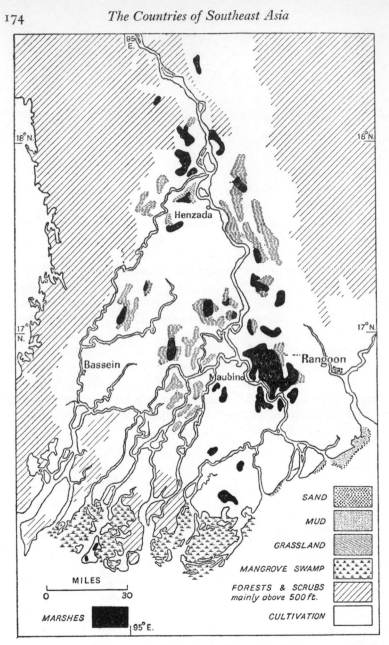

FIG. 57.—Land Use in the Irrawaddy Delta

paddyland on the delta. The high rate of increase of Burmese paddy-lands at certain phases of the '8o's might justify calling it a scramble for pioneer lands—a "rice rush" to use an expression more common for gold and tin rushes. The main rush to the Delta had taken place before census figures became available and after 1880 an evening up throughout Burma was already apparent. The first rice rush seems not to have drained population significantly from other parts of Burma so much as to have formed an outlet for the population which here, as over all parts of Southeast Asia, was rapidly expanding.

POPULATION CHANGES IN BURMA

Year	Lower Burma			All Burma	
	Millions of persons	*Percentage of 1881*	*Percentage of all Burma*	*Millions of persons*	*Percentage of 1881*
1881	3.57	100	61	5.9	100
1891	4.41	122	57	7.72	131
1901	5.41	150	51	10.49	178
1911	6.21	173	51	12.1	205
1921	6.86	191	52	13.2	224
1931	7.77	215	53	14.7	249
1941	8.92	249	53	16.8	284
1951	10.4	289	56	18.6	315
1961	12.49	351	56	21.5	368

Gradually, however, the labour question arose, as it has done in every pioneer territory; the land under rice increased beyond the capacity of the traditional Burmese family and communal systems to deal with. It was difficult enough to get the new lands cleared for rice-farming and as crops came along, the situation was worse because every rice seedling is plucked separately by hand and every ripened head is cut by sickle. That the crop was for cash sales led inevitably to hired labour, mainly from India, and it was not long in the Burmese community, traditionally not organised on a cash basis, before the rate of spending, whether on non-essentials, on labour or on mere subsistence during poor years, as in the depressions of the 19th century, exceeded the average income, leading in turn to loans of money from outsiders, to mortgages and very soon, instead of a pioneering community owning and working its land, it became a money agriculture on farms in the hands of mortgagees. Thence it became an estate agriculture renting to tenants or employing labour at wages, and the wage earners included the original peasant farmer, now landless and no longer assured of getting his staple rice for his family consumption, and also the landless group which originally farmed as labour hired by the peasant farmer. By 1936 over 9 million acres of Lower Burma agricultural land had transferred from

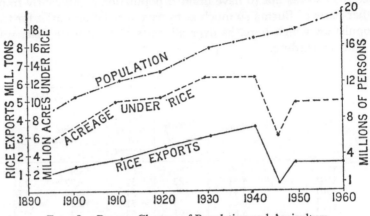

FIG. 58.—Burma: Changes of Population and Agriculture

peasant owners to mortgagors and landowners who rented it back to the peasants: a reversing of this is now taking place.

This delta agriculture has ultimately led to the disintegration of the original Burmese system of cultivation based on personal landholding and family or communal co-operation, which is now confined to Dry Zone farmers who continue on their smallholdings as subsistence farmers, only lightly touched by the system of farming for cash. But the paddylands of the Delta are still the chief source of Burma's commercial rice, and the rental system developed there at any rate assures a steady flow of rice into trade, because the farmer must immediately after his harvest get cash to provide the rent, which is a fixed money payment on a short lease of two or three years. Thus agricultural land became a social problem in Lower Burma, as within a century it changed from the system of pioneer landowing peasant to one of short-term tenants who found themselves in a more prejudiced and unfavourable position than has arisen in the very oldest land systems of Europe, where at any rate *latifundia* are broken down into farms rented on a percentage of crop basis (as opposed to a fixed cash rental) which buffers the tenant from some of the worst evils of external price changes for the commodity he produces.

The Second World War had a great impact on the weak agricultural structure of Lower Burma where three million acres of paddy were abandoned over the period 1941–48 and not restored until the 1960s.

As a result both of the opening up of the new paddylands of the delta and of the progressive squeeze to sell rice brought about by the changing social systems, Burma's outflow of rice into commerce has expanded enormously, at a rate considerably faster, until the present decade, than the population increase (Fig. 58). The following figures make a picture of rapid expansion of Burmese agricultural production which has grown faster than that of the pioneer wheat producing areas (the U.S. and Australia), accompanied though these were by greater proportional popula-increases and rapid mechanisation of field work:

Year	Burma's Rice Exports (million tons cleaned)
1881	.52
1891	.82
1901	1.42
1911	1.78
1921	2.45
1931	3.00
1941	3.50
1951	1.29
1961	1.59

These exports represent surpluses over internal consumption which in 1965 was about treble the amount exported.

The bulk of the deltaic paddy crop comes from "rainfall" swamps, which receive the necessary floodwater direct from the heavy rains of Lower Burma rather than from systems of irrigation drawing water from the Irrawaddy itself (Fig. 59). There are bunds (*kazims*) round every paddyfield and systems of channels to drain away the surplus in due course, and relatively little is fed to the fields from the Irrawaddy in spate. This is a peculiar inter-action of physical conditions in the Delta, where local rains pro-duce floods well in advance of the peak heights of the rivers, which behind their levee-like banks often run at higher levels than the rain-flooded fields on either side of them. Farmers of the Irra-waddy Delta thus have the problem of protecting their paddyfields from flood by the river, not the more usual one of using the river floods to irrigate the paddyfields. Because the Irrawaddy comes to the sea in a rainy area and not a dry area, the control problem resembles that of the Lower Rhine rather than that of the Nile. Only on the right bank of the Irrawaddy have major embankments been built to protect fields that side. The technique of using local

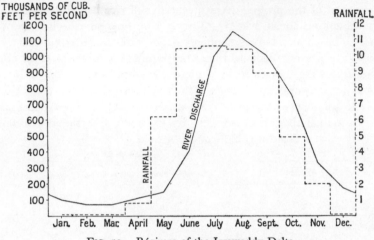

FIG. 59.—Régimes of the Irrawaddy Delta

rainstorm floodwater (and to some extent the spates in small streams originating within the delta area) implies that the Irrawaddy load goes almost exclusively into the sea and does not contribute much to building up the delta surface.

The process of rice cultivation in Burma is the one common to most of Southeast Asia. To work the ground, local ox-ploughs are simple, consisting of little more than a light wooden sole tipped with iron and intended to break the ground, not to turn it in the European manner. In addition, farmers make very extensive use of a form of harrow upon which they depend for levelling the fields, puddling the wet surface at planting time and clearing the weeds. All delta rice is transplanted, usually with many female helpers, from a nursery or seedbed, usually one-tenth the area to be farmed. Transplanting has only so far been possible by hand, so that it makes a high demand on labour over the short planting period. Upon the seedbed, animal manure from the farm cattle is usually spread, but the other fields are not manured. Very little land is left fallow and no rotation has been devised, so that symptoms of over-cultivation have quickly appeared, hastened by the dependence on rain floods rather than on silt-laden river floods. Only in Akyab has broadcast sowing become the tradition, where it yields somewhat less than the transplanting system. This is less a mere convention and more the result of the character of local rains, because there must be careful correlation between the rising flood in the fields and the height of the growing rice plant which needs just to show above the water surface without either being submerged or drying out.

Between planting and harvesting, little attention needs to be given to the growing rice. High winds in the late-growing period or cyclonic storms during the ripening period may cause crop damage and call for palliative field work. It seems incredible that all Burmese paddy is cut by hand, using only the sickle; it is traditionally a male activity, which explains the great need for male labour at harvest time, the labour peak of the Burmese farming year. Threshing is still done upon sunbaked mud floors where the paddy sheaves are stacked and then trampled by the buffaloes or oxen until the grain is loosened. Afterwards hand and wind winnowing separate the grain from the chaff with the help of a rough bamboo tripod from which the threshed mixture is slowly poured so that the grain falls below and the chaff is blown to the side. After this stage, the grain is sacked and goes into the circuit of transport and brokers to the rice mills. For seed and local use, about 17 per cent of the Lower Burma crop remains on the farm.

At least 95 per cent of Burmese lowland rice may be called a winter crop. The rhythm of planting activity reaches its peak in July and that of harvesting in November and December, a period of much more concentrated activity than at planting time. From mid-December to mid-January the bulk of the crop is moving towards the mills, firstly by cart towards local collection points, then by water to the milling centres. Burma's elaborate river system is an essential part of its rice commerce because upon these rivers, in small country boats and barges or—on main streams—in river steamers, most of the rice moves. Little cutters travelling coastwise bring the rice to the major centres from patches of riceland up and down the coast. Without this water transport, we may doubt whether commercial rice production would have been possible at all, because trade in rice has for a century been possible only by maintaining very low prices.

Rice milling ranks as a separate industry. It has steadily changed character, having been for most of last century a Europeanised industry near the ports, but in the present century dozens of small capacity mills owned by local people have been set up along the main rivers at the foci of paddy-growing areas, where the gaunt structures of corrugated iron mills make an unusual note on a landscape otherwise still dominated by traditional Burmese forms. By 1960 about 710 mills were in operation; of these 640 were small, dealing with less than 100 tons of rice a day, and the larger ones were in Rangoon, Akyab, Bassein and among the distributaries south of Henzada.

Until the milling operation removes the outer skin, the cereal is frequently called by terms differing from those used for the grain after milling. The actual words vary from country to country. In the rice trade, which is no less complex in its nomenclature than the wheat trade, there is the grading of broken or unbroken rice, the broken being grain fractured by milling. Technical terms distinguish grain containing various proportions of broken rice, the more broken being *pari passu*, the cheaper. Another process is that of polishing, a milling process giving a shine to the grain. Increasingly popular among Asiatic people, particularly in India, is parboiled rice—grain which undergoes steaming, boiling and drying processes, said to give it a better vitamin content and keeping quality, the latter being specially attractive to labourers wishing to make one cooking of rice which will last through the whole day.

Those Burmese farmers who retain some rice for their consumption during the year use hand-milling methods involving both pounding and milling, but they have increasingly sold all unhusked paddy except that needed for seed, and purchase milled rice for their domestic use.

Although the harvesting is almost completed in the two months, November–December, milling is fairly evenly distributed through the year, the spread arising from varying distances and brokerage considerations in a territory where transport is simple and slow.

Rice in 1964 accounted for 76 per cent of Burma's export values. Its significance for revenue is even greater and its bulk induces a high shipping tonnage between Burma and its rice markets. About 80 per cent of the rice moves out through Rangoon. The ports of other rice-growing areas, Bassein (9 per cent), Akyab (6 per cent), Moulmein (5 per cent), handle a relatively small volume of the rice exports which derive overwhelmingly from the Irrawaddy Delta. At Rangoon, Akyab and Moulmein shipping of rice is in sacks by way of lighters, which load steamers at Rangoon with the output of mills situated in minor creeks. At Okkalapa outside Rangoon a satellite town for mills and jute factories is planned.

The rhythm of export is distinctive. Each of the months October, November and December exports about 5 per cent of the year's total, and the monthly outgoing thereafter increases to a peak in March when nearly 15 per cent of the year's export leaves Burma. Then the rate of outflow diminishes again. The hurried post-harvest export is explicable by the absence of large storage space at the ports and the rapid deterioration of any rice stored through the wet season.

The Delta had 43,000 acres under jute in 1965, so as to be self-supporting in the sacks (gunnies) needed for the rice trade.

While the direction taken by Burmese rice exports changed in detail according to the state of the rice harvest in surrounding countries, in 1940 about half went to India, 12 per cent to Ceylon, and 6 per cent to Malaysian ports. Long-distance rice trade was never large. For 1957–60 the pattern of outflow was new, Ceylon taking one-quarter, India a third, Indonesia a sixth, Japan a sixth and Malaysia 6 per cent. Trade in rice is state-controlled.

HILL AGRICULTURE

In the Burmese hill districts may be seen examples of cultivation types at various stages of evolution from "shifting cultivation" called *taungya* (literally "hill-field") in Burma, to sedentary cultivation.

The whole hill zone outside teak reservations is peopled by groups whose basic and traditional form of farming is *taungya*. Their experience with the more amenable valleys leading into the Irrawaddy Basin has encouraged the fixation of agriculture, particularly in the Shan Highlands, yet shifting agriculture still goes on and probably at least 7 million acres at any one time are temporarily occupied by people who set up their villages near a clearing and move their villages every four or five years as they shift their interest to a new clearing. Formerly shifting cultivation went on even in the Irrawaddy Delta and it continues to be customary in the contrasting types of level open country round Myitkyina and Mergui. Cotton continues to be an important *taungya* crop at Thayetmyo. Migrant farming partly accounts for the mobility of the clans and tribes who have been constantly moving over the Burmese hills for centuries (Fig. 62). The forms of farming evolved in this tropical jungle, from the hunting-collecting type to the shifting agriculture and so to the fixed agriculture in the valleys, make an interesting contrast with parallel conditions in tropical Africa where the evolution largely turns upon variants of animal farming; apart from pigs and chickens, animals have no great place in Burmese hill agriculture, which centres upon subsistence crops of dry rice, millet, yams and sugar.

Though simple in its scheme, hill farming is not easy. With the limited labour and simple tools at its disposal, a family finds the clearing of new fields from virgin forest represents most of a whole year's work. These hill farmers are far more mutually dependent than fixed farmers of the plains and their clan or tribal structures are the tighter, making their style of farming, their general culture and tradition remarkably uniform over wide areas, irrespective of language or origin.

The physical problem of erosion caused by extensive shifting cultivation has not been fully studied in Burma. Probably 14 million acres lie bare to the torrential rains at any one time, allowing for existing cultivated areas and those recently abandoned. In addition, the hill peoples have been steadily increasing in numbers over the last 150 years at least, and the rapid silting of the Lower Sittang in recent years may quite well reflect greater erosion arising from more intensified cutting of the hill cover by the increasing hill population. At present about 2½ million people in Burma are estimated to be engaged in *taungya*, an activity more elaborate and widespread in this continental sector than elsewhere in Southeast Asia. The Shan Highlands have in part a fixed agriculture, often including plants of temperate latitude, concerned with market gardening and fruit farming for Rangoon. *Tung* trees have proved a successful cash crop introduced from the Chinese side of the border; the oil extracted makes a high quality varnish. Tea is grown by Shans for the Burmese market only. Farther south, in Tenasserim, the rubber and coconut plantation techniques of Malaysia have been introduced this century on a small scale.

The overall picture of agricultural activity in Burma provides interesting correlations with Malaysia. In both countries there has been a rapid change-over from subsistence farming to cash farming. In Burma the key item of cash farming is the local staple food, rice, while in Malaysia it is the non-indigenous, locally-unusable rubber. Both zones have been pioneering areas, the one on the basis of immigrants, the other originally on the basis of indigenous Burmese peasants. The whole structure of trade and commerce for both countries has been built up on a large-scale production of single commodities, rice and rubber, whose value depends on external assessments.

Chapter Eleven

THE SOCIAL GEOGRAPHY OF BURMA

THROUGHOUT Upper Burma, the history of tribal clashes has left a tradition of tightly nucleated settlements enclosed by a stockade situated in valleys near enough to the fields yet well out of the *chaungs* or torrential water courses. Bamboo, timber and palms are the universal structural materials and they provide domestic utensils produced by a wide range of cottage industries.

Upon the Irrawaddy Delta, the pioneer tradition, foreign influences and the long period of social security, have led to loose settlements designed to take advantage of slight embankments across the swamps, and houses are strung along levees beside the distributaries and along old spits paralleling the seaward edge of the deltas. For urban settlements, brick and imported corrugated iron are the structural materials. In the Delta landscape, the greater security and the linear village form combine to eliminate the conventional stockades, and the cash economy is made apparent in the frequent show of foreign textiles and domestic utensils among the peasants.

POPULATION PATTERN

Essentially an agricultural people, the Burmese concentrate on the best agricultural lands (Fig. 60). Even so, Burma has the lowest nutritional density (population per cultivated acre) (Fig. 61) of any Southeast Asia territory, rivalled in this only by Malaysia. Greatest population density lies roughly within the triangle Henzada, Bassein, Rangoon, in the upper and older part of the Delta where average densities are 250–500 per square mile. The rest of the Delta and most of the Irrawaddy Basin up to Thabeik-yin have densities averaging 125–250 per square mile, which occur also in the narrow sedimented zone round Akyab. Outside these areas, in the far north and in the Shan Highlands, population thins out until in the Western Ranges there are less than 25 persons per square mile.

The pools of peoples to the north and in Central Asia have

combined with the basin topography of the terrain to produce a steady compression of many peoples at differing stages of development into the relatively dead-end location of Burma (Fig. 62). Of these people, the Burmese have established greatest coherence and set the ethnic character of the whole Irrawaddy Basin, which is almost exclusively occupied by them as far as the latitude of Bhamo; they constitute two-thirds of the whole population (24.7 millions in 1965). Towards the south they have inter-bred with Mon Khmer groups (known as Talaings in Burma) who, part of those highly developed Indo-Malayan peoples found also in Thailand, Indochina and Malaysia, preceded the Burmese in the Irrawaddy Basin.

The national nucleus of modern Burmese is the Dry Zone whence they have in more recent historic times pressed out southwards. Their physique, culture and character is Mongoloid with cultural assimilations from the Mons. Their speech is tonal and monosyllabic, related to Tibetan but with script and grammar derived from Pali through the Buddhist priesthood, the literary tradition of which has made 50 per cent of Burmese males literate—a higher vernacular literacy rate than anywhere else in Southeast Asia. Burma has sometimes Burmanised other and later waves of peoples from the north, sometimes diverted them, as in the case of the Shans who migrated southward later and were forced into the eastern highlands and Thailand. Another Mongoloid group, the Karens, was pressed in turn to the southern highlands and to the Pegu Yoma. Today the distinction between these rival groups persists and 9 per cent of the people of Burma describe themselves as Shans and 7 per cent as Karens. Isolation, differences in language, and transport difficulties have perpetuated differences which appear sharper than the similarity of social and cultural habits justifies.

In the more thinly populated areas of the western and northern hills, ethnic fragmentation has proceeded farther. These hills have been called an ethnological maze of tribes stratified by altitude and by inter-digitations along valleys. Burmese call all tribes of the Western Mountains Chins, though among the tribes at least 60 different languages are in use and the tribal names are equally varied. While they have played little part in the modern evolution of Burma, a number of not too difficult ways cross these hills from Assam; of them, the Myittha route through Manipur, the

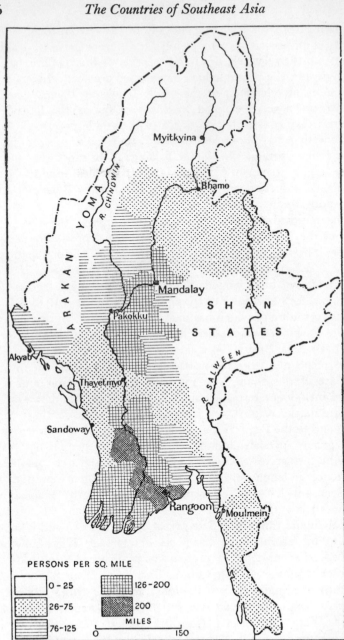

FIG. 60.—Density of Population in Burma

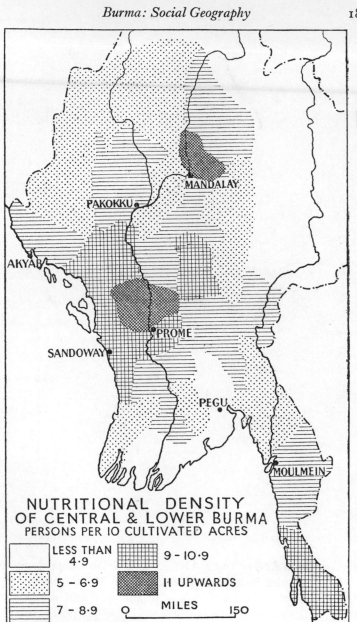

NUTRITIONAL DENSITY
OF CENTRAL & LOWER BURMA
PERSONS PER 10 CULTIVATED ACRES

LESS THAN 4·9	9 – 10·9
5 – 6·9	11 UPWARDS
7 – 8·9	MILES 0 150

Fig. 61.—The Relation between Cultivation and Population in Burma

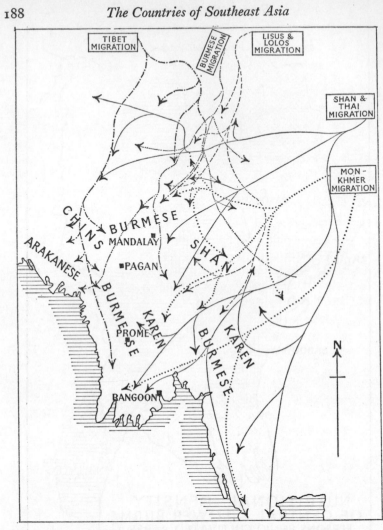

FIG. 62.—Burma: Overland Migrations and Communal Patterns

An route from Arakan to the Dry Zone and the Taungup route to Prome were used in historic times, though travel through these tropical valleys is by no means easy and overland movement is better facilitated on the drier uplands. From the north, the Hukawng Valley and the Tuzu Gap have been lines along which known groups have entered. From Assam and the north by these routes came peoples of a Mongoloid or Tibetan type resembling those already in Burma. A contemporary parallel to the historic migrations from the north has become evident by the repeated pressure of Chinese people from Yunnan into northeast Burma and the Shan States, where at times the Chinese have ranked as a political problem.

Though Buddhism has become the characteristic expression of Burmese cultural life, its entry into Burma was neither caused by, nor cause of, subjugation to India. Into the Arakan deltaic zone have steadily filtered peoples from India over the past two millennia, followed by interbreeding with indigenes so that the Arakanese people differ slightly from the main Burmese stock with which, however, it was constantly in contact through the Arakan Yoma.

Large-scale Indian contacts are relatively modern features of Burma and came in two distinct stages. Firstly in mediaeval times the trade and interchange between India and China skirted Burma to the north by way of Tibet over the mountain routes, and, more significantly, southward round the coast, where points of call for shipping grew up from Akyab to Pegu, Moulmein and Mergui as successive laps on that trade route partly seaborne, partly over-land, which crossed the Kra Isthmus. Buddhism came to the Burmese along this sea-route, followed in its time by Islam which has established little more than a minor cultural influence in the Akyab area only. This formed part of a trade movement skirting the nucleus of Burmese people, whose agriculture and state organisation was inland, in the Dry Zone. At that stage the skirting trade influenced the Burmese very slightly and their traditions developed in their own way and at their own pace within the protective isolation of the interior.

Yet it was along the coast that the momentum of activity gradually increased, to create influences centrifugal to Burma and out of harmony with the centripetal influences of the Dry Zone. Following the coastwise trade route came the East India Company, through which the British became associated with Lower Burma. As a result of the administration of the East India Company from Calcutta, the centrifugal influences round Burma drew that fringing zone within the commercial and organisational orbit of India, and, although the control from India ceased by formal governmental separation in 1935, commercial ties with Calcutta continued and governmental forms and traditions in Burma had already received the indelible impression of the Indian pattern.

Then came the migration of Burmese as pioneers to the new delta paddylands which were brought under control in Akyab, the Irrawaddy Delta, the Lower Sittang and, to a less extent, Tenasserim. The new cash agricultural system developed in these pioneer areas led to a heavy demand for labour, far more labour than Burma could supply—and it was met by seasonal migration from the congested areas of Bengal and Madras. Over later decades the flow decreased so that the movement of Indians to Burma in 1937 was half that of 1927 and stopped in 1942 when over half a million Indians fled to India.

The movement both ways was governed by general economic conditions in Burma relative to those of India; in 1928, for example, there was a net immigration of 85,000 Indians, declining to a net emigration from Burma of 57,000 in the 1931 depression. It is to be stressed that the peak period of developing new paddylands, 1880–1900, was not the peak period of Indian immigration, showing that the rice pioneering was largely by indigenous Burmese peasants in the first place. The great increases in rice acreage in the 1960s was not accompanied by renewed immigration.

Thus the commercialisation of Lower Burma has led to the introduction of foreign populations, just as has been the case in Malaysia. These Madrasis and Bengalis came originally as seasonal migrants, making for the Irrawaddy Delta in the harvesting season and returning to India immediately afterwards, or in the next dry season, having done a series of jobs from harvesting, reaping, and milling to repairing the field bundings. To this extent the duration of one man's stay was on the average shorter than was the case with non-seasonal migration into Malaysia. Gradually they came in also for the non-seasonal work of running the railways, the harbours, the river shipping, milling, lumbering and the other industrialised occupations established by the commercialisation of Burma over the last hundred years. Early labour difficulties in these occupations were in part met by subsidies to encourage Indian immigrants.

Thus a steady settlement of Indians and their families took place and by 1941 over a million Indians were living in Burma, principally in the urban and commercial centres of the coastal and deltaic zones. Hindustani became the second language of the country, and the professions and the administration for a time were almost exclusively Indian in personnel. In this way the multiplicity of peoples already in Burma was complicated by commercialisation and urbanisation based on Indians.

How the early Burmese pioneers of the newly opened rice areas of the deltas gradually lost their independent smallholdings and became tenant farmers has already been described. To complicate the issue, the hands into which the mortgaged lands fell were Indian, mostly of the Chettyar Indians, who became owners of half the Delta's agricultural lands by 1931. They were foreign, absentee non-agricultural landowners, which added to the Burmese farmers' economic difficulties the passion of racial animosity which had scarcely arisen while the immigration of foreigners was confined to the temporary agricultural labourer type. Thus, the Irrawaddy Delta was not only foreign to Burma in its agricultural system of cash crops; it was more concerned with overseas interests and overseas trade. The port of Rangoon was almost the sole entry and exit of the country; land on the Delta was largely in the hands of foreign Indian owners who encouraged still further cultivation by compatriot Indian labourers. This split Burma into the centripetal zone, the Dry Zone, essentially Burmese and poor, and the centrifugal zone, the wealthy Irrawaddy Delta and Rangoon, essentially foreign and mainly Indian, an exit rather than a nucleus of Burma. While, then, Burma's earlier history was one of a dead-end to Mongoloid migrations, the relative emptiness of the new, most fertile part of the country made it a magnet for the impoverished, loose-footed peoples of congested eastern India.

URBAN CENTRES

Only two places, Rangoon and Mandalay, can be called big towns; of the others, only Moulmein, Bassein and Akyab contain over 50,000 people. Towns may be classified as minor ports and estuarial rice centres, such as Akyab, Bassein, Moulmein and Tavoy. In addition there are river ports in a string from Henzada to Bhamo, lining the great Irrawaddy waterway, which is commercially navigable to 900 miles inland. Many small towns like Myingyan have the rural industries of oil pressing and cotton ginning. Yenangyaung and Namtu are garish and makeshift oil and mining towns. The railway and administration centres often have a long history, as is the case with Pegu, Shwebo and Toungoo.

All these places have been described by Spate as little more than overgrown villages, sprawling vaguely round a few buildings often of the "corrugated iron" period; they were pioneering settlements in character, whatever their history.

Rangoon (about a million inhabitants in 1962) stands at a point where converge the Irrawaddy waterways, an overland route to the foothills of the Pegu Yoma and overseas steamship routes. Itself accessible by ocean-going steamers, Rangoon thus commands the approaches to Burma by both the Sittang and Irrawaddy waterways and valleys, as well as along the Pegu Yoma, which is a well-drained land route followed today by the railway. The town has the rectangular pattern common in pioneer towns and it had no local significance until external trade developed over the last century or so. Its pre-1941 aspect was distinctly Indian though Burmanisation of the administration has gone on rapidly since Burmese governments were established there. In its function as chief port, Rangoon has handled over four-fifths of the country's external trade and been the gathering point of great numbers of Indian migrants with a seasonal volume of passenger traffic to and from India, which totalled over half a million annually for the period 1921–31. Overseas shipping and interests gave Rangoon a cosmopolitan air, the most modern and westernised town in the country. Though the port suffered to some extent by being off the general run of major ocean-going steamers, its international significance was increased when it became a half on transcontinental airlines linking it to India and Europe, Bangkok and the Far East, and to Singapore and Australia. About one-third of a million Chinese had settled in the different ports of Lower Burma as traders, more resident than migrant. For a time the Rangoon–Lashio–Kunming route to wartime Yunnan produced a feverish activity among Chinese traders, but this route seems unlikely to be much used. There has arisen no change in the function of Rangoon as the administrative capital of Burma in its independence (1948). The city suffered more from war in the Far East than any other capital of Southeast Asia except Manila: its transport facilities were destroyed and this, together with the breakdown of internal organisation, paralysed trade which, despite greatly increased prices, was in 1964 worth less than in 1938, reflecting Burma's withdrawal from world affairs.

Mandalay, historically associated with Burmese kings, is a much smaller and now war-scarred town which never ceased to be entirely Burmese in its tradition. It has more than 212,000 inhabitants, and before 1941 had a cultured and matured social atmosphere in the Oriental manner, with an elaborate and indigenous art, music and drama which was paralleled in few other parts of continental Southeast Asia, where the pioneering spirit is only now maturing to artistic things.

Moulmein (112,000 in 1960) has coastwise trade in rice and timber from the Lower Salween.

Urban Burma still shows many scars from the two military campaigns fought through it in 1942 and 1944. The countryside remains much the same, with minimum change on the subsistence farms of Central Burma and maximum change in the commercialised deltas where Indian migrant labour has ceased. The Indian population has changed considerably because 600,000 Indians trekked through the Arakan Hills into Assam in 1942 and few returned.

REGIONAL GEOGRAPHY

Four relatively densely populated regions are the core of Burma's geography (Fig. 49):

1. *The Dry Zone*, whose dry climate, subsistence agriculture and exclusively Burmese tradition make it the most distinctive region, centring on Pagan and Mandalay. Its boundaries are partly the 40″ isohyet, emphasised by sharp marginal relief changes.

2. *The Lower Burma deltas*—where, centring on the Irrawaddy Delta, and spreading through the Sittang Delta, a commercialised agriculture based on rice, foreign trade and foreign labour has created a composite non-Burmese region whose evolution has given Burma a second and powerful focal point, Rangoon.

3. *The Arakan deltaic coast*, a minor paddy-growing area and historic line of Indian approach to Inner Burma, with less population than (1) and (2). Sharply confined to seaboard by "Pacific type" mountain ranges inland, it has tended in the last half century to be related commercially to Bengal rather than to Burma.

4. *The Tenasserim Coast* is a highly varied region of ranges, fringed by small cultivated lowlands hedged in by mangrove swamps where the setting and the pattern of local life resemble those of Eastern Malaya. Rubber, tin and coconut production give it

a commerce distinct from that in the rest of Burma and relate it more to the Kra Isthmus.

All the remaining regions of Burma have hill or mountain landscapes, thinly populated, with agriculture still evolving from migrant cultivation to fixed cultivation and at different stages of Burmanisation going on among the many tribes and clans living there. These regions are:

5. *The Western Forest Belt*, a completely forested region, stratified into types altitudinally and having rain forest on the western flanks and deciduous forest on the seasonally dry eastern flanks, the whole drained by longitudinal and trellis patterned rivers, the chief ones flowing to the Irrawaddy.

6. *The Northern Irrawaddy Basin*, north of the latitude of Bhamo, where the basin merges into the Himalayan mountains, and becomes a series of high N–S. ranges, trenched by headwaters of the Irrawaddy River and leading up by high mountain wastes into Tibet and Inner Yunnan. Through this very thinly populated territory came many of the present Mongoloid tribal groups now in Burma.

7. *A transitional region* of rising altitudes, increasing rainfall and teak forests between the Dry Zone, the Northern Irrawaddy Basin and the Shan Highlands.

8. *The Pegu Yoma*, a thinly peopled inlier region of young warped rocks between the Lower Irrawaddy and the Sittang, with vestigial volcanic cones to the north, oil on its NW. flank and commercial teak nearly everywhere.

9. *The Shan Highlands*, a zone of cool seasons (due to altitude) and more rainfall than the Dry Zone, producing deciduous forest and a subtropical mixed forest, reflected in subtropical agriculture with rice cultivated only in the warmer lowlands. Occupied by Shan peoples who are related to the Thai, it connects as readily to Thailand as to Burma. Commerce has intruded towards Lashio and Kalaw which are rail terminals for the routes into Yunnan, and at Bawdwin where there are lead mines and a growing *tung* plantation industry. This terrain is thought to have considerable prospects for agricultural and population developments. The Salween runs through it without providing a negotiable line of approach.

The nine regional units are linked together simply:

(*a*) By the Irrawaddy waterway, which suits the needs of the middle and lower Irrawaddy basins for cheap and bulk transport; and focuses on Rangoon as terminal and entrepôt. Inland waterways carried 13.1 million tons of freight and 4.9 million passengers in 1964.

(b) By the Rangoon–Myitkyina railway running first along the Pegu Yoma foothills to join the Irrawaddy at Mandalay, and by the Mandalay–Lashio branch leading to the Yunnan road. From Mandalay, lines reach Yeu, from Thazi they reach Myingan and some miles beyond Kalaw, to Heho, from Pyinmina a line crosses the Pegu Range to Kyaukpadaung; in the south there are links from Rangoon to Prome, to Henzada and Bassein, and from Pegu to Moulmein and Ye. Freight on the railway roughly halved from 1937 to 1957. In 1965 it carried 40 million passengers and 2.7 million tons.

(c) By an elaborate coastwise traffic of small sailing and steam vessels, centring on Rangoon.

(d) A road from Rangoon to Mandalay and Lashio crisscrosses over the railway and duplicates its function. Another reaches the Shan States on the east and Prome and the oilfields on the west. In general, the road system in Burma has remained undeveloped and frequently dead-end. In 1965 commercial road vehicles numbered 4,400 and private cars 21,000.

Modern Phase

The 1941–5 breakdown of links by river and railway brought a drift towards regionalism. Feeling for Mandalay as capital was, however, stemmed because the city had been so badly damaged. Internal tensions, communalism and Communism prevented the writ of Rangoon reaching very far inland. Rice came forward only in small quantities and armed bands claimed a share as it passed. Government agencies controlled rice which became the sole support to the machinery of state, so that while independence produced a tendency to isolationism, almost a socialist hermit-state, overseas trade remained vital. In 1965, the trade outflow chiefly of rice and teak was $600 million, the inflow $679 million, chiefly textiles and manufactured goods.

[*One Burmese kyat or rupee was officially about 64 Malaysian cents, 21 U.S. cents or 1s. 6d. during 1966.*]

Chapter Twelve

THE EAST INDIES

THE WESTERN ARCHIPELAGO—SUMATRA

THE EAST INDIES

THE East Indies is a non-political term for that group of islands lying off Southeast Asia from the Sulu Sea southwards, terminating at Weber's Line west of Irian. Broken down into some minute land fragments, the groups (except for East Malaysia and Portuguese Timor) was subject for four centuries to political administration by the Dutch, for a few years by the Japanese and now by the Javanese, a historic continuity upon which is based the conception that the archipelago has a geographical unity. The region is undoubtedly one of broadly related ethnic groups dispersed through a sprawling island world, of similar physical environments and of similar human adjustments.

The East Indies is the one example of large portions of equatorial environment sufficiently penetrated by stretches of sea to make them accessible, so that human beings have been able to enter the region easily and to experience the environmental factors at work. The human response has varied widely; the teeming millions of Java contrast with the forest-covered emptiness of Borneo, and the primitive tribes still wandering in the mountains of Sumatra scarcely relate to the elegance and refinement of Balinese cultural life, or the sophistication of Jakarta.

That the archipelago stretches through 2,000 miles has effectively kept apart the people of individual islands whose forested terrain operated also to isolate coastal people from those of interiors. Against these impediments have been working the ease and fluidity of movement by water, on seas smiling and benevolent for weeks at a time, on rivers, the only natural paths through forests and swamp, and on sheltered lagoons behind the coast. The waterways that provided the easiest lines of movement for indigenous people made this zone equally accessible to foreigners, obliged to travel among the islands by reason of the long Malay Peninsula thrusting far south of the Asiatic mainland, so that people of India,

China and Europe have moved freely for millennia among the islands, adding to the mixture and diffusion of diverse ethnic and cultural types and stages of technological development. None of the islands has height sufficient to create large areas of other climates or vegetation, but the volcanic highland zones of young fertile soils have drawn to themselves very dense populations of intensive agriculturalists who have pressed farming almost to the lips of active craters, a single outburst of which may bring calamity to thousands of people. Political power in Java was centred round the productive volcanic zones; other sultanates centred on the coastal fringes, to form amphibious political units. Modern Indonesia controls most of the islands from Jakarta.

With the justification of geomorphological, faunal and floral differences, the East Indian islands may be subdivided into: (*a*) The Western Archipelago, to include Sumatra, Java, Borneo and other islands related to the Sudan Platform, a group where routes between major parts of the Asiatic continent have converged to make a strong impression on local ways of living, especially by introducing modern commerce; and (*b*) the Eastern Archipelago from Bali and the Macassar Straits eastwards, off the track of international routes, much less influenced by Asia, little touched by modern commerce, but with a Russian-sponsored oceanographic station at Ambon.

For the Indonesian regions. Dutch phonetic renderings of local place names will be used for easier reference to maps and sources.

[*One hundred Indonesian rupiah are called one* new rupiah *worth officially about 3 Malaysian cents, 1 U.S. cent or ¾d. in 1966, often available at large discount.*]

THE WESTERN ARCHIPELAGO

Although Borneo is by far the largest of this group, most interest attaches to the much smaller island of Java, where the greatest population and the intensest cultivation have evolved. Sumatra is in these respects intermediate in type between Borneo and Java. Small islands like Banka and Billiton have significance only for their tin mining.

SUMATRA

(*a*) *Physiography*

About 1,600 miles long and fairly equally divided by the Equator, Sumatra is itself surrounded by islands. Paralleling it

SLIGHTLY DISTURBED
SEDIMENTARY PIEDMONT

OLD MOUNTAIN
SYSTEMS

OLDER VOLCANIC ROCKS
MAINLY BASALTIC

RECENT ALLUVIUM
AND MARSH

YOUNGER VOLCANIC
ROCKS

VOLCANOES +

DJAMAT
BASIN

TRIPA BASIN

G. LEUSER

LAE-ALAS
BASIN

POESOEK
BUKIT

ANGKOLA-
GADIS BASIN

BOEALBOEALI

B. SOEMPOER
BASIN

G. MERAPI

B. KOEANTAS
BASIN

LAKE
KERENTJI
BASIN

G. KERINTJI

G. DEMPO

MILES

0   150

FIG. 63.—Landforms of Sumatra

in the Indian Ocean are the Nassau - Mentawei islands, mountainous, neglected, thinly peopled and off the track of world interests. On the Malacca Strait side are flat, marshy islands slowly building up seaward, and progressively linking by sedimentation to the Sumatran mainland. Farther east still are the islands of the Sunda Sea, submerged extensions of Sunda Platform ranges in W. Malaysia. The ranges of Sumatra extend northward as the islands round We and southward into the Sunda Strait where the great Krakatau volcano marks the meeting place of lines of tectonic weakness running lengthwise through both Sumatra and Java. None of these marginal islands supports many people. The Sunda Platform, mostly concealed by sediment, lies roughly east of a line between Tandjoengbalai to Oosthaven.

Sumatra is remarkable for the huge flat alluvial lowland extending along two-thirds of the East Coast, from Tandjoengbalai southwards. This region, a forest-covered swamp masking the edge of the Sunda Platform and merging into the shallow Malacca

Strait, is an obstacle to settlement and approach from the east, sparsely inhabited and undeveloped, the longest and most continuous example of Southeast Asia equatorial swamp still beyond the control of human technology. More than any other single factor, this repellent East Coast has operated against the development and peopling of Sumatra. These alluvial swamps in places extend inland for as much as 150 miles, and are chiefly responsible for the bulging shape of southern Sumatra today.

The Sumatran mainland (Fig. 63) is formed by a complex series of mountains well to the west, establishing a watershed rarely over 35 miles from the Indian Ocean. It has no generally accepted name except in the southern two-thirds where it is called the Barisan Range (Barisan means "line of hills"); to the north the terms Atjeh and Batak Highlands apply.

These mountains and the plateaux they enclose are partly tilted from west to east so that a mountain wall, edged by raised coral beaches and trenched by short, violent streams, forms the western landscape, hindering approach and human development on that side. Throughout its length the mountain system has been accompanied by faulting to produce longitudinal rift valleys arranged as a discontinuous trough through most of the mountain region, from the Basin of Goja and Alas in the north to Semangka Bay in the south. The Angkola-Gadis (Padangsidipoean), Upper Soempoer, and Bukit Tinggi (Koentas) depressions are other basins along the medial trough.

To this triple division vulcanism has added the complication of lava outpourings of several ages and types, from andesite to ash. Erosion by the torrential rains has carved and removed much of the older lava yet large deposits of it remain in the south and at points on the west. Most of the outflow seems to have spread east as great sheets of pumice, tufa and ash, partly in the original state, partly redistributed as water-borne alluvials. The East Coast swamps are largely built of redistributed debris from more recent volcanic eruptions of South Sumatra. In the Batak Highlands tufa from recent vulcanism has obliterated all earlier relief over an area of some 5,500 square miles; south of Sorikmerapi occurred another large outflow of lavas. One effect of these outpourings of volcanic material has been to block parts of the medial trough, interrupting and diverting its drainage for a time, often creating temporary lakes which have left fertile alluvial basins attractive to farming and accessible only through gorges at what was the debouchment of the lake, as at Lake Tawar. The whole drainage pattern is one of interaction between the alignment of the medial trough, the general tilt eastwards, and the tongues of volcanic debris.

Between the mountain system and the East Coast is a strip of piedmont varying in continuity through the length of Sumatra. It has a distinct character set by only lightly folded sedimentaries crossed from the west by entrenched streams, and containing oil-bearing substructures exploited at various points from Atjeh to Palembang. This piedmont comes almost to the coast north of Medan, to narrow the line of coastal swamp, but it stands well inland elsewhere.

In the Batak Highlands, the volcanic outpouring of acidic rocks 2,000 ft. thick has concealed the medial troughs and the adjoining eastern piedmont down to the East Coast. Huge dormant cones still stand on the inner Batak landscape round Lake Toba. Steeply graded rivers have cut gorges to break up the plateau-like landscape, and carried the easily eroded volcanic debris towards the east coast; upon these transported soils has grown up the plantation agriculture (Fig. 66) west and south of Medan. In contrast to the acidic rocks elsewhere on the Highlands, from the dormant Batak volcanoes in the north came basic ejecta, weathering into fertile soils which alone make possible the tobacco plantations behind Medan. Elsewhere the acid volcanic cinders have spread a porous mantle on the plateau, upon which the normal Tropical Rain Forest will not grow, so that a semi-arid savannah vegetation scattered with giant ferns covers the landscape. Probably, too, this zone has been overcut by shifting agriculturists and regrowth of the secondary forest hindered by soil porosity and by the dry föhn winds coming across the mountains from the south and east. Lake Toba, 50 miles long, 3,000 ft. above the sea and covering over 500 square miles, is surrounded by cliffs often 2,000 ft. high, at the foot of which are narrow alluvial belts intensively farmed for rice; its outlet to the southeast (Soengai Asahan) plunges through tremendous gorges.

Farther south from the Batak district, the dormant Boeal-boeali volcano is the first of the Barisan Mountains where the typical form of two ranges separated by a series of fault depressions becomes emphatic. These depressions are swampy or occupied by lakes. The Western Range, built of recently dormant cones and less resistant volcanic materials, presents a torrentially scored face to the Indian Ocean where only scanty and small alluvial fans, separated by cliffed headlands, attract settlement. In the Eastern Range appear more resistant metamorphic rocks, schists, slates and limestones, descending less steeply to the east and enclosing a few depressions, such as the Batang Oembilin Basin, site of the chief Sumatran coalfield, linked by railway to Padang.

At about 1° 30″ N. the whole mountain structure narrows to a low waist not more than 20 miles wide through which it is possible to cross without rising above 2,000 ft., at Padang Sidimpoean. A highland road threads the medial trough from this small town through the Angkola and Soempoer Valleys to the Bukit Tinggi Basin, thence splitting to traverse the West Coast southward from Padang and the eastern piedmont to Djambi, Palembang and Lampoeng Bay. Lake basins are present in this section of the medial trough (Manindjau and Singkarak) each fringed by minor agricultural areas.

South from the Batang Hari rises first the active Kerintji volcano (Piek van Indrapoera), highest and most naked peak in Sumatra (12,470 ft.), and thereafter volcanic cones, mostly active, dominate the landscape as far as the Sunda Strait. Granite, crystalline lavas and tufas spread everywhere. Where the medial trough appears, its alluvial fillings attract cultivators and settlements, but transmontane routes are few. In this zone begins the great Air Moesi which, very mature in contrast to most Sumatran streams, is at this stage broad and shallow, with gently sloping sides. Many of the volcanoes of South Sumatra discharge tongues of mud (lahars) which drain into the lowlands.

Half the area of Sumatra lies on the plains east of the Barisan Ranges, and does not exceed 100 ft. in altitude. Apart from the piedmont, where oil and coal frequently occur, the recent alluvium from the volcanic highlands plasters all other formations, Since mangrove and tropical swamp are progressive growths, there are by now some slightly higher and drier sections, well away from the rivers which, heavily laden with mud and decaying vegetation, have lost the power of vertical aggrading so that they abrade sideways to form constantly changing courses and to leave numerous abandoned channels quickly choked with thick-matted vegetation. Much of the swamp is inundated each rainy season, and twice

FIG. 64.—Land Use in Sumatra

daily the large deltas and a zone up to 12 miles broad along the coast may be flooded by tides. While the rivers across the swamps are navigable to some extent, depending on shifting sand-banks, villages along their banks are separated by great distances. Some of the channels near the coast are surprisingly deep, probably due to tidal scour; the Kampar, for example, has a powerful bore. The navigable streams establish an E-W. line of communication, met inland on the piedmont by roads and a railway with a NW–SE. alignment. The natural vegetation is of two types: (*a*) Tropical Swamp Forest, predominating in the eastern half of the island, and (*b*) Tropical Rain Forest, occupying most of the rest of the island, with a few variations due to changing altitudes and porosity of soil (Fig. 64). Along the East Coast, corals do not appear, inhibited by the muddy shores and extensive mangroves. On the West Coast there are both live corals and coral terraces on raised beaches.

(b) Climate

Sumatra's climate broadly resembles that of Malaysia. The high mountain barrier induces very heavy rains (over 150 in. p.a.) at all seasons with maximum during October-November north of the Equator and during December-January south of it. Seasons of less rain (not amounting to drought) are more pronounced to the

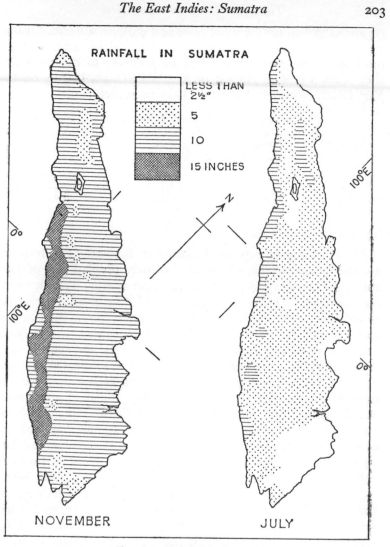

Fig. 65.—Rainfall in Sumatra

north (as in West Malaysia) and some of the mountains basin have low rainfalls because they are shielded from rain (Fig. 65).

Considerable differences of weather from district to district occur in the Barisan Ranges where föhn winds are very pronounced on the eastern flanks during southwest winds. Cool drier climates upon some of the plateaux create minor variations in the equatorial régime of violent convectional rains and uniform warmth. Strong, east-moving squalls, the "Sumatras" of the Malacca Strait, blow most frequently across the north in January; to the far south they reach a peak in August on the West Coast, in July on the East Coast. No tropical cyclones have been recorded.

SUMATRA: AVERAGE RAINFALL (inches)

	Rain-days (over .02in.)	*Jan.*	*Feb.*	*Mar.*	*Apr.*	*May*	*June*	*July*	*Aug.*	*Sept.*	*Oct.*	*Nov.*	*Dec.*	*Total*
Bukit Tinggi (3,018 ft.)	195	9	7.2	8.4	9.9	7.0	5.4	3.7	6.0	6.7	8.7	8.7	9.6	90.3
Padang (230 ft.)	190	13.4	10.9	11.4	14.3	12.0	12.8	10.9	13.4	16.4	19.4	19.9	18.7	173.5

(c) Population Patterns

Medan, the *most* populated district of Sumatra (Fig. 66), has a density equal to that of the *least* densely peopled part of Java and contained 464,400 people in the 1961 census. This developmental contrast, while reflecting physical differences, relates also to accidents of recent history. In the Hindu colonisation period travellers visited Sumatra frequently, recorded the relative grandeur of principalities centred there and did not suggest then the contrasts between Sumatra and Java were so great as they are now. During the last few centuries, Sumatra has been off the track of the international trading interests threading these seas, and the East Coast swamp and the West Coast cliffs made it far more difficult to approach the populated interior than was the case in Java. Operating to its disadvantage also was the late arrival of modern organisation and transport systems; Sumatra only came under Dutch control early this century. The island escaped that impulse to population expansion, the Culture System, which had much influence in Java last century, and it has never in modern times attracted large-scale immigration. These are negative factors. The present population (15.7 million in 1961) has an average density of 85 persons per square mile; about 18 per cent of Sumatrans live in towns, a proportion of urbanisation trebled since the previous 1930 census.

The pattern of people in Sumatra may be summed up thus. The densest population spreads behind Medan; somewhat lesser densities cover the Bukit Tinggi basin, the adjoining depressions of the medial trough, and the Batak Highlands. Fringing the northernmost and southernmost tips, in the fertile little estuarial bays of Atjeh and Lampoeng, are minor concentrations of people. Least populated is the East Coast swamp where over large areas there are densities well below 25 per square mile, indicating that the same swamp has acted as a major barrier between the people

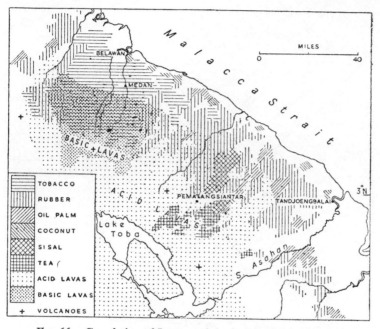

FIG. 66.—Correlation of Lavas and Agriculture behind Medan

of Malaysia and Sumatra, more so than the Malacca Strait itself, which is a means of contact for sea-going people. Fertile soils of basic lava origin are found only in Lampoeng, in the foothill country west of Palembang, in the Padang Basins, and on the Batak Highlands, all attracting agricultural populations. Of the 12 towns, mostly peripheral, only Palembang, Medan and Padang are substantial, with over 150,000 each.

Menggala is the centre of a fairly prosperous farming region whose population barely reaches 60 per square mile. In the middle and upper valleys of the Air Moesi, the alluvial soils and the controllable water supply permit rice farming, flanked by rubber and coffee plantations; this zone attracted interest because

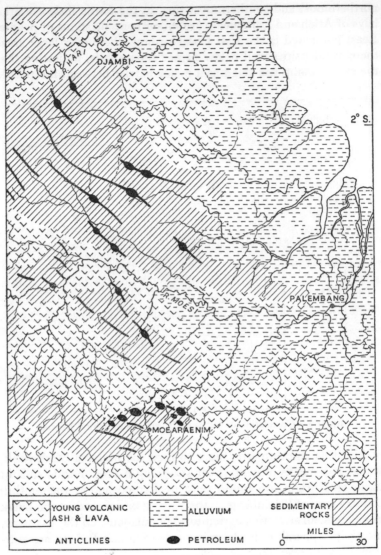

FIG. 67.—Petroleum Deposits near Palembang

it is near productive oil wells (Fig. 67). Palembang (1961 pop.
458,700), where a line of low hills approaches the Moesi, has
been the chief centre of this region for long historical periods;
although the settlement was mentioned by early Indian and

Chinese travellers, its modern revival as almost monopolist commercial centre of Sumatra is connected with the oil refineries of Pladjoe nearby and its accessibility from overseas by ocean steamers and from Central Sumatra overland through the piedmont. Djambi has a rather similar location and historic value with respect to the Batang Hari river. The Bukit Assam coalfield, linked by rail to Palembang, has special economic significance for this region deficient in coal because it resumed production quickly, combining with Oembilin to give 444,000 tons in 1964.

Where the eastern piedmont comes to the coast, on either side of Medan, relatively dense populations have settled recently in connection with tobacco, rubber, coffe, tea and oil palm plantations. Medan itself (351,000) originally developed into the regional capital because, located on the Soengai Deli, riverine and coastwise routes centred there. Shipping difficulties in so shallow a river made necessary in course of time the creation of an outport at Belawan, which handled mainly an export trade of bulky primary commodities (1960 exports 300,000 tons, imports 140,000 tons). Belawan once dealt with more shipping tonnage than any other Sumatra port, multiplying its tonnage five times over the inter-war period, but it suffered from much silting during the Japanese Occupation, and now ranks far behind Palembang.

Few mountain districts in Sumatra have more than 50 people per square mile, and though the youthful soils round the Kerintji volcano rank as well peopled, the density of that region is only 70 per square mile. A longitudinal highway links the various medial troughs, encouraging their agricultural development. Among the Padang Highlands there is more intensive settlement than elsewhere in Sumatra, based on the fertile volcanic soils round Merapi. Thus densities of over 950 people per square mile occur in the Bukit Tinggi (51,000 in 1961) country where tobacco, coffee and coconuts are grown. Nearby at Sawahloento, coal is mined. This dense population extends to the west coast where Padang (161,000) is chief town of West Sumatra and third in the whole island. Even here, however, an artificially sheltered outport has had to be built farther south (Telok Bajur) because the shallow, exposed bay does not suit modern shipping. To this Dutch-built outport, now part of Padang, is routed for export the agricultural produce of the Highlands and the heavy output of the Oembilin coal mine, one of the few sources of coal regularly available for archipelago railways and shipping. Transport proved a costly overhead to these remotely located coals which, after railing to seaboard, still have considerable distances to cover before reaching convenient selling points at Sabang or in Java. The Batak Highland is the only other mountain zone with fairly dense settlement (over 350 persons per square mile). It has good links to Medan and to Sibolga. The Batak setting has not only stimulated a vigorous agriculture among local people, but also encouraged hill resort development around Lake Toba.

(d) Human Types

While numerous clan groupings developed here where evolution in isolation was facilitated by the terrain, two ethnic types settled in Sumatra. Long-headed Caucasoid types (Nesiots) are represented by the Bataks, the Gajo and the people of the Nias-Mentawei islands. Broad-headed Mongoloid types seem to have migrated hither from Continental Asia, by way of Malaysia, and may be recognised today among people of the Sumatran East Coast, the Menangkabau and the Atjeher who fringe all the northern tips of Sumatra. Among Sumatrans no less than fifteen languages and a wide range of dialects are in use today; though their customs vary, they are variations on a similar pattern closely associated with the uniformity of environmental conditions.

Three groups of peoples may be distinguished:

(a) *The Menangkabau,* distributed from the middle of the island to the West Coast. This is a people more broad-headed (Mongoloid) than neighbouring groups; Menangkabau are Muslim now but retain their older matrilineal social system and its strong family ties which have led to the housing of many branches of the one family under one roof, and to customs resembling those of the Hindu family system, calculated to keep family property intact. The elaborately-decorated quarter-moon-shaped houses evidence a fairly high cultural standard, producing skilled wood and metal work. Menangkabau agriculture has considerable complexity, based on wet paddy and buffalo breeding. The Menangkabau have a commercial reputation as the only Sumatran community astute enough to be able to hold its own in trade against the Chinese middlemen established everywhere else in the island.

To the east of the Menangkabau, other types of Malays live on the East Coast and its adjoining islands. They are Muslims with a patrilineal system and they gravitate towards village sites close to tidal water. Some Malays near Palembang have a tradition of originating from Malacca. They are not located well enough to be more than indifferent agriculturalists but they are active fishermen, among whom much overseas influence is apparent.

(*b*) North and south of (*a*) are *Batak and Lampoenger*. The word Batak, originally a derogatory Malay term, covers a number tribes of the uplands round Toba and reaching to the west coast at Natal. These people are chiefly influenced by Hindu and animistic traditions, though conversion to Islam and Christianity has taken place among southern tribes. Patrilineal inheritance and class distinctions, related to the caste system, govern Batak customs, which are associated with multi-family houses and a subsistence agriculture now emerging from the shifting cultivation type. The Gajo people of inner Atjeh resemble the Bataks yet they have been subject to Atjeh influence long enough to adopt many Atjeh ways.

Lampoeng people have had long associations with the Bataks, weakened now by influence of Sunda people from across the strait and by the belt of Malay peoples stretching east-west through Middle Sumatra. Though Muslim, they are not far from the head-hunting stage. Their several-storeyed houses are distinctive, each standing in its own stockaded compound on high piles. They are almost vegetarian and have an elaborate literary culture.

(*c*) *Atjeher.*—The Atjeh people comprise many tribes among which there are marked differences between more agricultural coastal types, much influenced by foreign contacts, and the more mobile interior types. Atjeh was invariably touched by the peoples crossing the Indian Ocean over many centuries and it has had longer associations with Arabia and travellers from that direction than with any other single foreign interest. It was historically the first part of the Indies to become Muslim. All peoples of the group have an aristocratic society whose fanatic Muslim tradition has welded them into a community which fiercely resisted subjugation by outsiders in modern times. Atjeher land is tribally owned but individually cultivated on a subsistence basis. The influence of Arab traders has been very strongly superimposed upon much older cultural traditions.

In addition to more settled communities, there are in Central Atjeh very primitive peoples resembling the forest wanderers of West Malaysia. Incompletely Muslimised, they are hunters, gatherers and fishermen. Odd migrant tribes of shifting agriculturists have been found farther inland but the nomadic hunter-gatherer types predominate. Among the non-Muslim Mentawei-Nias islanders. Polynesian affinities are very marked and cultivation is based on yams.

Upon this pattern of indigenous people has been imposed the more recent immigration induced by modern agricultural mining activity, bringing Chinese labourers into the Medan district and into Palembang. In 1960 Sumatra contained about 600,000 Chinese who were prominent as plantation and mining workers, as fishermen at Bagansiapiapi, and as retailers and middlemen in nearly all the towns.

(e) *Land Utilisation*

Most of Sumatra remains under its natural vegetation cover (Fig. 64), the Tropical Rain Forest being interrupted only by patches of secondary forest and savannah where local soil conditions are inferior. The largest patches of secondary forest are upon the eastern side of the southern mountain system (west of Palembang) and marginally round all agricultural zones.

Indigenous agriculture continues to be more dependent on shifting cultivation than on sedentary farming. Hence the zones of densest indigenous population are being extensively cut over by the predatory shifting system, accounting for the fringe of savannah round all settlement areas. So far the population has not reached a density sufficient to weaken the tradition of shifting cultivation which still supports about 6 million Sumatrans. Many of the hill people depend on roots, the older indigenous interest in food cultivation. Rice and maize, which the more developed groups cultivate, are definitely the result of external contacts and practised close to lines of external communication.

Wet paddy farming is confined to a few deltaic embayments on the Atjeh coast, and to the upper valleys of the Moesi and Hari rivers on the flanks of Kerintji, as vestiges of the prosperous principalities of the first millennium when Indian colonisation reached its peak. Elsewhere dry paddy on temporary forest clearing is more usual. There are a few permanent rice-producing zones scattered round the Lampoenger coast. These agricultural activities are on a subsistence basis, yet Sumatra as a whole is not self-supporting even in rice, so that maize has become well established as secondary food crop. Only in the Padang Highlands has a more intensive indigenous agriculture produced rice for local commerce. In Atjeh and Lampoeng rice acreages have rapidly expanded over recent years, made possible in Lampoeng by soil rejuvenation from last century's Krakatau volcanic explosion which spread fertile ash in south Sumatra. Much of the difficulty of agricultural expansion has been the scarcity of people. In modern times, officially encouraged immigration to Sumatra has been slow and reluctant even from nearby Java which faces the problem of too many people and inadequate land. The Javanese immigrants needed to be farmers to be suitable as permanent settlers, yet they were wanted as labourers upon European plantations as well. Under this double demand for labour, the expansion of Sumatran food agriculture scarcely kept up with the rate of immigration. Indonesians are renewing efforts to colonise for rice farming in South Sumatra, where "transmigration" from Java is now national policy. Over the 1930–61 census period, while Sumatra as a whole increased population by 87 per cent, the immigrant area of its south coast increased by 141 per cent, and of its central east coast (Riau and Djambi) by 274 per cent. The west coast remained nearly static.

Rubber ranks as an important crop of the indigenous farmers of Sumatra, a development fitting in both with the shifting cultivation when undergoing transition to sedentary farming, and with cash crop farming. The smallholdings are worked partly for food and partly for rubber. Other crops grown by smallholders for cash are tobacco, coffee, tea, kapok, coconuts and pepper. The actual acreage under rubber, the chief smallholder cash crop, cannot be listed accurately because the units are small, widely dispersed and irregularly worked. The most convenient index comes from Sumatran statistics of smallholder rubber exports which from nothing prior to 1915 grew to 224,000 tons in 1956; this included 46,000 tons from Djambi, 77,000 from Palembang and 70,000 tons from the northeast coast. A rough estimate of the smallholding acreages may be made on the basis of 15 acres producing a ton of rubber.

Sumatran agriculture has not closely followed the Malaysian pattern. European-captitalised plantations under foreign management began late last century. The oldest (1863) were for tobacco in the sultanate of Deli behind Medan, where high-quality tobaccos are still grown in plantations totalling 29,000 acres upon basic lava soils. Large rubber plantations gradually occupied lands adjoining these old tobacco plantations and now exceed them in importance. Similar large rubber plantations were established inland from Palembang and Djambi. During the labour confusions of 1961, .51 million metric tons of rubber were purchased from Sumatran smallholders as compared with the estate production of .10 million tons. The Medan area (Fig. 66) has a diversified plantation agriculture rather than the monoculture typical of Malaysian plantations and oil palm, tea (particularly near Pematangsiantar), coffee and sisal estates alternate in strips roughly at right angles to the coast to take advantage of transported volcanic soils. Attracted by these plantations, many Chinese labourers have immigrated round Medan which exported 16,000 tons tobacco and 25,000 palm kernels in 1961.

Minerals were also largely worked and managed by foreigners. The Atjeh and Northeast Coast oil wells were handled by refineries at Sabang and Medan, those farther south at Palembang and Djambi. Much of this oil went to islands near Singapore for final distribution. In 1940 over half the Sumatran crude oil production (5 million tons) came from the Pladjoe fields and another quarter from Djambi. During 1962 a total of nine million tons of crude oil was again being produced in Sumatra. Chinese miners have regularly washed for gold in the alluvials of West Sumatra, the output being more important as a symbol than it is in fact.

SINGKEP, BANKA AND BILLITON

Offshore from Sumatra and connected with it administratively are the islands of Singkep, Banka and Billiton whose over-mature relief repeats that of Malaysia. They are the largest of that maze of small coral-girt, granite-cored, thinly peopled and almost uncultivated islands known as the Rhio and Lingga archipelagos, scattered south of Malaysia, restricting movement of shipping now,

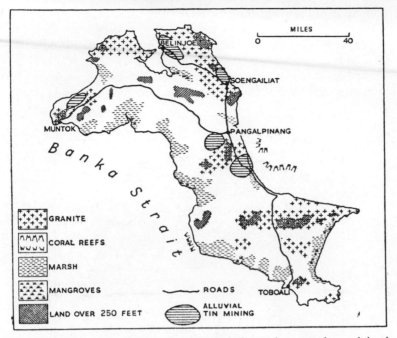

FIG. 68.—Banka. This island is almost entirely forested except where mining is carried on.

though they facilitated the inter-continental movement of people for millennia in the past. The form of the Sumatran coast curiously parallels those of Banka and Billiton (Fig. 68 and 69). These two islands have rich alluvial tin deposits under conditions recalling those of the Kinta Valley though here partially deposited in the sea—hence locally known as "sea tin". These alluvials are still worked by Dutch dredges and some lode tin is mined in Billiton. Large colonies of Chinese labourers have settled on these mines as temporary immigrants; of 115,000 persons on Banka in 1940, 43,000 were Chinese and there were 20,000 Chinese among the 58,000 people on Billiton. The islands support about 250,000 people and the mining centre, Pangalpinang, contained 159,000 people at the 1961 census. The ore has variously moved to the Singapore smelter, to Arnheim in the Netherlands, to the U.S.A. and since 1967 to the Muntok smelter (capacity 13,000 tons). Mining fluctuates with world tin prices and dropped 40 per cent from 1956 to 1962 when 16,600 tons ore came 65 per cent from Banka, 25 per cent from Billiton and the rest from Singkep. Modest amounts of pepper are exported.

From Poelau Bintan in Rhio comes the greater part of Indonesia's total bauxite production (516,000 tons in 1964).

Farther south, the volcano Krakatau has little significance in human geography, although it is notorious for a tremendous out-

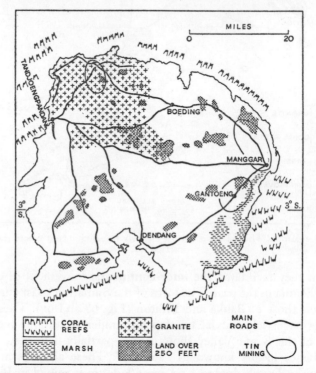

Fig. 69.—Billiton. Apart from mining areas the island is forested

burst in 1883 which, by spreading ash over huge areas of South Sumatra and as far as Singapore and Jakarta, exemplified what devastation and changes by inundation and by covers of ash can be produced quickly in the unstable sectors of the archipelago.

TRANSPORT

While much of the East Coast is repellent to settlement, transport now gravitates in that direction on account of the navigable rivers leading to the international artery of the Malacca

Strait. Thus, Singapore, not far from the middle of the East Coast, has tended to be the focus of Sumatra's external trade, especially as link to Europe, and as port of call for shipping moving from all East Coast ports to Jakarta, the administrative capital of the archipelago. The configuration of the Strait led local and international shipping through the narrows close to Singapore whose long-standing significance in relation to Sumatra was reflected in the Japanese device of making Singapore the administrative capital of both Malaya and Sumatra. By 1955, Singapore still handled 21 per cent of Indonesian exports but only 1 per cent of its imports, even greater quantities passing through without transhipment and consequently unmentioned in trade records. In 1958, Penang's entrepôt trade included $89 million imports from Sumatra which received, however, only $6 million exports from Panang. Sumatra's trade through Malaysian ports was restricted 1963–6 by the Indonesian government embargo following the institution of the Federation of Malaysia, after which smuggling was intensified.

The bulkiness of Sumatra's exports, chiefly rubber and petroleum, causes Palembang and Belawan between them to be responsible for over one-third of all Indonesian outflow. In 1957 at Palembang began operating the first catalytic oil-cracking plant in Southeast Asia, now producing from local crude over 6,000 barrels a day of high-octane petroleum.

Chapter Thirteen

THE EAST INDIES

THE WESTERN ARCHIPELAGO: THE NATURAL LANDSCAPE OF JAVA

Just over 6,000 miles long, the prolific island of Java is set slightly askew to latitudes and located farther away from the Equator than the northern parts of West Malaysia. It tends to have an emphatic dry season and a rainfall diminishing east of a meridional line through Goenong Merapi, though these tendencies are over-ridden in detail by relief. Middle Java (Cheribon to Semarang) scarcely exceeds 60 miles in width, but east and west of this "waist" the island broadens to about 100 miles, so that its form is distinctly elongated, emphasised by a lengthwise arrangement of the structure and the landscape types, whose continuity is more pronounced to the south than to the north. The island of Madoera, always bracketed with Java administratively, is a structural extension of North Java.

Beginning from the south, the landscape types may be summarised thus (Fig. 70):

1. The south coast limestone platforms.
2. The medial "ridge and valley" belt of disturbed sedimentary rocks.
3. The line of volcanoes forming the axis of Java.
4. A belt of alluvials from Bantam eastwards through the Loesi-Solo valley to the Madoera Strait and enwrapping the volcanoes.
5. The North Coast limestone platforms of Rembang and Madoera.

THE SOUTH COAST LIMESTONE PLATFORMS

Five platforms, a small one in S. Buitenzorg, a large one in S. Priangan, the extensive Goenong Sewoe between Kali Opak and Patjitan Bay, the plateau between the bays of Popoh and Sipelot, and an eastern outlier forming the Blambangan Peninsula, are built of little disturbed massive limestone rising precipitously

from the coast and forming
a landscape of tropical karst
type. The formation is thick
and porous and its subterranean drainage leaves the
surface generally waterless
and barren, negative to agriculture and to population.
Goenong Sewoe sets the
type, as a platform rising to
about 1,000 ft. in a series of
steep bare hills and hollows,
uncrossed by modern routes.
Those platforms to the west
receive regular rains and have
a more profuse vegetation,
while those to the east serve
to emphasise the arid note on
a landscape naturally subject
to a long dry season.

THE MEDIAL RANGE AND VALLEY BELT

The Medial Range and
Valley Belt is a maturely
dissected landscape on marls
which give rounded relief
forms. These sedimentaries
which, with the limestone,
cover 33 per cent of the
surface, were derived on the
south from eroded volcanoes
of previous geological eras
and have been much folded
and fractured. There tends
to be a medial trough among
the ranges, after the
Sumatran pattern, showing
as various basins (e.g.
Bandoeng and Garoet) to

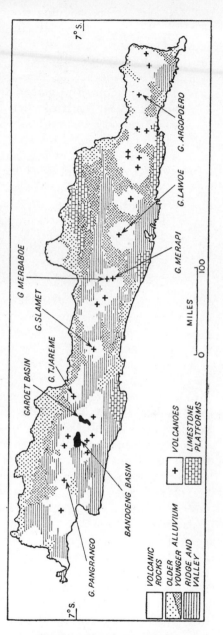

FIG. 70.—Landforms of Java

the west and as a broadening trough to the east where it opens and loses altitude until partially inundated by the Madoera Strait. The sedimentaries reach altitudes over 4,000 ft. and form the substructure af Java's highlands. They involve on the north lignite and oil deposits. To the south the highlands come to the coast as cliffs, frequently marked by raised beaches and only in a few places, as near the Banjoemas Plain, does the highland stand back from the coast behind alluvial belts. It is among these sedimentaries that fossils of "Java man" (*Homo soloensis*) have been found as evidence of the contact of this region with Asia over long geological periods. Upon these marls and associated rocks there is abundant surface water, exemplified in the rolling maturely-eroded landscapes of Preanger, but the formations are not extensive in dry East Java and their detail is much influenced by volcanoes and the superficial material derived from them. On the north, these sedimentaries do not reach the coast.

THE VOLCANOES

Volcanoes dominate the Javanese landscape everywhere, disrupting the sedimentary structures (Fig. 72) and masking the older landscape forms with lava and ash outpourings. Scarcely any long distance view can be found which does not include a volcanic cone. Java's volcanoes rise in steep slopes, scarred by torrential rains, to greater heights than any other of the relief forms: 44 cones are between 6,000 and 10,000 ft., and 14 are even higher. In few parts of the earth are structural weaknesses and lava flows crowded together in such profusion. The degree of explosiveness among the volcanoes varies so that the ash sometimes builds up round the vent a steep, narrow cone with a funnel-shaped centre, and sometimes spreads farther afield. The pattern of volcanic materials depends on whether the ejecta comes as molten lava or as the ash of exploded lava; the former flows like a viscous tongue down the sides of the volcanoes, usually from a point where the crater rim is lowest, while the ash is carried as a cloud whose direction depends on the wind. Because the rainfall is generally so heavy, the effect of tropical storms and of altitude, the craters tend to become lakes. Extinct cones invariably have rounded lakes within them for a time until erosion breaks down their rim. Other craters may become explosive by reason of the steam pressure set up in them by the percolating water, or become

Fig. 71.—Physiographic Sketch of Goenong Oengaran

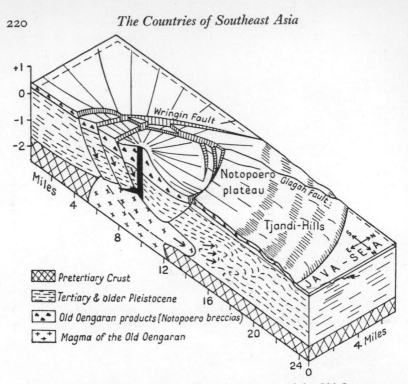

FIG. 72.—Block Diagram of the Volcanic Structure of the Old Oengaran

hot mud lakes which periodically spill over as lahars, devastating the countryside round the volcano, or emit ladoes, which are scorching clouds of hot dust of equally devastating effect. Gas vents (fumaroles) and hot springs of sulphuretted water or mud (solfataras) occur round some Javanese volcanoes. Poisonous heavy gases may lie in valleys for long periods, converting them to "death valleys" where fauna cannot live.

Javanese volcanoes erupt more frequently with ash than with lava and when lava flows it is generally basic, so that soils on the lava and on alluvial ash derived from the lava, contain high proportions of calcium, nitrogen, magnesium and phosphorus in soluble form, to the great benefit of agriculture. Erosion, especially as great landslips, is, however, severe, because the ash is unconsolidated, the slopes steep and the rainfall heavy. All these features mean that the landscape form close to the volcanoes is abrupt and severely scored, unrelieved round the active vents by vegetation cover.

Goenong Merapi (fire-mountain, a common local term for volcanoes) may be cited as example of one of Java's most destructive volcanoes (Fig. 73). Nearly 10,000 ft. high now, it was continuously active for long periods over the last hundred years. To the north, within a few miles, there towers another cone, Merbaboe. On its other side, Merapi slopes into the teeming, fertile and congested plains of Magelang, Jogjakarta and Soerakarta where intensive agriculture has been possible on the volcanic ash spread out by the torrents. Farmers push their settlements and their terraces of rice to within a

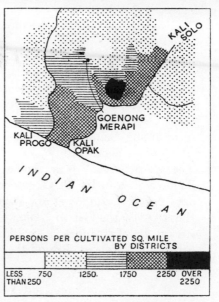

PERSONS PER CULTIVATED SQ. MILE BY DISTRICTS

| LESS THAN 250 | 750 | 1250. | 1750 | 2250 | OVER 2250 |

FIG. 73.—The Irregular Nutritional Densities on the Flanks of G. Merapi. These probably relate to the prevailing wind direction (from northeast) at time of ejection

few miles of the vent, so that the regular lahars, ladoes, avalanches and eruptions may cause heavy destruction of life and property. Nevertheless farmers press back again on the devastated hillsides whatever the risk, so great is the value of the volcanic soils. Close observation is kept on this volcano and siren warnings are given to the population at critical times.

The volcanic axis is inland, with the exception of Karang in Bantam and Moeria in Rembang which are volcanic outliers within a few miles of the coast. Lavas, however, reach the coast at points south of the Madoera Strait and at Wijnkoops Bay (South Bantam). In West Java the volcanoes are arranged in a loop enclosing the Bandoeng and Garoet Basins which were lake-filled at one time owing to the obstruction of volcanic outpourings. In East Java too, the vents form a continuous group, but in Middle Java the volcanoes are in twos or threes, separated by sedimentary uplands. Most volcanoes are distributed along the medial trough which their ejecta have obliterated at many points. Only the volcanoes of South Bantam erupt acidic lavas, largely explaining the low fertility and thin agriculture on the flanks of Bantam volcanoes (Fig. 75).

The Bandoeng and Garoet Basins merit special attention because an intensive agriculture had developed within them.

(a) Formerly a lake, the Bandoeng Basin, now about 800 ft. above sea level, is drained westward by the Tjitaroem which has a gorge marking its break through the ring of volcanoes surrounding Bandoeng. Small lakes still stand in the basin which has a high fertility.

(b) The Garoet Basin is a similar feature separated from the Bandoeng Basin by G. Goentoer lavas. The two basins may have been continuous at one stage. Floored by fertile volcanic alluvial soils, the Garoet Basin still has vestigial lakes. Its main stream, the Tjimanock, leaves it by a deep gorge through the encircling volcanoes. Round the Garoet are numerous tea and cinchona plantations.

THE NORTHERN ALLUVIAL BELT

Here the water-transported debris of the volcanic interior has been spread out, concealing the Sunda Platform and forming the floor of the shallow Java Sea which is steadily being reclaimed by natural sedimentation and by cultivators pressing seawards with their skilful reclamation methods. These alluvials form a fertile coastal belt west of Semarang and continue eastwards as the depression occupied by the middle Loesi-Solo rivers. Eastwards from Merapi, too, the isolated groups of volcanic cones are surrounded by alluvium. The portion of the alluvial belt to the north may be divided into two parts. The inner portion, closer to the uplands, is lined by low terraces roughly parallel to the coast, marking pausing levels in the progressive uplift associated with Java's recent tectonic history. The outer and later alluvials are flat and less than 50 feet above the sea. Between these two alluvials is a distinct terrace or break of slope though the transition is gentle in some places. Settlement, as at Bekasi for example, tend to concentrate at this break of slope, which is healthier and safer from flood than the lower alluvials. It attracts railways (the Jakarta-Cheribon Railway) and roads for the same reason. The lower alluvium is given over very largely to rice, with elaborate drainage, irrigation and water control channels threading the landscape and acting also as lines of settlement and transport. Rapid delta formation is still taking place at a rate increasing temporarily whenever there is an outburst of volcanic activity in the interior to provide heavy loads of ash for the rivers (Fig. 19).

The inner belt of alluvial terraces is not continuous, varying from gulfs reaching inland almost to Bogor to complete disappearance, as in the Tjitaroem Valley. The upper alluvials rise in places to altitudes of 300 ft., providing a diversified landscape due to the incision of watercourses below the terrace level. Rice occupies much less of this upper surface, which must be irrigated artificially to control the run-off. Many plantations have been set in this area which has a more scattered, evenly distributed population than the lower and younger alluvials nearer the coast.

The Loesi-Solo Depression, drained both eastwards and westwards by the two rivers after which it takes its name, has an almost imperceptible watershed and a confused meandering drainage system through a number of swamps and lakes (often used as fishponds (Fig. 77).) Large areas of it are under paddy, but the several limestone islands jutting through it have a teak forest cover. A fair density of people runs right through the Depression, especially along the Solo, whose banks carry almost continuous villages.

Among the volcanoes east of Merapi, the transported alluvial filling between the vents has formed zones of major human interest because they have been nurseries of Javanese culture and tradition. Large principalities grew up there on the basis of intensive agriculture:

(a) *The Soerakarta Basin,* part of the Solo Valley, lies between the volcanoes Merapi and Lawoe and is scored by streams so that its intensive agriculture depends upon elaborate artificial terracing to produce rice and sugar. This is one of the highly productive areas, whose soil has been frequently renewed by Merapi ash (Fig. 73).

(b) *The Madioen Basin* between Lawoe and Wilis-gebergte is narrow and flatter, enabling it to be well covered with permanently irrigated paddyfields. Terraces have in addition been pressed up the sides of the Basin to heights of 3,000 ft. on Lawoe. This Basin ends sharply to the south against a wall-like range of sedimentaries. To the north is the Solo River which the Madioen River joins just before it enters its narrow course through the northern range of sedimentaries.

(c) Discontinuous with the Soerakarta and Madioen troughs, *the Kediri Basin* is twofold. An upper part, the narrow plain of Toeloengagoeng, lies at the foot of the Popoh-Sipelot limestone platform. The lower section, below a bottleneck at the town of Kediri, broadens northwards and eastwards into one of the most fertile rice and sugar districts of Java, with terraces carved along its sides far up the adjoining mountains. The eastern loop of the Basin, often known as the Brantas Plain, continues to the Madoera Strait, the lower, younger alluvials round the Strait being lined with fishponds.

(d) *The Malang Basin*, communicating by the middle Brantas Valley with the Kediri Basin, is unlike the other intravolcanic basins in broadening to the south. It is probably an old lake basin (cf. Bandoeng) whose floor is more concave than flat, at about 1,200 ft. above sea level. There is no easy way through from this basin to the south coast and the direct road and rail route north to the Madoera Strait has been difficult owing to the steep slopes.

THE LIMESTONE PLATFORM OF REMBANG AND MADOERA

The north coast limestones of Rembang and Madoera give East Java a coast unlike that farther west. These massive limestones repeat the karst character of their counterparts on the south coast:

(a) A very narrow fringe of alluvial plain lines the Rembang-Bodjonegoro coast and the cliff-like limestone hills press well to the north. Much of the Rembang limestone, of which considerable areas exceed 900 ft., is covered with teak forests and there are oilfields south of Rembang itself. The width of the limestone is greatest towards the middle, tapering to a mere two miles near Brondang, where it approaches closest to the coast. Several roads and light railways cross this limestone which is in general an area of negative human interest.

(b) In the extensions of this limestone into Madoera, the alluvial fringe is discontinuous. Only small embayments of alluvium separate the steep limestone cliffs. Flat-topped limestone at heights of 800 ft. is nearly continuous over Madoera. Undualting relief develops upon the marly sedimentaries which

form a low central longitudinal belt through the middle of the
island, yet rivers frequently run right across the island from
north to south, little influenced by the marly depression.
Most of Madoera has a barren aspect and its vegetation is
distinctly deciduous owing to the East Monsoon drought.
Farming concentrates in three alluvial pockets on the southern
coast but most activity centres on coastal saltpans and fishponds.

RIVER SYSTEMS

About two-thirds of Java drains north to the Java Sea as a consequence of the watershed lying well to the south. From Jogjakarta to G. Mohomeroe the watershed is actually only a few
miles from the Indian Ocean. The relatively simple pattern of
the rivers is complicated in detail by (*a*) radial drainage from the
volcanoes, (*b*) old lake basins and the medial trough, which break
the symmetry of streams flowing meridionally, (*c*) the E-W. fault
and fold systems, which impose their lines on the rivers to make
dislocated trellis patterns. The longest rivers are in the middle-
east where Java is broadest. The Solo drains over 600 square miles.
The Brantas is curious for turning at some place in its 340 mile
course towards every point of the compass. Javanese streams vary
tremendously in volume at different seasons, accounting in part
for their heavy deposits at the coast. They have greatest volume
from October to May when rains are heaviest, bringing floods
from the torrential downpours and from the overflowing streams,
despite elaborate engineering precautions. From May to September is a dry season, most pronounced in East Java, when rivers
are low and desiccation prepares the soil for rapid erosion after
rains begin again. Some Javanese streams have been proved to
denude their basins in a day of torrential rain by as much as the
Marne denudes its basin in two centuries. Part of the heavy load
forms a network of levees across the northern plains.

CLIMATE

Well into the southern hemisphere, Java receives its wind-
seasons from directions differing from those of the rest of Southeast Asia. The northern tropical air arrives as northwest or
westerly winds bringing equatorial downpours from October to
May, which is a wet season throughout Java, rainshadow effects

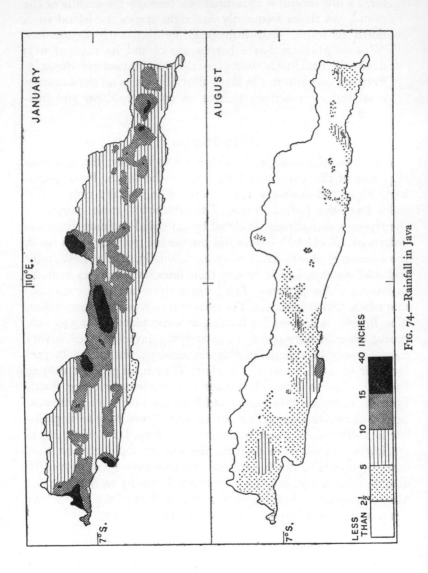

Fig. 74.—Rainfall in Java

being negligible because the high relief is conical rather than in ranges. Southern tropical air remains as southeast or easterly winds which bring to East Java a pronounced drought from these warm latitudes (Fig. 74).

JAVA: AVERAGE RAINFALL (inches)

	Rain days (over	*Jan.*	*Feb.*	*Mar.*	*Apr.*	*May*	*June*	*July*	*Aug.*	*Sept.*	*Oct.*	*Nov.*	*Dec.*	*Total*
Jakarta (26ft.)	138	11.9	13.4	8.0	5.6	4.1	3.7	2.6	1.6	2.8	4.5	5.7	7.6	71.5
Pasoeroean (16 ft.)	94	9.6	11.8	8.0	5.2	3.5	2.3	1.1	0.2	0.3	0.8	2.5	6.3	51.6
Tosari (5,692 ft.)	142	12.4	14.6	10.8	6.9	4.6	3.3	1.5	1.1	1.0	3.4	7.8	11.8	79.2
Bandoeng (2,395 ft.)	146	7.6	7.7	9.2	9.2	5.2	3.7	2.5	2.2	3.5	6.6	9.2	8.7	75.3

Among the western mountains, particularly on the southern side, this drought is less pronounced. Rains come in violent thunderstorms which reach a peak to the north in December and to the south in May. The dry season has long sunshine periods, a factor encouraging intensive farming. Yearly rains vary considerably; in Bantam, averages above 160 in. per annum are common, while the north Cheribon Plain receives less than 40 in. per annum and all the northeast plains from 40 in. to 80 in. per annum.

FORESTS

Although about a quarter of Java is still forested (Fig. 75), the high population density implies that forest gives way to agriculture where at all practicable. Commercially the Javanese forests are of interest for the teak-growing on the porous and infertile limestone soils of Rembang, Semarang, Madioen and Kediri. This timber is extracted chiefly for local use, so that Java's teak export has steadily declined.

Chapter Fourteen

THE EAST INDIES

THE WESTERN ARCHIPELAGO: THE CULTURAL AND SOCIAL LANDSCAPE OF JAVA

JAVA has for over three centuries been associated with agricultural conceptions brought by the Dutch who imposed cash farming upon the agricultural systems traditional to the country. For most of the colonial period, this western influence aimed to obtain from Java exportable agricultural products rather than minerals, and to procure them through local farmers rather than from European plantations, although these gradually appeared. Dutch techniques have largely been responsible for the great intensity and variety of Javanese cultivation, unequalled in any other unit of Southeast Asia and representing a tropical variant upon the intensive horticultural style evolved by the Dutch in Europe. The possibilities could not have been realised had it not been for the soil conditions of Java which are largely derived, both inland among the mountains and along the coast on the river-transported alluvials, from volcanic ash of basic character which weathers to a soil of high fertility and is constantly renewed by further ejecta from the volcanoes. The importance of this renewal is evident on the flanks of Merapi, for example, which show the most intensive agriculture and densest populations where the winds prevailing at the time of ejection have deposited the ash, the windward sides being distinctly less cultivated and less populated (Fig. 73). Zones of sustained fertility are zones of constant soil renewal—hence the pressure of farming to areas as close as possible to the cones where ash deposition is most frequent, and also to those alluvial areas where streams are bringing silt from the new ash on the volcanic uplands.

These circumstances, the physical and the traditional, combine to make Java the most outstanding example of a mixed agriculture, aiming both at subsistence and at cash sales (Fig. 76). Indigenous agriculture has gradually adopted some of the crops for export which were first introduced and cultivated on highly capitalised plantations, creating rival systems of production.

By now, shifting cultivation has nearly disappeared from Java and farming has become sedentary, though the *"desa"* system, under which communal land is periodically redistributed and re-assigned to individual village cultivators, may be seen as a continuation of principles once evolved among shifting cultivators. Except in the wetter, cloudier west, much land is cropped twice a year, and in Semerang and Malang the area cropped is often 50 per cent more than the area farmed, so great is the double cropping.

Much of the variety of crops (Fig. 76) arises from the variety of environments; tea is apt for the wet uplands of the west and sugar for the sunnier irrigated lands of the east; the flat lowlands of the north suit paddy growing, which is practised in a continuous belt from one end of north Java to the other, broken only by the teak-covered limestone plateaux, as at Rembang. To supplement the inadequate rice production for so teeming a population, tapioca and maize

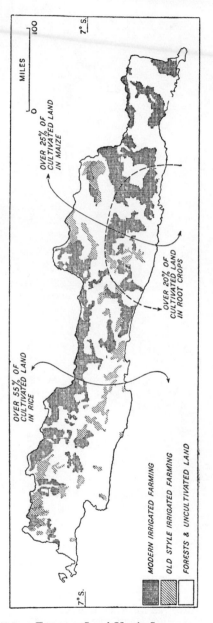

FIG. 75.—Land Use in Java

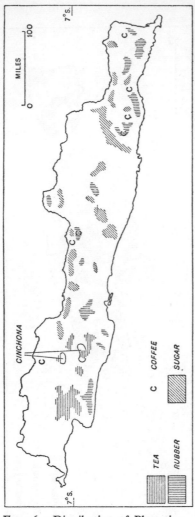

FIG. 76.—Distribution of Plantation Crops in Java

are widely grown as second crops, even exceeding the area under rice, along the northeast coast and in the eastern intra-volcanic basins. Pulses are extensively but unevenly distributed. Of the cash crops, sugar has for many years been the mainstay, grown at times on almost all village paddy-lands from Cheribon eastwards, wherever permanent irrigation is possible. Sugar has become an integral part of village farming as well as of permanent European plantations (Fig. 76). Because religion, social custom, tradition and family life are all intimately tied into the ecology of indigenous farming, to make agricultural innovations is extremely difficult and extremely slow. To have established such an innovation as commercial sugar growing by smallholders and to have obtained exportable produce from them has been accepted as a mark of Dutch administrative success in Java. European plantations and indigenous farming systems went on simultaneously, but the latter were supplying about a fifth of the 1965 output of 650,000 tons, and it is a local policy to increase smallholdings of sugar. Sugar for a time entirely displaced spices, the chief trading interest of the first Europeans in this region, as the key agricultural export. Here, as in other tropical areas, the huge and rapid production of the tropics quickly tends to saturate the market, so that sugar later slumped and lost importance in Java, where its acreage in 1963 was, however, about 50 per cent greater than in 1951.

Though the island has had a significance in agricultural exports out of proportion to its size, subsistence agriculture is still dominant. In 1956, about 20 million acres were farmed for local foods and only one million acres for export crops, which, however, were valued at a large proportion of all exports from the East Indies. Few commercial crops could be called exclusively European or exclusively Javanese, but rice, by far the largest single crop, is almost entirely produced by Javanese. Sugar, tea, cinchona and oil palm are mostly plantation grown, pepper comes generally from local farmers, while tapioca and coconuts are grown roughly equally by plantations and by smallholders. The Javanese did not at first take up rubber smallholdings and by 1937 practically all rubber from Java was plantation grown— a great contrast with conditions on the other islands and due to the preoccupation of farmers in Java with more immediately necessary food crops, whereas the other islands had much cheap virgin land; by now many European estates have been sub-divided.

The staple food crops of Java are invariably irrigated and the cultivated landscape is extensively bunded, serving to prevent soil erosion and to conserve soil qualities. The torrential rains, loose topsoil and steep relief would otherwise cause quick erosion. The elaborate terracing of the loose ash on the side of volcanic uplands is thus a soil conservation necessity as well as a device for water control and an expression of population density. Much ingenuity with limited means has been shown by Javanese farmers whose irrigation methods are of great antiquity but still very effective. Large modern irrigation systems have been built by the Dutch to cope with violent, erratic or entrenched streams beyond control by older methods. Over $2\frac{3}{4}$ million acres are irrigated with modern canals from the Tjimanoek, Tjitaroem and Brantas rivers, and 6 million acres with native systems.

PATTERNS AND METHODS OF FOOD CULTIVATION

Of about 20 million acres cultivated by local farmers in annual crops, 52 per cent is in wet paddy, 25 per cent in maize and 18 per cent in tropical root crops (yams and tapioca), the latter an association with the root agricultures of Central Pacific islands. Groundnuts and soya have greatly increased in acreage since 1952.

So closely has wet paddy-growing become integrated with local farming that *sawah*, the Javanese word for it, is used to mean farming in general. A fluctuating total of about 4 million tons of rice is produced each normal year and eaten within the island. The amount of rice produced often reflects the general economic condition, so that greater profits in export crops cause less cultivation of rice. When sugar for export slumped over the period 1930–37, sugar land reverted to rice cultivation, whose total annual acreage over that period increased by 1.2 million to 9 million in Java alone. To this extent the agriculture of Java is more fluid, versatile and responsive than is the case with most countries of Southeast Asia, certainly more so than in other tropical sugar-growing regions. The average yield of rice (1,000 lbs. per acre) is usually higher than any state in Southeast Asia, except Malaysia varying considerably within Java and being highest in the east.

While the greatest production of rice comes from wet lands, which are most abundant in the Cheribon and Pekalongan Residencies, one-sixth of the total paddy acreage is dry, a technique concentrated in the Jogjakarta, Bantam and South Bogor areas. This older method yields less than two-thirds of the wet method and the increase of dry paddy over the last decade indicates considerable pressure on food crops and the full use already being made of irrigable land. Dry paddy farming exhausts soil far quicker than the wet method and it cannot be continued indefinitely on the same patch of land.

The methods of ploughing, planting and harvesting paddy in Java differ little from the hand methods of the rest of Southeast Asia. Most processing of the grain is also by hand, only a small proportion leaving any one locality to go to middlemen for mechanical milling by Chinese firms, For the heavy work of reaping, local labour is sufficient, the whole community participating if necessary and sometimes taking for the service a percentage of the harvest (varying from 10 per cent to 20 per cent). Essentially a cooperative communal activity in each village, Javanese rice farming still uses systems of common seedbeds and communal seedstores. Often the payment in kind for reaping services goes into a community pool.

Because of the double cropping and of the great variety of local conditions, the rhythm of activity is more spread than usual elsewhere. Rice seed begins to be sown in October for the West

Monsoon rains. Transplanting may be deferred until January or February. The harvest takes place 3½ to 6 months after transplanting. January is the peak sowing month for Java as a whole, but some sowing goes on in parts of Java every month. Similarly, the harvesting peak occurs in May and June, although havesting takes place in one district or another throughout the year.

Tapioca has been occupying about one-tenth of Java's cultivated area and, besides being an important local supplementary food, it is exported (supplying three-quarters of the world's prewar needs) for industrial starch, gums and textile sizes. The woody refuse after the starch has been extracted is used as cattle fodder.

About a quarter of the cultivated area is under maize, which is eaten in large quantities by the Javanese, and exported to nearby islands, in at least one of which (Timor) it is a staple food.

In 1940 Java and Madoera produced 6.1 million tons of paddy in the ear from wet lands and .5 million tons from dry lands, a total of 4.2 million tons of clean rice. While, however, this production (80 kgms. per person) was not adequate for direct consumption by the Javanese, who ate 86 kgms. per person each year over 1936–40, there was an export of finer grades to Sumatra, Sulawesi and Borneo and an import of poorer rice from Thailand.

Java's postwar rice situation has been precarious. Official reports for 1957 showed a paddy acreage of 10.5 million (one-eighth higher than prewar) and over one-sixth rice in production, but importing rice has become a chronic feature of Java's economy which brought in 1.3 million tons of rice for 1963.

CULTIVATION FOR EXPORT

Sugar occupied about 650,000 acres in 1931, 65,000 acres in 1935, 240,000 in 1940, almost ceased in 1945, and was 270,000 in 1964. This great fluctuation in acreage and of labour demand resulted from external prices and the varying impact of international control. It missed causing a rural catastrophe in Java only because of the method of farming. Sugar is by nature a crop of the wet lowlands, of land suitable for rice. A three-year rotation system was normally used by which the planters, at first European, rented acreage for sugar from local farmers, who did the cultivating and harvesting for the planter at wages and between-times cultivated the rest of their land in the usual subsistence food crops. Thus in years of bad external sugar prices it was not a matter of sugar lands going out of cultivation, but of the land being put to other uses by the local farmer. Radically different from conditions in the West Indies, this is a relic of last century's "Culture System" of forced cultivation for the government, a system which, whatever its social effects, successfully produced large quantities of sugar, then the mainstay of exports. Sugar is a long-term crop compared with most of those in Java: it is planted between April and October under the planter's supervision for harvesting after twelve months. The heavy demand for labour at cutting time is readily met because the plantation is invariably in densely populated lowlands; altogether about 60,000 temporary wage earners were used for sugar plantations in 1940. Across the sugar-growing lowlands, light railways have been built to bring the cane to the mills. Before 1929, Java had 179 sugar mills, 47 in 1940 and 25 in 1965, when estates had only 80,000 acres under sugar.

Produced by combining estate and smallholder methods, Java's sugar went mostly to Britain and India, owing to the expansion of a protected beet-sugar industry in Holland. Javanese farmers also cultivated some sugar on their own account, obtaining lower-grade sugars for local consumption and not using the mills owned by the large planters. Local cultivation of sugar was a steadily expanding business and Javanese consumption was rising. The smallholder may ultimately set the character of this industry, much as rubber smallholders tend to do elsewhere.

Over the inter-war years, Javanese sugar production underwent changes as abrupt as in the acreage involved. It dropped from 2.9 million tons in 1930 to less than half a million tons in 1936, and rose to 1.4 million tons by 1939 when India alone was taking about half a million tons from Java. It was evident before 1941 that, from being a producer of food products for Europe, Java was becoming a producer for the countries of Asia, a tendency which is becoming more apparent as time goes on. For 1949 the exports of sugar from Java were barely one-seventh of those of 1938, evidence of stagnation and destruction which have taken so long to rectify that other tropical producers are eliminating old markets for Java's sugar (650,000 tons output 1965).

Coffee and tea have at different times been the incentive to planters for export from Java. Coffee became highly speculative and proved very susceptible to devastating disease, besides quickly

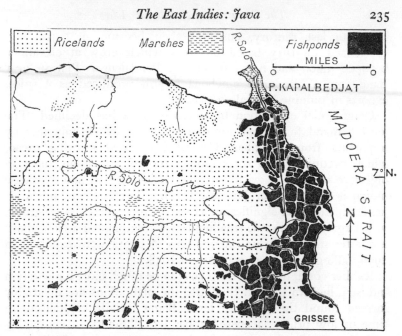

FIG. 77.—Land Utilisation at the Mouth of the Solo River

exhausting the soil, so that, after being forcibly introduced under the Culture System, it has become a crop of smallholders who produced barely 45,000 tons in 1961. Tea, begun as a British plantation interest in Java, particularly in the cool, rainy Preanger Highlands, because the tea bush is limited to areas whose driest month has not less than 20 rainy days, to a great extent displaced the older Dutch coffee trade. Some 85,000 lbs. of tea were being produced annually before 1941, local smallholders supplying about 15 per cent which they sold green to the planters for processing. In 1965 tea estates in Java produced 46,300 tons using only 14 factories: smallholders produced almost as much. Individual tea factories were slowly re-established and cooperative processing is becoming the normal. A change of direction in exports has appeared; instead of two-thirds of the Java tea going to U.K. and U.S.A., nearly half the output is going to other Southeast Asia territories. Smallholders grow tobacco in eastern *sawah* and produced 410,000 tons of groundnuts in 1963.

Cinchona, whose bark is the basis of quinine, has had a varied success. Nearly stifled commercially by a monopolistic buying ring late last century, cinchona then became an expanding, specialised industry based on trees which grow at elevations between 3,000 and 6,500 ft. on the Pengalengan Plateau near Bandoeng. While some cinchona is still produced as a spice, exports of quinine have almost ceased.

Commercial cultivation of spices in Java has declined. The local demand for cloves, for example, is more cheaply met by importing from Zanzibar. Central Java tried growing cacao, which occupies 3,900 acres (1965). Indigo cultivation, once an objective of Dutch agricultural policy, has ceased and synthetic indigo is imported for Javanese textiles. The coconut, however, has assumed major significance as a cash crop. Coconuts are grown very largely by Javanese smallholders whose planted area is about a quarter million acres; 189,000 tons of copra were exported in 1956, falling away to 44,000 tons in 1958.

Rubber continued even until 1965 to be much more a plantation industry in Java than in Sumatra; the plantations are invariably located round the 1,500 ft. level. Being heavily capitalised, in time of low prices Javanese rubber has difficulty in competing with the smallholder production in other parts of the Indies and with crops in other parts of Java. Plantations were occupying 1.4 million acres of Java and Madoera, of which area 41 per cent was in rubber, 19 per cent in tea and 17 per cent in coffee. Java's production of rubber was over 90,000 tons in 1937 and 107,000 tons in 1956, since when estates found it difficult to continue.

Because cattle are necessary as draught animals for fields and local transport, they are reared for this purpose and serve as peasant investments as well. Over 5 million cattle (40 per cent buffaloes) are distributed rather unevenly over Java and Madoera. This represents a cattle density of over 100 per square mile in Java and over 300 per square mile in Madoera where some districts have a density equalling that of European cattle-breeding regions. Buffaloes are preferred in the damper, cloudier west where rough haulage has to be done, while oxen are more numerous in the rice areas of the east. Cattle breeding is a widespread minor occupation and in Bantam and Preanger large herds are kept. Madoera is a major centre of the cattle trade, exporting over 90,000 annually for meat as well as large numbers for draught in the nearby islands.

INDUSTRIALISATION

As a development of this century, a considerable amount of industrialisation has proved possible by extending the domestic industries already existing and by village industries of a type developed in Japan. European-style factories employed farm labourers at off-seasons to process sugar, rice and tapioca or to weave imported cotton. Rubber manufacturing, including tyres, is going on in a total of 70 factories. In Madoera large-scale salt extraction developed to take advantage of the high evaporation rate and the large market in Java whose salt output was 445,000 tons in 1963. Industrial self-sufficiency is aimed at despite technical difficulties and foreign competition. To this end textile mills are encouraged. In 1965, 75 mills produced 56 million yards of cloth, sarongs and towels being the specialities.

Extractive industries of Western pattern were based on the manganese ores of Jogjakarta and Preanger, on sulphur from various craters (as a Kawah Poetih), on iodine springs at Soerabaya and on the china clay of Preanger. About 66,000 tons of petroleum are being produced from old wells in Rembang and Soerabaya, and oil refining is done at Tjepoe Wonokromo and Kapoean (Blora) for the Java market. Mineral production is, however, a very minor part of Java's activities.

THE CULTURE SYSTEM

The Culture System which strongly influenced the form of agriculture in Java was operated by the Dutch after the Dutch East India Company failed by other means to obtain a substantial export of agricultural products. Introduced in 1830 and withdrawn in 1870, this system, an unusual one for colonial territories, compelled Javanese farmers to give a part of their land and their labour for cultivating, under Dutch supervision, prescribed export crops (sugar, coffee, indigo) to be sold in Europe for the benefit of the Dutch Government. By thus treating Java for a period as a money-making concern, the Dutch Government soon obtained a huge revenue surplus, for the first time in Java's colonial history. More important in the long run, the system incidentally taught the Javanese new types of intensive cultivation and an understanding of the principles, new to Java, of large-scale agriculture for export. It proved a very heavy tax on the fertility of soils and on the families which had to provide labour, to the extent of impeding subsistence farming, so that the Culture System offended the spirit of the times and was soon resented in Europe no less than in Java. Although at maximum it only affected five per cent of Java's cultivated area, it led to new cash crops, and planters (for sugar see p. 233) continued to cultivate on lines established by the Culture System long after it had been abolished. Coffee, sugar and indigo, the objectives of Dutch policy, soon faced depressions due to rival producers in Europe (beet sugar) and elsewhere in the tropics, so that an increasingly diversified and more scientific type of planting had to be adopted.

One of the reasons for imposing the Culture System had been the Javanese tradition that the village or tribe has land rights as a community, a tradition admirably suiting the interests of self-contained communities but not of exporters. Hereditary personal possession of land has gradually displaced the periodical redistribution of communal land, an old tradition persisting in some areas. While in 1882 only 18 per cent of villages followed the personal property land system, 39 per cent did so in 1927 and the rest redistributed land at various intervals. One effect of the Culture System was to establish among Javanese the idea that personal land owning is a heavy burden. The regular subdivision of agricultural land by sharing among the huge rural population has produced very small farms and the average farm rapidly diminished in size as the population increased. In 1930 the average holding of wet and dry land together was 2.45 acres, decreasing to 1.7 acres in 1965. So closely is farming and subsistence integrated with social and religious life that only in very recent years, as a long term effect of the introduction of money crops, has there been much sign of Javanese farmland falling into the hands of absentee mortgagors.

POPULATION PATTERNS

One of the most densely populated islands of the world, Java by 1966 contained at least 71 million people with twelve cities of over 100,000 each (Fig. 78). Within the island many localities have even greater congestions. In the states of Soerakarta and Jogjakarta, over 3,500 people live on each square mile; these very dense regions are directly associated with wet paddy which occupies more than 40 per cent of their surface. Southern Bantam and the southeast corner of Besoeki, which are dry or infertile areas, show on the population map a density averaging less than 350 persons per square mile.

The reasons for this concentration of people are complicated and manifold. No one reason is significant on its own. Propitious climate, constantly rejuvenated basic volcanic soils and extensive irrigable lowlands suiting rice, provide the physical basis. Long association with western methods and interests has led to a remarkable interlocking of subsistence and cash crops, combining oriental and western techniques which have here achieved a balance. Java had until 1941 an exceptionally long period of social security coupled with the increasing communal stabilisation by major irrigation and drainage systems. The Culture System, short-lived though it was, proved to be an incentive to population increase, because it placed on the community a pressure to obtain extra hands, so that towards the end of the Culture System period population was increasing at the then fantastic rate of 33 per cent per decade.

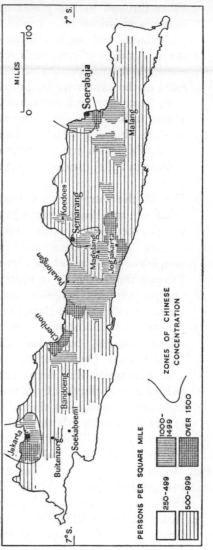

FIG. 78.—The Distribution of People in Java

The population concentrates in three zones

1. Throughout the northern alluvial plain, from the Jakarta

Plain through to the plains of Probolinggo and Pasoeroean, dense populations have grown up in association with the wet paddylands and sugar cultivation. In this belt are Adiwerno (near Tegal), a district with 6,500 persons to the square mile, the highest rural density anywhere in Java; and also the chief exits of the export trade, Jakarta (3.1 million in 1963), Cheribon, Semarang and Sourabaya. Jakarta, the original base for Dutch influence in the archipelago, now lies too far inland for modern shipping which is handled at its outport, Tandjong Priok. Of Java's 800,000 tons exports (1961), Sourabaya (1.3 million in 1962) handles 40 per cent and Tandjong Priok 20 per cent.

2. Within the intra-volcanic basins of Central Java (the Solo, Madioen, and Brantas basins) lives about a third of the Javanese people, occupied almost entirely in agriculture, the urban centres of Jogjakarta and Soerakarta (each over 350,000 people) containing only a very small proportion of the people. Despite the frequency of eruptions causing heavy losses of life and property, the volcanoes are ringed by crowded villages and farms pressing up the slopes to the newer ash deposits.

3. Subsidiary concentrations of people are in the Bandoeng-Garoet Basins, connected with plantation agriculture on western lines. On the south coast the only densely populated zone is between Kali Serajoe and Kali Progo, where a narrow belt of deltaic alluvials from the Central Java volcanoes permits a rural life resembling that of the northern alluvial plains and extending southwards the high densities common to the intro-volcanic basins. Tjilitjap, the only fairly deep-watered harbour on the South Coast and sheltered from the violence of Indian Ocean storms by the Noesa Kambangan, is an outlet for the southern portion of densely-populated Central Java. Its trade is mainly sugar and tapioca for export (52,000 tons, 1961).

4. Although the relief of Madoera consists predominantly of dry limestone, its few coastal plains are highly productive, and it sustains an average density of 1,300 per square mile, which is higher than the average for all Java. The medial trough is barren and thinly peopled, but elsewhere rice, maize and tobacco-growing, cattle-rearing and salt production are important activities. From Madoera there is steady migration into Java to relieve the pressure of population.

These zones of concentrated population and agricultural activity are linked by roads and railways threading the northern plain, with offshoots southwards into the fertile intro-volcanic basins and to the Tjilitjap. Few patches of Java are over ten miles from a road or railway, which, with the ample coastwise shipping, give Java a close, poorly maintained transport system.

On Java, river and canal bank settlements occur in lines upon all the rice-growing plains. Along both north and south coasts are linear sand-dune and sandspit settlements, with further linear settlement on the old marine terraces. Girdles of villages surround the cones of basic volcanoes. Defensive stockades disappeared after centuries of policing, yet may be used again to meet modern conditions. Cattle pens are unusual on the village landscape except in the breeding areas of Madoera. Javanese houses are bamboo and thatch structures without stilts, differing from Malay-Burmese house forms.

Two Javanese cities, Jakarta and Sourabaya, are of "million" rank and ten others exceed 100,000, with 8 million people thus urbanised.

JAVANESE PEOPLES

The people of Java are more homogeneous than those of neighbouring territories. Only three main languages are used, permitting the diffusion of literary, musical and plastic arts which over centuries have reached and maintained very high standards and continue to play an intimate part in Indonesian social and cultural life. Justifiable pride in this culture, modified to some extent by Islamic influence, is the basis of Javanese nationalism, to which the communal system adds the preference for the communal solution of difficulties, and which expresses at the same time the urgencies arising from a teeming population in a territory now closer to the limits of its capacity to support people.

There are distinctions between the Javanese, the most numerous group, whose homeland is the eastern two-thirds of the island, the Sundanese of the west, and the Madoerese, who spread into Java from their own congested island. Among Javanese, the Hindu and Buddhist influence of the first millennium Indian colonisation period, whose stone monuments are at Borobodur, Blitar and Kedoes, expresses itself in many ways, not least as the aristocratic tradition and as the self-contained community of the *desa* or village. Upon these smouldering traditions is imposed the different communalism of Islam. Sundanese people speak another language and show their cheerier outlook by using brighter coloured clothes. Their villages are characteristically broken into small hamlets and their cultural development is not considered to have reached Javanese standards. The Madoerese are dour, dogged and more individualist than the Javanese, befitting their function as the chief cattlemen of Southeast Asia and their origins on an island where it is a struggle to survive.

Though the population is extremely dense, it has led to only a trickle of migration from Java to the other islands, despite the increasing difficulties of living in Java. Pressure of population has been met so far by increasing the intensity of agricultural production, by pushing cultivation to the maximum within Java, and by industrialisation.

IMMIGRANTS

While Java has itself a great indigenous population, more than 500,000 Chinese have settled there, their presence dating from the very early days of Dutch colonial activity, when local labour could not be detached from its own ecology and Chinese were brought in for sugar plantation work. Since then Chinese have become a key community of urban middlemen and shopkeepers and they play a large part in inter-island commodity trade. One-third of Java's Chinese live in Jakarta, Semarang and Soerabaya, indicating their association with external trade. Most of the Chinese retain associations with China, to which they have expected to return. In addition, about 50,000 Arabs, mainly Hadramautis, live in Java, engaged also as middlemen, but tending to merge with the Javanese by marriage. They are highly respected for religious reasons and cause a large traffic in religious pilgrimages between Java and the Arab Countries.

Unique in Southeast Asia colonial developments was the settlement on Java of nearly 200,000 Dutch citizens. Until 1870, only Dutch officials lived there, but from then onwards permanent migration of Dutch people steadily increased until 1940. The Dutch chiefly settled in Jakarta, Bogor and Bandoeng, working as officials, traders, professional men and primary producers. Independence reduced this group to 10,000, which included Indo-Dutch Eurasians or "Indos", who have not all left.

Java escaped most of the effects of large-scale immigration of temporary foreign labourers and its cultural landscape has retained the character of a mature indigenous life well adjusted to and traditionally corporate with its environment. Having multiplied ten times 1815–1930, the people of Java were obliged to pioneer in quite a different manner from those of Malaysia and Burma—by developing an extended, intensified and diversified farming combining both subsistence and cash economies.

THE POST-1946 PHASE

After 1946, Java experienced a revolutionary breakdown involving upheavals of a kind it had escaped in the war period. Commercial agriculture came to a stop, many factories were destroyed, transport collapsed and central control ceased. Long-standing regionalisms reasserted themselves in the guise of petty autonomies, revived chieftaincies and gangsterism (see p. 258). Dutch technical cadres disappeared faster than Indonesians could make up from their own ranks. Financial collapse (see p. 197 for currency) was for a time staved off by restriction of tin and rubber dealings and restricting imports. Huge U.S. aid funds were given but national policy was to be self-contained, except that rice imports from Burma and Thailand had to be substantial to prevent urban distress when the expectation of being self-supporting in food proved ill-founded. Chinese traders were consistently penalised as nationality issues became acute. Political pressure came from China, but racial feeling has not completely eased and some enforced repatriation to China has been going on. By 1952 there were signs of normal external economic relations appearing but internal administrative and social machinery has not been rehabilitated. All ties between the Dutch and Indonesian governments ceased after 1955 and were only partly renewed in 1964. Even in early 1963 domestic political tensions overshadowed all else to produce an atmosphere of simmering civil unrest and disorder and the embargoes on trade with Malaysia, coupled with trade union violence against foreign businesses, worsened the economy and devalued the currency on the free market. Open civil war occurred in 1965.

The poor trade position in 1964 is shown on p. 379. All domestic statistics from Java must be viewed with reserve.

Chapter Fifteen

THE EAST INDIES

THE WESTERN ARCHIPELAGO: BORNEO

LARGEST of the Sunda Platform land units, Borneo takes its name
from Brunei, the now diminutive west coast sultanate which once
controlled most of the island. It bestrides the Equator and is
predominantly covered with Tropical Rain Forests, merging at
altitudes to great stretches of Mountain Moss Forest and in the
coastal lowlands to Freshwater Swamp Forest and Mangrove
(Fig. 79). Flanked to west and south by shallow seas scarcely
200 ft. deep, Borneo has only a narrow continental platform to
north and east where the sea floor slopes steeply to great depths
of the order 12,000 ft.

BORNEO: AVERAGE RAINFALLS (in inches)

	Rain days (over .02in.)	Jan.	Feb.	Mar.	Apr.	May	June	July	Aug.	Sept.	Oct.	Nov.	Dec.	Total
Sandakan (105 ft.)	—	18.2	10.4	7.9	4.1	5.8	7.4	6.4	7.9	9.5	9.8	14.8	17.4	119.6
Pontianak (10 ft.)	182	10.6	8.5	9.6	11.1	10.7	8.9	6.5	8.6	8.6	14.7	16.1	13.1	127.0
Balikpapan (16 ft.)	137	7.7	7.5	9.0	7.6	8.7	8.3	7.8	6.9	4.8	5.7	6.4	7.5	87.9

Divided for most of a century into a smaller north-western
portion under British influence (North Borneo, Brunei and
Sarawak) and a larger Dutch portion to south and east, the island
has shared little in the innovations and advancements of adjoining
territories. This backwardness is no recent thing, though there is
evidence of very old Chinese interest in NW. Borneo (for pearls
and bird's nests) and of some first millennium Hindu penetration
along South Borneo rivers. Borneo exemplifies today conditions
which four or five centuries ago were probably widespread in the
archipelago and nearby territories. That they persist in Borneo is
due (a) to being off the track of Southeast Asia routes; (b) to low
fertility of its surface and the low sunshine of its climate; (c) to the
non-discovery of any valuable mineral to attract a "rush" deep

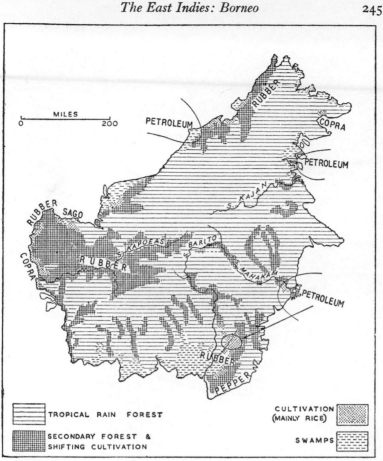

FIG. 79.—Land Use in Borneo

into Borneo; (*d*) to the compactness of the island; (*e*) to the difficulty of approach by Borneo rivers which invariably have shifting bars across their mouths so that even shallow boats can only cross at highwater or, on the east, dangerous barriers of coral reef, and (*f*) to the absence of any strong agricultural tradition among the people.

Over the interior of Borneo moves a scattering of aboriginal peoples, many of whom have not advanced beyond the collecting-hunting stage, and where they practise agriculture it is by the shifting system. Activity and settlement are peripheral (Fig. 80) and the interests centrifugal; even on the coasts the cultural

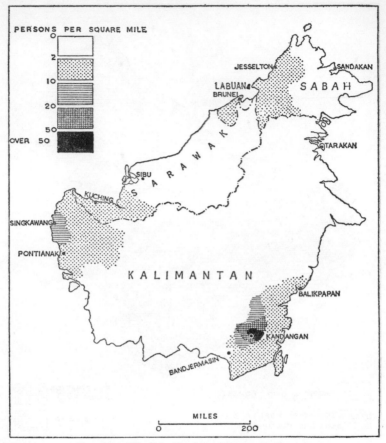

FIG. 80.—The Distribution of People in Borneo

landscape is that of crude tropical pioneering settlements poor-look-
ing and squalid, mostly peopled by immigrant Chinese and Malays
from nearby territories. To the people of the interior applies the
collective name "Dyaks" although they are subdivided into many
groups at widely different cultural levels (Fig. 81). On the coast,
settlements are often like lake dwellings built out over shallow
tidal waters. There is little transport except on the rivers or by
jungle paths. Of 5.9 million people now in Borneo, only 1.4
million are in the north-western sector now called East Malaysia.

The landform, hilly rather than mountainous, and generally
below 6,000 ft., is one of advanced maturity, varying from the

rounded slopes of igneous rocks to the flat-topped interfluves of sandstone country, as in the Madi Plateau, and the striking fretted landscape of limestones, as in the Boelit Valleys, which are covered with vegetation because their porosity is offset by the even and heavy rains. The mountain systems reflect structural lines deriving from old E–W. fold-fault systems with some NNE–SSW. trend lines evident in the long watershed boundary of Inner Sarawak. Round the river mouths spread great swamps upon which the distributaries are constantly dividing and reforming.

Northern Borneo

This region includes Sarawak, Brunei and Sabah (until 1963 called British North Borneo), an area of 80,000 sq. miles, of which 60 per cent is in *Sarawak*, draining mostly by streams to the west and north. The Rejang is the longest river but its great deltaic swamps form an impediment to penetration along it, though Sibu, 60 miles from its mouth, ranks as a port for the 125,000 local people of the Rejang Valley. About 1.4 million people live in Northern Borneo; of these nearly 820,000 are in Sarawak, mostly close to the coast. There are about 170,000 Chinese immigrants and an even larger number of immigrant Malays, the newcomers dominating retail and export trades and working on the oilfields. Kuching, the Sarawak capital, is a river port set away from heavy deltaic silting. Refineries at Lutong, handle part of the oil piped from Seria in Brunei where in 1964, 3.4 million tons crude were obtained from 110 wells. In 1960 the oil output showed first signs of declining. About 166,000 tons bauxite were exported.

Sabah contains 507,000 people (1964), with Muslim seafarers scattered round the coasts. Its chief towns, Jesselton (pop. 12,000) and Sandakan, include many Chinese immigrants.

Brunei, while only a small unit, has continued to be predominantly Malay and very wealthy due to oil exports worth over $170 million in 1964 when the population was 97,000.

This large undeveloped territory was never agriculturally self-sufficient. Brunei produces only a third of its rice needs and Sabah less than half. Chief interest has centred on rubber and coconuts to take advantage of the cheap land, although labour has been a major difficulty. Last century there were attempts at commercial tobacco growing which failed; timber is now its mainstay, accounting for 1.8 million tons of exports which include

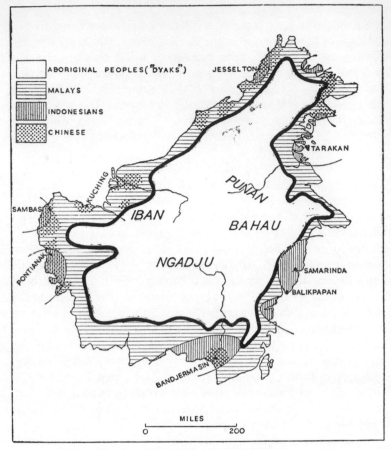

FIG. 81.—Ethnic Distributions in Borneo

70,000 tons rubber. While company plantations of rubber had been started, smallholdings represented an expanding interest, worked in conjunction with rice. For these pioneer areas, statistics are not detailed. Some 290,000 acres altogether are in rubber, mostly in coastal Sabah, which also exported 15,200 tons of copra in 1965. Rice occupies a total of 390,000 acres (1965) in small poorly-kept patches, but recent development schemes intend to create new rice-growing areas in these territories on the basis of imported Chinese labourers, with the object of relieving chronic rice shortages in West Malaysia. Sarawak was always a key sago producer (from 70,000 acres sago) and exported pepper worth $41 million in 1965.

Much pioneer development was destroyed in 1941 but oil wells were speedily rehabilitated to reach by 1959 an output nearly seven times that of 1939. Political skirmishing by both the Philippines and Indonesia occurred 1961–6. 1963 Sabah and Sarawak federated with Malaysia and together form East Malaysia.

KALIMANTAN

The greater area and coast of Indonesian Borneo are responsible for its higher population (4.1 million 1961) which does not indicate any development more intensive than that in Northern Borneo. The population has a slightly different composition on the coast, where there are Bugis from Suluwesi in the southeast, Javanese in the south, and Chinese in their very old settlements at Sambas (where their colony is about 1,000 years old) and Pontianak in the west. Local people who are Muslim are all described as Malays, a term which covers many different types; the others, generally called Dyaks, are tribes of Kajan, Kenja and Bahau in Central Borneo, Ulu, Ngadju in the south and east, together with many nomadic tribes such as the Punan. Among Dyaks strong family ties have replaced the more usual village systems and often the whole of a large family lives in a single "long house," located on ridges and containing what is almost a village of related people.

Only the valleys of the west and southeast are well peopled, and all five towns, Bandjermasin, Pontianak, Balikpapan, Tarakan and Tandoengseilor are coastal, containing over 25,000 people each. Round Pontianak (151,000 in 1962) much land is under coconut, rubber and pepper; the middle Kapoeas Valley is fairly well cultivated with similar crops round Sintang whence the products go by river to Pontianak. In the southern lowlands between Soengei Barito and the Gunong Meratoes is a well-populated farming area less rainy than elsewhere and less severely leached, so that rice, pepper, rubber and coconuts are grown for export through Kandangan which several good roads link to Bandjermasin (214,000 people), the most populous district of Kalimantan. Much colonising for paddy has been going on in Kandangan to relieve dangerous pressures in Java.

The East Coast is everywhere thinly peopled. Coal was mined prewar at Poelau Laoet, but the greatest postwar exploitation has been at Loa Koeloe and Parapattan which yielded 100,000 tons in 1960. Balikpapan was the focus of the lower Mahakan Basin where Samarinda, one of the largest fields in the archipelago, produced the oil which formed most of Balikpapan's export of 600,000 tons in 1961; in the same year the outlying field at Tarakan shipped about 100,000 tons. The Samarinda crude oil production is still half that of prewar, but the Tarakan field, heavily damaged during the war, is practically restored and had about 250 wells pumping in 1962. Food cultivation is negligible except where Javanese have settled. Pepper for export is grown on Poelau Laoet. Smallholdings of rubber are becoming popular and produced 130,000 tons in 1960. Over recent years fishing has become prominent, the sea-catch being 130,000 tons in 1964— over three times that of 1951. A big programme of constructing polders in the freshwater swamps is in hand which, given enough immigrants from Java, could make this a new "rice-bowl" area. Timber production is substantial but erratic (10 million cu. ft. rough in 1960). Kalimantan is now putting into trade about half of all Indonesia's copra (108,000 tons in 1964) though its copra fluctuates widely from year to year and always suffers from Philippine competition.

[*In Sabah, Brunei and Sarawak, the Malaysian dollar is currency; in Kalimantan the Indonesian rupiah, as shown on p. 197.*]

Chapter Sixteen

THE EAST INDIES

SULUWESI, BALI, LOMBOK, TIMOR, AND WEST IRIAN

EAST of Borneo and Java, the population of the islands thins out and development is both recent and not far advanced, so that geographical references diminish almost to those of a gazetteer. These islands are mostly volcanic, set in very deep seas. Coral reefs invariably surround them, often as double palisades preventing access from the sea. The maze of small islands, often ill-surveyed and scarcely above water, presents a worrying obstacle to navigation. Today the strait between Bali and Lombok is the most frequented international shipping highway through the region yet the Portuguese in their phase as Far Eastern traders for a time used the Macassar Strait as route to and from China, and Macassar as a watering place on their way to the Moluccas. Halmahera, which so curiously resembles Suluwesi in form and its offshore islands, the Moluccas, were the magnet for spice traders from the Roman to the Portuguese periods, because they produced unrivalled cloves. That interest has disappeared and there is no commercial activity drawn towards these smaller eastern islands, apart from minor copra production which has varied much in prosperity, tending now to be formally and reliably cultivated on plantations farther west rather than in small patches among these islands, where the collection costs are high and the copra standards uncertain. Suluwesi, Bali and Lombok merit special interest since upon them live 12 million of the approximate 13 million people settled in this eastern island region, which, for a time, became the separate political unit called East Indonesia. Distance, isolation and a self-contained economy here emphasise the tendency for Indonesia to fall apart.

The southern part of the Macassar Strait was a most difficult sea passage for sailing ships and is still considered dangerous to shipping in stormy seasons. Innumerable coral-girt islands and reefs lie across it, forming in one place the Great Sunda Barrier

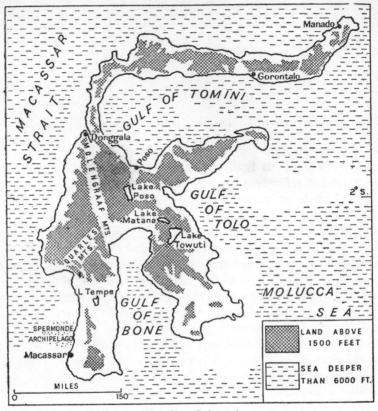

Fig. 82.—Suluwesi

Reef, only slightly smaller and more dangerously located than the comparable Great Barrier Reef at Queensland; it thrusts nearly 250 miles out from the Borneo coast, leaving a narrow gap of deep water between it and Suluwesi. The Reef extends southward irregularly, to the Lima and Kangean Islands, making a shallow coral-edged bank over 50,000 square miles in area (Fig. 7). Other coral masses are scattered between this bank and South Suluwesi of which the Spermonde Archipelago off Macassar is the largest.

Suluwesi

Though larger than Java, the tentacled island of Suluwesi (once Celebes) is remarkably attenuated, its 3,000 miles of coast enclosing 73,000 square miles, so that little of Suluwesi is more than 25 miles from the sea. This does not make for greater accessibility because rocks and corals line the coast almost without break, probably explaining why the island escaped the flood of early Indian colonisation, was largely bypassed by early European traders and became Islamised at a later date than most parts of the East Indies.

An extension of that arcuate series of folds and faults already observed in Sumatra and Java, Suluwesi has been subject to tectonic stresses from many directions; its shape relates to the Java-Sumatra mountain system on latitudinal lines and the Philippines system on meridional lines. Its precipitous shores and the uplifted blocks and rift valleys which form its surface evidence the strong influence of faulting processes which at a later stage involved vulcanism, still apparent in the extreme northeast tip behind Minahasa and in the extinct Lompobatang of the south. All except its northern limb lies below the Equator but the whole island has the typical humid, warm unvarying climate which permits Tropical Rain Forest over its whole surface.

THE EASTERN ARCHIPELAGO: AVERAGE RAINFALL (inches)

	Rain days (over .02 in.)	*Jan.*	*Feb.*	*Mar.*	*Apr.*	*May*	*June*	*July*	*Aug.*	*Sept.*	*Oct.*	*Nov.*	*Dec.*	*Total*
Manado (30 ft.)	164	17.7	15.1	11.6	7.9	6.3	6.5	4.6	3.7	3.4	4.6	8.7	14.4	104.5
Macassar (13 ft.)	134	26.6	23.2	16.4	6.0	3.4	2.9	1.4	0.4	0.6	1.7	7.2	23.5	113.3
Koepang (148 ft.)	80	15.2	15.8	8.5	2.6	1.1	0.4	0.2	0.1	0.1	0.7	3.6	9.5	57.8

The rivers deriving from this setting are large in volume, but at a very youthful erosional stage; their short courses are frequently broken, in places with great waterfalls, elsewhere by deep incisions and gorges. Very little of its surface is below 1,500 ft. and Suluwesi ranks as a most mountainous terrain, the only significant lowlands being the Sidenreng-Tempe lake belt which almost isolates the southwest limb, and the valley of Sampara at the southeast tip. Lakes are numerous, particularly towards the middle of the island, and in some cases are graben lakes of great depth; Lake Poso, one of a group of lakes on NNE–SSE. lines, has a depth of nearly 5,000 ft. Other lakes have filled up to form inland marshy flats.

While gold, nickel, iron and petroleum have been traced in Suluwesi, they have not been worked.

On Suluwesi there are over 7 million people, of whom about a million are in Minahasa. Large tracts of the country are still un-populated except by a few wild tribes. The Minahasa district has a density of 75 person per square mile whereas Macassar on the southwestern limb has as many as 325 per square mile. Dense settlement is confined to the coast, and the interior has only a wandering population in the isolated valleys and basins. Most numerous of the indigenous people are the Bugis and Macas-saris, 2 million of whom live in the southwest. They were his-torically one of the most active Muslim seafaring peoples of the Indies, acquiring a notoriety as pirates and slavers; they now rank as an inter-island trading people whose little sailing ships may be found anywhere between Singapore and Port Moresby. The Portuguese recruited Bugis to work in W. Malaysia, a very early sign of colonial labour shortages there, and a group of them settled inland from Malacca. Tribes of the interior are collectively known as Toradjas whose animism has distinct Polynesian associations; they practise the shifting cultivation of yams. In the northern Suluwesi limb are Muslim Gorontales and Christian Minahasis which latter are thought to resemble Filipinos and to be the most progressive and advanced people in Suluwesi—probably because they are well educated on western lines and European mannered.

The concentration of people in the northeastern tip, Minahasa, results largely from the more intensive agriculture made possible by young volcanic soils. Only a valley agriculture is practised there and none of the volcanoes of this corner are terraced to the maximum as in Java. The narrow fertile lowlands are vigorously farmed, centring on subsistence rice with coconuts and maize for export from Manado (population 60,000). In the southwestern peninsula too, large populations are supported on volcanic ash soils from Lompobatang, which are cultivated for rice, maize, coffee and coconuts. On the south-west limb, Macassar (district pop. 395,100 in 1963) acts as outlet to the belt of dense population which extends along the coast to the low-lying area round the Sidenreng-Tempe lakes, through which zone, and radiating from Macassar, has been built the only noteworthy road system of Suluwesi. Westernised farming styles and plantations are negligible in Suluwesi and the exports derive from smallholders. Rubber has not been taken up to any appreciable extent.

That Macassar is so central to seaways among the easternmost islands causes it to be considered the capital to East Indonesia in the schemes for a federal structure of Indonesia re-calling a pattern evident in the later Portuguese period among the lands.

BALI AND LOMBOK

The islands stringing from Bali to Timor are known as the Lesser Sunda Islands, of which only Bali and Lombok are densely populated and well studied. They are thus interesting geographically while by no means representative of conditions in the islands east of them. Separated by the Lombok Strait, the safest and deepest channel through the western Lesser Sundas, the physiography and patterns of Bali and Lombok have close similarities. They are to be considered as extensions of relief forms already met in Java. Thus the southern parts of both Bali and Lombok are low limestone plateaux, as in South Java; the outcrop

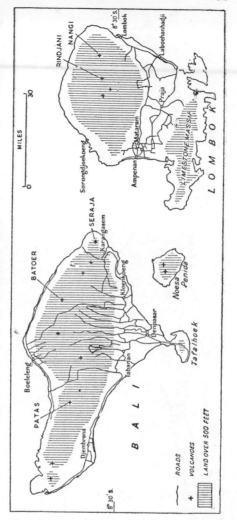

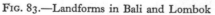

FIG. 83.—Landforms in Bali and Lombok

in Bali is small, forming the bare, unpeopled Tafelhoek, which is linked to the island by a tombola or sandspit, but Lombok has a large out-crop forming a waterless karst upland (about 1,000 ft. high) thicketed with bamboos, barren and unpeopled, with a similar limestone outlier in the sterile zone between Djembrana and Tabanan (Fig. 83).

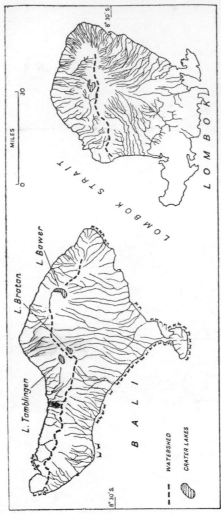

FIG. 84.—Drainage Patterns in Bali and Lombok

While the substructure of Bali and Lombok to the north is undoubtedly an extension of the fold-faulted sedimentary ranges of the Java axis, it is completely obliterated by volcanoes whose ejecta dominate both landscapes.

In Bali there is a line of active volcanoes well to the north (Piek van Tabanan, Tjatoer, Batoer and Agoeng) scored on their northern sides by short streams too torrential for irrigation and dry for half the year. Large streams fan southward (Fig. 84) to build up a most fertile inclined alluvial plain, constantly rejuvenated by water-borne volcanic ash upon which dense settlement and paddyfields on ingeniously irrigated pre-Dutch terraces extend inland and upward to about 2,000 ft., slightly thinning thereafter, although settlement and cultivation extend up to the western rim of the Batoer caldera at about 5,000 ft. Rivers on this side are incised in the loose, high-level ash; they vary greatly in volume because the watertable in the scoria quickly lowers during dry seasons. These streams are in torrential spate during the rains and almost dry up during the east monsoon (May to November). Upon this sunny tilted plain the fertility of the transported ash soils exceeds even that of Java and the population density is accordingly very high (Fig. 85).

The volcanic zone of Lombok is more like an elliptical cone and there are few caldera—Rindjani (12,200 ft.) and Nangi. Here the steep dry northern slopes are notably unpeopled and the gentler southern slopes lead down to an inclined rectangle of intensely cultivated and irrigated land. Towards the east, the climate becomes distinctly drier, taking on an almost Australian aspect, with prickly pears and cockatoos indicating the migration of Australian flora and fauna.

The people of Bali are still Hindus. They have descended from high caste Hindu Javanese pressed eastward during the Islamisation of Java, yet retaining an aristocratic society and strongly communal life which finds expression in an elaborate artistic culture reaching higher forms here than anywhere else among the island peoples. Their

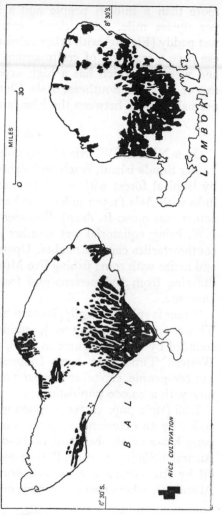

FIG. 85.—Rice growing in Bali and Lombok

temple architecture is unusually striking and complex. In Lombok the Balinese are outnumbered by "lax Muslim" Sasak people. Population in each island concentrates upon the fertile southern volcanic slopes. In the Gianjar district of Bali there are 2,300 people per square mile and the whole island exceeds 1,500 per square miles, to total 3.5 million. Lombok has little more than a million people and a lower average density—810 per square mile. Each island contains about 250,000 acres of wet paddy (Fig. 85) with other subsistence food crops. The Balinese have a tradition of craftmanship in wood, stone, gold, silver and weaving, which has a high export value. Balinese rear and export pigs for Southeast Asia Chinese. International shipping normally passes between the islands without stopping.

TIMOR

On a NNE–SSW. axis of 310 miles, Timor is the easternmost Lesser Sunda island, reaching heights of 7,300 ft., largely covered by tropical forest with eucalyptus and having plant and animal links with Asia (1,500 miles away) and Australia (420 miles away across seas 9,000 ft. deep). Summer (Dec.-Feb.) winds from the NW. bring equatorial wet weather and for the rest of the year southeasterlies cause droughts. Upon poor coastal farms of paddy and maize with some fishing live Muslim and Christian Timorese, differing from Indonesians and from Melanesians in build and language.

Timor is split politically. Its eastern 60 per cent forms Portuguese Timor (1964 pop. 543,000), administered from Dilli, a port founded by the Portuguese in 1668, now with 52,000 inhabitants. Western Timor has been Indonesian since 1947, containing 450,000 people, capital at Koepang founded by the Dutch in 1668, now with a 20,000 population.

Dilli (1960 pop. 52,100) exports gums, sandalwood for joss and coffee by an occasional ship on Australia-HongKong runs. Koepang has a small shell and bêche-de-mer trade by ships on the Australia-Singapore runs. Portuguese Timor is being explored for oil by Australians who started boring in 1959 at Ossulari and Aliambata, where surface seepage occurs.

WEST IRIAN

In 1962, the Netherlands relinquished West New Guinea whose population of over half a million in a thickly forested, a little developed mountainous area of 167 sq. miles has been incorporated into Indonesia as "West Irian" (cap. Kota Baru). Apart from Javanese immigrants, the West Irians have little historic, ethnic, linguistic or economic relations with Indonesians.

Chapter Seventeen

THE NATURAL LANDSCAPE OF THAILAND

IN many respects, Thailand resembles Burma. Both countries have a south-facing trough form, similar climates of alternating wet and dry seasons, similar interest in a single major river system, considerable cultural likenesses between their people, and similar economic structures based on the export of rice and teak. Their differences derive from Thailand's more southerly latitude, and from aspect, which influences the Thai climate adversely from the rice-growing point of view, and draws Thailand into seaborne relations with China (they share no border) and towards the trade streams of Southeast Asia. It is, however, the least documented country of Southeast Asia and even its place names have not yet been uniformly phoneticised. Thailand was once called Siam.

Thailand is laid out very simply (Fig. 86). To the west are strung out old mountain systems which extend into Burma in the one direction and into W. Malaysia in the other. To the north, an eroded plateau forms a broken upland terrain, resembling the Shan Highlands, of which it is an extension. To the east of Thailand is a low platform, the Korat Plateau, with two scarps facing west and south as ramparts separating it from Central Thailand and combining as a high bastion to the southwest where Kao Lem (Khao Khiaw) reaches 4,100 ft. Between these three units is Central Thailand, a trough comparable to the Irrawaddy Basin, forming the heart of the country though less dominated by a single stream. Into Southeast Thailand juts a small extension of the Cardamom Mountains between which and the Korat Plateau is a broad low corridor drained by the Prachin River and leading from the plains of Tonle Sap to the Gulf of Thailand.

The eastern boundary, mostly one of natural repulsion, runs for miles along the Middle Mekong, then follows the south Korat scarp to become a watershed boundary in the Cardamom Mountains. With Burma, Thailand shares a long watershed boundary zigzagging down the skew coulisses of Tenasserim and Tavoy in such a way that near Sam Roi Yot the boundary approaches so

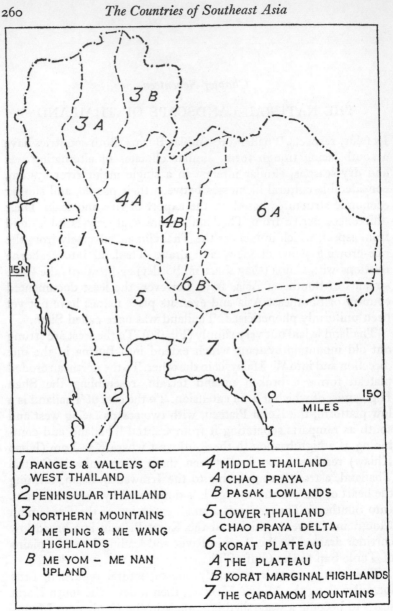

1 RANGES & VALLEYS OF
   WEST THAILAND

2 PENINSULAR THAILAND

3 NORTHERN MOUNTAINS
  A ME PING & ME WANG
    HIGHLANDS
  B ME YOM – ME NAN
    UPLAND

4 MIDDLE THAILAND
  A CHAO PRAYA
  B PASAK LOWLANDS

5 LOWER THAILAND
   CHAO PRAYA DELTA

6 KORAT PLATEAU
  A THE PLATEAU
  B KORAT MARGINAL HIGHLANDS

7 THE CARDAMOM MOUNTAINS

Fig. 86.—A Regional Division of Thailand

near to the Gulf of Thailand that Peninsular Thailand, the Kra Isthmus, is almost separated from Continental Thailand. To the north in the Shan country, the boundary is also a watershed boundary, though it runs for some miles along the Salween gorge and even returns to the Mekong at its incised mountainous section near Chieng Sen.

Landscape Types

1. *The Western Mountains* (Fig. 86) follow patterns already fully described in the comparable parts of Malaysia and Burma. In detail these alternations of low corridors separated by lines of high granite mountains flanked occasionally by patches of limestone producing a landscape resembling the karst, show varieties of disposition though not of landscape type—and these dispositions moulded historic overland routes. North of Sam Roi Yot, the mountain lines run NNW. to SSE. and the parallel wet valleys drain two ways, to Burma and to Thailand converging upon Moulmein and Radburi respectively, and used as mediaeval trade routes particularly along the Meklong Valley. South of Sam Roi Yot, the granite ridges first assume a line NNE–SSW., becoming meridional farther south when crossing into Malaya. Here the Kra Isthmus is at its narrowest (about 35 miles in lat. 10° N.) and the short torrents have laid down tin-bearing alluvials on the flanks of nearly every granite outcrop. This was also the location of overland routes between east and west, of which the Takuapa-Bandon route was typical. It was largely a route for small river boats, only a short section needing portage which, in so forested a setting, was always critical and difficult for traders. None of these trans-isthmus routes have modern significance; on the Radburi-Sisawat-Moulmein route the Japanese began a wartime railway which is now out of use. A Kra Canal seemed practicable enough to merit prohibition in the Anglo-Thai treaty of 1946.

2. *The Northern Mountains*, an intensely folded old-mountain system of shales, schists and limestones, are in an advanced erosional stage and their intrusive granite cores are exposed on distinctive N–S. lines. Many streams flow south from this extension of the Shan Highlands and through the Central depression. Between Lampang and Pre is one of the few volcanic outcrops in Thailand, which has no active volcanoes. The

region contains the country's highest relief and in its valleys are fertile pockets of alluvials which have attracted peoples from the harsher north. Its southern limit is a latitudinal line about 17½° N.

3. *The Korat Plateau* (Fig. 93) has features unique in Thailand and Southeast Asia. It is a practically horizontal bed of red sandstone lying unconformably and almost undisturbed upon that general mass of eroded faulted rocks apparent at the surface in most adjoining regions (Fig. 87). This sandstone plateau,

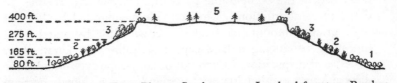

FIG. 87.—Section of Korat Plateau Sandstones. 1. Lowland forest. 2. Bamboo with isolated trees. 3. Tropical rain forest. 4. Dwarf trees capping barescarp 5. Savannah with scattered pines

while averaging about 500 ft. above sea level, tilts slightly from scarps of above 1,500 ft. at the east and south, towards the Mekong, shedding eastwards its streams, the Nam Chi and Nam Mun, and giving the whole region an outlook towards the Mekong and away from Central Thailand. The landscape is square-cut with broad, flat, incised valleys and flat-topped interfluves like mesas in which the watertable stands well below the surface for most of the year. The sandstone plateau terminates in linear scarps (possibly of fault origin) to the west and south as the Dong Paya and Dong Rek, in the neighbourhood of which small outcrops of ancient volcanic tufa have been found. Equally sharp is the termination of sandstone north and east overlooking the Mekong Valley. Along the Nam Mun and Nam Chi wide marshy flats extend latitudinally almost right across the Plateau, as the only well-watered areas in an otherwise dry area, and they are subject to inundation by Mekong spates as is the case with Tonle Sap. Below the Nam Mun junction, the Mekong enters a gorge-like bottleneck where sandstone barriers in places extend almost from side to side. During heavy rains this rocky impediment causes the Nam Mun to be inundated far upstream by a rush of water from the Mekong, aggravated by rain-floods on Korat itself. A similar condition occurs in most of the lesser streams flowing from the sandstone into the Mekong, though most Korat drainage goes to the Nam Mun before reaching the Mekong. The Nam Mun valleys is thus a flat bed of seasonal marsh (Fig. 90) which remains the longer because the main stream has built levees which prevent quick drainage of flood-water back to the river. Upon the Plateau capillarity causes salt frequently to flower at the surface during the summer, when it is collected for domestic use and traded by caravan routes into Yunnan as well as into Central Thailand. An outlier of Korat is found at the Mieng Hills northwest of Petchabun. In the southwest corner of the Plateau appears a line of granite hills in continuation of the Cardamom Mountains.

4. That portion of *the Cardamon Mountains* in Southwest Thailand repeats features found in Cambodia (see Chapter 19) with a difference of aspect: the Thai section has a number of fertile alluvial valleys opening south to the Gulf of Thailand. These valleys are moderately peopled and cultivated. The low hills of these peneplained folded rocks extend to the straight eastern side of the Bight of Bangkok where a fault structure extends the line of the Dong Paya scarp.

5. *Central Thailand* may be described as a depression floored by highly eroded complex-structured sedimentaries mostly reduced to levels below 300 ft. and is generally masked by river alluvials. It extends to lat. $17\frac{1}{2}°$ N. north of which mountains appear, to the scarp of the Korat Plateau where it terminates as a meridional line, and to the west where it ends in a fairly straight line against the Tanon Tong Chai and Tenasserim Ranges. It remains to be verified geologically whether this is a fault depression or an erosional basin.

While Central Thailand is often called the Menam Valley, there is no River Menam; Menam means "The River" in Thai. Four main streams enter the depression on practically N–S. lines from the Thai Northern Mountains. Three of them, the Metun, Ping and Wang combine near Ban Sop Woung and are joined near Nakawn Sawan by the Nan and the Yom to form one single stream for about 25 miles, but from Chainat southward these combined waters braid into distributaries of which the chief are the Tachin on the west and the Chao Praya to the east. It is this main distributary, the Menam Chao Praya, which is meant conventionally by describing the "Menam" as the chief river of Thailand. The easternmost distributary receives near Ayuthia the waters of the Pasak, a river which distinctly parallels the Dong Paya scarp.

The Prachin (Ban Pa Kong), draining between the Korat Plateau and the Cardamom Mountains, makes a sharp bend southward so that it does not join the main drainage system of Central Thailand but separately enters the Bight of Bangkok. The Meklong flows from the Western Mountains southeastward to make a similar separate entry to the Bight, though artificially connected to the Menam Chao Praya by parallel canals (for irrigation and transport) across the deltaic plain along one of the old transisthmus routes between east and west. These rivers periodically have great volume and heavy silt load; they have built up large alluvial fans and deltas and are still steadily filling the Bight of Bangkok.

As with the Irrawaddy Valley, we may distinguish two distinct parts of Central Thailand:

(a) *Lower Thailand*, the flat deltaic alluvials forming a trapezoid from the Bight to the points Prachinburi on the Prachin, Saraburi on the Pasak, Peiyuakiri on the Chao Praya and Raiburi on the Meklong. Within this area the relief of levees and alluvial banks alone rises above the surface, which is only a few feet above sea level (Fig. 92).

(b) *Middle Thailand*, the northern part of the trough, characterised by rolling hill and valley relief crossed by lines of muchfolded shales and schists. The narrows below Nakawn Sawan indicate that the substructure runs athwart the drainage lines to form an almost enclosed basin to the north. Beside the main rivers are alluvial flats containing braided streams, thus extending far inland long fingers of landscape resembling that of Lower Thailand. The Pasak Valley is large and disproportionate to the present river within it; it follows a linear form apparent on the Mekong between Luang Prabang and Paklay and is in turn extended south by a tributary of the Prachin, suggesting that the Pasak once flowed separately to the Bight as an old course of the Mekong.

Mineral exploitation is slight apart from dredging tin from the estuarial and offshore gravels of Kra. River gravels yield gold in the Nam Nigau valley and in Kra valleys, though these last can be relics of old trade routes rather than signs of local ore. In the Nam

Wa of North Thailand, at Chon Luk in Dong Paya and at Muang Kut in the east, the copper mines no longer operate. Galena occurs at Kanchanburi. Kra produced 500 tons of scheelite (tungsten ore) in 1963. A few gems continue to be found in the Cardamoms. Iron ore is widely distributed, producing 810,000 tons (1965) for a local oil-fired smelter. There is unworked lignite near Nakawn Sawan. Tin ore from Kra was shipped to Penang or Singapore. Exclusively an investment of European or Chinese capital, the tin mines worked with Chinese labour (23,000 persons in 1964) on systems already used in Malaysia. Thailand in 1964 produced 15,840 tons tin ore, double the 1958 output. A tin smelter with 20,000 ton capacity is starting in the south.

CLIMATE

The Thai climate relates to climates of the adjoining territories of Burma, Indochina and W. Malaysia. The Kra Isthmus experiences the North Malaysian type of climate with rains at all seasons and two distinct maxima. The Central Depression is distinctly dry (Fig. 88), receiving rains only when the summer airstream comes directly from the south, otherwise the Western Mountains shield the Menam Chao Praya Valley, producing a dry zone resembling that of Central Burma. The high surroundings of Central Thailand deny the regions any significant amelioration of drought by occasional cyclones. Typhoons from Indochina and the South China Sea rarely reach even the Korat Plateau.

Thus, excepting the Kra Isthmus, Thailand has less than 1 in. of rain for each month from December to April. Rains then set in with an abruptness like those of India and Burma, at the end of April, to continue until mid-November. The volume of rain varies from district to district according to aspect and altitude so that in July, for example, southeast Thailand and all the mountain areas receive over 10 in. of rain, while Central Thailand and Korat receive less than 10 in. By October the rains diminish throughout Central Thailand.

Relief largely determines the pattern of annual rainfall totals, according to the few long-period records which have been kept. The higher edges of Korat receive as much as 120 in. p.a. whereas the lower plateau areas receive less than 60 in. and even less than 40 in. in the rainshadow east of the Dong Paya scarp.

Central Thailand everywhere has less than 60 in. while on the

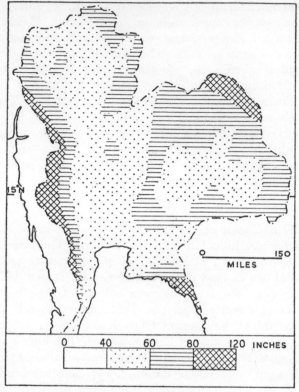

Fig. 88.—Rainfall in Thailand

eastern foothills of the Western Mountains a narrow belt of rain-shadow from Prau Kao on the Bight to Raheng on the Ping River has less than 40 in. p.a. Thus Central Thailand has a rainfall resembling the Dry Zone of Burma but there is no increase of rain towards the southern plains, which continue dry all the way to the

THAILAND: AVERAGE RAINFALL (in inches)

	Jan.	*Feb.*	*Mar.*	*Apr.*	*May*	*June*	*July*	*Aug.*	*Sept.*	*Oct.*	*Nov.*	*Dec.*	*Total*
Bangkok	.9	1.0	1.3	1.9	6.8	6.4	6.9	7.3	1.6	7.8	2.1	.7	54.6
Kanburi	.9	1.0	1.3	2.3	6.4	5.2	5.3	3.8	7.8	6.9	.7	.4	51.3
Nakon Nayok	1.0	1.1	1.9	2.3	7.9	11.6	14.5	16.5	16.7	7.3	2.6	.5	83.9
Chiengmai	.4	.1	1.0	1.6	6.0	5.1	5.7	9.1	9.5	6.7	2.3	.5	48.0
Udorn	nil	0.7	3.0	3.7	9.1	10.4	8.6	8.4	9.9	2.2	1.2	nil	57.2
Takuapa	1.1	1.3	6.1	7.5	17.7	20.5	23.8	23.9	33.3	21.2	9.2	3.1	168.7

Bight. Upon the Korat Plateau a similarly low rainfall is emphasised by the porosity of the red sandstone and comes in a season of about 200 days, during which high temperatures prevail to lessen the effectiveness of the low rainfall.

A climatic drawback is the wide variability in the Thai rainfall from year to year, always a critical factor in drier climates. Over the period 1914–25 the wettest years differed from the driest years by as much as the average rainfall at Bangkok, and the length of the wet season varied from 174 to 236 days per year.

Low rainfalls in Central Thailand have several effects. Because the streams are relatively short and originate within the Thai climatic régime, their volume fluctuates widely during the year and their load at the onset of the wet season is abnormally heavy, due to the ease with which rain scours the dry dusty surface. Such an alternation in the rivers produces bars across their mouths. The Chao Praya at Paknampoh has a flow of scarcely 4,000 cub. ft. per second during the dry season, becoming 54,000 cub. ft. per second in the wet season. At Bangkok the flood discharge is of the order 95,000 cub. ft. per second. The rise begins rapidly in May and continues until the end of October, after which it falls gradually to a minimum in April. For fifty miles inland the distributaries of the Chao Praya are subject to tidal influence, particularly during the dry season, making the lower reaches of the river brackish and creating a problem from the farming and potable water point of view, while helping to scour the channels slightly. The Chao Praya mouth can be entered only by regularly dredging the sandbars which are very little modified by marine currents because the Bight is so sheltered. Other streams are unsuited for navigation even at their mouths; the smaller rivers, like the *chaungs* of Burma, dry out to a trickle among banks of gravel during several months, when water shortage dominates Thai life everywhere outside the main river valleys.

VEGETATION

The Korat Plateau and Central Thailand are covered by the dry deciduous type of Monsoon Forest (Fig. 89) in which bamboos predominate, much subject to fires in the dry season and becoming savannah or scrub in type after frequent burnings, whether caused naturally or by shifting cultivators. Higher altitudes everywhere induce an approach to Tropical Rain Forest because they receive

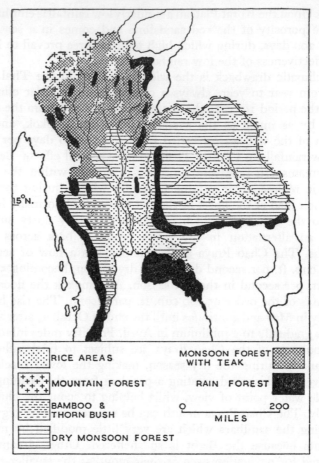

FIG. 89.—Vegetation in Thailand

heavier and more regular rains and the Kra Isthmus is practically entirely of this type of forest. North of about 17° N., apart from the occasionally cultivated alluvial valleys, the landscape is deciduous Teak Forest, Northern Thailand repeating in this respect the pattern of the Irrawaddy Basin. Some six foreign firms had leases to extract teak from this area up to 1942 and over a million logs a year were cut from Thai forests, dragged to the water-side by elephants and floated down to the coast during the wet season beginning in May and June. Thai teak partly moved out by way of the Salween and the Mekong but at least three-quarters went by the Chao Praya to Bangkok. About half the commercial teak is from the Yom valley, and a quarter each from the Wang and Ping Valleys. Recently legislation stipulated re-forestation after cutting the teak because it was becoming apparent that the extraction rate was faster than the natural replacement and was causing hill erosion to increase. Near Bangkok are many teak mills though logs also go to Singapore

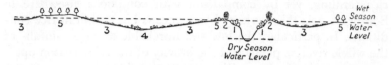

FIG. 90.—Rivers and Swamps in Korat. 1. Evergreen shrubs and small trees. 2. Thorny bamboo lining levees. 3. Grasses. 4. Marsh. 5. Park-like savannah above wet season water level

for milling, in company with much Thai rattan, for which Singapore is also an entrepôt. The timber trade had been declining after 1907 and the demand for Thai teak fluctuated widely, its pace being set by Asiatic rather than by European or American consumers. After 1946, teak extraction expanded to exports worth $27,000,000 in 1964.

Peculiar to the valleys of Korat is the great development of seasonal Freshwater Swamp Forest. The flat lands away from the rivers (Fig. 90) are inundated during the wet season, which encourages a profuse vegetation and this in turn becomes an impassable forest in the dry season. Thus the landscape when dry resembles the worst savannah-scrub, lined with bamboo on the slightly higher ridges, and when wet resembles young swamp forest found in latitudes much farther south.

Chapter Eighteen

THE CULTURAL AND SOCIAL LANDSCAPE
OF THAILAND

THE agriculture and the social structure of Thailand hinge upon rice farming, yet by comparison with conditions elsewhere in Southeast Asia this territory by no means has optimum rice conditions. In particular, the low and unreliable average rainfalls of the whole riverine plains and the brevity of the rainy season operate against rice farming. Zimmerman considered at least three-quarters of Thailand was unsuited to rice cultivation.

OLDER FARMING SYSTEMS

Probably almost a million Thai people in the northern and western mountain districts and on the Korat Plateau still regularly depend for their food on shifting cultivation. The amount of land used in this way is probably half a million acres in any one year.

Outside Lower Thailand where special conditions operate, farming is of the subsistence type and agricultural produce does not move in an appreciable quantity from one district to another. To the north the farming is based upon transplanted glutinous rice, less because the glutinous type is preferred and more because that type matures in about 4 months; transplanting makes it a safe crop for a district whose rainy season is unreliable and never longer than $4\frac{1}{2}$ months. The same consideration causes Korat to devote 70 per cent of its farmland to glutinous rice.

Supplementary to this staple peasant food are many other crops for local use, all of them tolerating the low rainfall, short wet season and long dry season, but the riceland is never re-cropped in any one year. Tobacco, a little cotton, fruits, tea (on the uplands) and vegetables are produced in this subsistence system. For the whole of Thailand outside Kra, the non-rice crops occupy in total less than 3 per cent of the cultivated land, the 1965 acreages being 105,000 tobacco, 1,085,000 maize, 375,000 sugarcane, 172,000 cotton. For rice growing, areas away from the main rivers depend on direct rainfall supplemented by direct flooding from the smaller rivers where this takes place naturally. Controlled irrigation with dams and distributary canals operates for only a small fraction of the arable area.

In the Korat valleys rice grows on the fringes of the seasonal swamps and the timing of planting and harvesting is related to their natural floods. Any cultivation behind the levee banks of these swamps must wait for the river itself to subside, because no method has been evolved to drain to the river which is then standing at least as high as the water in the fields. Frequently there arise communal clashes of interest in the Korat swamps: peasants who live by catching the freshwater fish brought to the swamp by the river in spate, work for the quickest possible draining of the swamp as the river subsides; paddy-farmers on the other hand need the water to be retained behind the levees as long as possible. It is remarkable in this Southeast Asia region, where water control has generally reached a high standard by methods devised under and for local conditions, that paddy farmers of north and east Korat, where conditions are unreliable, should have evolved no irrigation of their own, not even the simple water-gate to use the swamps behind the levees as water storage tanks. Water scarcity sets the key of all Korat activity; the combination of low and unreliable rainfall, high evaporation, porous sandstone and low watertable leaves the people critically dependent on the brief natural floods of the river valleys. Less than 7 per cent of the Plateau is cultivated, much of this being on the shifting system and less than 2 per cent being in crops other than rice. All processing and cultivation is haphazard here. Of land reported to be under rice in the 1960–61 season, 11 per cent was in Central Thailand north of Nakawn Sawan and about 45 per cent in the Korat Valleys where there is always quick response to rice prices, a rise of which encourages catch-cropping in marginal areas. Only a little of the rice moved out of these localities.

The Kra Isthmus, with a landscape like North Malaysia, has all Thai tin mines, 110,000 acres of rubber, and a million acres rice.

COMMERCIAL AGRICULTURE

The deltaic plain of Lower Thailand (Fig. 92) is the zone of specialised rice agriculture, resembling in its position within the state and in the economic machine the commercial rice-producing zone of Lower Burma but with differences in method. For 1962–63,

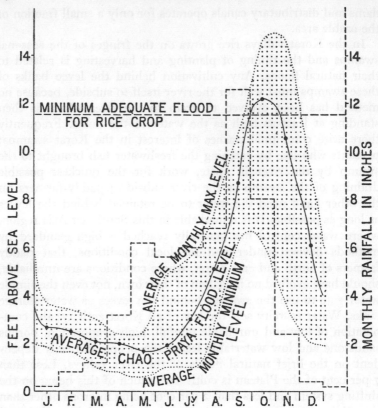

FIG. 91.—Rainfall and River Régimes at Ayuthia

about 9.5 million acres of paddy were being cultivated in this restricted region, representing over 51 per cent of the Thai paddy area. Precipitation everywhere in Lower Thailand is less than 60 in. p.a. and is only just over 50 in. at Ayuthia in the heart of the rice country, as against the minimum wet paddy requirement of 70 in. p.a. The effective rainfall is considerably less—about 40 in. only for the critical months when paddy is in the ground (Fig. 91). Thus we have the unusual circumstance of a large-scale commercialised rice production—almost all rice export derives from Lower Thailand—in an area without adequate rainfall for rice.

All rice grown in Lower Thailand for trade is non-glutinous and wet-cultivated. Rainfall deficiency is made up by direct floods from the rivers whose spate in the deltaic sector of the Chao Praya is about a month after rains begin in the mountains of the north. The whole plain is canalled for simple distribution of the spate. Because most of the fields are fed by gravity without an artificial head of water, the duration and depth of flooding are uncontrollable and the crop risks are very great. There are the risks of inadequate depth of flood, too much depth, inadequate duration and too prolonged duration, so that the harvest has a wide variability. At Ayuthia over a century of observation, only 32 per cent of the years had adequate floods, 22 per cent of the years they were barely adequate, 30 per cent of floods were far too shallow and 15 per cent too deep. These are the consequences of having neither dams to store, dykes to protect nor adequate canals to distribute and balance the supply of field water.

To provide adequate floods for the rice areas, the Chao Praya waters at Ayuthia must rise to at least 11.5 ft. above the average level of the Bight of Bangkok and the success of any one crop depends on maintaining this level for a sufficient period to mature the rice. Maintenance of level depends in turn on the continuation of rains at the headstreams of the Chao Praya; should August and September be unusually dry in the north, a sharp drop in Lower Thailand floods occurs and the rice plants cannot mature—with serious results for the Thai commercial economy. Thus in 1919 when the minimum 11.5 ft. of flood at Ayuthia was not reached at any time, over 2½ million acres (43 per cent of paddy) were destroyed.

Such uncertainty has led to canalisation at Klong Rangsit, N.E. of Bangkok, where Pasak and Pakong water irrigates .55 million acres of paddyland. West of the Chao Praya, ponds and mobile pumps offset the inadequate natural floods. At Chainat, a barrage has been completed across the unruly Chao Praya (whose variation of level averaged 38 ft. for 1950–54) to regulate its height and assure water for 3.7 million acres.

Since the Chao Praya has a heavy load in spate and varies in volume rapidly, silting is a constant problem in the channels and in the fields. Distributaries build up levees, which in time they penetrate, leading to a change of course (Fig. 92). There are signs of steady migration of distributaries to the east, leaving what were once good rice areas with every expectation of floodwater to become relatively unimportant and unreliable producers, as in the Suphanburi district where a heavy rice production was obtained

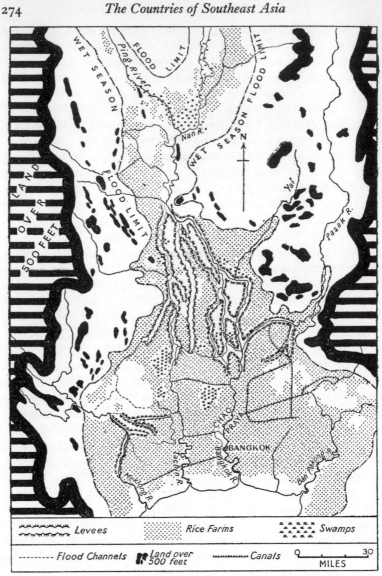

Levees   Rice Farms   Swamps

Flood Channels   Land over 500 feet   Canals   0   30
                                                          MILES

FIG. 92.—Landscape and Land Use in Lower Thailand

in the 14th century when the Chao Praya reached the sea by way
of what is now the silted up Thachin River.

During floods, Lower Thailand is under water to depths
varying from a few inches to as much as 10 ft. The canals (*klongs*)

are aids to water distribution and do not significantly drain the landscape. They are, however, the only practicable routes and the rural areas are linked by shallow-draught boats along these *klongs* which are at once agricultural aids, the high street, the sewer and the water supply to local people. The nature of the floods is a factor maintaining fertility but the migration of the waters and the frequent silting up of channels cause a shift in the location of the most favoured and reliable rice-growing areas. Without controlled irrigation, any area built up above the general level by sedimentation will no longer be flooded and must fall out of cultivation.

RICE

The Lower Thailand plain is almost a one-crop area. Rice farming dominates all else, but there is a little vegetable growing near Bangkok and fruit and peppers are produced at Chandburi. Farmers on the plain always grew beans and maize for local use, but over 1948–63, the area of maize has increased elevenfold. In the technique of rice cultivation, great differences may be found close together. The areas with most dependable floods follow the transplanting system, timing the field work so that preparation of the ground by ploughing is done as soon as the beginning of local rains softens the baked fields, and transplanting into flooded fields takes place later when the spate reaches the plain. If the local rains and the spate happen to come almost simultaneously, then broadcast sowing is adopted, as it is also where the farmer has inadequate assistance for transplanting. Broadcast sowing yields poorer crops and permits less accurate adjustment to local floodwater vagaries. The vegetable and legume-maize-pepper-tobacco cultivations are in areas working from direct rainwater rather than from floods. In every case cultivation and processing are effected by manual methods until the rice leaves the farm. Half of Lower Thailand's paddy is broadcast.

The rhythm of activity in Lower Thailand is notably short and more sharply defined than in most paddy areas. July is the peak planting month and December the peak harvesting month. A spread of activity arises from differences in the date when spates appear in different parts of the lower Chao Praya and in the middle Mekong (which controls Korat planting seasons).

Though cultivation in Lower Thailand has been non-intensive

and precarious (commonly a fifth is lost each year), the acreage under paddy has increased, spectacularly so since 1950.

Between 1910 and 1940 an additional 5 million acres came into cultivation, less than expansion in Burma for the same period but an impressive additional acreage put under rice by Thai

PADDY FARMING IN THAILAND

Quinquennium	Area under paddy p.a. Million acres	Production clean rice p.a. Million tons	Average exports clean rice Million tons
1916–1920	5.50	1.92	.7
1921–1925	6.45	2.76	1.1
1926–1930	7.14	2.71	1.2
1931–1935	7.93	2.94	1.5
1936–1940	8.45	2.71	2.0
1946–1950	10.40	3.40	.87
1951–1955	13.2	4.5	1.33
1956–1960	13.4	4.9	1.16
1961–1965	15.1	6.2	1.47

farmers alone. Foreigners played no part in the increasing farming labour, all of which has been done by Thais. From 1950 to 1966, farms increased by nearly 6 million acres, by nearly the total rice acreage of Japan.

THE LAND QUESTION

Until early this century, land had little value. It was often communal and held on squatters' rights. There were still large individual land holdings dating from the period when Thai officials were granted land in lieu of salaries. At that time so much land was unclaimed that it could be had by anyone able to farm it. Confusion began to arise in land questions as population increased and the best lands were fully taken up. The farms were often unsurveyed and without deeds. In the delta, floods regularly obliterated land-marks, making identification of property difficult. After 1912 when rice began to have money value in Thailand, new lands were offered to encourage smallholders, but in effect, big landowners obtained even bigger holdings and land speculation intensified with the expansion of rice exports. Delta farming has become concentrated into large units and commercial rice today comes from great estates cultivated by tenant farmers supervised by a rent collector for the absentee landlord.

Round Bangkok and in Rangsit farms are larger than anywhere

else in Thailand and at Dhanyaburi nearly 85 per cent of peasants are tenants. Tenancies average 40 acres each, usually on a yearly basis, so that village life is fluid. Thus the commercial rice is produced by migrating farmers who pay rent, who cultivate very little food for themselves and have no reason to improve the land. Naturally they extract as much as possible from any field they rent, irrespective of overtaxing the soil, which may pass to other hands the following year. Hence, after the progressively heavy rice exports of the 15 years to 1935, came an alarming decline of yield which continues to be one of the lowest.

RICE PRODUCTION (average 1961–64)

	Area Million acres	% change over decade	% irrigated	Production p.a. million tons cleaned	Yield change over decade
Central Thailand	6.7	+ 4	46	3.2	+22
Korat	6.2	+25	4	1.9	+13
North Thailand	1.0	+13	3	0.6	+42
Kra	1.2	+13	7	0.5	+14
Total	15.1	+13	24	6.2	+18

The system of renting ricelands led to borrowing from moneylenders. Tenants bore the losses arising from Nature's variations, which are very considerable. Where farmers started off by possessing a little family land and rented a field or so in addition, their personal property was steadily lost to cover the risks. The landless population has thus swollen, to total 46 per cent of the families in Lower Thailand by 1950, making available the labour which is needed seasonally on commercial rice farms. Outside Lower Thailand, harvesting and planting are communally organised Within Lower Thailand it must be done with hired labour—an additional burden on tenant farmers, whose outgoings are in cash, for rent, land, taxes and wages.

Milling.—Over 1,000 rice mills are located near Bangkok and on the major water channels by which rice moves. The movement of paddy to mills is loosely organised. Paddy leaves the farm in small units and the tenant does not negotiate directly with the mills. Hence there has grown up a complex middleman system mostly run by Chinese, which handles all movement and storage from the farms to the mill. It is this phase in which holding for a market rise may take place. The tenant must turn his rice into

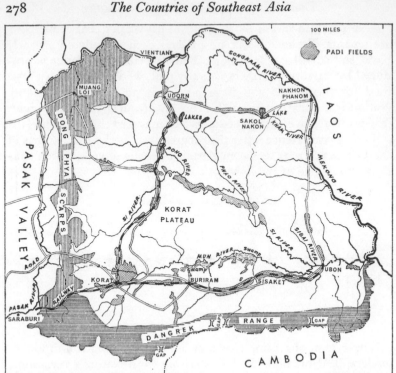

FIG. 93.—The Korat Plateau

cash quickly to meet his obligations, a situation in which middle-men, whether Chinese merchants or Thai officials, profit. Thus the benefits of improved rice prices are largely denied to the farmer and were for a long time taken by the Chinese dealers who com-mercialised Thai rice. From 1946 to 1954 the Government ran the rice trade, purchasing from the peasant at a price which was often only about a quarter of the export value so that the producer gained little.

Of the 1.6 million tons of rice exported annually on an average over 1961–5, 20 per cent went southward for Malaysian con-sumption, 10 per cent to Hongkong, 16 per cent to India and 11 per cent to Japan. In this movement, carried out by foreign ship-ping from the one port, Bangkok, the proportion to Hongkong and Indonesia tended to decrease in recent years, but India, Japan, and Hong Kong are usually Thailand's best customers, in that order.

CATTLE

Related to rice-farming is the cattle breeding which goes on in Korat. Rice farmers throughout Thailand use buffaloes and oxen as their draught animals. Usually each family has a pair of animals, buffaloes being preferred in Lower Thailand and bullocks elsewhere. In Korat, however, the average smallholder owns just over four of these animals and the savannah setting plus fodders from the local subsidiary maize growing, suit this small breeding activity, which supplies draught animals to the cultivators of Lower Thailand. But Korat has no specialist cattle farming. The animals come from smallholders, not from herds. Caravans of these small cattle make their way from Korat to Lower Thailand throughout the year. On the Plateau live about 5 million cattle, 7 million buffaloes an average of 3.2 per acre of riceland as against .7 per acre in the Thai plains. From Korat, too, comes a steady supply of pigs for the Chinese of Bangkok and elsewhere. In 1964, Thailand had 5.4 million cattle and 4.9 million pigs, and was exporting 82,000 pigs and 67,000 cattle.

THE POPULATION PATTERN

Thailand is as thinly populated as the greater part of Burma and North Malaysia. A general average of 290 persons per square mile is distributed so that Lower Thailand has a density of over 350, the Korat Plateau and the teak country of the north have between 50 and 100 people per square mile, while the Western Mountain zone has less than 50 per square mile. Densities round Bangkok resemble those of congested parts of the Red River in North Viet Nam where emigration resulted, while the Bangkok zone ranks neither as over-populated nor a source of migrants. The difference is largely one of "nutritional density," population per acre of paddy (Fig. 95). Lower Thailand has only .96 persons per cultivated acre as against 3.1 per acre in North Viet Nam. In the same sense, the nutritional density of Lower Thailand is far below that of most other regions of the country, which helps to account for the paradox of a large population and a large agricultural production for export (compare also Fig. 61).

Of Thailand's total population, 14.5 million in 1937 and 30.6 million in 1965 estimates, 1.7 million are in Bangkok itself, the only significant city in Thailand, with nearby Thonburi contain-

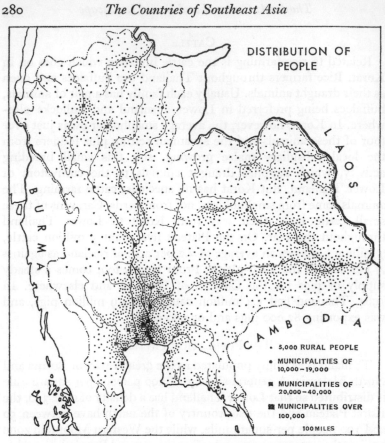

DISTRIBUTION OF PEOPLE

BURMA

LAOS

CAMBODIA

· 5,000 RURAL PEOPLE

● MUNICIPALITIES OF 10,000–19,000

▪ MUNICIPALITIES OF 20,000–40,000

▪ MUNICIPALITIES OVER 100,000

100 MILES

FIG. 94.—Distribution of People in Thailand

ing 410,000 people. Four-fifths of the Thais live in rural villages. Thai census reports are difficult to correlate but that of 1960 gave the current national increase as averaging 3.29 per cent per annum. The crude birth rate is about 2.4 per cent and the death rate 8.5. Over the period 1929–37, 3 million locally born people were added to the population and from 1937 to 1965 a further 16.1 million were added, more than doubling the population in the last 27 years, a rate of expansion unequalled elsewhere in Southeast Asia (except Singapore) (see p. 385).

The rise of population has made it necessary for the Thai paddy acreage to be nearly quadrupled in this century though rice exports rose much more slowly. This fast rate of increase may

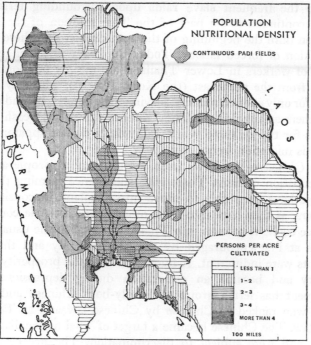

FIG. 95.—Nutritional Densities in Thailand

hot, however, be a modern peculiarity because an estimate of the total Thai population for 1854 was 6 million. Such a sustained natural increase of population justifies questioning Zimmerman's assertion that malaria, arising from the uncontrolled floods, has undermined the Thai people. Indiscriminate drinking of canal-water has repeatedly produced epidemics of cholera and the panicky abandoning of whole centres of population, particularly on Korat, yet the Thai rate of increase scarcely indicates progressive and cumulative debility, notorious though Thailand may be for its swarms of mosquitoes and other disease-carrying pests. Historically the focus of population and of agriculture has steadily shifted south from Chiengmai to what would appear to be the more unhealthy yet more productive settings of Ayuthia and Bangkok.

Thailand has for two or three centuries suffered from labour shortage rather than over-population. This was the background of the slow approach on to the more fertile ricelands of the south and to the frequent slave raids upon surrounding territories. Slaves continued to be part of the Thai solution of the labour question until the beginning of the 20th century and there is still a tradition of forced labour. Today the heavy seasonal require- ments of workers in Lower Thailand are met by temporary mi- grants from the northeast (the Korat Plateau), who stay in the plains for only about 6 months, leaving their families behind to look after their smallholdings. They return with a little cash which suffices for two or three years. Individuals do not apparently re- peat this migration frequently.

The Chinese.—It follows from the shortage of people and the preoccupation of most Thais with subsistence farming that the Chinese have been able to move into Thailand in considerable numbers, as they have into most other Southeast Asia countries. Chinese coolie migration into Thailand has taken the usual form. It was at first encouraged by the Thai nobility and the Thai peasants were indifferent. It fluctuated with the prosperity of the country and became an emigration during depressions. The movement has left a group of locally-born Chinese and Sino- Thais who ranked as Chinese by Chinese law and as Thais by Thai law. The Chinese became a target of Thai nationalist indig- nation and were subject to discrimination. The net movement of Chinese for the period 1925–30 was into Thailand at an aver- age of 37,000 per annum, while for the period 1930–35 it was an average loss of just under 1,000 per annum. By 1960 there were in Thailand a million people described as "of Chinese race," though China claimed its nationals there numbered over 3 million. The Chinese community controlled the middleman and milling aspects of the rice trade, they were the artisans and skilled workers, the miners and the rubber planters of Kra, and the principal importers. They took little direct part in agriculture except as market gardeners near Bangkok, though they dealt in all agricultural produce, kept village shops, and commanded a key position in public affairs, more so than in any neighbouring country.

Indigenous Groups.—Among the indigenous people a wide ethnic range may be recognised. In Lower Thailand, the Tai group (Tai is an ethnic term, Thai is for nationals) dominates. North of Sukotai and in the Korat Plateau live Laos, part of that group widespread in inner Indochina and closely related to the Tai. In all the virgin forest areas are scattered nomadic peoples, of which the most numerous are the Karens who overlap the border with Burma, normally living at altitudes of 1,500–3,000 ft. Among the Northern Mountains at still higher levels are the "hill people" of whom the Miao, Lissu and Yao are representative. Round Chantaburi in the southwest are remnants of Khmer-Cambodian types and a few Annamites have moved round the coast as far as Bangkok. In Kra are the Semang aboriginal types, found also in Malaysia. Along the Kra coasts are the Chao Nam, a group of "gipsy fishermen," Malays totalling about 600,000 occupy the border area south of a line from Singgora to Puket which is an ethnic-religious boundary well north of the political boundary. About 85 per cent of people in Thailand are Tai-Lao, between whom there are only minor differences, so that Thailand is fairly homogeneous, apart from the Chinese traders of Lower Thailand and the Malays of the far south.

Customs.—The preponderance of Tais means that a single language runs throughout Thailand except for the hill and jungle people (Fig. 118). Laos speech is a dialect variation of standard Thai rather than a distinct language. While the Chinese and Malays keep to their own languages in private, they are educated to use Thai publicly. Thai is a tonal language of the Tibeto-Burman type strongly influenced by Pali as a result of long Buddhist missionary activities, and written in a script of Indian origin.

Because the Buddhist tradition is strong, pagoda-type temples have been built in the well-populated zones. Villages have pagodas located outside the house group and not as the nucleus of the settlement, though the religion is integrally associated with social and agricultural life.

It is through the Buddhist priesthood that intellectual life in Thailand relates so much to the tradition of the early Indian colonies, an influence which appears also in the traditional Thai dress, the *panong*, a cloth wrapped round the lower body and through the legs after the manner of the Indian *dhoti*. This dress, common to Thai men and women, differs from the *sarong*-like dress of the rest of Southeast Asia and of the hill and jungle people surrounding the Thais.

Settlement Types.—Village forms resemble those of all Southeast Asia. There are linear villages along levees and similar locations naturally above flood-level, and along the drier edges of the flood plains. Proximity to water is everywhere the chief site consideration. The only landscape of flimsy pioneer type is in the newer commercial rice-farming areas of Lower Thailand where tenants are too mobile to concern themselves with formal village construction. House forms are generally raised, built upon bamboo legs, beneath which the simple farm tools and draught cattle are kept. In Korat and in the Western Mountains defensive village forms are more usual, the houses standing in a rough ring surrounded by earthworks and a bamboo stockade; these in part reflect the need for coralling the cattle and also the social insecurity of these remoter areas. Among Laos the word for a town, *"wieng,"* meaning a fortified place, emphasises this defensive interest. During the flood season, Thai cultivators of the lowlands may become water-borne, putting their whole family on small boats until the waters subside. Many houses are in fact built on bamboo rafts, rather like Noahs' arks, and nucleated as villages on the *klongs*, even in Bangkok, where the network of waterways lined by these house-boats has caused it to be described as the Venice of the Far East.

TRANSPORT

That North Thailand had two-way trading associations with the Shan States and with Burma until 1921 caused Burmese currency to be used there. The anomaly resulted from the difficulty of reaching North Thailand from Bangkok on the Chao Praya whose waters and sandbanks vary so much and so quickly. It was a centrifugal tendency increased by the Thai teak trade being in the hands of those who also held teak concessions in Burma. Burmese, Indian and Chinese traders were at that time dominant in the North. When the Bangkok-Chiengmai railway was built (by 1921) it created a tie, bringing North Thailand into the hinterland of Bangkok rather than of Burmese ports. The teak trade continued to use the Chao Praya system seasonally, while the new railway operated for passengers and minor trading goods.

A similar centrifugal tendency existed in the Korat Plateau which has easier routes towards the Mekong (by shallow boats) than towards Central Thailand with which the connection was by cattle-caravan. Very little trade went into Korat; the outward movement involved agricultural produce and the cattle carrying it to Bangkok were sold to farmers of Lower Thailand. The

Ayuthia-Korat Railway, the first major Thailand line, was intended to establish centripetal forces and the line was extended to Ubon more from political motives than because any trade stream was expected. This railway and the newly macadamised highways to Nongkai and Nakhon Phanom bring Korat rice to Bangkok (300,000 tons per annum of poor grade rice which releases better grades for export from Lower Thailand), together with cattle and pigs. The inflowing traffic to Korat is normally smaller in volume and value, consisting of fish, sugar and manufactured goods, now boosted by supplies for American forces.

The Bangkok-Singapore railway assisted the development of Kra and aimed to tie the southern province to the capital. Its actual flow of freight is small and rubber and tin moving by railway from South Kra to Penang did in practice add to the centrifugal tendencies in the isthmus. In 1961, the total railway freight was 4.7 million tons.

Thailand for years was nearly roadless. In part this results from the technical difficulties of building roads safe from the Lower Thailand floods, in part from doing nothing to rival the railway. Local freight and passenger movement is largely by the rivers and canals. In 1940 the railways carried well below a million passengers and this was quoted to justify not building roads. Southern Thailand is without trunk roads and Bangkok road traffic (67,000 private and 87,000 commercial motor vehicles in 1965) was isolated from the roads built as feeders to the railways rather than national trunk routes. Bullock caravans are being replaced by small "mosquito buses" on new all-weather Korat military roads.

The Chao Praya system is navigable during high water seasons by steam launches as far as 120 miles above Paknampoh. Thus it carries major traffic inland only for about 260 miles, even in the most favourable season. In the dry season launches can scarcely reach 100 miles from the sea. This is a great contrast with navigation on the Irrawaddy and helps account for the slower opening of the north. Ships of 1,500 tons net can reach Bangkok but most rice goes in lighters beyond the bar to the ocean-going streamers. 1,940 vessels took on 4.5 million tons of freight at the port in 1965.

TOWNS

The Thai are traditionally rural but in 1960 12 per cent lived in towns. *Bangkok* (1.7 million, 1965) is the political, social, economic and commercial capital. Thailand is almost a city state, because what Bangkok says is acted upon, the rest of the country being the seat of power. Bangkok became the capital only in 1782, before which Ayuthia was the principal city with Bangkok merely an outpost. The only modernised city in the country, Bangkok has stood apart from the interior. It is a delta port with the disadvantage of a shallow, winding and variable river across which lie great sandbanks impeding access. To its west is industrialised Thonburi (410,000), with rice and teak mills. Many Chinese are to be seen on its streets, sign of their prominence in Thai commerce. Bangkok has an advanced artistic tradition, expressed in ornate temples and palaces of distinctive style, often juxtaposed with other buildings of ultra-modern design.

Besides the Bangkok-Thonburi complex, eight towns each exceed 100,000, urbanisation having been rapid since 1947.

Ayuthia, repeatedly described by 18th-century travellers and twice destroyed in Burmo-Thai wars, has a tradition in Thailand comparable to that of Mandalay. It is a river port and though the main railways pass through it, only farmers and shopkeepers live there in a light and flimsy settlement containing less than 20,000 people, many living upon houseboats threading the creeks surrounding the town.

Chiengmai on the Ping River was once the capital of a Laos kingdom for which Burmese and Thais fought frequently. This is evidenced by the elaborate fortifications. It organises teak rafts which go downriver to Bangkok. Junction of caravan routes into Yunnan (Southwest China) and the Shan states, it has recently become a strategic military base.

POLITICAL UNITY AND RELATIONS

Thailand is unique in Southeast Asia for having remained intact despite European colonisation going on all round it. Its independence of this influence was originally based on the function of Thailand as buffer state between French interests in Indochina and British interests in Burma and Malaysia. Thus independence was tolerated by others rather than maintained by the Thais whose country was steadily commercialised. Its finances were until 1941 linked to sterling and its trade to Singapore. To some extent the Chinese influence in its commerce and trade overseas made

Thailand a Chinese colony. Upon its Chinese community Thailand partly depended for its role as a rice, rubber and exporter.

The country escaped military destruction during the Japanese War, so that its agriculture quickly created the largest post war outflow of rice. Thailand's political structure, sometimes thought to be dangerously inflexible, now shows national stability unmatched by newer independencies. Hence it has become less a buffer state and more the continental keystone of the whole region which looks on China as perilous. British and American influences rivalled themselves to support Thailand, hoping to assure stability and rice for India, Malaysia, Indonesia and Japan. Its rice exports are significant and profitable as never before. Thailand is wooed internationally. Bangkok has grown cosmopolitan, world airways converge there. The new function of Bangkok has made it also the focus of the United Nations Food and Agriculture Organisation (F.A.O.). Several hundred thousand American troops have been for some years in the north with great impact on roads, airstrips, modernisation and commercialisation of previously remote border communities. By 1966 no less than 130 factories were established to supply cement, fertilizers, steel and domestic equipment.

[*One Thai tical or baht was officially about* 14 *Malaysian cents,* 4¾ *U.S. cents or* 4*d. in* 1966.]

Chapter Nineteen

THE NATURAL LANDSCAPE AND REGIONS
OF INDOCHINA

"INDOCHINA" is now a conventional term for the region divided since 1954 into Cambodia, Laos, South Viet Nam and North Viet Nam (sometimes called Vietminh, a party name). The Viet Nams, each aspiring to absorb the other, succeed the previous states of Tonkin, Annam and Cochinchina, under which names they are treated in the extensive French research and source materials and older maps (see p. 316).

It is built round a resistant crystalline Central Massif of great geological age now forming that part of the Chaine Annamitique roughly south of the river Song Buong (Fig. 97). The fractured rocky coast marginal to this massif is part of the northeast edge of the Sunda Platform. Differential movements between this massif and another in South China led to compressional structures between them and the extrusion of igneous rocks. West of the Central Massig, sandstones conceal the substructure.

Between the Central Massif and the Cardamom Mountains and also between the Chaine Annamitique and the South China Massif level expanses of alluvials are still being laid down by the rivers, forming fertile and cultivated lowlands contrasting with the forests of the crystalline highlands Limestone. occurs extensively to the north, intricately eroded by solution into that bizarre karst landscape of the Baie d'Along.

CLIMATE

The climate of Indochina (Fig. 96) is transitional between the continental extremes centring on Asia to the north and the equability of the archipelagoes to the south, complicated by the changing streams of air described in Chapter 2.

Over the period mid-September to March, continental Asia dominates the meteorology and airstreams from the north and northeast bring low temperatures to Hanoi, rains to the eastern

288

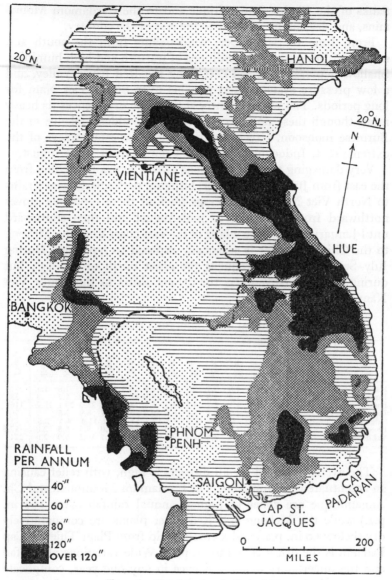

Fig. 96.—Precipitation in Indochina

flanks of the Chaine Annamitique and to the Cardamom Mountains, and dry, sunny weather to the rest of the country.

From June to September, windstreams from the south and southwest bring tropical conditions of warmth and high humidity. Shallow depressions travel east along the Red River Valley, and a low pressure system often remains over South Viet Nam for long periods. The whole country at this time experiences its heavy rains, though these do not come with the sudden violence of the Burmese monsoon. Except in the enclosed coastal valleys of the extreme east, Indochina's maximum rains fall in July–August.

Very damaging tropical typhoons sweep across Indochina from the east from July to November, bringing particularly heavy rains to North Viet Nam. The average track of these typhoons moves northward from February to mid-August and then southward until January, so that the whole of the east coast from the Mekong to the Chinese border is seasonally exposed to typhoons. During July–September they frequent the coast north of lat. 15°, but during October–November, the danger shifts to the South Viet Nam coast (Fig. 14).

RAINFALL IN INDOCHINA (inches)

	Jan.	*Feb.*	*Mar.*	*Apr.*	*May*	*June*	*July*	*Aug.*	*Sept.*	*Oct.*	*Nov.*	*Dec.*	*Total*
Hanoi	.9	1.4	1.8	3.7	8.7	0.7	12.8	14.3	10.7	4.1	1.8	1.1	72
Luang Prabang	.8	.5	1.3	4.5	6.2	6.7	8.9	12.6	6.8	3.2	1.2	.3	53
Hue	7.0	3.1	4.1	2.1	4.4	3.2	3.3	4.6	14.4	25.5	29.1	15.2	116
Dalat	.3	1.1	2.2	7.1	8.1	6.4	10.2	8.6	12.7	8.9	3.5	.9	70
Saigon	.7	Nil	.6	1.6	8.4	13.7	12.3	11.3	14.1	11.4	4.4	2.5	81
Phnom Penh	.1	.6	1.9	3.8	5.0	6.0	5.9	6.4	9.0	9.6	6.8	2.0	57.5
Val d'Emeraude	1.5	1.7	7.2	8.8	22.4	30.6	41.6	41.5	33.7	19.5	9.9	2.6	221

The average rainfall for all districts is high, with relief causing an accentuated precipitation. The Cardamom Mountains and Ch. Annamitique are zones of highest annual rainfall (over 160 in. p.a.) while the Mekong and Red River plains are comparatively dry (below 60 in. p.a.) and a coastal strip from Phan Thiet to Cap Padaran is the driest zone (30 in. p.a.). Wide variations of rainfall and the uncertainty of its incidence in any one year, complicate the agriculture. These irregularities are greatest to the north, worsened by long sunny seasons of high evaporation which accentuate the drought. Uncertainty of rainfall incidence, a factor fluctuating more here than in other Southeast Asia territories, is

most critical for Indochina rice farming and the crop may fail
entirely when the timing of rain or of sunshine is widely irregular.
Thus in Indochina a year with a normal rainfall total may prove
to be agriculturally calamitous if one or two critical times of the
year are abnormally dry or wet. Rains in the north fall as seasonal
drizzles; farther south, they come with more tropical intensity.

NATURAL VEGETATION

Indochina is naturally a forested region of which some 14 per
cent has been cleared for agriculture and another 50 per cent modified by cutover to stand now as savannah.

The forest types discussed in Chapter 4 are well represented in
Indochina (Fig. 104). Tropical Rain Forest occupies most plains
and foothills to 2,500 ft., though lowlands of particularly porous
subsoil may have only Monsoon Forest. While rain forest which
has scarcely been cut at all remains in the Cardamom Mountains
and near Savannakhet, elsewhere shifting cultivation has modified
it to secondary forest. The Ch. Annamitique and the Mountains
of Tonkin carry Tropical Rain Forest broken by great patches of
Monsoon Forest, particularly in the drier uplands adjoining the
Middle Mekong Valley. Stands of teak do not develop extensively
in the Monsoon Forests except in association with crystalline rocks
round Pak Lay in Laos. In South Viet Nam and behind Cap Padaran extensive savannah is a response to the low rainfall. Tropical
grass (Imperator cylindrica), called *"tranh"* in Indochina and
used for thatch, is widespread. Round the Tonle Sap where
seasonal inundations occur, the Freshwater Swamp Forest
contains many Hydrocarpus or *chaulmoogra* trees whose oil is
used for leprosy. The higher altitudes and cooler winters of
Western Tonkin Mountains have produced fairly large areas of
pine forest, with P. Merkusii and P. Khasya as common types.

Mangrove Forests are restricted to three zones of the coast,
the rest being too rocky or too steadily attacked by currents:
(*a*) a discontinuous fringe to the Red River Delta, (*b*) a continuous
fringe to the Mekong Delta, extending northwards into the Gulf
of Thailand from Pointe de Ca Mau, and (*c*) fringe round the
southern end of the Cardamom Mountains.

On the dunes of bays between the rocky promontories of the
Viet Nam coast, are stretches of Casuarina Forest.

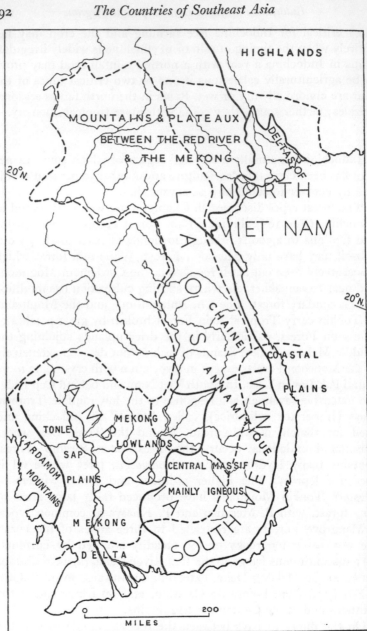

Fig. 97.—The Indochinese States (broken-line boundaries) and their
geographical regions (continuous lines)

REGIONAL LANDSCAPES

Indochina divides into distinctive regions (Fig. 97) which are:—

1. *The North Viet Nam Deltas*, including those of the Red River and adjoining rivers.
2. *The Lower Mekong and the Tonle Sap plains.*—These regions differ from their surroundings in possessing great population densities (Fig. 102) and large-scale agriculture (Fig. 104), both having served as nurseries for distinctive cultural and communal developments (Fig. 103), though the rhythms of development have differed.
3. *The Highlands of North Viet Nam*, north of the Red River.
4. *The Mountains and Plateaux between the Mekong and the Red River.*—These are zones of sharp internal contrasts arising from very broken relief in which population is low and scattered and human development has been slight. The Highlands are transitional to South China and through them has been a constant, poorly channelised, coming and going of peoples between Tonkin and Canton. The negative region of mountains and plateaux relates mostly to Northern Thailand and Yunnan, and has functioned as a refuge for human groups pressed from the north and from the east.
5. *The Viet Nam Highlands* or *Chaine Annamitique*, between the Mekong and the South China Sea, is a composite region politically subdivided into Laos, the wild country draining westward to the Mekong, and both Viet Nams, centring on small coastal and fertile pockets of intensive agriculture and dense population backed inland by negative uplands.
6. *The Mountains of West Cambodia*, including the Cardamom Mountains and the Elephant Range, an undeveloped and repellent region throughout its known history.

NORTH VIET NAM DELTAS

In historic Lower Tonkin, the terrain is flat, almost entirely built up of river alluvium (Fig. 98). Minor differences of level on this flat landscape have major significance for agriculture.

The Red River delta, thickly peopled and intensively cultivated, is edged landward by highlands of rugged limestone. Dunes have been built up on the seaward fringe, and are most developed towards the south. The delta, a large part of it less than 10 ft.

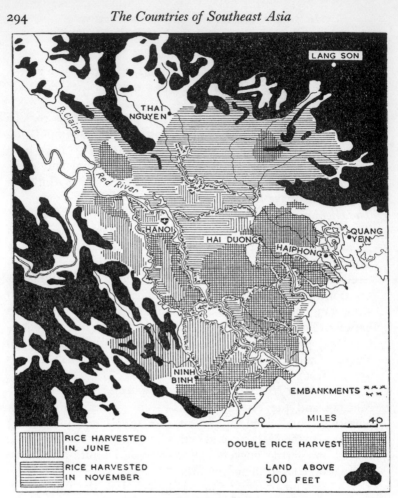

FIG. 98.—The Red River Delta of North Viet Nam

above sea level, is a network of distributaries carrying off water of the Red River and of many shorter streams, such as the Song Cau, from the deforested northern highlands. A distinct drift of the main distributaries towards the south has been going on under the influence of heavy sedimentation from these northern tribuatries. The deltaic surface merges northwards into deltaic fans built by tributary streams. Numerous embankments, some old terraces and old levees, provide drier and safer zones for settlement and also model the delta surface into shallow basins which suit the needs of rice cultivators. Towards the north, little of the delta is embanked and tides spread far inland, especially in the dry season when the outflow of fresh river water is least. Adjoining deltas, the Song Ma, Song Chu and Song Ca, extend the landscape of the Red River delta southward, but the highlands approach closer to the sea and in places isolate parts of this southern alluvial extension, whose agricultural development differs from that of the Red River delta because there is a broken inland

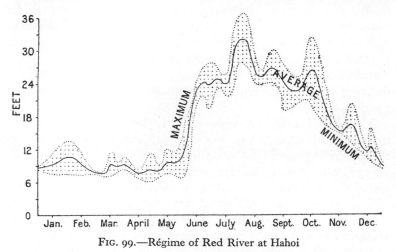

FIG. 99.—Régime of Red River at Hahoi

belt of coarse, sandy soil (probably marine) without natural or artificial embankments to control spates.

The North Viet Nam deltas are difficult to approach from the sea and the water channels across them are subject to frequent changes (Fig. 99). These features have impeded overseas trade and make even Haiphong (outport of Hanoi) not easily accessible by modern shipping. Towards the south, the delta extends seaward at the rate of about 300 ft. a year under the influence of heavy river alluviation and longshore drift.

Upon the delta daily temperatures fluctuate sharply, especially in winter, when temperatures are lower than in any other Indochinese lowlands. Rainfall, while showing some seasonal contrasts, is more evenly distributed than farther south, benefiting from South China cyclones in winter and from rain showers brought across the Gulf of Tonkin by the northeast winds. Winter rains come as prolonged drizzles which have high effectiveness and make second cropping possible. Annual rain totals are very variable, which, added to wide variations of river flooding, make for unreliability in the rice farming.

Red Delta rice cultivation depends on flood regulation, which has become more difficult following continued deforestation of the surrounding hills, irregular sedimentation and slow migration of the distributaries. Major embankments have been built at various times to control the floods, but have often led to more disastrous floods, as when in 1926 about one-third of the delta was under water following a break in the embankments. As the height of embankments is being progressively increased, the whole river profile tends to rise above the delta level. This admittedly aids the distribution of water to the fields, yet makes more difficult the draining of the inter-embankment basins when once these are flooded.

Modernised irrigation goes on side by side with primitive irrigation. About 6 million acres of lowland are under rice; of these 2 million acres (in the centre and east) are double or treble cropped each year, 1.3 million acres being harvested only in summer, and 1.5 million acres only in winter. In response to the great variety of soil, weather and flood conditions from place to place in the delta, over 300 different types of paddy are grown. These produce almost 3.2 million tons per annum, with an average yield of 17 bushels per acre, though it may vary from 37 to 5 bushels per acre in different localities. Of this production less than a tenth goes into the provincial markets; the rest is locally consumed by the farmers who are working largely on a subsistence basis. Farms are small; 36 per cent of cultivated land in 1943 consisted of properties of less than 5 acres each, and land hunger was acute, giving rise to a tradition of communally held land which was redistributed to clan members periodically. By 1905 about a fifth of the farm land was held under this system, resembling collective farming, and thereby conditioned people to Communist land policies.

Through the war years, North Viet Nam acreages under paddy remained fairly close to prewar figures, indicating the predominant interest in subsistence farming.

The delta carries 13 million people with a rural density averaging 1,950 per square mile which is equivalent to figures in the crowded lowlands of China and Japan (Fig. 102). The urban population is small and while Hanoi, the capital, has over 640,000 people, most other towns contain less than 10,000. Highest rural densities (over 2,800 per square mile) are in districts lining the Red River and in a belt towards the sea, round Hanoi and round Ninh Binh. These concentrations are in the more fertile zones, particularly on newer alluvial soils. To the east and north, delta populations do not reach such densities, except near the manufacturing town of Haiphong (369,000 in 1960), the Yunnan railway terminus, where cotton mills and cement works are operating. The dense rural population is nucleated for communal help in agricultural work and located where there is some physical security against flood risks. Villages are levee settlements, embankment settlements, sand-dune settlements and groupings round the foot of hills rising above the plains.

THE HIGHLANDS OF NORTH VIET NAM

A terrain of igneous mountains and plateaux of sandstone or limestone, the Highlands have a pattern aligned from NW. to SE. Through them flow rivers on similar lines, but of varying maturity, most of them having sections of deep narrow gorge. A small portion of the Si Kiang drainage system (Song Tso Kiang) carries water northward from the Highlands. Much deforestation has gone on, leaving naked hill landscapes recalling those of South China. Only a scanty farming population is in this region, chiefly settled by hill peoples (Mau, Lolo, Tho and Nung).

BETWEEN THE MEKONG AND THE RED RIVER

An extensive mountainous area between the Red River and the Mekong reaches greater average heights than the North Viet Nam Highlands. To the east, this unit has a NW–SE. trend in its relief which is of massive limestone or crystalline rocks forming inaccessible blocks of country. Towards the Mekong the structural trend becomes NE–SW., and involves old sandstone which forms plateaux, such as the Plateau de Tran Ninh, south-east of Luang Prabang. The rivers are here deeply incised in narrow valleys which are infertile, uncultivated and sparsely peopled. The chief stream is the Black River, paralleling the Red River before joining it, and navigable to Cho Bo; despite its rapids this is the artery of local transport.

Both these mountainous regions west and north of the Red River delta are deeply ravined, generally forested and left to isolated groups of Laos (or Laotians), Man, Miao and Lolo hill people who have moved in from Yunnan over the centuries. They are stratified in distribution, Laos occupying valley floors and growing wet paddy, and Man groups living at slightly higher altitudes and practising shifting cultivation. Higher still, above 3,000 ft., live the Miao who maintain an energetic mixed hill farming of dry paddy, maize and cattle, and are the militant late-comers to North Viet Nam. The Lolos are less localised but frequently appear settled beside the Laos.

The population of these highlands totals barely 2 million, with a density of 48 per square mile which, while very low compared with the delta populations, exceed that of other Indochinese uplands. North of the Red River is somewhat more densely populated than to the west, where there are large virtually un-inhabited areas.

THE VIET NAM HIGHLANDS

An extensive region, geographically so far, between the Mekong and the Col de Dong Trai Mit and Cap St. Jacques, mostly known as the Chaine Annamitique, is less a chain and more a sequence of weathered plateaux sloping more gently to the west than to the east, where high spurs reach the sea to enclose between them small coastal plains which have been attractive to settlement. From the Song Buong valley northward, the chainlike character is more pronounced as a consequence of the fold-fracture structure involving extensive sandstones and limestones. South of the Song Buong are ancient crystalline masses partially covered by lava flows and flanked to the west by old tabular sandstones leading down to the Middle Mekong and the province of Laos. Upon the basalt lava flows, a laterised soil, called "terres rouges," has proved more fertile than most other upland soils surrounding it.

On the east, the small coastal plains vary considerably in size, fertility and population. They are isolated landwards by broad stretches of negative country edged by abrupt scarps and cliffs and they relate more to the sea than to the mainland. They lack modern harbours and suffer from violent seas which build bars and lagoons across the mouths of the short torrential rivers.

Across the Highlands during midsummer blow the "Winds of Laos," which are föhn winds bringing hot, dry, violent winds to the coastal plains and imperilling agriculture by causing rapid desiccation. At other seasons the coast induces local variations of climate by shielding certain areas and varying the incidence of land and seas breezes. To these factors attaches special importance because the regional rainfall is highly irregular and torrential. The coastal plains are subject to the dangers of typhoons and the risks of local floods because it is difficult to regulate the torrential rivers which frequently have a régime resembling that of the *chaungs* of Burma.

Within the coastal lowlands live 8 million people in patches of great density associated with the deltas of Song Ma, Song Chu, Song Ca, Huong Giang, Quang Ngai and Quang Nam, separated by virtually unpeopled, barren uplands with a few nomads. Hue (120,000) and Da Nang (Tourane, 115,000) are the chief towns. Towards Cap Padaran the coastal lowlands contain less people, a result of droughts and greater agricultural risks. These lowlands are almost entirely peopled by Vietnamese who have steadily migrated southward from the northern deltas.

Over towards the Mekong, population thins out, consisting in the uplands of Tai, Nung and Miao tribes derogatively called Moi (savages) by the Vietnamese. The many tribes of Moi operate interesting transitions between, and combinations of collecting-hunting, shifting cultivation in the forest, and sedentary agriculture. Laos, the state of the Middle Mekong, is peopled by Laotians who are ethnically related to Tais. They live in small agricultural hamlets, have historic Buddhist associations and semi-feudal customs. Their thinly settled forest country concealed infiltrating guerilla armies during over twenty years of the Viet Nam struggles.

The settlements of Laos are beside the Mekong, with Vientiane (capital, of 100,000 in 1963), Luang Prabang, Pakse, Savannakhet and Tha Khek as the largest. The river is a line of transport, especially between Savannakhet and Vientiane, but external contact by the Mekong is impeded by rapids, narrows and shifting sandbanks, the signs of immature drainage.

Rice occupies $2\frac{1}{2}$ million acres of land scattered through the Viet Nam coastal plains, the larger units being towards the north. Irrigation methods in these plains are primitive. To the north double harvests (June and November) are normal, while farther south, three harvests a year may be gathered, as at Quang Ngai, where harvest occur in April, September and January. About 1 million tons of rice are produced annually, the low yield

FIG. 100.—Cambodia, Tonle Sap and the Mekong Confluence

arising from soil poverty and irregular rainfall. Salt water fishing is fairly intensive along the rocky coast: a large portion of the catch is salted or fermented into the sauce *nuoc mam*, which are readily exportable forms of fish.

THE LOWER MEKONG AND TONLE SAP PLAINS

The plains south of the Phnom Dangrek Hills, Pakse, on the Mekong, and the Plateaux du Muong and Djiring (which end the

Chaine Annamitique), and east of the Cardamom Mountains, have three subdivisions:

(a) *The Tonle Sap Alluvial Plain* is one of the most interesting features in Southeast Asia. The area has been converted from an arm of the sea into a plain containing a lake, the Tonle Sap, as the result of Mekong sedimentation which has taken place within probably historic times. The transition was slow enough to retain in the lake fish which are adaptations of marine species. The Tonle Sap (Fig. 100) is shallow (not deeper than 6 ft. anywhere in the dry season) and in process of further subdivision by lacustrine deltas built out by the Stung Sen and Stung Chikreng, and it is blocked at the eastern end by sedimentation which forms the Veal Phoc (Plain of Mud).

The amount of water in the lake varies widely. At low water (November to June) its area is about 1,000 square miles and its breadth 22 miles. Its water then drains to the Lower Mekong across the Veal Phoc through great floating islands of tangled vegetation. At high water (June to October) its area may be 4,000 square miles, its width 65 miles and water flows into it from the Mekong. This reversal of flow at the flood season reflects the fact that the Mekong is so sedimenting its distributaries that it has seasonal difficulty in discharging to the sea. The Tonle Sap thus acts as safety valve for the Mekong, probably explaining the low flood risk in the Mekong Delta, which needs no embanking such as is essential in Tonkin.

(b) Through the lowland east of Tonle Sap, the Mekong continues a southward course as an elaborately braided stream over flat clay lowlands above which small sandstone outliers rise as low hills, as near Khone. Rapids in the Mekong below Khone are caused by an east-west belt of basalt and there are minor obstacles of similar type near Kratie.

(c) *The Mekong Delta* may be considered to begin from Phnom Penh (Fig. 101) where the Tonle Sap outflow joins the Mekong and the whole river divides into two major distributaries, the Fleuve Anterieur and the Fleuve Posterieur, which in turn subdivide before reaching the sea. The delta merges and is continuous with the Vaico-Saigon deltas on the north which are less fertile and less populated. The whole is built of sticky

Fig. 101.—The Mekong Delta

mud with occasional belts of fluvial sands. Except at the
mouth of the Saigon River, the delta's coast is not approach-
able by major shipping and the distributaries are unnavigable
except for very small boats. The Ca Mau Peninsula (Presqu'ile
de Ca Mau) is a gigantic spit, built from Mekong materials
carried southwest by marine currents. It is extensively forested
and advancing seaward at 200 ft. a year, so that charts of it
are unreliable.

For nationalist reasons, the Cambodians plan a new outport across
the delta, at Kompong Som, south of Kompot on the Gulf of Thailand.

On the Mekong Delta, a midsummer drop of the otherwise
high temperature is caused by rains which here derive from
southerly winds in a monsoon régime; at Saigon 76 in. of rain fall
from April to December (with peaks in June and September)
and only 4 in during the rest of the year.

The delta floods resemble those of Lower Thailand. Cultivation depends entirely on the natural flood rhythm and there is practically no control of the water. At Bathé, for example, on the border of Rachgia and Long Xuyen, from October to January the Mekong is flooding its delta to depths from 18 in. to 6 ft.; during July and August the delta is flooded by local rains. For these conditions, "floating rice" was devised and introduced at the end of the eighteenth century, an innovation which alone made possible the great increase of paddyland on the delta this century. "Floating paddy" is sown without using a seed-bed in the dry period of March and left to grow through the river-floods for harvesting in January when they subside. Strains of this paddy may have stalks as long as 18 ft., which permit the plant to continue growing through floods which would drown normal types of paddy.

Of the population of this whole lowland, about 7 million are in the South Viet Nam portion and over 6 million in the much larger Cambodian portion (Fig. 102). In the former, the average rural density is about 230 and in the latter 75 per square mile. In the Mekong Delta itself densities reach 600 per square mile, well below those for the Red River delta, an interesting contrast between two deltaic regions of similar climate and agriculture. The explanation lies in the physiography of the Mekong Delta which has been the scene of faster deposition and more dangerous inundations (comparable with the Chao Praya floods) than the technology of earlier Cambodians could deal with. The Indian colonial period here is fairly well documented: at that time interest centred round what is now the Tonle Sap, more particularly at Angkor on the line of overland routes into Thailand, an area where there appears to have been prolonged social disruption by disease and flood. The parts of the delta most densely populated and intensively cultivated today are those where Annamites have immigrated from seaward causing population to increase very rapidly this century.

Though elsewhere generally rural, the population of the lowlands is urbanised at Saigon and Cholon, twin towns on the northeast margin, whose population was 1.9 million in 1955, dropping sharply to 1.3 million in 1961; they are on the Vaico-Saigon rivers linked by creeks to the Mekong distributaries across a complex of merging deltas. Saigon, whose site relative to the Mekong resembles that of Rangoon to the Irrawaddy, has fluctuated widely in population and economy during the unrest and civil war which have been almost continous since 1946.

Where the deltaic soils are specially fertile and water control has been developed for paddy cultivation, new populations have settled; towards the coast the population thins, where tides make the subsurface water brackish and prejudice farming. Away from the distributaries, on the interfluves or mesopotamia, the population also thins out. Distinct linear patterns of settlement along the river banks and along the lobate lines of old dunes, now well inland from the sea, are apparent throughout the delta.

In the Cambodian plains, densest population spreads across the lowlands from the South Viet Nam border towards Kompong Chhnang and Kompong Cham. Phnom Penh, the state capital (460,000 pop. in 1963), is fairly central to this lowland though eccentric to the state as a whole. Population round Tonle Sap is confined to a narrow band between the marshes bordering the lake and the forested hills. Most villages are above the limit of summer floods and therefore well away from the lake itself, though some pile villages have grown up close to it. Angkor, the ancient capital near the provincial market of Siem Reap, lies well north from the lake today, though its old importance probably hinged upon waterside location during the Indian colonial period. Battambang (pop. 29,000 in 1961), second town of Cambodia, lies far south of the lake on a well cultivated lowland now connected by rail to Phnom Penh. (See Grostrer.)

In South Viet Nam 6.2 million acres are now under paddy, with a further 6 million acres round Tonle Sap and its adjoining Cambodian lowlands. This cultivated area has increased fivefold since about 1875 and rice monopolises it more than anywhere else in Indochina, though the farming is much less intensive than in North Viet Nam. On the delta zone, where the pioneers have been most active and effective, the rice yield averages in places 1,200 lb. per acre; characteristic of the landscape are special granaries for storing that rice which is paid as rent-in-kind by the tenant farmers. A variety of floating paddy is grown in the fields liable to specially deep floods round Tonle Sap. About 5.1 million tons of paddy are being produced on the delta with another 2.1 million tons from Cambodia. The former is derived from compact holdings averaging 22 acres each held on a system by which the tenant halves the harvest with the landlord. In Cambodia 80 per cent of the holdings are less than 10 acres and mostly owner-cultivated.

The rural situation differs from others in Asia by being strongly affected by civil war. While acreages under rice quickly rose in Cambodia, in South Viet Nam they declined by half and, after full-scale modern war developed with the presence of North Viet Nam and American armies, the farming position became blurred.

The second activity is fishing in the Tonle Sap which produces 123,000 tons fish annually, one of the world's largest inland fisheries. The fish are dried, smoked or fermented for export from the region by junks which move out of the lake to the Mekong by way of the Snoc Trou or mud flats. In many places the junks must be pushed through mud and vegetation rather than floated in the ordinary sense, taking 15 days to reach Phnom Penh from Kompong Luong. There is a sea-fishing industry round the Mekong Delta where the river discharge contains much food for fish. South Viet Nam landed 375,000 tons in 1965.

Saigon-Cholon form the capital and chief port of South Viet Nam, on a river accessible by ocean-going vessels despite shifting bars, which make an awkward entry worse by being off the main shipping routes. Now in decline (only 2 million tons shipping entered in 1962, cf. 5.2 in 1937) and French in layout, Saigon has depended on rice exports and still handles almost all the Cambodian and South Viet Nam outflow. That trade links it characteristically to ports elsewhere in Asia, though the rice it handled was only 310,000 tons in 1962 against 1.5 million in 1935.

The isolated *Mountains of West Cambodia*, the Cardamom and Elephant Mountains, resemble an island surrounded on the one side by the Gulf of Thailand, and on the other by the fertile Mekong lowlands and their extensions westward to Lower Thailand. Densely forested and very rainy, the Cardamom Mountains are the highest points of a plateau over 3,000 ft. high, a little known area of crystalline and calcareous rocks with short, violent and deeply entrenched rivers. Its coast is lined with miles of inaccessible cliff, broken by low-lying estuaries supporting isolated farmers. The zone is negative, isolated and very thinly peopled.

Chapter Twenty

THE CULTURAL AND SOCIAL LANDSCAPE
OF INDOCHINA

THE POPULATION PATTERN

CIVIL war has recurred in Indochina for the last twenty years during which armies have been raised and civilians shifted about by force or by fear, increasing the urban populations and changing the rural areas so that the next true censuses must show much modification of the patterns as they appear on the estimates we now have to use.

As Fig. 102 shows, the Indochinese countries are most unevenly peopled, a consequence of being most unevenly farmed. The arable areas compared with state areas of Laos, North Viet Nam, South Viet Nam and Cambodia are respectively 2, 6, 9 and 12 per cent. Some districts have densities reaching 2,500 persons per square mile, but 1961 state densities were 20 per square mile in Laos, 215 in South Viet Nam, 271 in North Viet Nam and 79 in Cambodia.

The region's empty spaces have been repugnant to people of the crowded coasts and deltas because the forests and mountains are considered to have endemic malaria from which the lowlands are relatively free, preventing permanent internal colonisation in modern times and undermining the stamina of people already settled there. The barrier of malarial forests largely accounts for the greater success of coast-wise migrations into Southeast Asia from the north. The rise and fall of historic kingdoms in Southern Indochina may also be related to disease.

Of the 41.6 million people in the Indochinese region (1964), 18 are in North Viet Nam, 15.7 in South Viet Nam, 5.9 in Cambodia and 2 in Laos. Scattered irregularly between the major communities are about a million hill tribesmen. The Vietnamese of old Annam were migrant for years, creating minorities beyond their borders. Chief non-indigenes are Chinese and their offspring, prominent in markets, ports and Cholon. The population is three-quarters rural, only eight towns exceeding 100,000 each.

Because the population is rural and dependent both for income and for subsistence on the one crop, rice, the people are largely concentrated in the rice-growing areas. The ratio of population to rice areas, the "nutrition density," is thus more relevant than the ratio of population to state areas. There are fairly wide variations of nutrition density state by state. Many districts have far greater nutritional densities than those of the state as a whole. Cua Bang, for example, is a North Viet Nam province with a nutrition density of eight per acre!

Population pressure is clearly most acute in North

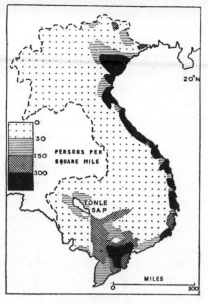

Fig. 102.—Density of Population in Indochina

Viet Nam and is rapidly increasing in the lower Mekong Valley.

In this century, the Indochinese states, like many colonies, increased rapidly, largely by high birth rates. Over 1937–57, the region added ten millions (45 per cent) to its population. For

INDOCHINA: NUTRITION DENSITIES BY STATES

	Persons per acre of paddy (1961)
North Viet Nam	2.9
Cambodia	1.8
South Viet Nam	2.5
Laos	1.2

1957–61, South Viet Nam and Cambodia both increased at 3.9 per cent p.a.

The contrast in population density between the crowded alluvial lowlands and the thinly peopled uplands reflects differences in agricultural potentiality, differences in outlook, and different forms of land utilisation. The communities in the deltaic lowlands round the Red River have grappled with the difficult conditions there and acquired a reputation as hardworking farmers; the Mekong lowlands, originally developed without continued success by Cambodians and Laotians, later received large numbers of Annamites who settled and coped satisfactorily with the Mekong paddylands, which thus were some of the last in Southeast Asia to be brought into production. Why Cambodians should thus have lagged behind other communities in agricultural initiative is not easily determined, especially in view of their historic importance, of which we have evidence at Angkor. It is probably less an inherent defect of Cambodians and more a combination of progressive debility, high disease rates and a long series of Mekong inundations which for a period were beyond control by the techniques available.

MIGRATION

Migration in Indochina has assumed several forms. When the agricultural potentialities of the Mekong Delta began to be realised early this century, large numbers of Chinese from South China and Hainan immigrated to take up land, and later to specialise in trade along the inland waterways. Few of these farm immigrants are still agriculturists. The Chinese community has fluctuated with the state of trade, although local nationalism in modern times has put a brake upon it, but Chinese are important as rice dealers (recalling the situation in Thailand), rural moneylenders, fish dealers and middlemen. Indochina contained 293,000 people of Chinese origin in 1912, the 1960 total being over a million—750,000 in South Viet Nam, 230,000 in Cambodia and 58,000 in North Viet Nam.

More significant, though less easy to trace, has been the migration of Annamites from the old overcrowded kingdom of Tonkin and Annam to the Lower Mekong. Transport difficulties hindered the movement of Annamite peasants, who had their usual aversion to leaving their traditions and their home fields, however congested. They moved on short contracts to plantations in the hill zones, but they avoided the mosquito-infested forested areas when they sought permanent settlement. Despite these factors, about 4 million Annamites now live in the paddylands of South Viet Nam and 350,000 immediately over the Cambodian border, the result less of recent events and more of that southward drift of

Annamites which has gone on since the 14th century and irrespective of the French influence. Most of the migration was uncontrolled but as many as ten thousand contract labourers a year were reported. Thus the population balance has steadily changed, hastened since 1954 by the migrations of some 80,000 peasants away from North Viet Nam, complicated by regrouping farmers into fortified villages.

ETHNIC GROUPS

In Indochina is found again the contact between earlier people of Indian and Far Eastern origin who have left influences in culture, religion and language (Fig. 103). The old Hindu tradition is centred in Cambodia, the Imperial Chinese in North Viet Nam, so that the two major population foci, the Mekong and the Red River lowlands, differ ethnically; the areas between are zones of interaction between these peoples and the migrant hill people at different stages of development, who are partly wanderers overland from the north and partly refugees from the lowlands. Thus Indochina's physiographic differences are paralleled by different population densities and differing ethnic groups, and the impediment of the Chaine Annamitique has served at once to separate the major groups and to conserve a few hill peoples.

Among the peoples we may distinguish two distinct types:

1. The South Mongoloid people, fairly short, brachycephalic, with short flattened nose, straight black hair, the epicanthic eye and a yellowish-brown skin. Vietnamese often show these features clearly, retaining their slight build even after considerable intermingling with other types. The Laos of the Middle Mekong Valley are of this Mongoloid group which has spread south and east from Tibet and Thailand (see also Fig. 62)

2. A short, long-headed, moderately broad-nosed people with wavy black hair and straight eyes is a type widespread in the East Indies and represented here by the Cambodians who, while mostly a cross between South Indian colonists and Mongoloids, are smaller, darker and better built people than Vietnamese. The physical types among the Mois are generally Nesiot, though some (Ho, Yau, Meo, Lao, Neua, Dam, Deng and Lu) relate to woolly-haired Negritos.

These physical distinctions between North and South Indochina are emphasised by language (Fig. 118). The Tonkinese

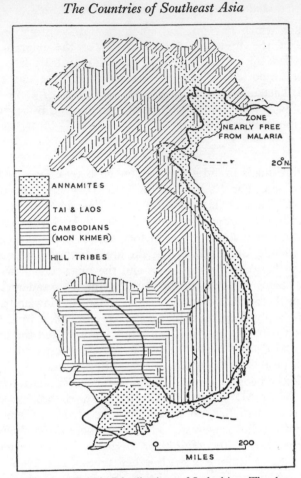

FIG. 103.—Ethnic Distributions of Indochina. The dotted line marks the boundary of the kingdom of Annam until 1948

and Annamites have monosyllabic tonal languages, related to Cantonese, once ideographic and now rendered into a romanised form. Southern and western parts of Indochina use Cambodian or Khmer languages, which have no tones, are polysyllabic and written in a derivative of a South Indian script. Tai, used close to the Thailand border, while tonal, has many Cambodian roots. The hill peoples speak languages allied with Malay, Burmese and Tibetan, and many languages without literatures are preserved among them.

INDOCHINESE AGRICULTURAL TYPES

Agriculture in Indochina has been largely of subsistence type, direct use of home-grown produce limiting the circulation of commodities and of money among the peasants. Plantation agriculture, under European direction, has developed only this century and the area involved is less than 1 million acres as compared with 18 million acres of indigenous cultivation, and Indochina's total area of 185 million acres. The indigenous agriculture concentrates in the lowlands, the plantations in the uplands more especially in the more fertile "terres rouges" over laterised basic lavas in the southern Chaine Annamitique.

The Red and Mekong Deltas are the key farming areas, with small but well-cultivated patched in the innumberable small coastal basins of Annam. The Red Delta has been built up of alluvial loams, sands and clays in proportions varying from place to place. North of the Red River and west of Hai Duong the alluvium is sandy, elsewhere a loam of red, yellow or grey colour predominates. These soils are laterised, accounting for the tendency to bake hard when left bare for a time. Cultivation and repeated flooding by the heavily silted Red River seems to be stemming the worst effects of laterisation, enabling soil fertility to be maintained despite very heavy cropping. In South Viet Nam the most fertile areas are of recent Mekong alluvium which has a high nitrogen and potassium content but is deficient in lime and phosphorus. Certain alluvials round Saigon appear to have suffered podsolisation, to become infertile sandy grey earths not suited for agriculture.

Three types of indigenous land utilisation (Fig. 104) have grown up in different regions:

(*a*) Coastal plains to the east as far south as Binh Dinh are intensely cultivated with two or three crops each year, on a subsistence basis with negligible trade in agricultural products.

(*b*) On the plains of the Lower Mekong and Tonle Sap, land is farmed more extensively. Only one crop is usual each year and much potential farmland remains unused, though acreage has doubled since 1938. From this lightly-peopled zone, a large surplus of rice is produced, forming the chief source of Indochinese rice exports.

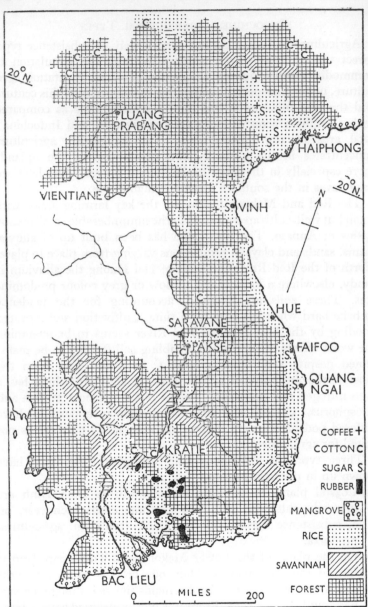

FIG. 104.—Land Use in Indochina

(c) In the jungles, the hill tribes follow the self-sufficing system of shifting cultivation.

The human ecology of rice shows clearest in the older, more intensive agriculture of historic Tonkin and Annam, where personal or family farming (as opposed to tenant farming) and seasonal communal co-operation is customary. There the peasant has a small thatched wooden house, stilted for security and nucleated into small hamlets (an isolated farmhouse is unusual) but at the same time close to his small fields.   A few fowls and pigs are his only livestock and produce little cash income. On an average, individual peasants do not own buffaloes or oxen, but a group of them shares one animal for ploughing. The simple farming tools are everywhere home-made, almost entirely of wood, for rural Indochina is still largely in "the Wood Age."

Gourou, reporting a 1934 field enquiry on these self-sufficient farms, showed that the net annual cash receipts of a Tonkin farmer averaged $32 (probably $160 at today's rice prices). Additionally such farmers produced enough for home use and charges-in-kind. The position has worsened since due to the reduced size of holdings.

In South Viet Nam during its rapid pioneering phase—1920–40—large personal holdings were staked out before development actually began so that cultivation through tenant farmers was usual. Immigrants from North Viet Nam found it difficult to get virgin land and formed a floating labour population including many who were desperate to remit money to families elsewhere. A tenant family rented 12–15 acres of paddyland which all members helped to work, paying half the crop as rent. The family consumed most of the balance and its adults would do as wage earners for short periods to get a cash income when sale of the home rice surplus was insufficient. Gourou says such tenants averaged $85 annual cash receipts (say $425 today).

In all parts of Indochina the farmers became involved with moneylenders, who were often the Chinese merchants upon whom the peasant depended for selling rice and purchasing his other needs, as has been the case with Burmese peasants.

Of 15 million acres cultivated in 1940, 12½ million acres were under paddy, which provided about 6 million tons of cleaned rice, supplying 90 per cent of the Indochinese diet and 70 per cent of the exports. The whole rhythm of rural life centred on rice, which set the pace also for general commercial activity The margin of rice exported, 1.3 million tons per annum for 1936–40, was only about 20 per cent of the annual production, so that given normal wide fluctuations of climate, yield and price, Indochinese commerce always depended on a narrow margin.

Colonial struggles halted farming in Indochinese states more than did World War II and 6 million acres went out of cultivation by 1947. The regional farmed area in 1961 was about 19 million acres (17.1 under paddy) but production was proportionally less at 7.1 million tons rice of which barely 6 per cent was traded externally; Cambodia was exporting a quarter of its product.

Maize became a common supplementary food crop on paddylands of uncertain water supply. Cambodia has 350,000 acres of maize on the fringe of Tonle Sap floods. Both Viet Nams use maize as a cottage garden vegetable but North Viet Nam is also bartering it to Eastern Europe for capital equipment.

Tropical root crops (sweet potatoes and yams) and tropical fruits are grown as dry season crops in small patches, generally for home use. The limit of coconut cultivation is in South Viet Nam, north of which winter temperatures are too low. Extensive coconut plantations have been located near Bong Son, Binh Dinh, Faifoo, Quang Ngai, My Tho, Ben Tre and Vinh Long. Groundnuts were grown in the Tonkin Delta but vegetable oils entered little into trade, because of competition with vegetable oils in other French territories and of the French preference for olive oil in domestic use.

A quick-growing dwarf mulberry peculiar to Indochina is often grown in combination with rice round Hai Duong in North Viet Nam, and Thanh Hoa, Quang Nam and Binh Dinh in South Viet Nam, for feeding silkworms as a cottage industry, now fading out. Cotton cultivation was tried in Thanh Hoa and in Cambodia, but the crop does not attract peasants. Pig-farming has greatly increased: Cambodia and South Viet Nam exported over 230,000 pigs in 1961 (to Hong Kong, Malaysia and Borneo) when Cambodia also exported 15,000 cattle.

Sugar is grown as a peasant crop, now occupying about 100,000 acres of which the majority is in South Viet Nam, in the Vaico Oriental, Saigon and Dong Nai Valleys. North Viet Nam is building a sugar mill near Hanoi. The crop has shown poor yields so that production (South Viet Nam 1.1 million tons cane 1964) has been less than consumption.

The well-populated districts of Nam Dinh in Tonkin, Tourane-Faifoo in Annam, and Gia Dinh, Hoc Mon and Kompong Cham in the Mekong lowlands cultivate poor quality tobacco, which needs considerable labour and forms a dry-season cash crop for peasants, although it is unsuitable for export.

Indochina has been one of the world's largest pepper producers. Characteristically a product of Chinese cultivators on the Kampot plains of Cambodia, 1,200 tons pepper were exported from there in 1961.

Plantation agriculture was started in Indochina as part of the colonial system and concentrated mainly along the Saigon River and the Dong Nai in South Viet Nam, in the "terres rouges" districts, near Kompong Cham in Cambodia, and scattered through Laos and North Viet Nam. Of the large plantation holdings by Frenchmen, nearly two-thirds were under paddy and sublet to tenant farmers, a condition unparalleled in any other Southeast Asia colonial territory; the rest was in rubber, coffee and tea.

Indochinese rubber plantations appeared later than those elsewhere in Southeast Asia, totalling in 1940 less than 150,000 acres spread over 350 plantations. The industry was state-fostered and once enjoyed a tariff-protected market in France. In 1965, South Viet Nam was producing 69,000 tons and Cambodia 49,000 tons, the value of their rubber exports having in some recent years exceeded the value of rice exports.

Coffee, an early plantation enterprise in the hills near Phu Ly, shifted south as soils became exhausted, to small estates on the "terres rouges" near Vinh and Quang Tri, producing 3,500 tons in 1961 (cf. 2,600 tons in 1938). Tea occupies 25,000 acres in the South Viet Nam uplands, yielding 5,000 tons for local use in 1965.

THE POLITICAL UNITS

Indochina was so named by the French who exercised political control over the different physical, economic and human regions which were divided into the following administrative units mostly evolved from older states:

1. *Cochinchina*, which became a French colony in 1862, was never before a unit on its own. It consisted of the seaward fringe of the Mekong Delta colonised by Annamites and Chinese.

2. *Cambodia*, a kingdom which began as a Hindu colony, is centred in the Tonle Sap agricultural basin.
3. *Annam* was a historic "empire" which had been expanding southward since the 14th century.
4. *Tonkin* was also an "empire" but for long under Chinese suzerainty until conquered by the French in 1884. Later it became the focus of militant nationalism and the Viet Minh party.
5. *Laos* was originally a group of small principalities pulled politically between Annam and Thailand.

Nationalism mixed with racialism and Communism after 1946 produced civil war. In early 1955 the independencies were:

(*a*) *Cambodia*, roughly the kingdom as in (2) above, using Phnom Penh as its capital and the riel as currency.

(*b*) *Laos*, a consolidation of (5) above with Vientiane as its capital and the kip as currency.

(*c*) *South Viet Nam*, "the Republic of Viet Nam" since 1956, consists of old Cochinchina and Annam south of lat. 17°, with Saigon-Cholon as capital and the piastre as currency.

(*d*) *North Viet Nam*, a Communist state called "the Democratic Republic of Viet Nam," formed of Tonkin and Annam north of lat. 17°, with Hanoi as capital and the dong as currency.

North Viet Nam, while needing China's aid, dreaded the resumption of colonisation from Peking. Using Sino-Russian equipment, it engaged in a devastating guerrilla civil war by the Communist Viet Cong (a party name) against the U.S. alliance with South Viet Nam.

INDUSTRIES

Local industries have been limited to small-scale production by cottage workers of pottery, basket-work and woodwork for domestic use. Haiphong has recently built two cotton mills.

Of the worked minerals, coal, and tin with its tungsten associate, have been by far the most important, but anthracite pro duction amounted to over 3.5 million tons (cf. 2½ million for 1941) and tin concentrates totalled 1,450 tons in 1964.

Coal was mined almost entirely from the Quang Yen field which stretches in a fairly large arc close to the coast north of the Red River. Close to the surface and fairly horizontally bedded, the coal, of anthracite, smokeless and high calorific type, was first mined opencast. As mining moved east into descending strata, shaft systems became necessary. Capable of over 2 million tons per annum, the fields have the advantages of accessibility, proximity to shipping and the best type of coal in all Southeast Asia, where coal deposits of any kind are few. There are small unworked inland coal beds at Tuyen Quang, Phan Me and Nong Son.Using nearby coal, Haiphong makes about 300,000 tons of cement annually. Its installations have been heavily bombed.

Tin came into production very late in Indochina, whose total annual output was only 1,500 tons by 1940. It occurs at two centres:

(*a*) Near Cao Bang in the Pia Ouac Massif of North Viet Nam close to the Chinese border, where an outlier of Yunnan tin lodes appears. Here at the mining village of Tinh Tuc the lode tin includes some wolfram: its output once went by Haiphong to Singapore for smelting. About 2,500 are now employed on this mine using newly acquired Russian equipment, producing about 900 tons annually for a local tin smelter. This tin is prominent in government to government barter between North Viet Nam and Eastern Europe.

(*b*) Near Nam Patene beside the Mekong in Laos is an alluvial tin deposit whose cassiterite has impurities hindering smelting. Its export of 480 tons ore in 1965 was the most valuable single item of Laos' exports.

Small quantities of silver, lead, antimony, iron ore (from Kampong Thom in Cambodia and Thai Nguyen in North Viet Nam), gold, phosphates, zinc (from Cho Dien in North Viet Nam) and precious stones have been mined occasionally.

COMMUNICATIONS AND TRADE

The road pattern consists of a fan of roads round Hanoi, another opening through the Mekong lowlands from Saigon, and the two linked by the coast through the Viet Nams. The road from Saigon is only seasonally usable to Vientiane and the Mekong has little immediate prospect of serving as a highway into Asia.

The railway system is more sketchy, though designed by the French to link together the northern and southern zones of population. The main line, now interrupted, ran between Saigon and Hanoi, keeping close to the east coast. A separate line from Phnom Penh to Mongkol Borey provides an isolated system intended to link Cambodia to the lower Mekong river shipping and avoid the mud flats below Tonle Sap. From Haiphong and Hanoi a railway overcame relief difficulties to run northwest as far as Kunming, the only railway to inner China: the new Hanoi-Linchow line is vital for North Viet Nam military supplies and has been heavily bombed.

The external routes are shipping lines to Saigon, a few local shipping services to Haiphong and airlines linking Saigon to Bangkok, Singapore and Hongkong. Coastwise shipping links the coastal population and trades with Thailand and South China. The American military supply base at Danang could become a major new port.

The Indochinese states export agricultural produce of low value to weight. Of the total exports in 1964, valued at $446 million, rice formed 28 per cent, rubber 51 per cent. Their imports are processed goods and capital equipment. Of the 1964 imports valued at $1,294 million, the greater part was textiles and machinery from the U.S.A., Japan and India.

The collapse of this region's rice export has been crippling internally and serious for elsewhere in Monsoon Asia. The Indochinese states combined only exported about 218,000 tons rice in 1963 (cf. 1.4 million in 1940) and this trade may never recover to earlier volumes. Only 30 of Saigon's rice mills were used in 1964.

The situation is confused. The new states are not well established in geographical literature. Most accessible data is in reports of ECAFE which has projects for developing Tonle Sap and harnessing the middle Mekong. In 1965, widespread military action in South Viet Nam paralysed trade which became a one-way flow of military material. Major transfers of people and changes brought by mechanised armies in the Viet Nam war mean that few topographical maps and economic statistics can be relied on.

[*One South Viet Nam piastre was officially 5 Malaysian cents, 1¾ U.S. cents of 1½d. in 1966. when it was accepted as equal to the Cambodian riel and four times the Laotian kip. The North Viet Nam dong, being Communist currency, is not quoted internationally but, originally equal to the piastre, it now has an estimated value of 1 Malaysian cent, ¼ U.S. cent or ⅛d. sterling. These currencies are very weak.*]

Chapter Twenty-one

THE PHILIPPINE ISLANDS

PHYSIOGRAPHY

ELEVEN islands, Luzon, Mindanao, Samar, Negros, Palawan, Panay, Mindoro, Leyte, Cebu, Bohol and Masbate, in that order of size, account for 95 per cent of land area in the Philippines. The other 7,000 islands of the group are mostly a few rocks or corals showing above the sea, with areas of less than one square mile each. Themselves separated from the Asiatic mainland by deep seas, the Philippines are flanked to the east by one of the world's profound oceanic trenches (over 7 miles deep) and they form part of the "fiery girdle" of volcanoes, earthquakes and tectonic instability, which rim the Pacific on meridional lines. A knot of different structural lines sets the pattern of these islands. Through Luzon, Samar, Leyte and Mindanao distinct N–S. fold-fault systems are apparent in continuation of that line of structures paralleling the eastern edge of the Sunda Platform. To complicate the physiography, volcanoes and their ejecta dominate the landscape from the south as far as the southern peninsula of Luzon, an extension of the volcanic line evident in Minahasa. Athwart these meridional trends lies another continuing the ancient SW–NE. form lines of East Malaysia and marked by horst and graben landforms such as the deep collapsed block now containing the Sulu Sea which is edged with linear fracture remnants forming the Palawan and Sulu Islands. It may also be traced in the alignment of the Zamboanga Peninsula of Mindanao and in the islands of Negros and Panay.

The Philippines can be conveniently grouped as (1) Luzon, the large, well-populated island of the north; (2) the Visayan Islands, arranged roughly radially round the Visayan Sea, and including Samar, Negros, Panay, Leyte, Cebu, Bohol and Masbate; (3) Mindanao, the second largest island, well to the south; (4) Palawan and the Sulu Islands, stepping stones between the Philippines and Borneo. High relief is general throughout the islands which are surrounded by reefs and marine terraces of coral, accounting for the difficulty of approach in modern times. Luzon and Mindanao are the only units of sufficient area to have distinctive regional differences within them.

Upon the islands limestone, shales and sandstones occur in small outcrops and cause local variations of soil.

To the north in Luzon the Cagayan Valley flows meridionally in a tectonic trough between the eastern high Sierra Madre Mountains and the Central Cordillera on the west, to form one of the key agricultural regions of the Philippines. Roughly paralleling it farther east beyond the Central Cordillera, the Middle Luzon or Manila Plain opens to the sea at both ends, at the Lingayen Gulf and Manila Bay, and forms a densely populated farming zone. The Central Cordillera extends south to the latitude of Manila, whence it is interrupted by a graben-like lake plain, the province of Laguna. South and east of Laguna, Luzon loses its meridional form lines to become a fretted, varied country of volcanoes, spreading from the Taal volcano behind Batangas to Mayon Mountain near Albay. On the east of Mindanao the Diuata Mountains repeat the meridional structural lines and are separated by the Agusan Valley from the Lanao-Bukidnon upland where groups of extinct volcanoes cause the Cotabato River to have a complicated course in part meridional, in part related to the SW–NE. structure of the Zamboanga Mountains, and provide soils whose qualities make the valley the largest potential agricultural area of the territory. Mindanao otherwise has a landscape of high rugged mountains and rolling uplands; Mt. Apo at 9,450 ft. is the highest Filipino mountain.

Throughout the Philippines drainage is by short, violent streams of immature development.

CLIMATE

Insularity and latitude combine to make the climate of the Philippines distinctively even and mild in its temperatures which range between 75° F. and 85° F. everywhere and throughout the year. More variety from place to place and seasonally is evident in the rainfall régime yet even in this respect there are neither the extremes of total rainfall nor the seasonal contrasts found in comparable latitudes of Burma, Thailand and Indochina. Streams of the southern and northern tropical air masses play over these islands in a rhythm differing from the rest of Southeast Asia as a result of the northeastern oceanic location. The northern air masses exercise by far the most continuous influence, flowing over the islands from October to April without modification as northerly and later easterly winds. May is the month of equatorial calms, particularly to the west. From July to August southern tropical air comes as winds from slightly east of south bringing very heavy rains everywhere, especially to the western islands.

RAINFALL IN THE PHILIPPINES (inches)

	Jan.	*Feb.*	*Mar.*	*Apr.*	*May*	*June*	*July*	*Aug.*	*Sept.*	*Oct.*	*Nov.*	*Dec.*	
Baguio	1.2	.7	1.9	4.9	15.8	15.7	42.3	45.5	28.3	17.0	3.4	2.2	178.6
Paracale	18.1	10.9	8.1	4.1	7.0	8.5	11.4	6.8	9.6	20.6	19.5	20.0	144.6
Manila	1.0	.5	.7	1.2	5.1	9.9	17.0	16.6	14.4	7.7	5.6	2.5	82.2
Tacloban	14.0	8.7	6.2	5.3	6.2	7.9	6.9	5.5	6.0	8.0	10.9	14.0	99.6
Zamboanga	2.1	2.2	1.5	2.0	3.5	4.2	4.9	4.0	4.7	5.7	4.2	3.4	42.4
Cebu	4.2	2.9	2.0	1.7	4.5	6.4	7.2	5.7	6.9	7.7	6.4	5.0	60.6
Davao	4.8	4.4	5.2	5.8	9.3	9.1	6.5	6.5	6.7	7.9	5.3	6.1	77.6

These conditions interact with the variations of altitude and differences of aspect to produce four types of rainfall (Fig. 105):

1. An alternation of wet and dry seasons: a dry winter and spring followed by a wet summer and autumn bring to western parts of Luzon, Mindoro, Negros, Panay and Palawan a régime resembling that of Burma, though the cool season is more humid.

2. A wet season throughout the year with a distinct maximum in winter is characteristic of the Bicol district of South Luzon eastern Samar, Leyte and eastern Mindanao.

3. An important variant of (2) has no pronounced heavy rainy season, yet considerable rains fall most of the year with a minimum but by no means a drought for about two months in spring. The Cagayan Valley, the plains round the Visayan Sea, and north-central Mindanao, significantly the important agricultural areas, experience this rainfall régime.

4. An insular uniformity of rains at all seasons, without pronounced wetter or drier seasons, occurs as a coastal régime along northeast Luzon, southwest Bicol and east Mindoro, western Leyte and most of central and western Mindanao.

Total rainfalls vary between 40 in. and 180 in. with highest falls on southwest aspects.

The Philippines form probably the world's most typhoon-infested area because just east of the islands is the zone where

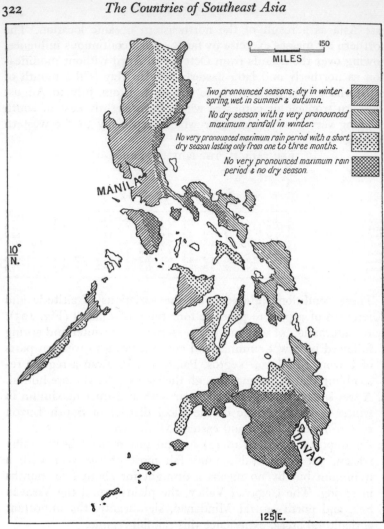

FIG. 105.—Régimes of Rainfalls in the Philippines

begin the typhoons moving towards East Asia (Fig. 14), so that the Philippines feel the effects, if not always the full force, of most of those typhoons which finally cross Indochina, South China and Japan. In the period July-September the typhoon tracks invariably pass across Luzon. During November-December, which are also months of intense cyclonic activity, the tracks more frequently cross the Visayan Sea. At the onset of the typhoon seasons, cyclones take a more south-to-north route across the Philippines. Very few typhoons ever cross Mindanao in which respect that island resembles the East Indies.

Soils

Recent and frequent tectonic changes have produced highly diversified soils upon which laterisation is the process operative almost everywhere in the Philippines, although mature laterites are infrequent. Large areas have immature transported or volcanic ash soils and many coastal plains have a fertile soil derived from weathering of extensive uplifted corals, as in Cebu. Regular soil renewal is here a prerequisite for the maintenance of fertility, and zones with regular local flooding by heavily silted streams (as in the Cagayan Valley) or with frequent addition of volcanic ash (as in Negros) support the intensest and longest established agriculture. A contributory factor in the general low quality of soil in the Philippines is the persistence of shifting cultivation (called *caiñgin*) coupled with a steadily increasing population, and few areas of the main islands are nor suffering from overcutting or overburning.

Land Utilisation

About 15 per cent of the Filipino surface is cultivated, though cultivation is most unevenly distributed (Fig. 106). On Luzon the Cagayan Valley and the west coastal fringe of the Ilocos and La Union are narrow cultivated belts. The Manila Plain and its extensions through the volcanic peninsula south of Laguna de Bay is now the largest and most continuous agricultural area in the Philippines. Coastal plains of the Visayan Islands, Panay, Negros and Cebu, are prosperous agricultural areas whose continued fertility relates to basic volcanic soils and weathered coral soils. Elsewhere agricultural units are small and isolated, often related to local alluvial fans and transported volcanic ash.

Forests and Mining

Large patches of Tropical Rain forest persist in northeast Luzon, on Samar, southern Negros, Palawan and, largest forest of all, on Mindanao, where the continuous forest cover resembles that of North Borneo. Tropical Swamp Forests having little

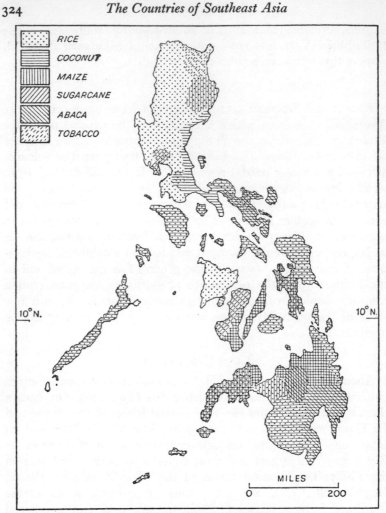

FIG. 106.—Agriculture in the Philippines

opportunity to develop in so youthful terrain, are only found round the lakes of the Agusan and Cotabato Valleys in Mindanao. Upon the Central Cordillera of Luzon relief has induced much pine forest. Large areas of Secondary Forest (called *cozon* in the Philippines) cover districts marginal to sedentary agriculture, where shifting cultivation is still widespread, i.e. on the flanks of the Central Cordillera, on Panay and Masbate and behind Cagayan and Cotabato on Mindanao.

Mining has had little effect on Filipino land utilisation and plays a subdued and limited part in the landscape pattern. That the region has igneous formations in its structure implies some mineralisation, against which have operated the difficulties of isolation and low yield. While Luzon gold and rumours about it drew external interest from as far afield as China and Spain at various times, large-scale exploitation of the gold is very recent, most mines dating from about 1913, since when mining rose to an all-time peak volume in 1940, when there were about 200 gold-mining companies, yielding 1.1 million ounces, valued at $76 million, chiefly in Mountain Province of Luzon working the lodes of Baguio and Bontok. Production declined to 426,000 ozs. in 1964 The absence of any lowgrade coals on Cebu and Albany retarded development of other minerals, but the domestic output of coal increased until heavy oils came into use; in 1965 about 96,000 tons of coal were extracted as against 41,000 tons in 1938. Iron ore, again mined at Camariñes Norte for export to Japan, had a 1965 output of over 1.4 million tons. Chrome ore produced in Zambales amounted to 468,000 tons in 1964, while manganese ores of Sequijor Island south of Cebu and of Basuanga (between Palawan and Mindoro) were producing 8,000 tons content in 1964. Copper, the once favourite metal of the volcanic East, is mined in Mountain Province and 60,000 tons copper content were extracted in 1964. The new mercury mines in Luzon now yield over 850 tons annually.

AGRICULTURE

Because it occupies a large area (estimated 25 million acres in 1965) and employs over 65 per cent of all Filipino workers, agriculture has been the primary activity of the Philippines (Fig. 106). The types of crop are much the same as those of Southeast Asia, though differing in emphasis and equally unconcerned with animal farming. About 37 per cent of the cropped acreage is normally in paddy, one quarter of it on the dry system; 24 per cent of the farmland grows maize; tropical root crops (yams and tapioca) occupy 3 per cent of the cultivated area. These are all food crops grown for local consumption. In addition, 25 per cent of the cropped area is for commercial production and the emphasis in the Philippines is on coconuts (on 15 per cent of the cropped area) with lesser acreages of hemp and sugar. The Philippines, by

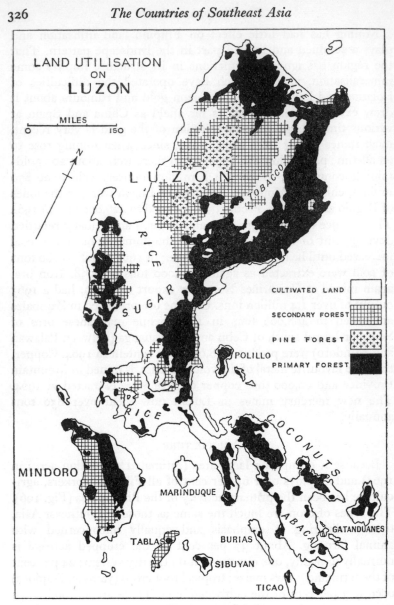

FIG. 107.—The Northern Philippines

specialising in coconuts, clearly differs from the commercial cropping of most of Southeast Asia and relates more closely in agricultural pattern to the easternmost East Indies.

For social reasons, agriculture aiming at both food and trade has become more commercialised in the Philippines than else-where and maximum return, rather than sustained return, has been the farming objective, facilitated by the reliable, evenly distributed rains and the continuous growing season. Hence double cropping is very common. Rice often follows rice on the same piece of ground and corn follows corn, and rotational schemes are not much practised except in non-irrigated farming among the hills. Thus in normal years Filipino statistics will show more acreage cropped than is cultivated, the explanation being that about 20 per cent of the fields are double-cropped.

Regional agricultural specialisation appears very distinctly, encouraged by spatial isolation and by great differences in soil. Rice will grow to some extent on every island, but the heavier soils, level landscape and alternating wet and dry seasons of Central Luzon cause that area to be specially suited to lowland rice. Coconuts, which need a climate without prolonged dry season, are extensively grown in South Luzon. Abaca (Manila hemp) has been found peculiarly successful under the even rains and high humidity of Davao where volcanic soils retain their fertility even with this exacting crop.

Luzon may be divided into five agricultural regions (Fig. 107):

(a) The Central Luzon rice area, where sugar cane is the chief subsidiary crop.

(b) The Cagayan Valley with large rice areas pressed well up the hillsides on the elaborate terraces of the Igorotes (whose skill pre-dates commercial farming), and supplemented by tobacco and maize.

(c) In the Ilocos-Mountain region of northwest Luzon rice, maize and potatoes are grown on the narrow coastal plain.

(d) In that part of South Luzon east and south of Laguna and including Tayabas, is a zone growing rice as subsidiary to coconuts on large plantations.

(e) In the extreme southern tip of Luzon, the volcanic region, rice fades out to give place to an agriculture specialising in coconuts and abaca, the latter invariably associated with volcanic soils in the Philippines.

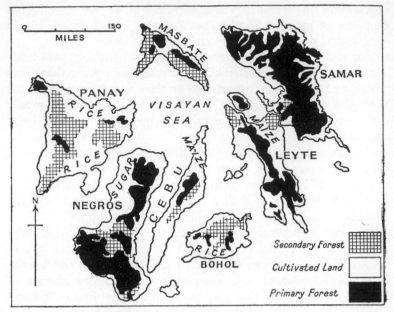

FIG. 108.—Land Use in the Visayan Islands

Among the *Visayan Islands* (Fig. 108), a zone of vigorous agricultural activity, Panay specialises in rice, and western Negros in sugar came. Cebu is a maize island with subsidiary rice. The other Visayan Islands have a poorer agriculture based on rice, coconuts and a little subsidiary hemp and maize.

Mindanao, a less developed island (Fig. 109), is fringed with subsistence farms cultivating a little rice, maize and coconut, except in Davao where half the cultivated land carries hemp and pineapples for canning. In recent attempts to colonise this island, the uplands were leased as cattle pastures, and the lowlands mechanically cleared for commercial paddylands largely irrigated.

Farming methods resemble those of all Southeast Asia. The hoe, the mattock and small sickles (*karit*) are used on rice farms, and the wooden ploughs are of the older soil-opening rather than the soil-turning type. While much discussion of mechanical methods went on during the American colonial period, in total the modern tractor and harvester have had no significant place in the Filipino agricultural system, which is essentially small-scale family farming. Over half the farms (as distinct from the proper-

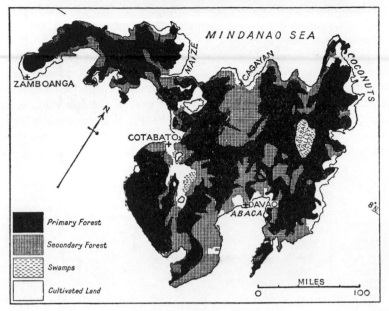

Fig. 109.—Land Use in Mindanao

ties) contain less than 5 acres each and about a quarter have only 2½ acres each. Farms are, however, much bigger in the commercial crop and pioneer areas of Mindoro, Mindanao, Negros and Masbate.

Irrigation is on 1,600,000 acres rice, aiming to distribute water rather than to counter drought, so that most systems have no storage or reservoir arrangements. Only upon the irrigated land is double cropping possible. Sugar has been farmed on irrigated land to a minor extent—differing in this respect from the technique in Java. The Igorote water systems of Mountain Province are at least twelve centuries old and repeat in the Philippines that skilled and intensive farming evident on the Javanese hills. While a substantial acreage in the Philippines is usually described as irrigated, in reality this consists of mere bunding to retain direct rainfall. Over three-quarters of the irrigated land is in the Manila Plain.

Over the period 1960–63, agricultural yields in the Philippines were only 680 lbs. cleaned rice per acre, lower than any other Southeast Asia territory. The Philippines is the heaviest user of chemical fertilisers in the region, applying 81 lbs. per arable acre in 1961. Agricultural development is, however, most uneven among the islands.

Rice.—Self-contained subsistence farming is less prominent in the Philippines, for historic reasons, than in other Southeast Asia territories, but local foods, of which the most important are rice, maize and yams, occupy nearly 73 per cent of the cultivated area and meet the major food needs of the Filipino population as a whole. Rice production before 1941 was about 1.4 million tons annually as against 2.8 million for 1966. The islands are complemen-

RICE PRODUCTION (average 1961–4)

	Area Million acres	*% change over decade*	*% irrigated*	*Production p.a. thousand tons cleaned*	*Yield change over decade*
Ilocos	0.36	+ 2	30	96	+19
Cagayan	0.81	+43	15	262	−14
Central Luzon	1.31	− 21	34	620	+32
South Luzon	1.01	+25	17	310	0
Bicol	0.75	+19	27	238	−36
Visayas	1.7	− 7	13	488	+ 9
North & East Mindanao	0.61	+40	12	136	−38
South &West Mindanao	1.4	+200	22	456	−20
Total	7.95	+18.5	21	2,606	+ 4

tary in their food production normally, yet there was a steady post-war inflow of rice until 1959, after which it was less than 9,000 tons p.a.

Rice stands upon 7.9 million acres or 36 per cent of cultivated land, providing the largest item in Filipino diet and in local cash crops. While grown by small farmers for domestic consumption, large commercial estates (*haciendas*) of rice exist in Central Luzon and Panay, districts containing 32 per cent and 12 per cent respectively of all Filipino paddyland. Mindanao carries 13 per cent of Filipino paddy, reflecting the size of Mindanao rather than a special interest in rice production. Half the total crop comes from Luzon, a quarter from Mindanao, whence rice is shipped to the other islands, particularly to the Visayas which, though intensively farmed have a net rice deficiency. At one time much was of upland varieties from shifting cultivators. Southwest Mindanao trebled its rice area over 1953–63 and mechanised to become a major source of Filipino food (see p. 331). Altogether a thousand distinct varieties of rice are recognised, indicating the subtle variations in local conditions. Transplanting is the usual method for lowland rice which has two seasons, as against one for upland rice, sown broadcast. The first lowland wet paddy is transplanted as early as May in Mindanao, but is deferred until July to the north in the Cagayan Valley. This will be harvested from September in the south to January or February in the north. Second cropping is not customary far south: on the Visayan Islands second transplanting starts about November for harvesting in April and in the Cagayan Valley starts in February for harvesting at the end of June. This latitudinal variation in the timing of heavy work periods has facilitated inter-island migration of labourers. Dry paddy activities are a month or two earlier than those of the first wet paddy cropping.

In keeping with the practice of other Southeast Asia territories, rice harvesting makes heavy demands on labour because the cutting is by hand with a small sickle or a knife (the Filipino *yatab* is like the Malay *tuai*) and even farmers with a few acres are obliged to use outside labour, customarily on the basis of giving the harvesters a portion of the crop. Communal farming help is less common in the Philippines than elsewhere. Only in commercial paddy-growing districts are modern rice mills found much milling still being done by hand. Commercial rice growing is becoming mechanised.

From Central Luzon milled rice goes to Manila by rail, road and coastal vessels, the largest surpluses originating in Nueva Ecija, Tarlac and Pargasinan. Thence it is traded exclusively by sea to Cebu, Davao, Albay and Negros, at two peak seasons of rice movement, January-February and August. This internal rice trade is largely done by Chinese dealers, paralleling the condition in most parts of Southeast Asia, with the result that Filipino nationalism was often directed to eliminating these "foreign" intermediaries even though they were frequently long-standing residents in the Philippines.

Maize.—Maize became one of the staples of Filipino diet as an effect of early and prolonged colonial association with Central America where maize was indigenous. It is grown a little on the upland belt with distinct wet and dry seasons, but is more general in areas without a dry season and it is very popular with shifting cultivators. For food, the maize is sun-dried, ground and eaten in various dishes resembling those of rice. It occupies 4.8 million acres, about two-thirds the area in rice, the greatest single producing area being Cebu where half the cultivated land is under maize, producing a quarter of the Filipino total. Negros, Leyte and Mindanao between them account for nearly half the total maize acreage and the people of these four islands have become principally maize-eaters. Maize is also prominent in Bohol, Masbate, Isabela and Cagayan. A moderate yield is obtained, to produce 1.3 million tons altogether (1966). In Cebu signs of soil exhaustion are becoming apparent in the maize yield which was there much lower than the Filipino average. Several maize crops can be raised each year and three seasons of planting-harvesting can be recognised though the first produces 60 per cent of the total, and the third crops are quite small. The chief seasons are (*a*) late winter or spring sowing (January to May), and (*b*) autumn sowing (October). Harvesting is in each case about three months after planting.

Other Foods.—While they occupy only a small dispersed acreage yams, sweet potatoes and tapioca are prominent in local diet. Root-crop acreages increased to 650,000 acres in 1966. Large quantities of legumes and savoury or peppery vegetables are cultivated to form a rounded diet which for most Filipinos is vegetarian, by necessity rather than by religious conviction. Protein food is chiefly from inshore fishing which landed 686,000 tons in 1965, and pork – 158,000 tons in 1964, having doubled over the decade. Animal farming is small. Buffaloes and oxen are rural draught animals though mules are common, relic of the Spanish period. The country is almost self-contained in cattle and pigs, the quantity of pork produced being higher than in any other Southeast Asian country.

Commercial Crops.—Of crops grown fundamentally for commerce, the most important have been sugar cane, coconuts, hemp and tobacco, together with small areas of crops which have been tried in nearby territories. Rubber has significantly not been taken up, although Mindanao has suitable climatic conditions; apart from about 1,300 tons produced annually by 8,000 acres in Zamboanga, interest in rubber remains negligible.

Influences behind the characteristically subdued development of Filipino commercial crops are:

1. The early Spanish colonial system did not encourage pioneer agricultural activities.

2. The change by which the Philippines became a U.S. colony towards the end of last century, followed by a Filipino-American War, brought a state of insecurity and uncertainty at the very period when most other Southeast Asia territoreis were going ahead with commercial agriculture. By the time pacification had taken place, other tropical areas were too competitive to encourage new rivals in rubber or rice production.

3. Association with the United States tariff systems and the virtual autarchy of North America operated against the production of Filipino sugar, which had to compete with Cuban and Louisiana cane, of Filipino fruits, which rivalled Californian and Hawaiian products, and of Filipino tobacco, rivalling that of Georgia.

4. There was a sufficient field for investment and pioneering in the United States to dissuade from similar initiative so far away in the Philippines.

5. The working of Filipino gold mines conveniently paid for United States manufactured imports without stimulating Filipino agriculture to long-term improvement.

6. Isolated by distances and by politics from the rest of Southeast Asia, the Philippines were little influenced by experiments, incentives, and developments taking place there.

Sugar.—Although coconuts occupy the greatest cash crop acreage, sugar cane had first place in value. It was estimated for 1940 that 2 million Filipinos depended on sugar for their livelihood, $500 million were invested in it, and over the quinquennium 1935–39 sugar formed 45 per cent of export values. Among the world's major sugar producers, the Philippines then ranked after India, Cuba, Java and Formosa. Sugar-growing practically disappeared in 1942 with violent repercussions in Filipino country economy which was geared to average a million tons sugar annually. Post-1946 expansion was rapid and by 1965 802,000 acres were producing 1.75 million tons sugar of which 1 million tons were exported, worth $370 million.

Commercial sugar-growing centres on Luzon and Negros which combine about equally to produce 85 per cent of the total output. The Luzon sugar zones are Tarlac, Pampanga, Batangas, Laguna, Pargasinan and Bataan. Negros sugar plantations concentrate to the west of the island. In Luzon, sugar grows in conjunction with rice as a smallholding crop, half the farms averaging less than four acres each of sugar. The estate or *hacienda* system is more typical of Negros where there are over 400 estates cultivating between 250 and 650 acres each. Upon each of these as many as 250 men will be needed during the milling season, tapering to about a quarter of this number for the rest of the year. Hence for the brief harvest period thousands of labourers must be brought from Panay and Bantayan. Because the cane grows best on a sandy loam which is not flooded even during the rainy season, upland locations are favoured. Haciendas use mechanical equipment for ploughing, smallholders the buffalo and wooden plough. Planting is begun in October to the south, continuing until January farther north. On Negros second cropping of new canes rising from the old root stock (ratooning) is common, as in the West Indies. Harvesting starts in November and may go on through April, labourers using the *bolo*, a form of chopping knife common throughout these wooded zones (*vide* the Malayan *parang*). Haulage to the mills, known as "centrals," is by narrow-gauge railway in the commercial areas, or by cart to small mills producing coarse sugar for local use.

The system of milling is the one common even in Europe in sugar beet areas; the mill is a private concern entering into agreement with growers who undertake to plant a certain acreage regularly over a pre-arranged period which may be as much as three years. In return, the mill extracts the sugar retaining 40–50 per cent for its service. The balance of sugar is sold by the grower. Mills do not purchase sugar outright nor engage in planting. Of the centrals in 1963, 14 were on Luzon, 20 on Negros and 6 on Panay.

Some fibre from the cane is used for papermaking and large quantities of potable alcohol are produced everywhere, the local rum being called basi. Production of sugar is roughly: Negros 59 per cent, Luzon 33 per cent, Panay 5 per cent.

Coconuts.—In acreage planted and number of people engaged, coconuts have been an outstanding feature of Filipino cash farming. Over 2½ million acres under coconuts give employment to 4 million Filipinos. By 1965, the Philippines produced three-quarters the copra of all Southeast Asia and coconut formed 36 per cent of its exports. Coconut cultivation proved remarkably elastic over the war period largely because the trees are perennial and production can be increased or decreased within wide limits solely by varying the intensity of collecting the nuts. Most small-holders have coconuts growing on their land; whether they sell depends on the inducement.

In 1965, copra production exceeded 1.4 million tons and exports of coconut oil or equivalent were near 890,000 tons, the Philippines making advances in this trade despite the competition of detergents with the soap industry.

Some 30 per cent of acreage under coconuts is in southern Luzon, on the wetter east side out of the track of the more damaging type of typhoon. On Mindanao is 25 per cent of the coconut acreage. Large plantations do exist, yet most of the crop comes from scattered smallholdings. The tree is a continuous producer after six years and smallholders harvest the dropped nuts rather than organise gathering from the tree. Ninety per cent of the nuts go to make copra, one-third by sun-drying, the balance smoke-dried. Over 1959–60, nearly .6 million tons of oil were exported annually. Copra is collected among the islands and ship-ped in small boats to Manila, centre of the oil extraction and export trade, and to Cebu which reships overseas without processing.

Abaca.—This perennial plant, yielding a fine hemp-like fibre (Manila hemp), resembles a related species, the banana, and reaches heights of 10–20 ft. The fibre comes from the leaf sheath on stalks or shoots, of which 12–20 may grow from a single root. It is native to the Philippines, whence most of the world supply now comes forming only 5 per cent of Philippine ex-ports.

Abaca grows on rolling hills of well-drained fertile soil where there is an even heavy rainfall; a dry season is unfavourable. It grows commercially in South Luzon and Davao, the former carrying 43 per cent of total acreage, on a mixed farming basis, the latter having been a Japanese mono-cultivation venture. From a total area of barely half a million acres, about 118,000 tons of fibre were produced in 1965 and nearly half was from Davao; the crop has not been diminishing. The fibres are extracted by a serrated or smooth knife drawn up and down the sheath. One plant may go on producing for 25 years.

Tobacco.—First introduced from Mexico by Spanish mission-aries, tobacco found the Philippine climate suitable and became

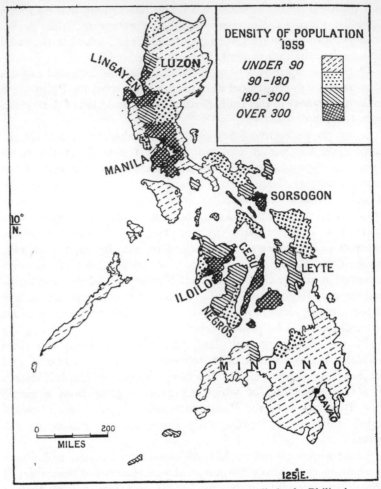

FIG. 110.—Density of Population per square mile in the Philippines

commercially important after Filipinos learnt the smoking habit.
During most of the 19th century tobacco was strictly a government monopoly and thereby restricted until the United States
became accessible this century as market for Filipino cigars.
Tobacco averaged 2 per cent of Filipino exports, for marketing
in U.S.A., Spain, France and Japan from the tobacco areas of
Cagayan, Cebu, Panay and Negros. Tobacco plants brought in
from near Medan (Sumatra) have become favoured commercially

in the Philippines. Tobacco acreage is now greater than in 1941, the 1965 acreage being 207,000 to produce 55,000 tons.

The minor cash crops are : agave, grown for its fibre which resembles abaca; cotton, which never prospered despite early Spanish hopes; kapok; coffee, which has last importance and derris, for insecticides.

THE POPULATION PATTERNS

An uneven distribution of people has developed in the Philippines (Fig. 110). Of 31.2 million Filipinos (1964 est.), 27 per cent live in the intensively farmed zones from the Lingayen Gulf southward through Manila and Laguna to Batangas. About 33 per cent of Filipinos live in the narrow congested plains encircling the Visayan Islands, forming a separate nucleation of people on the volcanic and weathered coral soils. Cebu (1.5 million) and Pargasinan (1.2 million) are by far the most densely populated islands. On the other hand, Palawan (162,000), Mindoro (313,000) and Mindanao each have low densities, though north Mindanao has fairly well peopled localities along the coast.

The picture is one of congested pockets and plains separated by nearly empty forested interiors where wander aboriginal tribes or an occasional pioneer practises shifting cultivation. The average nutritional density for the Philippines is over 1,100 per square mile of cultivated land. Peasant-style subsistence farming engages 70 per cent of Filipinos. Rural areas of Ilocos and Cebu have over 1,950 persons per cultivated square mile, so that the nutritional density is as high as anywhere in Southeast Asia.

Only to a very small extent did this local congestion produce migration to the emptier islands. Official encouragement to this end produced as little permanent result as in the East Indies. There have been two distinct types of migration:

1. An inter-island seasonal migration, at the end of which migrants returned to their home districts. The latitudinal extent of the Philippines and the consequent varying times of harvesting made possible this migration for wages which took the following lines:

   (*a*) From Ilocos on the west Luzon coast, to the tobacco farms of the Cagayan Valley.

   (*d*) From Ilocos and La Union to the paddylands of Central Luzon and the sugar haciendas of Pampanga and Laguna.

(c) From Iloilo, Antique and Cebu to Western Negros sugar haciendas.

(d) From Cebu and Bohol to the coconut and abaca plantations of Mindanao.

(e) From Capiz, Batangas and Pampangas to the sugar plantations of Mindoro.

In this migration the labourers went to the same sort of work they did in their home districts. Some three-quarters of a million workers usually involved in these movements, which varies in volume and direction with the market value of each crop.

2. Long distance migration: while Filipinos were still United States citizens they moved in considerable numbers into the western United States for a long period, leaving families behind and hoping to return with enough money to settle comfortably in their home districts. Much oriental labour in the western United States was Filipino. During 1934–38, the net movement was a return to the Philippines averaging 17,600 yearly because conditions in the United States were decreasingly favourable. For a time organised migration of sugar workers under contract to the Hawaiian plantations also went on until recruiting ceased in 1932, though Filipinos still drifted eastwards across the Pacific. In all cases there was some permanent settlement by Filipinos overseas, particularly in Hawaii where conditions resembled those of the Philippines. Since 1950 movement has been a net return to the Philippines or roughly 3,000 annually. In 1955 about 2,000 Filipinos emigrated permanently to the U.S.A., 630 to Japan and 280 to Australia.

There has been a gravitation towards the towns and in 1960 over 37 per cent Filipinos lived in towns. The Manila-Quezon complex totalled 2.5 million people in 1965.

Composition of the Population.—Like its neighbours, the Philippines has a complex people derived from stock of contrasting types (Fig. 118). Originally the Philippines was populated by Malayan types and for the period 1292–1478 it was under the influence of migrant groups from Java whose impact was greatest and most prolonged to the south. The Malay stock penetrated the islands from the sea, driving inland those aboriginal tribes of Negrito type still to be found in northeast Luzon, in the Sierra Madre, inner Panay and Negros, and in the Surigao Peninsula of

Mindanao. The Philippines escaped direct colonisation by Hindus, but Islam spread along that old trade route (Fig. 114) from Makassar and the Moluccas northwards, converting the Malay stock of southwest Mindanao and southern Palawan. The bulk of these southern peoples remained animists of the Borneo type, as they still are in inner Mindanao, Palawan, Mindoro and the Central Cordillera.

From 1565, Spanish influence was strong and emphatic, operating colonial methods and policies already worked out in Central America. The Spanish focus was Manila and the cultural influences of Christianisation and hispanisation spread from there radially southwards to have much effect in the Visayan Islands, but leaving Mindanao and Islamic area which Spaniards never completely controlled. They discreetly left the "Moros" alone. The Spanish cultural influence continued so long that 80 per cent of Filipinos are Christianised as against 4 per cent Muslim. This reflects the deep hispanisation, both by intermarriage and by education, of the Philippines today, though the Spanish colonial aristocratic group is rapidly diminishing. The place and personal names are strongly Malay to the south, and increasingly Spanish to the north.

Spanish infiltration into the stock was not the only process of mestization which has gone on in the Philippines. Chinese were well established in the northern islands when the Spaniards first came and they staged at least two risings against the Spaniards in the 17th century. Chinese have continued to trade and to act as middlemen during the two successive colonisation periods undergone by Filipinos, who were themselves not attracted by trading activities. For that reason in Luzon and the urban centres there has been a considerable cross-marrying of Chinese with Filipinos, evident in the more active personalities of Filipino public life. The cross currents of Malay, Spanish and Chinese stock have become confused and the distribution blurred so that the Philippines may be described as a mestizo territory, yet another point of resemblance to conditions of Central America rather than of Southeast Asia. The Philippines is unique in Asia for the mestization which has been achieved.

Equally complex is the language situation. Sixty-five languages and dialects have been officially recognised. The Visayan (sometimes spelt Bisayan owing to the Spanish pronunciation of initial

V's) language is that of the densely populated central islands and is spoken by the biggest single group of Filipinos (44 per cent) who distinguish between Cebu and Panay variants of it; it extends also to the agricultural fringe of Mindanao which has been settled by Cebu migrants. Tagalog, the speech of Manila and the more thickly populated provinces round it, is returned as the speech of 25 per cent of Filipinos and is slightly exceeded in importance by English, returned as the speech of 27 per cent Filipinos. Iloco is spoken by 15 per cent and Bicol by 8 per cent of the people, after which comes Spanish, now spoken by only 2.5 per cent of Filipinos and likely to disappear. Chinese is used by less than 1 per cent of the population, that is, by the more recent immigrants living in Manila, but it is in use in most trading centres of the islands.

English as a language dates from this century, a result of United States colonisation which ended in 1946. Following the Spanish example, Americans stressed an education in their own language, which has been most effective in the urban centres, leaving the countryside to use local dialects. Filipino indigenous languages are non-tonal and romanised, except in Mindanao where people use a flowing script of Arabic style. Ordinary Malay or Javanese is not spoken, the southern dialects being more related to North Borneo speech than to modern Malaysian or Javanese forms.

OVERSEAS INFLUENCE

Off the beaten track to and from Southeast Asia, the Philippines differs from all neighbouring territories in its long trans-Pacific association. Adjoining territories have been involved to various extents in the interchanges and interactions between India, China and Europe; the Philippines was for the last three centuries connected with Central America whence the Spanish colonists first came and to which they looked for economic, political, religious and social example in dealing with the Philippines. The last and final stage has been trans-Pacific association with the United States, as a poor relation rather than as an objective of major economic or social developments.

A heritage of Spanish colonial influence is the unusually high proportion of landless farmers in the Philippines, unequalled anywhere else in Southeast Asia. At the first postwar census (1948) less than half the farmers owned the land they worked, about 16 per cent owned some of the land they worked and 35 per cent were tenants on a sharing basis. This was at the end of strenuous United States efforts to undo the social evils and economic paralysis left by the Spanish aristocrats in rural areas.

Spanish Influence.—It is interesting to trace this Spanish influence on land holdings because they left behind problems resembling those in their American colonies and in Spain. They found in these islands the system of communal land holdings and communal help common to equatorial Asia and they observed that there was a head of this local communal activity with rights to direct it, but they did not realise or acknowledge that he was a communal centre-piece rather than the proprietor of village farmlands. Spaniards treated him, however, as the local landlord and gave him additional rights in return for his aid in taxation. They grafted into this their own colonial system of land grants to individuals who had feudal rights over property and persons living on the land. At that early time the population was much less than now (less than 90,000 people lived on Panay in 1586 and they had increased to 1.3 million by 1961), and huge grants of land (*encomiendas*) were given to encourage settlers from Spain as well as to reward people who had been useful. This was easily possible in newly developed territories.

The local leader thus became a *cacique*, as the Spaniards call one of these feudal landlords, or a foreigner came to act as one. The land became the property of one person and everyone on it lost his land rights, thereby forming a group of landless labourers. It was a system evolved in Spain when communal cattle-grazing lands became enclosed for cultivation. By this system the Spaniards created for the first time in the Philippines a landless population in a territory which had been one of subsistence farmers. Latifundia (large estates of absentee landlords) followed as a matter of course. The rural people were reduced to tenants or workers for wages, whereas they had been traditionally partners in their community, with equal rights and obligations in the food production. The degree of thoroughness with which this foreign system became established depended on the firmness of the Spanish hold, hence even now the highest proportion of landless farmers is round Manila and in Panay. Least tenancies appear where the Spanish system never became well established—in Mindanao,

Palawan and North Luzon. Operating to increase the concentration of property was the gradual acquisition of huge properties by the religious houses and the tendency, noted elsewhere, of people newly introduced to money systems to mortgage their property.

The *caciques* continued through the United States colonial period and reaped most of the advantages therefrom. Land was a major social problem in the Philippines, a circumstance not fully paralleled in adjoining territories. There was a highly educated class of landed proprietors, who were prominent in all agitations for political power, and an illiterate, defenceless landless group of rural workers, tending to migrate to places where wages were high, but often unable to move from their districts because they have become deeply indebted to the landlord.

The usual form of tenancy on rice land is the share tenancy (*kasama*) by which a proportion of the crop is retained by the tenant. The proportion varies according to whether he merely works the land and has seeds and animals provided for him (which gives him half the crop after half costs for these items has been deducted) or whether the tenant supplies his own animals, seed, harvesting labour, etc. (which obtains for him two-thirds of the crop). While at first glance reasonable, these terms in kind operate against the tenant, who in poor years may receive for his labour less rice than his family needs to feed it, so that he must borrow to get through the year and meet his taxes, whereas, whatever the state of the crop, the landlord gets a clear return which is probably worth more in cash to him in a scarcity year than in a normal year. It is a case of partial cooperation, seemingly fair, but inevitably getting tenants progressively into debt because they bear all the risks of cultivation. A modern evil has been subleasing; landlords lease *haciendas* on a cash rent basis to a few tenants, who in turn sublease on sharing terms to many smaller tenants, whose position and risk becomes increasingly desperate as pressure of population on the paddylands increases. Landed corporations were tending to maintain this system, which gave them returns at minimum bother to themselves. Expropriation of large estates became part of the Filipino constitution after 1936 and the laws prohibiting new large estates operated to divert United States plantation interest away from the Philippines to other parts of Southeast Asia. Tenant indebtedness in the Philippines has been as bad as in

Burma and Thailand. These land questions have constantly moulded the policies of modern Filipino governments.

The Philippines thus clearly differs from Southeast Asia in being far from the pioneering stage and also entangled with Spanish land systems. The coastal Filipinos have a traditional culture based on the wood and woven palm ecology of Southeast Asia which they have developed with artistry and enthusiasm. Their music, however, is of the Spanish guitar type rather than the pipe and finger-drum type of Indian and forest origins.

The largest empty space is Mindanao, a long-standing possibility for absorbing farmers from Luzon and the Visayan Islands. It remained uninviting for many years despite the success at Davao: as in the East Indies, social ties proved stronger than social distress. New roads and facilities are now opening Mindanao for thousands of settlers from the north and changing its population map—it contained 3.9 million in 1964, i.e. 12 per cent of all Filipinos.

So far there has been little evidence that modern industrialisation is practicable for the Philippines. A few cement plants, coconut oil mills, sweet and shirt factories have grown up, but there is neither much coal nor hydro-electric power. Only in cottage industry, particularly for hats and clogs, was there any considerable development, and this was rivalled by similar products imported very cheaply from China and Japan. Cigar making is shifting from the home to the factory. Embroidery too is changing from a cottage industry to small village factories. Over 1955–62, cement output trebled to a million tons and electricity output round Manila doubled.

The whole geography and ecology of the Philippines is a special extension of conditions similar to those of Southeast Asia, particularly of the eastern East Indies, but modified by several centuries of control and influence from America rather than from India, Europe and China. As in the case of Burma, the current problem of the Philippines is physical rehabilitation after two military campaigns, which have each caused extensive damage and disruption. The campaigns of the Philippines were firstly in Luzon and secondly in the Visayan Islands fanning out from Leyte. Manila suffered physically from the war more than most parts of Southeast Asia.

From the formalising of independence in 1946, there followed a period of anarchy outside the towns and of violent personalised politics within them, recalling the Spanish tradition. Remnants of wartime guerrillas (the Hukbalahups) roamed the hill-country, taking advantage of the geographical difficulties of contact between one part and another of the Philippines; they vied with district bosses and nullified national organisation. Piracy returned off southern islands. Land reforms were fiercely in demand by rural people, but the means and secure conditions in which these could take place without becoming a "free for all" did not exist. Mechanisation of farms and transport has taken place quickly and the population increases by a million a year. Economic aid in many forms from the United States was demanded and provided to a total of U.S. $755 million over 1945–58, despite the severing of old political ties; huge dollar funds were injected into the country (U.S. $21 million in 1966 with U.S. $20 million more for equipping Filipino forces) and some defence supplied by American bases in Luzon. The trade of the unit is now flowing again without substantial change from its pre-1941 pattern. For 1965, inflowing trade was worth $2,670 million of which 41 per cent came from U.S. and 26 per cent from Japan; exports were then worth $1,970 million going 41 per cent to U.S., 30 per cent to Japan and 4 per cent to the Netherlands.

PART III
THE HUMAN GEOGRAPHY OF SOUTHEAST ASIA

Chapter Twenty-two

SOUTHEAST ASIA AGRICULTURE

SOUTHEAST Asia has several agricultural types which are, however, less related to major climatic or environmental differences between one place and another and more to differing rates of agricultural development. To these rates of development the greatest impulses have derived very largely from conditions outside the region and most of the crops concerned have been introduced from outside. The system of shifting cultivation, often described as indigenous to Southeast Asia, is associated with all tribes and groups entering Southeast Asia overland from continental Asia, and the key crops of today, rice, sugar, tea, coffee, cotton, rubber and maize have all been brought from overseas and cultivated largely with the object of sales overseas. Prior to the introduction of these plants, agriculture centred on root crops, on sweet potatoes or yams, which are still staples for the more isolated and hence more primitive groups.

SHIFTING CULTIVATION

Of the agricultural types particular interest attaches to shifting cultivation because it represents a special stage in the evolution from hunting and food gathering to sedentary farming. Within this style considerable variations exist, from the clearing used for cultivating yams and bananas, probably the earliest form of land utilisation by peoples wandering through the jungles, to shifting cultivation of coffee and pepper by farmers intending to sell these crops, which are so exacting in their soil requirements. Some shifting cultivators are true wanderers: the whole group, family or tribe, moves on to a new location when it abandons one clearing for the next. Others are sedentary farmers, staying in one village all their lives, but varying the piece of ground they cultivate from time to time, abandoning the old piece to secondary forest growths, which can be thought of as a form of fallow. This last type has a long tradition in Java, the Philippines and Indochina, and has blended with the custom by which a tract of land belongs to a group, the individuals of which choose or are given, every now and again, different portions to cultivate for themselves.

Within Southeast Asia the shifting cultivation system has no relation to the needs of domesticated animals. There is no evidence here that the simpler tribes have been primarily cattle grazers, except in so far as all Mongoloid types coming south overland

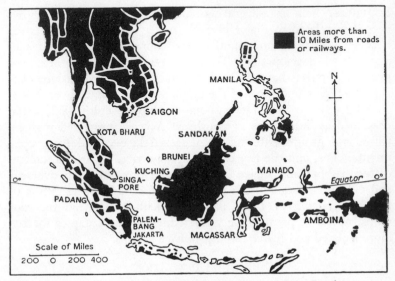

Fig. 111.—The Accessibility of Southeast Asia by Land

from the grazing grounds of Tibet and farther north may, at remote times outside this territory, have been associated with animals. Cattle, as distinct from buffaloes, do not fit into some Southeast Asia ecologies of climate, vegetation, pests and religious customs with meats; Buddhists and Hindus do not eat beef, Muslims will not eat pork and even the primitive animists have similar inhibitions. Wherever today there has grown up a cattle system, it relates to the ploughing needs and is concerned with buffaloes or small oxen and does not derive from an earlier tradition of cattle farming or nomadism.

Shifting cultivation is a system well adapted to large empty areas where soils are poor and the rate of soil erosion high. As soon as population increases, shifting cultivation, which needs each cutover area to stand unused for 7 to 10 years before being recultivated, rapidly overtaxes the capacity of the forest vegetation to reassert itself. Hence much of Southeast Asia has been progressively overburnt by the increasing forest population and the natural cover has selectively changed towards the savannah vegetation type, a progress speedier in the drier zones where the regrowth rate is slower. Overburning caused by overpopulation in turn induces rapid soil erosion, affecting the load and silting of river systems, possibly disturbing settled agriculturists far down the valley and remote from the overburnt area. For these reasons shifting cultivation has generally become illegal, yet it still persists in areas not easily accessible or amenable to control and probably even today as much as 5 million acres of temporary clearing each year is being cultivated over Southeast Asia, and between 40 and 50 million acres of clearing in the forests is being cultivated or is recovering from recent temporary cultivation—an area not far short of the total area of Thailand. From the shifting agricultural system, very little that is of trading or commercial significance derives; the proportion in coffee and pepper is negligible. As a whole, shifting cultivation is for subsistence only, yet it is an integral part of the regional farming tradition.

SUBSISTENCE FARMING

Farming of the ordinary sedentary type has in this region evolved from shifting cultivation as pressure of population on the land increased. Fixed cultivation can only be sustained where local conditions prevent soil exhaustion and soil erosion, or natural conditions counteract these inevitable effects of cultivation. Thus farming gravitates to the localities dry for a part of the year where leaching is a periodical rather than a permanent process, to localities where erosion and leaching are negatived by altitudes nearly at base level, to zones where the soil is the accumulation of fertile elements from other areas, or to zones of young soils rich in nutrient chemicals. The dry zones are away from the Equator and towards the "monsoonal fringes" of the tropics; flat flood plains beside mature streams are subject to little erosion and leaching; deltaic and basic volcanic soils remain fertile for long periods. These facts underlie the pattern of sedentary farming in Southeast Asia which occupies a total area of almost 100 million acres.

The greater part of this farmland, about two-thirds, is given over to subsistence farming, a system where practically nothing leaves the farm, which only grows what the family needs for food, the family needing all that it grows. Subsistence farming is at once deep rooted in the tradition of the people and at the same time isolation, difficulty of access and absence of communications largely force it upon much of the region, which remains for the greater part as isolated now as it was several centuries ago, and must even grow its own fibres for textiles. On subsistence farms the interest centres on rice, an almost universal staple in Southeast Asia, and only in the most congested areas, such as the Vizayas and Java, is there any well-established practice of growing some other food as substitute for rice. Rice dominates the diet even where local conditions seem unfavourable, as in the dry zones of Burma and Thailand or in the relatively gloomy, rain-soaked areas immediately round the Equator. At least 90 per cent of subsistence farmland is under rice, the balance of supplementary food needs (coconuts, spices, fruits and pulses) occupying a very small fraction of any one farm and often being gathered wild rather than cultivated. The dominance of rice, even among the hill peoples, is the more remarkable because the plant was apparently introduced by Indian colonists some time about the middle of the first millennium, since when thousands of varieties have been evolved to suit the subtle differences of local climate, seasons and soil.

In total, Southeast Asia subsistence farming has continued with methods evolved locally centuries back. The hoe or mattock and the dibble are still the only soil-working implements in many areas, even on paddyfields, but ploughs of the soil-opening rather than the soil-turning type have become widespread, generally home-made and entirely of wood, that raw material ubiquitous in this terrain. With the plough came the need for draught animals and most subsistence farms now have one buffalo or ox per family, the former being favoured towards the Equator, the latter in the drier or more seasonal areas.

COMMERCIAL FARMING

Farming for crops intended to be sold, that is, commercial or cash farming, came late to Southeast Asia. Except in one or two districts of the Philippines and Java, cash basis farming is scarcely a century old and many types of crude adjustment to this innovation may be found. The oldest cash farming of Southeast Asia was the spice trade of the Moluccas, but even at its peak that trade involved very few areas given over exclusively to spices, which for the greater part were collected from farmers each with a tree or two, rather than a number of acres devoted to a crop of spices. The crux of the matter at that period was that nothing cultivated in Southeast Asia apart from spice was transportable to or of use to the world's population centres overseas. To a large extent over the present millennium Southeast Asia has been an absorber rather than a supplier of goods or commodities; only in the last hundred years or so has the condition changed, not so much by new demands for Southeast Asia products as for crops transferred to Southeast Asia for production.

Rice.—Commercial agriculture in the whole region occupies about 40 million acres and has taken two forms, both strongly influenced by European interests: farming food crops for sale, and farming non-food crops for sale. Of the food crop, sugar was the earliest successful innovation established in Java and the Philippines soon after European colonisation began, and intended for export to Europe. Today at least half the area devoted to crops grown for export is in rice and, taking into account the amount of rice grown for cash sales in deficit regions inside each territory, the proportion may reach as much as three-quarters. Upon commercial rice production depends the possibility of workers leaving their own farms and devoting their full time to non-food cash crops, so that the workers on rubber, cotton, hemp, coffee, and sugar plantations have provided a great demand for Asia's staple cereal, supplies of which have been vital to the development of plantation and mining industries of Southeast Asia and, incidentally to the industrialisation of other parts of Asia. The bulk of the rice produced in Southeast Asia for export has gone to India and Indochina, where a condition approaching the limit of rice-growing has been reached, and to Malaysia. Japan was a rice importer before 1941 and now imports far more wheat. The rice export came, and still comes, from Burma, Thailand and Cambodia in that order of importance, areas which have pioneered in rapidly expanding commercial rice production to form the pool, the only rice-pool in the world, from which other areas have made up their deficits. Moreover the commercial production of rice in Southeast Asia has been steadily increasing over the last 20 years—

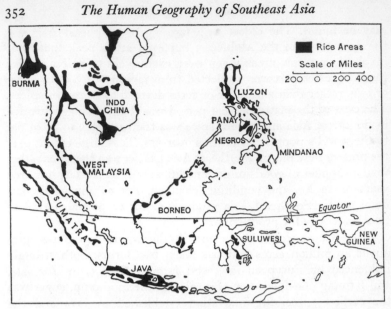

FIG. 112.—Distribution of Rice Cultivation in Southeast Asia

the average Southeast Asia acreage under ice each year of 1916–20 was 38.28 million, by 1939–40 it was 52.2 million and, in 1963, 67 million. These figures include both subsistence and commercial production of rice, and in 1965 by far the most extensive farming was still rice, which covered nearly 70 per cent of cultivated land in Thailand, 85 per cent in Indochina, 72 per cent in Burma and 42 per cent in the Philippines (see table, page 355).

SOUTHEAST ASIA AREAS UNDER RICE (million acres)

	1914–15	1924–25	1934–35	1944–45	1954–55	1964–65
Burma	10.0	12.1	12.7	8.5	10.0	12.5
Indochina	10.4	11.7	13.1	14.1	10.1	19.7
Thailand	5.0	6.8	8.1	5.5	13.8	15.1
W. Malaysia	—	.6	.7	.7	.9	1.0
Java and Madoera	6.9	8.7	9.9	7.7	9.5	10.0
Philippines	2.7	4.2	4.9	3.6	6.8	8.0

SOUTHEAST ASIA RICE PRODUCTION (million metric tons clean rice)

	1914–15	1924–25	1934–35	1944–45	1954–55	1964–65
Burma	3.73	5.15	4.6	2.4	3.8	5.4
Indochina	4.32	3.54	3.4	3.6	1.4	8.6
Thailand	1.93	3.08	2.86	3.7	4.1	6.4
W. Malaysia	—	.24	.33	.2	.46	.61
Java and Madoera	2.88	3.43	3.54	3.5	4.3	4.9
Philippines	.05	1.28	1.28	1.1	2.1	2.7

Cash farming for rice is the only extension of a Southeast Asia subsistence farming crop into commercial farming on a large scale; only the lesser part of coconut-growing is intended for export, though this too, is an extension of Southeast Asia subsistence farming. It has been inevitable that subsistence farmers and the techniques they developed for rice have set the character of commercial rice farming which has been pioneered by local people and continues to be essentially a non-mechanised produce whose volume comes more from area and less from intensive methods.

RICE IN SOUTHEAST ASIA:
ANNUAL AVERAGES PER QUINQUENNIUM

Period	Million Acrea Under Rice	Production Million Tons Clean Rice	Net Exports from SE.A. (Million Tons Clean)	Per Cap. Utilisation (kgms.)	Yield in Tons per Acre
1926–30	47.5	16.5	4.7	131	.348
1931–35	49.6	16.7	5.2	117	.337
1936–40	51.4	17.5	5.0	118	.339
1946–50	48.1	15.6	1.9	98	.325
1951–55	54.8	18.1	4.6	80	.332
1956–60	65.5	26.2	3.5	112	.395
1961–65	67.5	28.0	3.6	100	.408

Southeast Asia sowed 71 million acres in 1965 to produce about 32 million tons cleaned rice. National and personal absorption rose making it difficult for the region to have an exportable surplus of 3.8 million tons for which other Asian countries competed, causing rice to be dearer than wheat for most of the last decade.

Other Food Crops.—The other commercial food crops, sugar, coffee, tea, cinchona and oil palm total much smaller areas than rice farming. Broadly, these innovations were developed by European colonial planters opening up what were very largely virgin territories, normally in the form of large estates calling for a labour force which derived only in part from local people, the rest being obtained by introducing labour from outside. In the Philippines and in Java the first European essays in agriculture caused serious interactions on local land customs; in Thailand an aristocratic feudal system enabled commercialisation to be introduced without external intervention. These crops tended to be perennial cultivations, taking advantage of the continuous growing season of the region. In due course this has led to a large production, causing the external price to drop, especially as there has been similar commercialisation of the same crops in other tropical areas, all quickly reaching large-scale production of commodities which began as expensive luxuries and gradually cheapened to become low-priced semi-staple foods not offering any prospect of large returns for nominal outlays. Rivalries with other producing areas and speedy saturation of the world market has so far given these types of commercial agriculture a confused history of boom and depression, of rapid extension and then dereliction or scientific experiments to cheapen production. In these crops, techniques and methods more western than eastern have been used though mechanisation in the field has not been possible owing to the nature of the crops. The processing involved has often been modern and highly mechanised.

Rubber.—Commercial production of non-food or industrial crops in Southeast Asia has centred on rubber. Rubber has been an innovation peculiar to Southeast Asia (Central Africa and Ceylon took it up later) and its cultivation proved a remarkably successful transfer of a tree from another part of the tropics, developed here on plantation mass production lines, whereas in its original habitat the tree was wild and tapped on the "gatherer" system now only used for gums and damars collected from forest trees. Upon Southeast Asia rubber has depended the popularisation of the petrol driven vehicle, the incentive to petroleum production and the development of world road systems. Its cultivattion was on the European orchard pattern and at first it was only possible by companies sufficiently capitalised to wait 7 to 10 years for maturity and to recruit labour from other regions to make the plantations in virgin areas, at a distance from subsistence farmers or cash farmers of foods to suit the plantation workers. Smallholders gradually took up rubber planting as an adjunct to other crops and as part of a mixed farming system. Reversing the history of rice agriculture, rubber started as a large-scale plantation cultivation worked by non-indigenous people and gradually moved towards a smallholder, mixed-farming type. Altogether, some 10 million acres of Southeast Asia are in rubber, the greatest single block being in Malaysia. Rubber, too, is a perennial and a long-term crop and its history has been an alternation of high prices and low prices, and of rapidly saturating the market which has throughout been external to Asia. Malaysia, by almost exclusively specialising in rubber, proved very highly geared to external events and their effects on rubber price, to a degree not paralleled by other types of Southeast Asia farming which were, during a crisis, more closely related to subsistence farming and thereby buffered from external valuations.

TRENDS IN AGRICULTURE

Several long-term tendencies in these various farming types have become apparent. For all the commercial crops except rice, external events have obliged experiment and development towards higher and higher production per unit area; yields for commercial crops have progressively increased. In rice farming, however, methods have continued to be extensive, yields have steadily decreased and there has been little advance in either maintaining fertility standards or increasing the yield. Experimental farms exist throughout the territory to promote these improvements, which are showing effects.

NATIONAL SIGNIFICANCE OF RICE (average 1960–63)

	Rice area as % of total cultivated area	Rice as food % of daily intake	Rice as trade % value	Rice value as % total national product
Burma	72	70	71 (exports)	16
Cambodia	87	70	35 (exports)	23
Indonesia	48	42	11 (imports)	26
West Malaysia	17	45	5 (imports)	4
Philippines	42	50	1 (imports)	7
Thailand	68	65	38 (exports)	15
South Viet Nam	84	62	23 (exports)	14

The general movements of rice in Southeast Asia are evident from the table on page 356 which summarises surpluses and deficits this century.

Commercial rice production was associated almost exclusively with the expansion of agriculture to the deltas of the Irrawaddy, Chao Praya and Mekong and in varying degrees to increased control over flood waters. It is in this large-scale water control that the greatest long-term changes have been set going by western engineering techniques coping with the wide range of circumstances under which Southeast Asia floods occur. Effective small-scale water-control methods had in fact existed in this region before; the earlier technological interest was to expand rice production by increased water-control on specially fertile, generally volcanic, upland soils. The objective then and now was the same—to cultivate the most fertile areas; the difference was that the volcanic soils attracted local attention and were within the capacity of local people, considerably earlier than the deltaic soils,

SOUTHEAST ASIA RICE EXPORTS AND IMPORTS
(million metric tons clean)

	Exporters			Importers		
	Burma	Indochina	Thailand	Indonesia	Malaysia	Philippines
1925	3.32	1.33	1.18	.50	.41	.10
1930	2.95	1.02	.93	.62	.60	.01
1935	2.93	1.52	1.38	.36	.48	nil
1940	2.50	1.40	2.00	.06	.70	.1
1950	1.17	.09	1.48	.29	.47	.01
1955	1.63	.33	1.25	.15	.48	.15
1960	1.75	.77	1.20	.96	.59	.01
1965	1.13	.56	1.88	1.05	.60	.00

A trend has been a decline in Southeast Asia consumption of rice per person over the last 30 years, which made possible the expanding exports of rice at a time when population was rapidly increasing. The declining personal consumption relates to changing habits, especially along lines of trade movements. Bread, maize, potatoes, canned foods and move vegetables are entering into Asian meals. In towns a factor has been the steady advance in price— from $60 per ton in 1938 to $325 in 1948 and to $425 in 1952 at Rangoon—but even after official controls ended, comparable prices were high, averaging $391 in 1965 in Bangkok.

Commercial agriculture has largely revolved round tree cultivation (arboriculture rather than agriculture) in which the continuous growing period produces maximum effects. In this tendency may be seen a return to the tree vegetation which is indigenous to equatorial Southeast Asia, and away from the annual and deciduous plants more suited to ecologies associated with the seasonal margins of the tropics. Labour difficulties too are eased to some extent by tree crops whose periodicity is better spread than in the case of annual crops. To the labour difficulty also is due the trend towards devolving arboriculture from plantations systems to smallholders systems, leading to the smallholder becoming an exponent of diversified rather than single crop cultivation.

While the region has sought to escape the consequence of over-much dependence on one or two cash crops, Southeast Asia subsistence farming is really already highly diversified. Moreover, the region as a whole must be considered reasonably well diversified. Derris-root (basis of an insecticide) has ceased to be significant: the profitable innovation is oil-palm with cacao still increasing.

EFFECTS OF THE SECOND WORLD WAR

During the 1941-42 campaign, battles were fought through Burma, Malaysia and the Philippines. More military action took place in Burma and the Philippines over the year 1944-45. The direct long-term effects of these campaigns were not emphatic because agriculture and arboriculture cannot be "scorched" and denied to the enemy on a large scale. The war in these territories devastated internal communications, broke down the systems of internal trade, removed the means of communication between different parts of Southeast Asia and destroyed the channels to those overseas markets which had been the principal destination of commercial agricultural produce. Breakdown of external trade channels occurred in all Southeast Asia territories whether campaigns took place in them or not.

The first consequences of this disruption, as distinct from destruction, were to place a premium on subsistence farming, to cause all commercial cultivation to fall into desuetude, to undermine confidence in agriculture for cash, to cause the loss or destruction of draught cattle which were taken away for military use, to disperse labour forces, and to stimulate self-sufficiency policies. Very little of the perennial tree acreage, such as of rubber, was cut down—only 6 per cent in the case of Malaysian rubber—yet it was the commercial production which suffered most from disruption, which created in the postwar period considerable difficulties for those territories needing imported rice for the labour to rehabilitate commercial farming and industries. Agriculture itself, where labour was available, rehabilitated quickly; all but 2 per cent of Malaysian rice acreages were back in cultivation during 1945-46 and rubber made an equally quick comeback, so that about one-third of its prewar estate area was being tapped in 1947, representing two-thirds of the area tappable.

In the food crops, surplus margins were more slowly restored. Exports of Southeast Asia rice totalled about a million tons during 1946, as against a combined export of 5.7 million tons annually for 1936–40. The drop in production of this staple was greatest in the case of Burma because there the dislocation by war had been greatest, but by the 1950–51 season, about three-quarters of Lower Burma rice lands were back in cultivation, as against half in 1945–46. In Cochinchina only 70 per cent of the rice area was being cultivated in 1946–47. Thailand, which was untouched by military campaigns, reported 13.1 million acres under cultivation in rice for 1950–51 (64 per cent more than 1940–41)—the only territory to show a substantial increase of rice acreage in the war decade.

A feature after 1946 was initially a general decline in rice yields, mostly an effect of loss of draught cattle, though to report low yields was a convenient cover for black market sales. The consequence of lost production in local food was felt more in places like Malaysia which has specialised in non-food commercial agriculture, than in any other territories of Asia, which customarily needed to import only a small proportion of their rice. Maize growing increased spectacularly—over 1938–58 the Filipino acreage trebled and the Thai increased twelvefold from 1950 to 1965.

Since labour shortage has been prominent as a factor operating against postwar commercial agriculture, the subsistence farmer and the diversified smallholder have assumed far greater significance than before. Over 55 per cent of Malaysia's rubber production for 1946 was from smallholders, a proportion which had been as much as 85 per cent in the early months of that year, yet fell to 42 per cent in 1965 (cf. 39 per cent in 1940).

The vegetable oils soon came back into production and by early 1947 monthly production in Southeast Asia was not far short of 1941 production and now greatly exceeds it.

The lowering of food acreages per capita and of yields, combined with enforced reversion to subsistence agricultural forms, has had much significance for Southeast Asia food supplies over recent years, attracting foreign aid to expand food supply because population is rapidly increasing at the rate of over 30 million people per decade, and because social policy is to raise the standard of nutrition. These two factors have operated so that rice exporting countries have diminishing margins of their product to sell. How Asia's people will meet this basic difficulty of supply in their staple food is not clear; mechanisation is scarcely a solution, yields are very difficult to raise on a large scale, and there are few unused areas of high potential for rice farming, yet unless improvement is reached the labour force is likely to be uneasy in non-food-producing territories, rice may be for such areas no longer a cheap staple (see p. 356), and the costs of any production

CHANGES IN RICE FARMING (average 1960–63)

	Area p.a. *Million acres*	*% increase over decade*	*Production p.a.* *million tons cleaned*	*% increase over decade*	*Yield % increase over decade*
Burma	12.0	20.4	5.27	37.3	13.8
Cambodia	3.5	16.4	1.01	16.5	0
Indonesia	17.9	11.9	8.68	19.6	7.0
West Malaysia	0.96	13.9	0.60	34.9	19.0
Philippines	7.9	19.3	2.60	22.8	2.5
Thailand	15.1	17.5	6.07	32.8	14.5
Total	57.36	16.7	24.23	26.9	9.0

must remain high. Influences of this sort, in a region where average productive skill is low and slow, may cause it to become one of the world's most costly producer zones and hasten in Europe and the United States the exploitation of substitute commodities which lend themselves to mechanisation more than is the case with typical Southeast Asia agricultural products. Rapid peopling of the Sumatra, Borneo and Irian deltas may take place, much as the continental deltas of Southeast Asia were quickly peopled over the last 70 years; the fact that there has been previous reluctance to go to these places is no guarantee that there will be continued reluctance. Southeast Asia has at times become a consumer of rice cultivated outside Asia, absorbing 270,000 tons in 1951. South Americans exported 323,000 tons rice in 1961. Perhaps Brazil or Africa will change the outlook, much as Canadian, Australian and Argentine farms altered the European food economy last century. Already a change in diet shows—the region imported 740,000 tons wheat flour in 1962, of which the Philippines alone absorbed one-half. Maize production rose 110 per cent from 1950 to 1956 in which period Thailand increased its output over 31 times.

Chapter Twenty-three

THE FISHERIES OF SOUTHEAST ASIA

THE FISH POPULATION

BECAUSE equatorial waters have low salinity and low oxygen content, it has frequently been assumed that they have a low fish population. That view is difficult to maintain for the shallow waters of Southeast Asia where, according to Herre, the number of kinds of fish and their diversification is unrivalled by that of any other marine region. Whether this paradox disproves the theoretical view about equatorial seas or shows that the fish population depends more on the local supply of nutrients which so broken and well-watered a region as Southeast Asia discharges to the sea in extraordinarily large quantities, has yet to be demonstrated. There is no co-ordinated study of the fishing industry as a whole in this region.

Until recently, only the generic character of these Southeast Asia fish had been studied, from which it appears that, while by no means all of them have been named and identified, over 1,500 varieties are normally fished round Java, over 500 have been named as economically valuable round W. Malaysia, and similar large varieties are reported from all territories. Most of the fish known are inshore fish, closely dependent on food particles carried from shore to sea and on the great growth of plankton, seaweeds and corals which supply fish food. Because the shores of the landmasses in most of this region are frequently backed by swamps, there is a very considerable fish population in transition between shallow shores, swamps and ponds. Inland fishing is vigorous; during 1965 Indonesia landed 395,000 tons, Philippines 17,500 tons, Cambodia 395,000 tons, Thailand 72,000 tons, W. Malaysia 25,000 tons from freshwaters, swamps, artificial ponds, lakes and canals. Fish cultivation is increasing.

Though the deep-water fish of Southeast Asia have only in recent years been exploited commercially, by Japanese trawlers, they exist in these waters in surprising numbers. Schools of sardines some 10 miles long have been seen, together with frequent great shoals of mackerel and bonito. Porpoises (mammals which live on fish and are a guide to the fish density) have been seen in a school which packed an area 15 miles long and 2 miles broad. Plankton occurs at times in astounding quantities, practically smothering all other fish life in the neighbourhood. The movements and migrations of these fish of deeper waters have been little studied and the inshore fishing has been enough to meet local food needs, as well as not demanding too complex a technique or too great a capital outlay by the local fishermen who are generally very few, and too poor to equip themselves for long distance deepwater trips. A major impediment to introducing the elaborate systems of trawling and seining which have been developed in temperate seas is the frequency of coral reefs and knolls which, although attracting fish, catch the nets and ruin them.

FISH AS A STAPLE FOOD

Fish is a staple in the Southeast Asia diet as complement to rice. It supplies calcium, iodine and salt as well as animal protein, items otherwise not easily come by in these areas, or too expensive for the peasants. By habit Southeast Asia people are rice-fish-curry eaters and vegetables in the European sense enter very little into their meals. They are largely vegetarian but not interested in vegetables. Fishing has an importance in local ecologies second only to rice, yet fish is eaten in small portions more as condiment than as main part of a meal. Malaysians eat 80 lbs. fish per head each year: the total reported Southeast Asian catch was only 2.1 million tons in 1961, which is 22 lbs. per person (cf. 15 *tons* per capita in U.S.) The national statistics about fishing are thin because it is a mobile, dispersed activity without importance for revenue. Over 1955–65, regional landings rose by 89 per cent.

Several stages of commercialisation are met with but subsistence fishing predominates. In every paddyfield and swamp, villagers go fishing for their personal needs; on the coast many fishermen are part-time, sharing their labour between a paddyfield and a fishing boat. Some villages have specialised fishermen whose produce goes into exchange among the landsmen to make the village self-supporting. Gradually fishing for sale has become possible, yet there are major difficulties of transport to consuming centres, of organisation between fishermen and consumer, and of preserving the fish in good condition during transport.

TRADE IN FISH

Apart fron that fish eaten fresh on the coasts, the bulk is preserved for commerce and for storing during seasons when the sea is too violent, by sun-drying, salting or by conversion into one of the highly-spiced, partly-fermented fish sauces widely admired by Southeast Asia people (i.e. *blachan* in Malaysia, *trassie* in Java, *nuoc mam* in Indochina, *kapi* in Thailand, *ngapi* in Burma). Huge quantities of fish in these forms move inland within each country and there has developed a considerable movement of preserved fish between the different Southeast Asia territories, to supply the plantation and industrial workers. In 1961, the Philippines cured 170,000 tons fish, Thailand 52,000 tons and Indonesia 40,000 tons. That fish preserving is widely practised even for local use means that the activity is very largely buffered from the alternations of glut and scarcity which are common in fishing industries. The transport of the preserved fish both internally and externally tends to be by sea for cheapness, a paramount consideration in a food for peasants, and because there are few alternatives. Only in a few areas is there a speedy land service able to deliver fresh fish to inland urban centres. Much cheap canned fish is imported.

Commercialisation of fishing has brought in foreign personnel. Whenever fishing is carried on for export as cash sales, Chinese are frequently the principal fishermen, as at Bagansiapiapi (Sumatra) and Pangkor (W. Malaysia), in the deep-sea fishing centred on Singapore (once run by the Japanese) and even in the cultivation of fish in Javanese ponds. Moreover, Chinese are strongly represented as the middlemen who handle the trade from the actual fisherman to the ultimate consumer, and they are generally responsible for processing the wet fish into transportable forms.

FRESHWATER FISHING

While the absence of deep-sea and mechanical mass fishing methods is one peculiarity of Southeast Asia, equally remarkable is the emphasis on freshwater fishing. Very largely the methods of freshwater fishing—traps and small nets—have established the styles used for inshore sea fishing. For the most part the value of this freshwater production cannot be gauged though it has major importance in local diet. Two variations of freshwater fishing have exceptional interest. The Tonle Sap fisheries represent the most productive of the natural fresh fisheries. Half the Indonesian 1961 landings were from freshwater.

From Tonle Sap over 40 tons of fish are produced annually from each square mile of its surface, a productivity very much greater than that of the well-fished North Sea of Europe, and unique in its intensity. This exceptional production is possible because the large area covered from early June by shallow floods enables fish to spawn profusely in about 3,000 square miles of inundated forest, where abundance of vegetable matter makes the fish grow larger than those in any of the neighbouring rivers. Over 30,000 persons are normally fishing this lake and the full-time fishermen live in villages of pile dwellings scattered round it; of these lake-side fishing villages Snoc Trou is the most important. A considerable number of migrant fishermen, Annamese, Chinese and Malay, move into this area temporarily for the peak fishing season from October to January. Over 130,000 tons of fish are obtained annually and half of this is dried before leaving the region; some fish are sent alive towards the estuary of the Mekong in floating cages of bamboo enclosing what is virtually an artificial shoal moving through the water to the market, an ingenious device for transporting live fish. The commercial side of this fishing is almost entirely Chinese. Over-fishing has been going on in recent years and controls are becoming necessary.

In Java two types of pond fishing have been evolved. Near Jakarta, Sourabaya and Semarang where the demand for fish is great, mangrove swamps are partially enclosed to control the tidal water and into the enclosures are placed, between April and July, the spawn and young sea fish gathered among bundles of leaves which fishermen have previously placed in the open sea for the purpose. The spawn and young fish are carried to the fishponds in jars and there left to fatten on algae and water weeds cultivated for them. The milkfish (Chanos chanos) is popular for this purpose and reaches marketable size within a year. Elsewhere inland artificial freshwater ponds have been built, covering a total area estimated at over 100,000 acres, in which fish of the carp type are bred and fattened all the year round; 130,000 tons of fish are obtained every year by this means. Freshwater fisheries are now encouraged in every little tank or pond as a form of mosquito control.

INSHORE FISHING

Inshore sea fishing is by far the most usual in Southeast Aisa. The boats used are generally very small, often needing only a man and a boy to work them, indicating the small units of the industry. Land and sea breezes play a key part in the rhythm of activity, being the source of power to and from the shore. It is unusual for the boats to move more than a mile from shore and rarely do they lose sight of land. Much inshore fishing is done without boats at all. The beaches are netted by fishermen moving waist deep through water and, wherever fish are known to migrate along the coast, barriers of bamboo are built out, leading the fish into a square enclosure or trap from which they are periodically drawn up in a net by a fishermen who lives with his family on a platform above the trap. Probably three-quarters of Southeast Asia sea fishing is done where the sea is less than 10 ft deep. The fish thus obtained tend to be of the small type and a large proportion are crustacea, much favoured in local diet. Huge quantities of crabs, shrimps and mussels are obtained, and squids are regularly netted in large numbers for local use. Shells are baked and ground to powder and used in conjunction with the areca nut as a favourite old-fashioned chew common to the whole region. Because coastal fishing takes place so close to the shore where breakers are violent, it is markedly seasonal in character, depending on aspect relative to the seasonal winds. This seasonality is a great incentive to preserve the fish to last through that season when the little fishing boats cannot cope with the heavy seas. Inshore fishing closely relates to the shallow waters of the Sunda Platform; where the coast drops away to great depths, the intensity of fishing diminishes.

DISTRIBUTION OF FISHERIES

While fishing commands a wide interest, it is by no means uniformly developed through the region. Broadly, the coasts near densely populated areas are the most intensively fished and estuaries and deltas have major fishing developments, though neither at the Red River mouth nor the Irrawaddy mouth has fishing reached a high pitch of development. The Mekong, particularly at the seasons when the Tonle Sap water is discharging, has great attraction for fish and the whole coastal zone from the Mekong round the Gulf of Thailand to Singapore is well fished and is one of the few known tracks of fish migration in these seas, possibly relating to the southwesterly drift of the Mekong discharge. The Malacca Strait also has vigorous fishing industries, associated with the fishing at Bagansiapiapi and Pangkor which have been commercialised by Chinese. Along both sides of the Malacca Strait fish traps stand out from the coast almost continuously for mile after mile. Bagansiapiapi fish comes almost entirely from traps set across the creeks of the Rokan River. In the Philippines, themselves spread athwart the equatorial currents of the Pacific like a great trap, the annual catch of fish is second only to that of Indonesia yet the Philippines import much canned fish in addition.

For most Southeast Asia countries information about the significance of fishing activities is sketchy, although in every case fish ranks high in the basic foodstuffs. The total activity in fishing is enormous; probably 3 million people are engaged in Southeast Asia fishing and the amount of internal trade in fish must total far higher than so widely dispersed and so little commercialised an industry might at first suggest. There is always a substantial movement of fish in various forms from the coasts to the interiors and from one territory to another.

Burma.—That Burmese developed their tradition well in the interior may explain why it is only in Arakan and Tenasserim there has been intensive sea fishing. Within the Irrawaddy distributaries South Indians have taken to fishing and they deliver fish on ice to the rice farmers of Lower Burma, whose diet is more monotonously rice-and-fish than is the case towards the interior. The Buddhist tradition causes Burmese to disrespect fishermen on the grounds that they are responsible for the destruction of many living creatures. From Tenasserim and Arakan, surplus fish is exported to Malaysia and India, totalling about 2,000 tons a year. By trade, Burma appears as a fish deficit area, importing 10,000 tons yearly prewar and 4,000 tons postwar with only 44,000 Burmese engaged in fishing (cf. 71,000 in West Malaysia and Singapore).

W. Malaysia.—About 192,000 tons of fish were regularly landed on Malaysian coasts by some 23,000 fishing boats (1964) chiefly on the coasts of Selangor, Perak, Trengganu, Pahang and Penang. At Singapore were landed 10,600 tons of fish (1965) from traps and deep-sea motorised trawlers, working at long range among the remoter islands and off Borneo. In addition to this home production, 34,400 tons of fish (1964) was imported dry from E. Malaysia, Thailand and South Viet Nam, mainly as part of Singapore's entrepôt trade. The Peninsula has begun fish cultivation, producing 19,000 tons cockles alone in 1965. Prawns and carp are cultivated in both Singapore and West Malaysia.

Indonesia.—In Java intensive fishing is carried on, though its coast is small in proportion to its population and production has rapidly become inadequate, in contrast with the thinly-peopled coastlines of Sumatra, Celebes and Borneo. Java's fishing concentrates upon the northwest coast where 159,000 tons were caught in 1965; farther east along the north coast fishing diminishes. A part of the catch once moved to West Java and the Outer Islands for the plantation workers. Javanese interest in fishing fluctuated and declined till the island ceased to be self-supporting, leading to inflows of cured Thai and Vietnamese fish (10,000 tons annually).

To develop commercialised fishing in the Outer Islands was no easy matter, but in Sumatra and Borneo a start had been made. At Bagansiapiapi about 12,000 Chinese have established a large fishery producing annually about 100,000 tons of fish which go to Java (60 per cent), Singapore, Penang and Malacca. To salt the fish nearly 25,000 tons of salt move into Bagansiapiapi. In Borneo, Soekadana on the west and Pegaban and Kotabaru on the east were fishing centres, supplying the interior and exporting yearly about 4,000 tons of dried fish to Java; Macassar functions as a market for pearl and shell fishing and for the *abalone* (Holothuria) catch of the eastern seas besides exporting annually about 4,000 tons of *agar agar* (a seaweed for jellies).

To Java and Madoera just before the war 49,000 tons of cheap fish were imported from Thailand and Indochina by way of Singapore, 46,000 tons from East Sumatra, and 8,000 tons from other Outer Islands. The home catch of sea fisheries totalled about 425,000 tons in 1958, when fish weighing nearly 290,000 tons was also obtained from ponds and rivers. Lake Tempe (South Celebes) has been intensively developed for inland fishing. Over 250,000 Indonesians worked as fishermen in 1956.

Indochina.—Although the physiography of the Indochina coast appears to favour sea fishing, yet coastal fishing interests local people less than the inland fisheries. A luminant oil for peasants is extracted from Indochinese fish. South Viet Nam landed 375,000 tons sea fish in 1965. Only on the South Viet Nam coast, particularly near deeper waters round Tanh Hoa, is inshore fishing very active on the basis of trawling and seining, which are unusual styles for Southcast Asia. The Cambodian coast, meeting place of migrant fish from the Mekong mouth and the Thai and Kra coasts, produces fish of exceptional size. The Mekong distributaries are also considerably fished to supply Saigon as well as local markets. Of the freshwater fishing that in Tonle Sap is the best known and most productive, but there are others well developed in the streams of Tonkin and along the Mekong, where oxbow lakes and artificial ponds are used for seasonal fish cultivation.

Fish bulks large in Cambodian and South Viet Nam exports but is small in value. North Viet Nam landed 305,000 tons sea fish in 1963.

Thailand.—Every Thai is said to eat some fish with every bowl of rice. At any rate the Thai consumption of fish is estimated to be larger than for any single Southeast Asia unit. Much of the fish comes from inland fisheries and the floods of the Chao Praya and the Nam Mum create natural ponds which last long enough to fatten many fish. These inland fisheries produced 72,000 tons in 1965. Fishing is reported more carefully by method rather than by weight caught: the 1965 sea catch was 540,000 tons. Thai sea fishing provides that dried fish which is exported. Mackerel, sardine and pilchard types migrate along the attenuated coast and they are exhaustively fished as a whole, though individual fishing units are small and poorly organised. At certain seasons the sea offshore is almost solid with squid, which are caught in large numbers for eating. Probably 50,000 tons of fish are annually salted on the coast for transport and trade, but poor organisation and careless salting with lowgrade brine taken direct from the sea has given Thai fish a low reputation; it ranks as the lowest grade of salt fish in Southeast Asia markets. The catch in 1964 was valued at $180 million, of which about $8 million was exported to Singapore, Penang and Hongkong, largely for re-export. Because the local fish is inferior, some better fish are annually imported from surrounding areas to a value of some $2 million (1961). The fish trade was largely Chinese, but Japanese fishermen had worked along the coast for years, using large trawlers serving markets in Singapore and in Japan. Only 59,000 Thais were fishermen in 1960.

Philippines.—Fish is as important in Filipino diet as in that of peoples on the mainland, and it is likewise an inadequately documented phase of their activities. Only in 1939 was a census of fishing taken. The amount that went into inter-island trade was small compared with the catch and only 100 out of the 1,600 types of local edible fish were marketed. Filipino fishing resembles that elsewhere in Southeast Asia and both inshore and inland methods are used. In the last decade, some deep fishing has developed and trawlers land quantities of *bonito* (tuna). Deep-sea fishing centres on Batangas, Manila and Sulu, whereas the inshore types are most developed round Mindoro, Batangas and Bulacan. More than 90 per cent of inland fishing (from rivers, ponds and lakes) comes from Batangas, Bulacan, Laguna and Rizal. The Pampanga and Iloilo districts have many fish ponds. Pearl oysters are gathered sporadically round the Palawan and the Sulu Islands.

In 1960 about 250,000 Filipinos were fully engaged in fishing and another 290,000 fished part-time. The total catch for 1965 was about 686,000 tons, an increase of 44 per cent over 1960: over half was traded fresh.

FISHING TRENDS

Casually organised and producing a poorly graded commodity, Southeast Asia fishing has everywhere an important place in the diet of local people. The international trade in fish within the region has certain resemblances to the rice trade in direction, in variability from year to year, and in foreign monopolisation of the middleman function and trade organisation. On the other hand, the dispersed and loose organisation of Southeast Asia fishing proved an advantage in the war period. Its simplicity of operation, use of locally-made boats for fishing and bulk transport, and ease of replacement of locally-made equipment, meant it suffered lightly from the war.

The fish trade between Southeast Asia countries was paralysed over 1940–6, owing to difficulties of procuring bulk salt supplies and of transport, but the rice-eating people in rural areas were not seriously deprived of their supplementary fish, so much of which was caught nearby. The large towns which once consumed fresh fish trawled at a distance or brought on ice from the coast could not receive adequate supplies and suffered accordingly until transport became easier. Java suffered most from the breakdown of international fish trade because no other Southeast Asia territory normally imported such large quantities of dried fish. In every territory deliberate efforts are now being made to increase the harvest from the sea by introducing trawling and refrigerating techniques, smoothing market arrangements and exploring fishing zones outside the range of fishermen hitherto: the F.A.O. attempts to coordinate these from Bangkok. The total regional catch seems to have risen by 140 per cent over 1948–65 but detailed data is not collected consistently.

Chapter Twenty-four

INDUSTRY AND TRADE IN SOUTHEAST ASIA

IF "industry" be taken to include all activities connected with processing, then there is more industry in Southeast Asia than appears from the fact that "manufactures" in 1960 were only 12 per cent of its net domestic production. The territory is, however, overwhelmingly agricultural and in almost every part of the region it is subsistence agriculture which employs and sustains the largest number of people. Much manual processing is done by these subsistence agriculturists on their own little farms to prepare their production for their family consumption.

COTTAGE INDUSTRIES

The tradition of being self-supporting in each territory, the national counterpart of individual subsistence farming, is very strong even today, finding expression in the widespread cottage industry of weaving and in that Southeast Asia custom of making a single length of span-board, hand-made cloth the basis of a skirt-like dress—the *sarong, lungyi, panung* and so on. Today this domestic weaving, where it has managed to persist in spite of competition from cheap imported cloths, uses imported cotton yarn, although parts of Burma still weave homegrown silk, and Thailand and Indochina continue some home-weaving on the basis of local silk. Only in Java has the "cottage industry" become elaborated into a village factory industry for a more intensified and commercialised production of sarongs. Ninety-two per cent of Java's *batik sarongs* (printed cotton skirts worn by men and women alike) come from factories of less than 80 workers each; this specialised process of dyeing in patterns defined by wax is now done by the small factory working upon imported cotton cloth.

The other considerable domestic industry deriving from the subsistence tradition is that of making innumerable varieties of articles from plaited palm leaves. Containers of many sorts, hats, domestic utensils, house walls, mats, fish traps and agricultural tools are all made by villagers using the palms and bamboos of their setting. Baots, shoes and tools are made of wood by peasants mostly for their own use. While this type of industry usually secures no place in national statistics and has low monetary value, it plays a most important part in Southeast Asia life which may be described as still in the "Wood Age" so far as most peasant and rural life is concerned. Domestically-made cigars and cigarettes supply local needs and rapidly displace the *areca* or *betel* chewing habit. In Burma, the Philippines and Java cigar-making has become commercialised for trade and export; in Java some 12,000 tons of tobacco entered trade as cigarettes during 1954.

Throughout the region, too, are scattered remnants of a metal-working industry, as in the beaten silver of Malaysia and Java, the niello work of Thailand, and the gold settings for precious stones in Burma.

But these domestic industries rank as small by external standards and they play a negligible part in international trade. They must not be forgotten, however, because in the evolution of Southeast Asia we may see grow up forms of industrialisation originating in these domestic industries, as has been the case in the industrial evolution both of Europe and of the Far East. In these domestic industries little or no money is involved. At their simplest they are "subsistence industries" providing the family needs and scarcely anything more.

Thus most Southeast Asia people produce what food their families need and what articles they need. Their requirements from outside are very small and in any case their way of life involves so little money that they have small means to buy anything outside their local subsistence ecology. That was the earlier condition everywhere in Southeast Asia before the industrial revolution in Europe, and it continues both in the simple form and in many variations even today, when there have evolved groups of people in Southeast Asia who are entirely dependent on wages to buy food and what other articles they need. The subsistence principle is still strong in that very little money interchange goes on among the great majority of the population; some of them by doing part-time work earn wages, yet the money they earn has a very low average, indicated by the very low per capita revenues of the governments. For 1965, national revenues per capita in

Indonesia were $23, in Cambodia $34, in Burma, Philippines and Thailand about $55, in W. Malaysia $155, and in Singapore $280 the latter two states being those which have moved farthest from the subsistence principle and where work and other activities centre most on money.

It has to be noted that the small amount of money involved in such ecologies does not mean poverty in the European sense; it represents only that margin of necessities which is outside the subsistence ecology. In addition to the little money it obtains, each family in general has both its food and its domestic equipment produced by itself, or in conjunction with helpers from the village community. This is a state of society long since outgrown in Europe though we have to allow for it in every phase of Southeast Asia industry and trade and to assume it will continue to play a part in future changes.

AGRICULTURAL PROCESSING

Because Southeast Asia is so overwhelmingly agricultural its mechanical industries relate largely to agricultural processes. Rice mills, sugar mills, starch factories (from sago and tapioca) and sack factories, have all grown up in connection with agricultural processing in every one of these territories. In addition, rubber factories, oil presses and sugar mills have been established on western lines in association with European-style agricultural developments. The fabrication of rubber has not gone far within this region; tyres have been made in Java, and W. Malaysia now makes rubber tyres, shoes and piping for Southeast Asia markets. For the most part, mechanical processing industries are located peripherally to the countries concerned and they operate primarily for immediate export, though small rice, brick and sugar factories have spread inland away from coastal sites.

TEXTILES AND MANUFACTURES

Apart from food, the chief personal need of Southeast Asia people is cloth and the demand for textiles ranks as by far the greatest single item of fabricated goods. Most of the textiles recorded are imported; the domestic industry has tended to disappear except in the remoter districts, and textile factories have not been set up to any extent within Southeast Asia. Cotton spinning at Semarang, Tegal and Damak and some 200 small weaving factories in Java, were the leading developments in local textile industries, but the bulk of cloth and even of raw cotton has been brought in from abroad. Much of it is cheap cloth from Europe, India and Japan but there is a substantial need for the very finest cotton cloth produced anywhere and quite an exacting local standard of qualities. The region consumed an estimated 1,700 million square yards of cotton cloth in 1960 and offers great incentive to local textile production; Indonesia, Thailand and the Philippines have responded, their respective productions for 1965 being 57, 156 and 160 million yards.

Road and rail management, engineering maintenance and port industries form a leading group of mechanical industries directly affecting local techniques and introducing forms of industrialisation on western lines. The capital equipment for these activities is imported as are nearly all metal manufacturers for other purposes. Manufactured goods form the largest single category of the huge flow into Southeast Asia, worth over $14,500 million in 1965 even excluding North Viet Nam. These manufactured imports chiefly went to urban consumers, yet simple farming tools and articles like needles and scissors went in large quantities far into every country. Although this category was broad, the components were very varied so that the value of each ranked comparatively low. Manufactured articles of western type show only little sign of being made locally—as indicated in textiles (above) and footwear and tyres in Java and Malaysia, though conditions seem suitable for industrialising in the dispersed village pattern of prewar Japan, except that labour costs are high, being geared to rice prices. Thus the proportion of manufactured consumer goods to all imports remains high; in 1965 the proportion exceeded 75 per cent in Indonesia, Burma, Thailand and Cambodia.

MINING INDUSTRIES AND PROSPECTS

Mining industries of great value have developed in Malaysia, Burma, Sumatra, Borneo, the Philippines and the small islands east of Sumatra. Tin and petroleum have been the region's specialities so far and these have assumed great importance, combining to be chiefly responsible for the 1963 export value of about $2,050 million of mineral products from Southeast Asia to the rest of the world. Iron ore and bauxite occur in large quantities, but, without local fuels, they are mined on a large scale for long-distance export. Gold has had special significance in Philippines mining, yet though found at many points, it ranks low for the region as a whole. Both tin and petroleum give rise to processing industries of smelting and refining close to the streams of international traffic, the former associated with Singapore and Penang. They play little part in local life, employ few people and go on at isolated points.

These mineral industries (which have employed less than 260,000 persons since 1960) suffered from the war both by destruction in denial action and by neglect, so that they practically started anew from 1945. Southeast Asia provides the most prolific source of petroleum accessible to the Indian and Far Eastern markets and it is being rapidly developed by international oil groups, total output for 1965 being steady at 28 million tons crude. Tin came back into production again slowly because it needs mining equipment such as pumps and dredges which were not readily obtainable. There was doubt whether world need for tin would continue as great as prewar. The life of tin mines is limited, yet the little known islands south of Singapore are thought to contain extensive virgin deposits of tin likely to enter production in due course. The demand for tin has kept high despite pessimism about the competition of plastics. By 1955 the total tin output of Southeast Asia was about 107,000 tons concentrates, in 1958 cut to 62,000 tons when international tin restriction was operated to maintain prices, and back to 105,000 tons in 1966.

LABOUR AND POWER FOR INDUSTRIALISATION

Whether intensified industrialisation of Southeast Asia on the basis of these minerals is possible, turns upon two factors. Labour continues to be scarce; many prewar mining labourers disperse during the war years when mining stagnated, and any immediate diversion of labour from agriculture to mining, even if possible under the tight ecology of the prevailing subsistence farming, is likely to prejudice local food supplies which depend basically on hand-grown rice.

Furthermore, Southeast Asia has limited sources of mechanical power, a factor not only of consideration regarding expansion of industries derived from mining, but also regarding the general prospect of local industrialisation. While good qualities are mined near Haiphong, coals of Southeast Asia territories are of inferior grade and ill-suited to major industrial uses. This is an obstruction to developing the extensive iron ore deposits because only Haiphong coal can be used for smelting. Mineral oil has not suited heavy industrial processes though diesel type heavy oil engines are widely used in existing local industries, and will probably be the source of power for any new dispersed industries.

Water power resources are huge (est. 166,000 million kwh. p.a.) and widely distributed. Little has been harnessed, and it is remarkable that, although Southeast Asia people have evolved skilled techniques of using their water supplies for agriculture, they have shown little traditional interest in its use as power, even for textiles and rice-milling which might seem obvious needs. The high and fairly even rainfalls of the upland areas are assets for water power; only in the loose materials of volcanic flanks, as in Java, is there any great difficulty about the necessary damming. On the other hand, where the rivers have water enough and suitable relief, they are remote from the centres of greatest population concentration, where a labour corps is available. Hence of 26,000 kwh. p.a. estimated to be available from the waterways of Indonesian islands, hydro-electric stations with only a capacity of 1.4 million kwh. p.a. have been installed and three-quarters of these are in Java. Outside the equatorial zone, the irregular régime of rivers renders them less suited for water power, and scarcely any hydraulic power is developed in Burma, Thailand and Indochina. A single installation driven from a dam at Chenderoh across a major stream, the Perak River, motivates some tin mines of West Malaysia. On the other hand, electrification from imported oil has become widespread. Dispersed industrialisation based on water power could develop and Southeast Asia might, by industrialising on water power, heavy oils, and nuclear power, skip the phase of steam industrialisation through which Europe passed. In 1965 the region's electricity output was 9,000 million kwh., increasing but with a *per capita* production half that of the world and no atomic power in use.

Apart from teak extraction, Southeast Asia forests have provided little international trade, which is more remarkable now that the resources of temperate forests show signs of exhaustion. The defects of tropical forest for a timber industry have been explained; it is not clear why no interest has been shown in a pulping industry based on tropical trees most of which have the advantage of relatively quick natural replacement. Pulping of tropical woods may yet solve the world paper shortage, especially as woody or fibrous tropical plants might be cropped for pulping instead of depending on predatory deforestation as is the case in the pulping industries of temperate areas today.

The forests, however, supply the basic domestic fuel of the region. Charcoal and wood are the usual means of cooking outside electrified towns. For illuminants most people turn to their trees to coconut oil, second to which is paraffin oil from within the region. Industrialised road transport is lightly developed and motor vehicles are unevenly spread. Singapore Island alone has almost as many commercial motor vehicles as Burma and West Malaysia over twice as many cars as Thailand (1965).

From Commodity Production to Local Processing

Although producing raw commodities like rubber, copra, tin, petroleum, iron ore, bauxite and tapioca, all the basis of industrial processes elsewhere, has been the function of Southeast Asia this century, culminating in the 1960's in an outflow worth nearly $9,000 million annually, processing and manufacturing of these commodities may cease to be so exclusively done overseas: every state here attempts to make them the basis of local industrialisation, aiming to make use of local power resources and to obviate concealed unemployment among rural populations. A tendency in this direction was very evident in Java where skill and incentive were present; rubber goods, textile printing, preparation of medicines, confectionary and refining essential oils had grown to significant proportions by 1941 and the enforced isolation of the war years should have intensified them, though a resumption of normal trading relations has obliged these industries so to organise that they meet the rival processed goods of zones as varied as India, Europe and the Far East. The influence of India as a source of manufactured goods was evident, particularly in textiles, before 1940 and became even more prominent after India's additional expansion under the almost autarchic conditions of the war period. From 1958 India's exports to this region have been suffering in competition with those of China and Japan.

It is to be noted that the great markets for goods manufactured from Southeast Asia commodities so far have been in Europe and the United States. The little nations of Southeast Asia seem ill-prepared to absorb much of them for some years. Because food is produced in such large quantities in this typically agricultural zone, we may not overlook the possibilities of manufacturing foods in forms such as biscuits, jam and canned specialities. Hitherto the tight association with industrialised colonial powers has to some extent dissuaded intense application to the miscellany of industrial productions possible in Southeast Asia, yet the local nationalisms and the incentive to establish more diversified activities tend to encourage local industries. By 1965 the percentage of manufactures in the net national product was only 9 in W. Malaysia, 12 in Thailand, 14 in Burma and 18 in the Philippines (cf. 32 in Japan).

From the point of view of the rest of the world, a re-orientation of the tremendous quantity of Southeast Asia's primary agricultural materials now handled by processing industries already established in Europe and the United States, would have major effects. A nationalistic or racialistic Southeast Asia driving towards industrial self-sufficiency could drastically diminish the international streams to and from it. However, over 1960–64 these trade streams have continued to expand, only Singapore showing significant signs of levelling off both in imports and exports.

INTRA-REGIONAL TRADE

A total value of about $1,200 million is currently involved in the interchange of goods and commodities between one part and another of the Southeast Asia region. This intra-regional trade is relatively small because the component unit sof the region produce much the same commodities and goods, by reason of which the countries tend to be rivals rather than customers of one another. An historic factor was the pull of several metropolitan areas, Britain, France, Holland and the United States, which acted to lessen intra-regional trade and to lessen the regularisation and rationalisation of production in Southeast Asia as a whole. Food deficiencies of local people are largely met by intra-regional trade, particularly the rice and fish movements from Burma, Thailand and Indochina to the other territories. The layout of the whole region relative to transocean shipping routes draws much of the intra-regional trade to major foci like Singapore, from which point manufactured imports from other parts of the world are also distributed within the region. Singapore has functioned for a long time as entrepôt centre for the region, a trading place without means for itself generating much trade. Thailand has a very balanced trade relation with its neighbours, over 40 per cent of both its imports and its exports being related to Southeast Asia territories.

EXTRA-REGIONAL TRADE

The overall trade movements from the region to the rest of the world were huge; annually over the quinquennium 1936–40 commodities valued at well over $2,000 million went overseas from Southeast Asia and some $1,200 million of goods moved into the region, quite apart from the intra-regional trade. This disparity of values moving in and out of Southeast Asia has for years been paralleled in the trade of each country, the disproportion being least in the case of the Philippines and greatest for Burma. The imbalance went deeper; since the Southeast Asia output was of bulky, raw or partially-processed commodities, the outgoing tonnage far exceeded the incoming tonnage and the carriage involved made Southeast Asia one of the busiest oceanic shipping areas of the world, an activity swollen further by the great amount of coastwise shipping made necessary by the insular character of the region. It was largely the absence of this shipping which paralysed the region during the war years.

After 1946, the re-established regional trade proved very sensitive to political unrest. It showed new proportions (by major price changes) and new trends. Southeast Asia came to have persistent adverse trade balances; its total commerce in 1965 involved $16,400 million goods flowing inward and $14,200 million outward. The gap has often been much wider than this—most Southeast Asian countries absorbing more value than they export.

The imbalance soon after 1946 was replacement of war damage but the need for capital equipment in new developments and for more "consumer" goods to meet rising standards seem enough to cause the region to function more as a consumer than as supplier over many years. In 1965, only Brunei, Cambodia and the Federation of Malaysia exported more than they imported: South Viet Nam imported almost ten times the value of its exports. For 1965, the percentage of the regional commerce generated by the countries was Malaysia 32, Philippines 31, Thailand 21, Burma 9, Indonesia 4.

SOUTHEAST ASIA TRADE MOVEMENTS 1965 (million M. dollars)

	Imports	Exports	Export composition per cent
Brunei	98	185	petroleum 98
Burma	741	672	rice 76, teak 12
Cambodia	309	315	rubber 48, rice 33
Indonesia	1,863	2,064	rubber 51, petroleum 35
Laos	75	3	tin 91
W. Malaysia	2,556	3,042	rubber 51, tin 22, iron ore 5
Philippines	2,682	2,301	coconut 21, sugar 15, timber 12
Sabah	330	300	timber 45, rubber 13
Sarawak	474	426	petroleum 60, rubber 20, timber 20
Singapore	3,864	2,743	rubber 39, petroleum 13
Thailand	2,175	1,881	rice 52, rubber 33
S. Viet Nam	1,071	108	rubber 76, rice 18

CONVERGENCE OF ROUTES

This region stands at zones of convergence for transoceanic routes between the very densely populated areas of India and China, and also between those areas and Europe, Australia and North America, so that international shipping converges upon Southeast Asia independently of colonial considerations which once drew the Philippines into the U.S. shipping circuits, the East Indies into the Dutch, and the rest of Southeast Asia into the British. In 1964, about 27,000 merchant ships used the straits of Singapore as compared with 36,000 using the Suez Canal and 33,000 the Panama.

The convergence of shipping routes led to a system of convergent air routes which have tended to follow closely the shipping lanes, making Southeast Asia the terminus of the air lanes from North America down through the belt of narrow seas along the West Pacific (linking the United States with Japan, China and Java population centres) and from Europe across the "Eurasian Mediterranean" of Southwest Asia and India, as well as a junction for lines to Australia.

CONVERGENCE OF INTERESTS

There is thus much to be coveted in Southeast Asia, the raw materials and the food it produces, the manufactured goods it needs, the commission on the coming and going involved, are all desirable and those who share or have shared in its trade turnover (about $31,000 million in 1965) are inevitably defensive of their portion. Colonial powers have jealously divided up these assets in the past and it is to be expected that there will always be from India and China no less than from Europe, Japan and America, rivalry to share the trade of Southeast Asia.

Southeast Asia was for a long time divided by divergent colonialisms. It now is divided within itself by divergent nationalisms which leave it only too open to the covetous from East and West, more particularly as it is the only zone providing a surplus of rice and a zone able to absorb the shoddiest of mass-produced articles. From now on not only westerners will seek these great markets. The factories of Japan, China and India are equally interested so that the trading interests covergent upon Southeast Asia are increasing, now intensified by Capitalist, Communist and Nationalist rivalries. China sold nearly twice as much as Britain to Singapore in 1965.

ASIA AND SOUTHEAST ASIA

In its relation to the rest of Asia, Southeast Asia has functioned chiefly as a source of food (rice from Burma, Thailand and Indochina, and Filipino sugar) and of money derived from Indian and Chinese wages sent back to their homes by traders and labourers in the pioneer mining and planting zones. So far the region has been the only population and food "safety valve" for Asia, and the only "New World" for the teeming populations of China and India. Possibly it can continue to function in the same way for some time to come, but the food margin in Southeast Asia is decreasing. Other Eldorados of migration and food have in the past rapidly become overpopulated areas, needing imported foods—the rhythm of such a change-over may prove specially fast in a tropical region. Events of the last century in Burma, Thailand, Malaysia and Java have certainly shown how rapidly changes can be brought about and how when certain types of pioneering and initiative are concerned, the people of these territories are capable of large-scale action. Directed into forms of cooperative rural and industrial activities aptly fitting their traditional subsistence farming and communal mutual assistance systems, their rate of industrialisation may prove as remarkable as their rate of commercialisation of agriculture over the last fifty years. Just as commercialised agriculture on its own has produced disruptions and breakdowns of many aspects of local life and reduced it to a degraded form, so also industrialisation without planning to fit in with the ecology of Southeast Asia may reproduce for long periods only the more sordid phases of industrialisation from which the West is just starting to emerge. Commercialised agriculture in Southeast Asia has led to rural slums; industry uncoordinated with this special environment may merely bring squalor and bad living conditions which it has taken years to eliminate from the older industrial centres, but which can easily go on for much longer in a more ruthless oriental setting.

INTERNATIONAL AID

The post-1945 breakdown of security, public services and trade flows in Southeast Asia, and the fear of anarchy worsening or spreading led to international schemes for the rehabilitation of equipment and personnel. Many newly independent countries were bankrupt and stripped of experienced staffs by the war and its train of changes. Uncertainties inside and outside prevented private financing of replacement or development of plant and other means of production. The position was complicated by confused appraisals of Southeast Asian potentialities in the widest sense. To overcome the consequent stagnation, "the Colombo Plan for Cooperative Economic Development" and "the Economic Cooperation Administration" (which later changed its name to "Mutual Security Agency" and "Development Loan Fund") were evolved. The former was a sterling currency scheme, the latter worked to the same end through U.S. finance. Other aid schemes were afterwards set up by United Nations agencies. The ability of such aid to operate effectively within the human ecology of the region and to influence trade and industry permanently has yet to be seen; the need is great for a financing mechanism to counterbalance the natural reluctance of private investors to carry the risks of capital in territories insecure for so long and with untried, sometimes truculent new local governments.

Chapter Twenty-five

PEOPLES, POLITICS AND PROSPECTS IN SOUTHEAST ASIA

THE setting of Southeast Asia may be summed up as one of extremes of relief (deltaic plains and mountains) and a climate mostly approaching the wet limit for plant life but merging into monsoonal types. To this setting the people have made varying responses, ranging from migrant food gatherers and hunters in the jungles, to subsistence farmers in the plains, but all turning upon woody materials for weapons, implements, house-structures and domestic utensils, upon rice, the cereal of the wet extreme, and upon social systems of communal help. The whole social and economic life has been galvanised over the past century or two by being more and more drawn into commercial and industrial activities developed in response to and on the basis of external needs for the minerals and agricultural products of Southeast Asia, whereas prior to that time the region was touched only by a trickle of traders moving between India and China.

FACTORS IN THE HISTORICAL GEOGRAPHY

Several factors account for the difficulty of obtaining firm data to fill in our general picture of the historical geography of Southeast Asia. In the first place, there grew up no strong literary tradition to last through the centuries and record the past in a form other than mythical. Here tradition is largely oral and literature essentially Indian rather than indigenous. And whatever there was of local record and history has rotted away quickly, the climate, the ants, insect and moulds soon destroying anything on wood, paper, leather or cloth. Moreover, in this setting of swamps and forest, the most easily available material is wood, and artistic tradition expressed in wood, whether in carvings, buildings or tools, rapidly disintegrates, leaving little of that sort of evidence which is the basis of our facts about early periods in other regions. Buildings and carvings on stone were not normal expressions of Southeast Asia people where over large areas stone is not easily come by and where

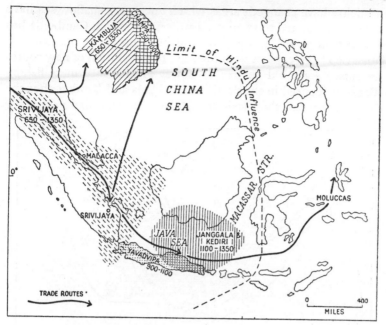

FIG. 113.—Historic Pattern of Southeast Asia during Indian Colonial Period

implements had not in any case developed far enough to deal with stone. Hence monumental evidence in Southeast Asia is so largely Indian, an introduction by foreigners using styles and techniques developed in their home settings, and most developed in the drier parts of this region, where stone is more accessible. On the clay lands, historic brick structures, also an Indian innovation, weather to nothing very quickly. At Angkor may be seen the power of quick-growing tropical trees to shatter and break down temples and palaces built of stone and lateritic blocks.

This has been a region of natural calamities, difficult though it is now to date them. Little Kingdoms have been wiped out in a few hours by Javanese volcanoes, as in A.D. 1006 when the flourishing city of Dharmavamsa (a great king of Central Java) was reduced to ashes by "a great calamity", probably an explosion and lava out-flow of the Merapi volcano. Settlements along rivers have been obliterated when huge mud-flows swept down from loose ashes on the flanks of new eruptions, possibly accounting for our ignorance of east Sumatran kingdoms. Coasts have altered through the years and deltas have changed; areas which once were shallow sea have become sedimented to swamps, a process by which Cambodia has been cut off as the Lower Mekong built up mud-flats isolating Tonle Sap from contact with the sea. The evolution of new routes has caused some old centres of power to fade into mere fishing villages, evidenced in the decline of Takhola and Bandon after the sea route through the Straits of Malacca became more generally

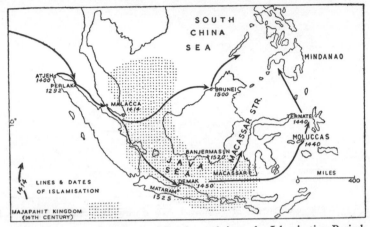

Fig. 114.—Historic Pattern of Southeast Asia at the Islamisation Period

used than that across Kra. Plagues have laid waste whole cities, as when Uthong in about 1350 was devastated by cholera and its population fled. The region is still one where malaria, dysentery, cholera and plague are endemic, more especially in the older, more congested territories like Java. These diseases have frequently flared up into appalling epidemics killing thousands of people, epidemics reflecting a relation between bacteria and the climate (which encourages bacterial reproduction), the population density, the difficulties of sewage disposal and social habits of indifference to hygiene (which has no ill effects among lonely settlements in the forest but becomes a social menace in towns). Fevers and virulent diseases have frequently ravaged the local people, debilitated them, and wiped out their settlements. The region is strewn with ruins of towns now abandoned, and with ruined groups of people who have degenerated physically by disease and under-nourishment. Southeast Asia proved capable of engulfing rather than enshrining those moving into it to live.

Further to complicate the historic geography was the fact that the literary people, the monks and religious men, were Indian or Indian-minded for long periods, disinterested in mundane records, and following the custom, still evident among many Southeast Asia people today, of avoiding personal names, so that anonymity, obscurity and confused nomenclature veil the past even in such records as do exist. Many experiments in writing styles were developed among these isolated and complex peoples and often inscriptions made in them cannot be translated today. Because of the dispersal tendencies within the territories themselves and the lack of focus to the region as a whole, no great depositories of learning were established in Southeast Asia to gather and conserve the record of its past.

POPULATION CHANGES

Broadly speaking, the region has been until recently one of very thin population had large patches of it still contain populations of remarkably low density. Direct evidence of densities are scanty for periods farther back than this century, yet it seems probable that the whole of Southeast Asia in 1800 contained only about ten million people, when the region was probably as thinly peopled in its most attractive areas as Upper Burma and Upper Thailand, the least attractive and developed areas, are today; Malaya then contained about a quarter million people, Java about four million, Burma probably less then two million. It was, even at the end of the 18th century, a zone of labour shortage and the objective of the local princelings of the times was to get hands, the basic power resource of their time, the one way of securing a small surplus from their fundamentally subsistent territories. Outsiders were not greatly attracted to Southeast Asia itself, as apart from the routes through it. To Spain its old colony, the Philippines, was no great asset and more related to Mexico than to Spain, remote and ready to drop from the Spanish orbit during the 19th century. To Holland, its colony in Java was a company venture that yielded little direct profit for many years and was at times on the verge of bankruptcy.

But the last 150 years brought tremendous changes in population. First, on the heels of the Industrial Revolution in Europe, came a revival and an expanded volume of trade between the Indian Ocean and the Far East, a stream which threaded the seaways of

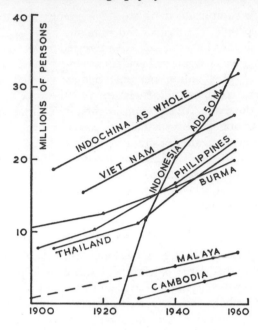

FIG. 115.—Population Expansions of Southeast Asia

Southeast Asia, diffusing new conceptions as it passed, re-estab-
lishing trading centres, drawing out huge volumes of Southeast
Asia produce and stimulating development of Southeast Asia as a
source of trade rather than a passage for traders. It has be n a
century and a half of tremendous population increases, causing
people to swarm upon the more fertile areas, upon deltas and
volcanic cones where people had not clustered before. In these
choice areas, the new deltas and the newer ejecta, the bulk of the
great population increase has concentrated, so that upon them live
teeming multitudes in limited zones separated by stretches of
forest-covered space scarcely more populated now than they were
several centuries ago. By 1920 the total population of Southeast
Asia had become 110 million; by 1940 it was 155 million and, by
1967, 240 million. These increases have not been even (Fig. 115).
This century Thailand has become more populous than Burma.
Since 1953 Singapore has been the fastest growing state (6.8 per
cent per annum), Burma the slowest (one per cent per annum).

SOUTHEAST ASIA NUTRITION DENSITIES

(Average number of persons per rice-acre per annum)

Quinqennium	*Burma*	*Indo-china*	*Thailand*	*Java and Madoera*	*Philip-pines*	*West Malaysia*
1916–20	1.23	1.75	1.66	4.12	3.13	—
1921–25	1.19	1.67	1.57	4.27	2.67	5.61
1926–30	1.14	1.67	1.57	4.50	2.69	6.13
1931–35	1.19	1.64	1.63	4.60	2.46	6.42
1936–40	1.25	1.63	1.74	4.96	2.79	7.02
1946–50	2.0	2.1	1.6	5.9	3.9	7.2
1951–55	2.0	3.1	1.3	5.9	3.2	8.2
1956–60	2.2	2.3	1.9	6.1	3.3	9.1

Because population and food production have increased *pari passu*, we should examine the local "nutrition density" (persons per acre in rice), since the surplus for export depends in part on low internal consumption. As the above table shows, Southeast Asian countries have considerable differences in nutrition density, it being highest in Malaysia (the plantation-mining specialist) and least in Thailand (the rice surplus specialist), yet increasing everywhere. Jumps in the postwar densities arise largely from natural rates of population increase far higher than the world average. The Southeast Asia crude birth rate for 1958–61 was about 4.4 percent per annum (cf. world rate of 3.4) and its death rate was 2.4 per cent (cf. world rate 1.8). In 1960, Burma had a higher crude birth rate than any country in the world and Singapore a lower crude death rate than either Britain or the U.S.A. Modern medicine and hygiene are making the old tag "Asia's graveyard" recede into myth.

CHANGING INTERNAL EMPHASIS

Today the very crowded places are Middle and North Java, Lower Thailand and the Red River Delta, where densities of over 2,000 people per square mile occur, with secondary crowdings in Lower Burma, the Lower Mekong, Central Luzon and the Visayas. These concentrations of people are pre-eminently in agricultural areas (Fig. 116), and they are in fact largely made possible by exceptional soil qualities within an area whose general soil fertility is low. These crowded areas have taken part in a commercialisation of local agriculture and their subsequent history has been firstly a

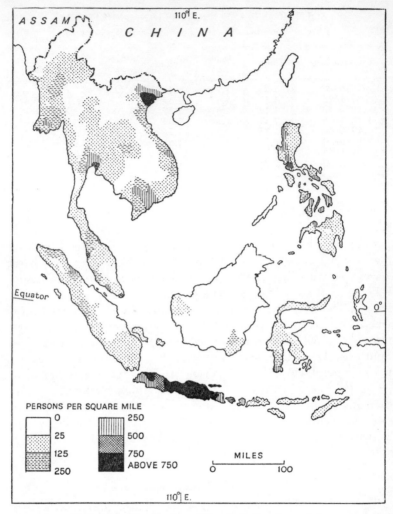

FIG. 116.—Distribution of People in Southeast Asia

rapid increase in people to a point where the new agricultural development ceased to be enough for the large population, leading to the second stage of slow migration and emphasis on commercial agriculture upon newer zones of similar type. Hence the change of emphasis from Tonkin to the Annam coastal plains and then to the Lower Mekong; from the Central Luzon area to Visayan Islands;

from the plains of Java to the dangerous upper limits of its volcanic country; and from Dry Burma to the Irrawaddy Delta. Sometimes there has been a little agricultural migration—very largely this change has been brought about by different rates of growth rather than movement of people to new places. Everywhere commercialisation of agriculture has led to population increase, because the agricultural technique has not changed from the Southeast Asia tradition of manual work at every stage. The bringing of new areas into cultivation has been followed by an increase in the number of hands to do the cultivating, partly a response to the need and partly made possible by additional nourishment and an added vitality arising from lower disease rates natural to the less populated area, because human diseases are diffused more slowly where people are isolated from one another, as in new areas. Thus Southeast Asia has been the scene of intense pioneering by people seeking, developing and filling new agricultural areas, to create for a time the eldorado of rice-eating peoples and the one safeguard of Indians and Chinese against the vagaries of their own harvests and against the congestions of their home districts.

Mineral in turn have attracted external interest. There has been the pull of gold in the Philippines, of tin in Malaysia and nearby islands, of petroleum in Sumatra and Borneo. These great gambles drew capital and pulled in crowds of labourers, wage-earners who were unavailable from local people so tightly held in their manual agricultural systems. Minerals drew millions of Chinese through the South China Sea in the tin rushes and oil rushes of the last hundred years.

Yet another form of comercialised agriculture developed, to provide the industrial raw materials of distant factories in Europe and America and based on crops entirely foreign to Southeast Asia. Sugar, coffee, hemp, rubber, oil palm proved highly successful in this terrain where they had never existed before. Large plantations of them were laid out, still more wage-earning labour was absorbed, a still greater production was obtained, drawing more and more people into virgin areas. Migrations from India and China were further stimulated to work upon the plantations whose uneven development, in successions of booms and depressions, alternately attracted migrants in the boom years and sent them home again in the depressions.

POLITICAL CONVERGENCE

These local products for commerce not only stimulated export trade; they stimulated import trades to feed the migrant peoples, to dress them, and to dress the agriculturists so preoccupied that they could no longer spare time to weave for themselves. And trade itself drew external interests; Chinese and Indian traders came in to monopolise middleman functions and Europeans came in and worked out here the complex balancing of their own industrial systems far away. Britain stimulated the commercialisation of Burmese rice production as an assurance of cheap food for an industrialising, overpopulated India. The Dutch fanned out from Java into the adjoining islands. Not to be outdone, the French moved into Indochina as a base for their China trade. Germans for a time controlled the copra trade of the farther eastern islands. The U.S.A. conquered the Philippines in a war with Spain. All major Western Europe powers and U.S.A. had colonial interests in the expanding peoples, the expanding production and the expanding needs of Southeast Asia. And the major oriental powers, India, China and Japan, had equally direct interest in the same area (Fig. 117) as an outlet for their people, a source of rice, a source of raw materials for their industries and finally as outlet for their own industrial products.

INTERNAL DIVERGENCES

The resulting pattern of people is one of unparalleled diversity in stages of evolution from subsistence to commerce, in densities of people, in ethnic types, in languages (Fig. 118). The similarity of setting, circumstance and products have disrupted Southeast Asia within itself by economic rivalry in producing similar commodities, and the divergencies of overseas connections with different colonial powers established divergent trade streams, currency differences, educational differences and political differences. Political and economic forces released in Europe and America had their repercussion within Southeast Asia, by means of which French protectionist policies virtually isolated Indochina from its neighbours and Filipinos turned their backs upon Asia. Thailand has been wooed, ignored or bullied, depending on the fluctuation of Anglo-French relations in Europe and the opportunism of the U.S. in building up its bloc in East Asia. All sorts of colonial systems have been

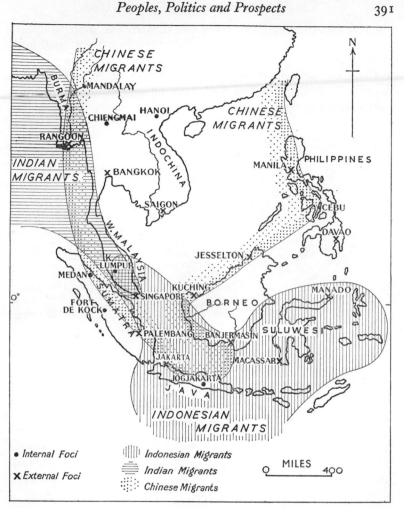

FIG. 117.—Pattern of Modern Migrations

experimented with, so that Southeast Asia has a great range of
constitutional forms, from fossilised oriental aristocracies to
democracies of a few intelligentsia and to would-be republics trying
to combine the appearances of democracies with the powers of auto-
cracies, the whole being permeated by complex trading systems of
both Western and Oriental types. All this may be summed up by
saying that the cross-currents and backlashes of the world's political and economic systems of the present and past still move

through Southeast Asia, irrespective of what the parts of South east Asia may have in common and overriding their traditional differences.

Every human type is represented in Southeast Asia. Successive peoples from East-Central Asia have filtered overland from the north, ranging from primitive Australoid types who left a few

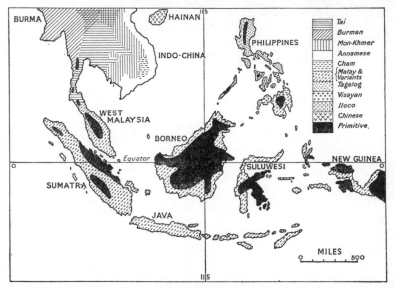

FIG. 118.—The Pattern of Languages in Southeast Asia

Negrito and Australoid people in the forests as mark of the greater stream which went island hopping to Australia, to the later Tibetan-Mongoloid peoples, forefathers of the Burmese, Thais and Laos of today. Then there were centuries of Indian migration early in this era, pressing overseas from South India across Kra, along the coasts of Sumatra and Java, into Lower Thailand and the Lower Mekong, leaving an indelible mark in the speech, culture and religions of people there today; this was a spread of Indian merchant adventurers and traders, and large-scale colonies exclusively of Indian settlers seem not to have been established, but in time there took place a great blood mixture between Indians and the older indigenous stocks. Later came a similar seaborne migration into Southeast Asia by predominantly Chinese people who first trickled south in the manner of sea gipsies, developed agricultural colonies as in North Viet Nam and merged with local people, followed by a stream of traders who started by being dealers in the India-China trade and became in time traders between one Southeast Asia people and another. Thus the migration to and settlement in South-east Asia of millions of Indian and Chinese labourers over the last fifty years or so (Fig. 117) is the modern expression of a process of convergence which has been going on for some two thousand years, differing only in that these latest migrants aimed to be temporary even though a portion of them never returned to their home countries, staying to marry and help change the character of Southeast Asia people. The predominantly Indian stream move east and south to a northern limit roughly running through Cambodia—Lower Thailand—Lower Burma; the Chinese stream moved into Luzon, into Borneo, Thailand, Lower Mekong, into the coastal fringes of Malaysia, Java and Sumatra, into Lower and Northern Burma. Never has any one people or any one power controlled the whole of Southeast Asia until the Japanese period 1942–45 which, repeating in form though not in character the Chinese migration, demonstrated a unity only of military and economic paralysis not of invigoration.

PLURAL SOCIETIES

Thus, though the ethnic types converging upon Southeast Asia have been of separate groups, they have extended over different lengths of time, with the result that the region's ethnic map shows different degrees of their absorption into the Southeast Asia setting. In some places the absorption is complete, in others it has scarcely started, and there are all variations between. Hence the units of Southeast Asia are peopled by a range of types from indigenes to raw immigrants, each with specialised functions in society, so that no unit is homogeneous horizontally: there are great variations of custom, speech and stock from one part to another of the same layer of society; homogeneous vertically, because there are generally communal differences between wage labourers, peasants, traders, administrators and aristocrats. Sometimes a religion is the only link. In other cases, education by the colonial power has been the chief link—as among the people of Indochina and of Indonesia. These conditions, added to the wide range of economic interests, mean that each political unit repeats in miniature the variety of peoples and interest which is typical of Southeast Asia as a whole.

The dualisms and pluralities of Southeast Asia society are relatively modern, becoming emphatic only over the past three hundred years, but plural societies and changing values within the units were long apparent in their changing political patterns. First there were the inland political nuclei; the kingdoms of Middle Burma, Upper Thailand, Inner Cambodia were matched among the islands by principalities set in the mountains of Sumatra and Java. Then came the little powers related more to the sea than to the land; the Sailendra kingdoms using the Malacca Strait as their bond and artery, the Majapahit sea kingdom whose territories in Borneo, Celebes, Java and South Sumatra may be thought of as footholds for a sailing people, fringing rather than entrenched in the islands (Fig. 113). At a later phase the move of power centres was to the lower rivers of the continental edge, to Lower Burma and Lower Thailand. In these historic patterns of political units may be seen operating the influences and traditions of widely differing human types, one rooted in the land, coming overland, depending on agriculture for its welfare and power; the other of seafaring people, many kinds and grades of them, coming to the lands of Southeast Asia by water, relatively mobile on their seaways, fishing and trading through the seas, and always peripheral to the land.

DUAL NATIONAL FOCI

In most of the constituent political units of Southeast Asia there is thus a split of interest (Fig. 117). Burma has a focus at Mandalay and a commercial-administrative focus at Rangoon; the Philippines has a dual nodality round Manila and round the Visayan Islands; Malaysia, which has only recently acquired clear internal focus, has two centres of different interest, Kuala Lumpur and Singapore, the former exclusively peninsular, the latter as much involved with all Southeast Asia as with Malaysia; Indochina has the double pull of the Red River (Hanoi) area and the Mekong Delta (Saigon); Java, its old internal focus at Jogjakarta, with Jakarta acting as external point of attraction. Sumatra is in the strange position of having several inland nuclei plus the tendency to use Singapore as its outport and route to Jakarta. Only Thailand can claim to have no second focus, yet even there the channelling toward Bangkok is only natural for the Chao Praya Basin; the Korat Plateau topography leads human and commercial interests towards the Mekong and the border country towards the northwest was once focused on the historic kingdoms at Chiengmai. Outsiders made and divided Borneo's fringe. Timor is split, its eastern part a political relic of Portugal's colonial period.

If this "balkanisation" be true of the individual political units, it is equally strong in the region as a whole, except that the intersection of major seaways and airways tends to make an internal regional focus on Singapore, a tendency diminished by India's economic pull on Burma and South China's pull on the people, trade and foods of Thailand and Viet Nam.

To some extent these dual foci to each territory have been stimulated by the arrival of Western trading systems which pulled in one direction while the traditional interests pull in another, yet in a sense all these political units have been created by colonial powers administering as a unit territories not previously politically unified or previously using the present boundaries. Spain and the United States enforced unity upon what is now the Philippines and in practice had continued difficulty in keeping Mindanao, for example, within the unit. France imposed a uniformity and a certain coherence upon Indochina which was novel to the constituent units. Malaysia as it exists today continues a British political creation. Before the Dutch colonial period all the islands of Indonesia had never been controlled as one state.

ENVIRONMENT AND STATES

The continental political units, Burma, Thailand and Indochina in some ways may be likened to little Egypts—nucleations of people within attractive, fertile valleys protected in these cases by the nearly empty space of forests and mountains. The combination of natural encouragement and natural protection conditioned major civilisations in Egypt and in Mesopotamia at one phase in history and appears to be equally encouraging in this tropical setting except for one difference, that although this environment on the southeastern fringe of Asia certainly suited the growth of states, its protective isolation was incomplete. In the north the growing riverine states were exposed to intruders. Thus in these riverside nurseries, states were environmentally encouraged to grow in a setting attractive as breeding grounds for nations, though the environment was not sufficiently isolating nor sufficiently protective to enable the nascent states to persist. So far as the main islands were concerned, on our maps they appear as more emphatic units than their elongated forms, difficult interiors and cliffed, marsh or forest edges in fact justify. Rarely has any one of the major islands been the locale of a single people singly governed, homogeneous and integrated into an island-state. These large islands have been dispersive and fragmentive to the peoples in them.

NATIONALISM

The effusion of nationalism after 1946 in Southeast Asia was thus a paradox. It is a nationalism of plural societies and substantial minorities, without homogeneity inside the states, and without a nation, as understood in Europe, and very much a culmination of the insecurity and uncertainty produced by the divergent influences which have long been at work, breaking down old social integrations and their warm, human associations, substituting for them nothing but commerce and the new myth "economic man," cold, inexorable and not adequately or fully integrated with Southeast Asia people and their setting.

The devolution of Southeast Asia from colonial into nationalist units took place at no propitious time. The cultivation of rice had been predatory, the accumulated effects of which were showing in diminishing yields, a trend not reversed until about 1955. Huge areas went out of cultivation due to war. Rubber, now competing with synthetic, has become static economy which may repeat the history of sugar. The demand for tin has expanded less then for most other metals. Plantation crops have lost labour, markets and opportunities. Yet Southeast Asia is still increasing its people faster than the world average. Its increase, however, has gone on at a slower rate in the already congested areas and at a faster rate in what had been the emptier areas of South Sumatra (with Javanese migrants), in Mindanao (with Filipinos), in Johore (by Chinese immigrants), as well as in Laos, Kalimantan and Inner Thailand, by local increases. Southeast Asia has been filling up despite hundreds of thousands of persons repatriated to the Netherlands, China and India over 1954–64.

DEVOLUTION

The Southeast Asia population is expanding now as the trade systems which provided its first impetus to expansion shrink and lose coherence. For 20 years now, decolonisation has gone on, the new states often starting more bankrupt than profitable concerns ripe for redistribution among new hands. Briefed in the theories and profits of a prewar economy, possibly even persuading themselves that something of the splendour of a 19th-century empire is theirs for the picking, these little nationalities are social liabilities, not assets. The policy of national autarchy may, under these conditions, reduce some new states to a condition approaching a low-pitched subsistence system, a reversion to the confusion and stagnation found there by the first European colonists. An era of political and material expansion has now ended and another of explosive instabilities has taken its place, a process of relinquishing and flinging off, possibly of disintegration. From a phase when Southeast Asia people were overwhelmed by the technological superiority of Europeans and Americans, the region is passing to one where this disparity becomes less as modern methods are injected by private initiative, by agencies like F.A.O. and by the U.S.A. and Russia in the Viet Nams. The tide of difficulties seems to be turning, though the pattern it will leave is vague.

How devolution will shape the political units of this region is still unclear. The divergences and dual foci produced by colonialisms, nationalisms and local wars have created states whence colonial administrators have gone and non-Asians remain only as diplomats, business agents or technicians. Millions of young Asian adults in 1967 never knew colonialism and they cannot endlessly accept that present failures can be blamed on history. All the states are weak, militant but militarily porous, their social structure cellular, their countrysides open to guerrillas and infiltrators.

The diminishing hold of European and American powers must increase the interest of China, India and Japan in this area where they have had traditional influence, whence they have derived great profits in the past, where many of their nationals are, where raw materials for their own industries can be obtained, and where the one rice granary of Asia is. Whatever the sentiment they profess, India and China in varying degrees may become involved with the control of Southeast Asia no less intimately than the colonial powers have been. Possibly these marginal, internally disrupted countries can only exist as satellites rather than as independencies.

Chinese Communism for Southeast Asia is the parallel of Japan's imperialism. Without seapower, militant China is an overland threat to Burma, Thailand and Indochina, where land-transport for armies is difficult but infiltration easy. It has access inside each country if Chinese Communists can use the Overseas Chinese. But the latter are traders, open less to Communism than to nationalism, being threatened by nationalism around them. Their link with China may be more nostalgic then real. Should China woo the native peoples, it faces their jealousy of Chinese already among them. Anarchy in the region, confused with and exploited by Communism, may be the political expression of the subsistence mode to which natives revert when their leaders cannot maintain security and efficiency upon which material progress hinges. An intelligence agency estimated Communist party members in 1966 to be 5,000 in Burma, 100 in Cambodia, 1 million in Indonesia, 2,700 in West Malaysia, 1,750 in the Philippines, 200 in Singapore, 700,000 in North Viet Nam and 31,000 in South Viet Nam.

In the readjustment of political, economic and social forces between the relinquishing of colonial power by one set of foreigner and its replacement by another or by indigenous party groups, processes of merging and reshaping the states may occur, because the metropolitan powers had, in effect, frozen Southeast Asia into a set of political units which bore little relation to local readjustments they caused. Nationalism and its social policies has first resulted in dividing Southeast Asia into some very small political units, possibly until their governments discover that adequate complementary components are more critical than nationalism or race to the smooth functioning of a state, which may lead to a regrouping into large units differentiated internally but integrated as a nearly self-sufficing whole. "National self-sufficiency" is for historic reasons a policy of great appeal to Southeast Asian electorates. Whether such fissions and re-groupings will be by arrangement, by force from within or by compulsions from without, depends as much on the persons thrown to the political forefront as on qualities inherent in the many-dimensioned pattern of Southeast Asia's political geography.

BIBLIOGRAPHY

The following books are sources of facts upon which the author has gratefully drawn and also additional reading on topics mentioned in the relative chapter.

CHAPTER 1: *Landforms of Southeast Asia*

BROUWER, H. E. *Geology of N.E.I.*, New York. 1925.
DALY, R. A. *Glacial Control Theory of Coral Reefs*, Am. Acad. Arts and Sc., 1915.
DAVIS, W. M. *The Coral Reef Problems*, New York, 1928.
GARDINER, J. S. *Coral Reefs and Atolls*, London, 1931.
GREGORY, J. W. "The Banda Arc," *Geog. Journal*, 1923.
MOLENGRAAF, G. A. F. *De geologie der zeeën van Nederlandsch Oost-Indie*, Leyden, 1921.
SCHOTT, G. *Geographie den Indischen und Stillen Ozeans*, Hamburg, 1935.
UMBGROVE, J. H. F. "Different Types of Island Arcs in the Pacific," *Geog. Journal*, 1945.
UMBGROVE, J. H. F. *Structural History of the East Indies*, C.U.P., 1949.
The Snellius Expedition Reports, Brill, Leiden, 1929–30.

CHAPTER 2: *Climatic Factors in Southeast Asia*

ALGUE, J. *Typhoons of the Far East*, Manila, 1904.
CLINES, I. M. *Tropical Cyclones*, New York, 1926.
DOBBY, E. H. G. "Winds and Fronts in Southeast Asia," *Geog. Rev.*, 1945.
DEPPERMAN, C. E. *Temperature Conditions in the Eye of Some Typhoons*, 1936; *Characteristics of Phil. Typhoons*, 1937; *Upper Air Circulation over Phil.*, 1940; *Typhoons originating over the China Sea*, 1938; pubs. Phil. Weath. Bur., Manila.
GARBELL, M. A. *Tropical and Equatorial Meteorology*, London, 1047.
WATTS, I. E. M. *Equatorial Weather*, London, 1955.

CHAPTER 3: *The Drainage Patterns of Southeast Asia*

DALY, R. A. *Changing World of the Ice Age*, Yale U.P., 1934.
MOLENGRAAF, G. A. F. "Modern Deep Sea Research in East Indian Archipelago," *Geog. Journal*, 1921.
MYERS, E. H. *Recent Studies of Sediments in Java Sea*, Science and Scientists in N.E.I., New York, 1945.
STAMP, L. D. "The Irrawaddy River," *Geog. Journal*, 1940.

399

CHAPTER 4: *Southeast Asia's Natural Vegetation*

CARTER, HILL & TATE. *Mammals of the Pacific World*, New York, 1946.
CURRAN, C. H. *Insects of the Pacific World*, New York, 1945.
MAYER, E. "Wallace's Line in Light of Recent Zoogeographic Studies," *Quarterly Rev. Biology*, New York, 1944.
MERRILL, E. D. *Plant Life of the Pacific World*, New York, 1946.
RICHARDS, P. W. "Ecological Observations in Rain Forest of Mt. Dulit," *Journal of Ecology*, London, 1936.
RIDLEY, H. N. *Flora of Malay Peninsula*, London, 1922.
SAUER, C. O. "Early Relations of Man to Plants," *Geog. Rev.*, 1947.
VAN STEENIS, C. G. G. *Maleische Vegetatieschen*, Buitenzorg, 1935.
WATSON, J. G. *Mangrove Forests of Malay Pen.*, Singapore, 1928.

CHAPTER 5: *Southeast Asia Soils*

CORBET, A. S. *Biological Processes in Tropical Soils*, London, 1935.
GLINKA, K. D. (trans. Marbut). *Great Soil Groups of the World*, New York, 1927.
HOLLAND, J. "Constitution, Origin and Dehydration of Laterite," *Geological Mag.*, 1903.
MOHR, E. C. J. (trans. Pendleton). *Tropical Soil-Forming Processes*, Univ. of Philippines, College of Agriculture, 655, 1930; *Climate and Soil in N.E.I.*, Bull. Colonial Institute of Amsterdam, 1938.
PENDLETON, R. "Laterite and its Structural Use in Thailand," *Geog. Rev.*, 1941.
POLYNOV., B. B. *Cycle of Weathering*, London, 1937.
THORP, J. AND BALDWIN. *Laterite in Relation to Soils in the Tropics*, Ann. Ass. American Geogs., 1940.
VAGELER, P. *Introduction to Tropical Soils*, London, 1933.

CHAPTERS 6, 7 & 8: *West Malaysia*

BLAUT, J. "Econ. Geog. of One-acre Farm on Singapore Island," *Mal. J. Trop. Geog.*, 1953.
BURKILL, I. H. *Economic Products of Malay Peninsula*, London, 1935.
CORNER, E. J. H. *Wayside Trees of Malaya*, Singapore, 1940.
DALE, W. L. "Rainfall of Malaya," *Mal. J. Trop. Geog.*, 1959–60; "Surface Temps. in Malaya," *Mal. J. Trop. Geog.*, 1962.
DOBBY, E. H. G. "Settlement Patterns in Malaya," *Geog. Rev.*, 1942; "Singapore," *Geog. Review*, New York, 1940; "Land Utilisation in Malacca," *Geog. Jnl.*, 1940; "Kelantan Delta," *Geog. Rev.*, 1951; "Recent Settlement Changes in S. Malaya," *Mal. J. Trop. Geog.*, 1953; (Ed.) "Padi Landscapes of Malaya," *Mal. J. Trop. Geog.*, 1955 and 1957.
Economic Development of Malaya, I.B.R.D. Report, Singapore, 1955.
EMERSON, R. *Malaysia*, New York, 1937.
FRITH, R., *Malay Fishermen*, London, 1946.
GINSBURG, N. *Malaya*, Seattle, 1958.

GRIST, D. H. *Outline of Malayan Agriculture*, Kuala Lumpur, 1950.

GULL, E. M. *British Economic Interests in the Far East*, London, 1943.

HODDER, B. W. *Man in Malaya*, London, 1959.

MAXWELL, C. N. *Malayan Fishes*, J. Malayan B.R.A.S., Singapore, 1921.

MILLS, L. A. *British Rule in Eastern Asia*, London, 1942.

MOHR, E. C. J. AND VAN BAREN, F. A. *Tropical Soils*, The Hague, 1954.

OOI JIN-BEE, "Mining Landscapes of Kinta," *Mal. J. Trop. Geog.*, 1955; "Rural Development in Tropical Malaya," *Mal. J. Trop. Geog.*, 1959; *Land People and Economy in Malaya*, London. 1962.

O'REILLY, J. M. M. "Malayan Tin Mining," *Mal. J. Trop. Geog.*, 1963.

PURCELL, V. W. W. S. *Chinese in Malaya*, London, 1948.

RICHARDSON, J. A. "Outline of Geomorphological Evolution of British Malaya," *Geolog. Mag.*, 1947.

ROBERTS, G. (DOBBY, E. H. G.). "Making Malaya a Nation," *Geog. Mag.*, 1946.

SCRIVENOR, J. B. *Geology of Malaya*, London, 1931.

SERVICE, H. "Explanation of Shallowness of Alluvium in River Flats of Western Pahang." *T.M.S. Chamber of Mines*, Kuala Lumpur, 1940.

SWETTENHAM, F. *Footprints in Malaya*, London, 1941.

WIKKRAMATILEKE, R. "Planned Settlement in Eastern Malaya," *Mal. J. Trop. Geog.*, 1963.

CHAPTERS 9, 10 & 11: *Burma*

ANDRUS, J. S. *Rural Reconstruction in Burma*, Madras, 1936; *Burmese Economic Life*, Stanford U.P., 1948

CHANG CH'ENG SUN. *Sino-Burmese Frontier Problems*, Peiping, 1938.

CHHIBBER, H. L. *Mineral Resources of Burma*, London, 1931; *Geology of Burma*, London, 1934; *Physiography of Burma*, Calcutta, 1933.

COLLIS, M. *Land of the Great Image*, London, 1945.

FITZGERALD, P. "Yunnan-Burma Road," *Geog. Journal*, 1940.

FURNIVALL, J. S. *Political Economy of Burma*, Rangoon, 1938.

JESSE, T. *Story of Burma*, London, 1946.

KAULBACK, R. *Salween*, New York, 1939.

KNAPPEN, TIBBETTS AND ABBETT. *Economic and Engineering Survey of Burma*, New York, 1952.

LEACH, F. B. *Future of Burma*, (2nd Ed.), Rangoon, 1939.

MILNE, L. *Home of an Eastern Clan (Palaungs)*, Oxford, 1924.

MOREHEAD, F. T. "Forests of Burma," *Burma Pamphlet*, London.

PEARN, B. R. "Burma Background," *Burma Pamphlet*, London.

SPATE, O. H. K. "Rangoon, A Study in Urban Geography," *Geog. Rev.*, 1942; "Beginnings of Industrialisation in Burma," *Econ. Geog.*, 1941; "Burma Setting," *Burma Pamphlet*, London.

SPATE, O. H. K. AND TRUEBLOOD, L. W. "Rangoon," *Geog. Rev.*, 1942.

STAMP, L. D. "Oilfields of Burma," *Jnl. Inst. Petrol Tech.*, 1929; "Burma; an Undeveloped Monsoon Country," *Geog. Rev.*, 1930; "Vegetation of Burma from Ecological Standpoint," *University of Rangoon Res. Mon.*, Calcutta, 1925; "Irrawaddy River," *Geog. Journ.*, 1940.
STEVENSON, H. N. C. "Hill Peoples of Burma," *Burma Pamphlet*, Longmans, London.
DE TERRA, H. "Quartenary Terrace System of Southern Asia," *Geog. Rev.*, 1939; "Component Factors of Natural Regions of Burma," *Annals Am. Assoc. Geog.*, Wisconsin, 1944.
WARD, F. K. "Irrawaddy Plateau," *Geog. Journal*, 1939.
ANON. "Burma's Rice," *Burma Pamphlet*, London, 1944.
ANON. *The Burma Petroleum Industry*, London, 1946.

CHAPTERS 12, 13, 14, 15 & 16: *The East Indies*

Atlas van tropisch Nederland, Amsterdam, 1937.
BARKENROAD, M. D. "Development of Marine Resources in Indonesia," *Far Eastern Quarterly*, New York, 1946.
BARNOUW, A. "Crosscurrents of Culture in Indonesia," *Far Eastern Quarterly*, New York, 1946.
BECCARI, *Wanderings in the Great Forests of Borneo*, London, 1904.
VAN BEMMELEN, R. W. *Mineral Resources of N. Indies*, Science & Scientists in N.E.I., New York, 1945.
BOEREMA, J. *Rainfall Types in N.E.I.*, No. 18 of Verhandelingen Konenklijk Magnetisch en Meterologisch Observatorium te Batavia.
BRAAK, C. *Het Klimaat van Ned-Indie*, No. 8 of Verhandelingen Konenklijk Magnetisch en Meterologisch Observatorium te Batavia; *Klimakunde von Hinterindien und Insulinde*, Berlin, 1936; *Climate and Meterological Research in N.E.I.*, Science and Scientists in N.E.I., New York, 1945.
TER BRAAKE, A. L. *Volcanology in Netherlands East Indies*, Science and Scientists in N.E.I., New York, 1945.
British Borneo Geological Report, ed. ROE, F. W., Sarawak, 1955.
BROEK, J. O. M. "Man and Resources in N.E.I." Netherlands Number, *Far Eastern Quarterly*, New York, 1946.
BROUWER, H. A. "Exploration in the Lesser Soenda. Islands," *Geog. Journal*, 1939; *Geology of the N.E.I.*, London, 1925.
COLLET, O. J. A. *Terres et Peuples de Sumatra*, Amsterdam, 1925.
DEASY, G. F. "Localisation of Sumatra's Oil Palm Industry," *Econ. Geog.*, 1942.
EVANS, C. *Among Primitive Peoples in Borneo*, London, 1932.
FURNIVALL, J. S. *Netherlands India*, Cambridge, 1939.
VAN GELDEREN, J. *Western Enterprises and the Density of Population in the N.E.I.* in "Effect of Western Influences on Native Civilisation in Malay Archipelago," Batavia, 1929.
HARRISON, T. "North Borneo," *Geog. Journal*, 1933; (ed.) *Borneo Jungle*, London, 1932.
HART, G. H. C. "Recent Developments in N.E.I.," *Geog. Jnl.* 1942.

VON HEINE-GELDERN, R. *Prehistoric Research in N.E.I.*, Science and Scientists in N.E.I., New York, 1945.

HOENIG, A. *Agriculture in N.E.I.*, Science and Scientists in N.E.I., New York, 1945.

KENNEDY, R. *Islands and Peoples of the Indies*, Smithsonian Institute, Washington, 1943.

KUPERUS, G. "Relation between Population and Utilisation of Soil in Java," *Compt. Rend. du Congr. Inst. Geog.*, Amsterdam, 1938.

LASKER, B. "Role of the Chinese in the N.E.I.," *Far Eastern Quarterly*, New York, 1946.

LEE, Y. L. *North Borneo*, Singapore, 1965. "Dev. and Planning Land Use, Br. Borneo," *Mal. J. Trop. Geog.*, 1961; "Long House Dyak Settlements," *Oriental G.*, 1962.

LEHMAN, H. "Morphologische Studien auf Java," *Geografische Abhandlesgen*, Stuttgart, 1936.

MILLER, C. C. *Black Borneo*, London, 1946.

ORMELING, G. J. *Timor*, Amsterdam, 1954.

PELZER, K. J. "Tanah Sabrang and Java's Population Problem," *Far Eastern Quarterly*, New York, 1946.

PRESTAGE, E. *Portuguese Pioneers*, London, 1933.

ROBEQUAIN, C. *Monde malais*, Paris, 1946.

STAUFER, H. *Geology of Netherlands East Indies*, Science and Scientists in N.E.I., New York, 1945.

VAN STEENIS, C. G. G. J. *Malaische Vegetatiescheten Tijdschrift*, v. h. Kon. Ned. Handrijkskundig Genootschap, 1935.

VAN STRAELEN, V. *Resultats Scientifiques du Voyage aux Indes Orientales Nederlandaises*, Brussels, 1933.

TENGWELL, T. A. *History of Rubber Cultivation and Research in N.E.I.*, Science and Scientists, N.E.I., New York, 1945.

UNGER, L. "Chinese in Southeast Asia," *Geog. Rev.*, 1944.

VERSTAPPEN, H.Th. *Djakarta Bay*, Hague, 1953.

VLEKKE, B. H. M., *Nusantara*, Cambridge, Mass., 1943.

WITHINGTON, W. A. "Population in Sumatra," *Mal. J. Trop. Geog.*, 1963.

WITTOUCK, S. F. "Exploration of Portuguese Timor," *Geog. Journ.*, 1938.

WILFORD, G. E. "Geomorphological Evolution of Brunei," *J. Trop. Geog.*, 1967.

WILLIAMS, M. *Five Journeys from Jakarta*, London, 1966.

CHAPTERS 17 & 18: *Thailand*

ANDREWS, J. M. *Siam, Second Rural Economic Survey*, Bangkok, 1935

BRAAK, C. *Klimakunde von Hinter U. Insulinde*, Hdb., d. Klimatologie, Bd. IV. Berlin, 1931.

COLLIS, M. *Siamese White*, London, 1936.

CREDNER, W. *Siam, das Land der Thai*, Stuttgart, 1935.

F.A.O. *Report on Siam*, 1948; *on its Fisheries*, 1949.

CROSBY, J. *Siam*, London, 1945.

DE YOUNG, J. E. *Village Life in Modern Thailand*, Berkeley, 1955.
LANDON, K. P. *Siam in Transition*, Shanghai, 1939; *The Chinese in Thailand*, Shanghai, 1941.
PENDLETON, R. L. "Land Use in N.E. Thailand," *Geog. Rev.*, 1943; *Soils and Surface Rocks of Siam*, Bangkok, 1953.
PUGH, M. *The Economic Development of Siam*, Bangkok, 1936.
ROBBINS, L. J. "A Journey in Central Siam," *Geog. Journal*, 1929.
STERNSTEIN, L. "Agricultural Land Tenure in Thailand," *J. Trop. Geog.*, 1967.
THOMPSON, V. *Thailand*, New York, 1941.
WILLIAMS, L. *Mysteries of Thailand*, London, 1941.
ZIMMERMAN, C. C. "Some Phases of Land Utilisation in Siam," *Geog. Review*, 1937; *Siam, Rural Economic Survey*, Bangkok, 1931.

CHAPTERS 19 & 20: *Indochina*

Atlas des colonies françaises, Paris, 1935.
BAUDRIT, A. *Le Fameux Song-Bé*, Saigon, 1936.
BRODERICK, A. *Little China*, London, 1942.
BRUZON, E. AND CARTON, P. *Le Climat de l'Indochine et les Typhons de la Mer de Chine*, Hanoi, 1930.
CHASSIGNEUX, E. "La Region de Hai Ninh," *La Geographie*, 1926.
COOLIDGE, H. J. AND ROOSEVELT, T. *Three Kingdoms of Indochina*, New York, 1933.
DELAHAYE, V. *La Plaine des Joncs et sa Mise en Valeur*, Rennes, 1928.
GAUTHIER, J. *Digues du Tonkin*, Hanoi, 1931.
GOUROU, P. *L'Utilisation du Sol en Indochine Française*, Paris, 1936; *Les Paysans du Delta Tonkinois*, Paris, 1936; *Le Tonkin*, Hanoi, 1931.
GROSLIER, B. P. *Indochina*, London, 1966.
LOUBET, L. *Monographie de la Prov. de Kompong Cham*, Phom Penh, 1939.
NULZEC, L. "Le Plateau des Cardamones Cambodgien," *La Geographie*, 1926.
ROBEQUAIN, C. *L'Indochine Française*, Paris, 1935; *Le Than Hoa*, Paris, 1929; *Economic Development of French Indochina*, N. York, 1944.
RUSSIER, H. *L'Indochine Française*, Hanoi, 1931.
SION, J. "Asie des Moussons," *Geog. Universelle*, Vol. IX, Paris, 1929.
YVES, H. *Terres Rouges et Terres Noires Basaltiques d'Indochine*, Hanoi, 1931.
Bulletin Economique de l'Indochine (annually).

CHAPTER 21: *The Philippine Islands*

ALLEN, J. S. "Agrarian Tendencies in the Philippines," *Pacific Affairs*, 1938.
BORJA, L. J. "Philippine Coconut Industry," *Econ. Geog.*, 1927; "Philippine Lumber Industry," *Econ. Geog.*, 1929.
BUTLER, O. M. *Philippine Islands*, U.S. Dept. Com., Washington, 1927.
CUTSHALL, A. "Trends of Philippines Sugar Production," *Econ. Geog.*, 1938.
FAY-COOPER, C. "Central Mindanao," *Far Eastern Quarterly*, New York, 1945.

FORBES, W. C. *The Philippine Islands*, Boston, 1928.
HAAS, W. H. *The American Empire*, Chicago, 1940.
HAYDEN, J. R. *The Philippines*, New York, 1942.
HERRE, A. W. "Philippines Fisheries," *Far Eastern Qy.*, New York, 1945.
KRIEGER, H. W. "Races and Peoples in the Philippines," *Far Eastern Quarterly*, New York, 1945.
KURIHARA, K. K. *Labour in Philippine Economy*, Stanford, 1945.
LASKER, B. *Filipino Immigration*, Chicago, 1931.
MILLER, H. H. "Principles of Economics Applied to the Philippines," *Geog. Rev.*, 1932.
ORACION, T. S. "Kaingin Agr. in S.E. Negros," *Mal. J. Trop. Geog.*, 1963.
PENDLETON, R. L. "Land Utilis. and Agri. of Mindanao," *Geog. Rev.*, 1942.
ROOSEVELT, T. "Land Problems in Puerto Rico and the Philippines," *Geog. Rev.*, 1934.
RUTTAN, SOOTHIPAN AND VENEGAS, "Changes in Rice Growing in Philippines and Thailand," *World Crops*, London, 1966.
SIMKINS, P. D. AND WERNSTEDT, F. L. "Migration of Philippine Population," *Mal. J. Trop. Geog.*, 1963.
VAN VALKENBERG, S. "Agricultural Regions of the Philippines," *Econ. Geog.*, 1936.

CHAPTER 22: *Southeast Asia Agriculture*

BARRETT, O. W. *The Tropical Crops*, New York, 1928.
DOBBY, E. H. G. "N. Kedah Pioneering for Padi," *Econ. Geog.*, 1951; *Food and the Changing Function of Southeast Asia* in *Southeast Asia in Coming World*, J. Hopkins, 1953.
GRIST, D. H. *Rice*, London, 1953.
KNORR, K. E. *World Rubber and its Regulation*, Stanford, 1945.
PELTZER, K. *Pioneer Settlement in the Asiatic Tropics*, New York, 1945.
WHITTLESEY, D. "Shifting Cultivation," *Econ. Geog.*, 1937.
WICKIZER, V. D. AND BENNETT, M. K. *Rice Economy in Monsoon Asia*, Stanford, 1941.
Devlpt. Upland Areas in F.E., 2v., I.P.R., New York, 1950–51.
Economic Survey of Asia and the Far East, annual reports.

CHAPTER 23: *The Fisheries of Southeast Asia*

CHEVEY, P. AND LE POULAIN, F. *La Pêche dans les eaux douces du Cambodge*, Saigon, 1940.
DELSMAN, H. C. "Fishing and Fish Culture in Netherlands Indies," *Bull. Col. Inst. Amsterdam*, 1939.
LEE, Y. L. "Chinese Fishing Village in S.W. Malaya," *Mal. J. Trop. Geog.*, 1962.
NICHOLS AND BARTSCH, *Fishes and Shells of the Pacific World*, New York, 1946.

CHAPTER 24: *Industry and Trade in Southeast Asia*

DIETRICH, E. B. *Far Eastern Trade of United States*, New York, 1940.
DOBBY, E. H. G., *Monsoon Asia*, London, 1962.
GULL, E. M. *British Economic Interests in the Far East*, Oxford, 1943.
SHEPHERD, J. "Industry in Southeast Asia," *I.P.R.*, New York, 1941.

CHAPTER 25: *Peoples, Politics and Prospects in Southeast Asia*

BAUER, P. T., *The Rubber Industry*, London, 1948.
BENEDICT, P. K. "Thai, Kadai and Indonesian," *American Anthropologist*, 1942.
BROEK, J. O. M. "Diversity and Unity in Southeast Asia," *Geog. Rev.*, 1944.
CHRISTIAN, J. L. "Anglo-French Rivalry in Southeast Asia," *Geog. Rev.*, 1941.
DOBBY, E. H. G. "Aspects of Human Ecology of Southeast Asia," *Geog. J.*, 1946; "Rec. Changes in Settlements of S. Malaya," proc. XVII, Int. Geog. Cong., Washington, 1952.
EMERSON, R., MILLS, L. A. AND THOMPSON, V. *Government and Nationalism in Southeast Asia*, New York, 1942.
FRYER, D. "The 'Million' City in Southeast Asia," *Geog. Rev.*, 1953.
FURNIVALL, J. S. *Colonial Policy and Practice*, Cambridge, 1948.
GOUROU, P. *The Tropical Lands*, London, 1953, and *L'Asie*, Paris, 1953.
KEESING, F. *Native Peoples of the Pacific World*, New York, 1946.
KERNIAL SINGH SANDHU, "Chinese Colonization of Malacca," *Mal. J. Trop. Geog.*, 1961.
LANDON, K. P. "Southeast Asia—Crossroads of Religions," *Chic. U.P.*, 1949.
LASKER, B. *Asia on the Move*, New York, 1945; *Peoples of Southeast Asia*, New York, 1945.
MAJUMDAR, R. C. *Hindu Colonies in the Far East*, Calcutta, 1944.
PANIKKAR, K. M. *Future of Southeast Asia*, London, 1943; *India and the Indian Ocean*, London, 1945.
PELZER, K. J. *Population and Land Utilisation (Pacific Area)*, New York, 1941.
PURCELL, V. *The Chinese in Southeast Asia*, London, 1951.
ROBERTS, G. (DOBBY, E. H. G.), "East to the Indies," *Geog. Mag.*, 1946; "South to the Indies," *Geog. Mag.*, 1946; "From Europe to the Spice Islands," *Geog. Mag.*, 1946.
TA CHEN, *Overseas Chinese in the South Seas*, Chungking, 1938.
THAYER, P. W. (ed.) "Southeast Asia in the Coming World," *J. Hopkins U.P.*, 1953.
WHEATLEY, P. *The Golden Chersonese*, I.B.G., 1955.
WIBO PEEKEMA, "Colonisation of Javanese in Outer Provinces," *Geog. Journal*, 1943.

INDEX

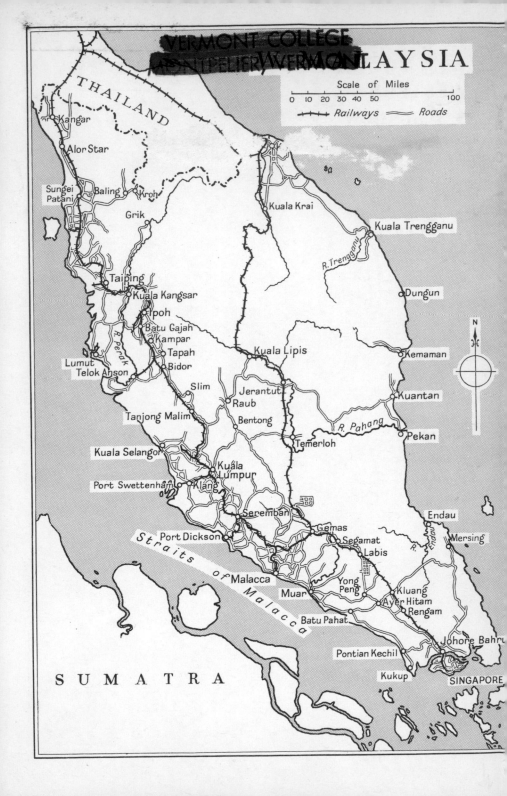

MALAYSIA

THAILAND

Scale of Miles

0 10 20 30 40 50   100

╂╂╂╂ *Railways*   ∽ *Roads*

Kangar

Alor Star

Sungei
Patani   Baling   Kroh

Grik

Kuala Krai

Kuala Trengganu

R. Trengganu

Taiping

Kuala Kangsar

Ipoh

Batu Gajah

Kampar

Tapah

Bidor

Lumut
Telok Anson

Dungun

Kemaman

Kuala Lipis

Slim

Jerantut
Raub

Bentong

Kuantan

R. Pahang

Temerloh

Pekan

Tanjong Malim

Kuala Selangor

Kuala
Lumpur

Port Swettenham   Klang

Seremban

Endau

Mersing

Port Dickson

Straits of Malacca

Gemas

Segamat

Labis

Malacca

Muar

Yong
Peng

Kluang

Ayer Hitam

Rengam

Batu Pahat

Johore Bahru

Pontian Kechil

SUMATRA

Kukup

SINGAPORE

N